The Sporting News

presents

HEROES
of the HALL

Baseball's all-time best

PHOTO CREDITS

T=Top B=Bottom

CONTRIBUTING PHOTOGRAPHERS:

The Sporting News Archives: 10-21, 26-28, 32, 34-45, 47, 48, 58, 59, 61-69, 73-79, 82, 83,86,87, 89-95, 98-101, 104-112, 114-119, 122-127, 129-133, 136, 137, 139-141, 144-152, 154-169, 174-177, 180, 182-187, 190-195, 198-210, 212- 219, 221-241, 244, 245, 248, 249, 251-255, 258-261, 266-272, 276-281, 283-297, 299-301, 303-310, 314-317, 319-325, 327, 331,332, 336-340, 342-345, 348, 350, 354, 357-359, 361, 364-366, 370-373, 375, 377-381, 384, 385, 390-395, 397-405, 408-411, 414, 415, 419-426, 428-431, 435-437, 441-443, 446-448, 450-453, 455-472, 476, 477, 480-482, 487-489, 491-494, 497T, 498, 499, 502, 504-509

Albert Dickson/The Sporting News: 4-5

Photos of Hall of Fame plaques courtesy of National Baseball Hall Of Fame Library, Cooperstown, N.Y.

NBLA/MLB Photos: 33, 49, 51-53, 72, 96, 113, 121, 128, 134, 135, 138, 142, 143, 178, 179, 188, 189, 211, 220, 257, 264, 265, 273, 298, 333, 341, 360, 374, 396, 418, 427, 434, 440, 449, 473, 478, 479, 486, 496, 497B, 503

MLB Photos: 25

PhotoFile/MLB Photos: 60, 88, 171, 181, 262, 274, 330, 334, 346, 347, 349, 351-353, 376, 382, 383, 386, 389, 432, 433, 483-485, 490

Rich Pilling/MLB photos: 80, 85, 172, 173, 246, 355, 362, 406, 412, 413, 417, 438, 444, 500

Louis Requena/MLB Photos: 22, 29, 30, 55-57, 70, 71, 80, 81, 84, 85, 102, 153, 170, 196, 187, 242, 243, 247, 250, 263, 275, 282, 302, 311, 312, 318, 326, 335, 355, 356, 363, 367-369, 407, 439, 445, 474, 495, 501

Louis Requena: 329

Tony Tomsic/MLB Photos: 54, 103, 328, 387, 388, 416

Bill Livingston/MLB Photos: 31

Wide World Photos: 23, 256, 475

Bettmann/Corbis: 454

Photo illustration of Ozzie Smith's plaque on page 429 by Steve Romer.

Copyright ©2002 by The Sporting News, a division of Vulcan Sports Media, Inc.,
10176 Corporate Square Drive, Suite 200, St. Louis, MO 63132. All rights reserved. Printed in the U.S.A.

THE SPORTING NEWS is a registered trademark of Vulcan Sports Media, Inc. Visit our website at www.sportingnews.com.

ISBN: 0-89204-688-0

10 9 8 7 6 5 4 3 2

ACKNOWLEDGEMENTS

The idea was simple and straightforward, a natural extension of the *Baseball's 100 Greatest Players* book published by *The Sporting News* in 1998. TSN, true to its rich baseball heritage, would put together an elegant Hall of Fame volume profiling and picturing all 254 members of the game's most elite society.

Execution, however, was not so simple. In addition to the monumental tasks of writing text, gathering hundreds of photographs, enhancing old images and designing 512 pages, special people, working quietly behind the scenes, contributed in ways too numerous to list. While their efforts, which often were provided beyond weekly obligations, did not gain a lot of attention, they were very much appreciated.

Special thanks goes to editorial director Steve Meyerhoff, who provides the direction and leadership that keeps the book department on course, and Dave Sloan, who jumped in to provide valuable editing and proofreading help. The outstanding photographs that give this book personality and life were gathered and researched by Peter Newcomb.

The design strategy, so crucial to any commemorative volume, was coordinated by creative director Bill Wilson and prepress director Bob Parajon and executed by a talented team that included Michael Behrens, Chris Callan, Matt Kindt, Jack Kruyne, Chad Painter and Christen Sager. The job of making good photographs look great was coordinated by Steve Romer, who received able assistance from fellow prepress specialists David Brickey, Pamela Speh and Vern Kasal. Russ Carr put the finishing touches on before sending the book to our printer.

◆ ◆ ◆

The statistical source for this project was *Total Baseball* and the display quotes were obtained from old issues of *The Sporting News* as well as newspapers, magazines and books from TSN's massive clip files. Information on Negro League players was pieced together from the clip files and the following books: *The Negro Baseball Leagues*, *Blackball Stars*, *The Negro Leagues Book* and *Voices from the Great Black Baseball Leagues*.

CONTENTS

FOREWORD
by Ozzie Smith

When the telephone call finally came, when I received the news that I had been elected to baseball's Hall of Fame, my emotions took over. I cried.

The call and the news had been anticipated. Ever since I retired after the 1996 season, people said I was a lock to make the Hall of Fame. I never felt that way. I tried to tell myself a lot of great players had come before me and had not been selected to enter the shrine at Cooperstown, for a variety of reasons. As had been the case throughout my career, I didn't want to take anything for granted.

I had played the whole scenario out in my mind a thousand times, anticipating what my reaction would be if the call came. What I had not prepared myself for, however, was the degree of emotion that overcame me when my election became official. I didn't

know how much this was going to touch me.

It was a long road from a childhood in South Central Los Angeles to the Hall of Fame. For the other 253 players featured in this book, those players enshrined before me, each has his own story to tell. The one common bond that I think links all of us is that we did not decide to play baseball because we thought one day we would be elected to the Hall of Fame.

My only goal, and I think the only goal of everybody else in the Hall, was to be the best player I could be. I didn't want people saying I was a defensive player, even though I was proud of what I accomplished defensively. I wanted to be a complete player, and if my defense was what caused people to notice me, that's fine. But I also know in my heart that I made myself into a good offensive player as well.

Former Cardinals shortstop Ozzie Smith, the only member of the 2002 Hall of Fame induction class.

My philosophy has always been simple — if you are good enough at what you do, you don't need to tell other people about it. They will see your ability, and recognize and reward you accordingly. What I am most proud of is that I don't think there was any time, not once, when I walked away after a game was over knowing I didn't give my best effort.

One thing I always tried to do was make certain fans were entertained, no matter whether they were cheering for the Cardinals or against us. I wanted those people to leave the game thinking they would like to come back because they had a good time and enjoyed watching the players perform.

I have been blessed in my career. I won a World Series championship and three pennants. I won Gold Gloves and started in All-Star Games. And now I've been elected to the Hall of Fame. It's a wonderful honor, and I am truly grateful. Who knows, when I walk up to that podium in Cooperstown I might even do a back flip.

Ozzie Smith

The Hall of Fame Museum was dedicated in 1939, after which everybody headed for Doubleday Field and a game featuring current major league players. Fifty years later, the induction spotlight belonged to Johnny Bench (opposite page).

OVERVIEW

HEROES OF THE HALL

They are immortalized in word, song, poetry and anecdotal hearsay and their deeds have been passed with enthusiastic exaggeration from generation to generation. Big and little, tall and short, fast and slow, strong and meek, they are part of an exclusive 254-member society that honors brains as well as brawn and celebrates such qualities as leadership, vision and fierce determination.

For the men who met and surpassed even the most lofty of our baseball expectations, the Hall of Fame is both an esoteric resting place and a physical reminder of special deeds and moments. The first exists in our hearts and memories; the second in a pastoral upstate New York baseball shrine that spotlights and immortalizes the most elite of the athletes and visionaries who have given shape and personality to the National Pastime.

More than anything, "Hall of Fame" is a concept that floods the mind with images — Babe Ruth's home run trot,

Mays robbing Wertz, the Marichal leg kick, Tinker-to-Evers-to-Chance, another Ryan strikeout, DiMaggio gliding, Brock sliding, Brooks diving left or right, Cobb snarling, Clemente beaming and Lou Gehrig, the luckiest man on the face of the earth — while triggering our senses with stories of human passion and dedication as well as weakness and frailty.

Beyond the Cooperstown museum plaques, beyond the mementoes and memories, are stories of men who, if not blessed with superior grace, agility, speed and hand-eye coordination, might well have been the laborers, bankers, firemen or teachers in a more ordinary life. Instead, they are nostalgic reminders of childhood and happy times, flashes of bygone greatness and heroism in brown paper wrappers. They are artifacts and exhibits of our memory, a feeling captured by writer Roger Angell in the New Yorker:

"They played so well and so long, succeeding eventually

at this almost impossible game, that we can think of them as something more useful than gods or heroes. We know they are there, tucked away up-country and in the back of our minds: old men, and younger ones on the way, who prove and sustain the elegance of our baseball dreams."

Elegant on the field, our Hall of Famers offer colorful, fascinating and sometimes-tragic microcosms of the society they entertain. Their stories allow us to glimpse the divergent spectrum of humanity that must be crossed to gain immortality.

Grover Alexander, so spectacular on the mound, battled alcoholism off it — a demon that surely affected a win total that still is tied for third best all time. A love for the nightlife and enormous appetite for food and drink is part of Ruth's persona, a polar opposite to the quiet, painfully shy, stay-at-

home lifestyle of longtime teammate Gehrig.

Others have shared Ruth's love for the spotlight, a fascination that drove 19th century hero King Kelly as well as future stars Dizzy Dean, Satchel Paige and Reggie Jackson. Some shared his affinity for the nightlife as well, a practice that took its toll on Alexander, Paul Waner, Hack Wilson and Mickey Mantle. Immortality, it seems, never comes easily.

Carl Hubbell, Dazzy Vance, Lefty Grove and Hoyt Wilhelm had to persevere through long minor league careers before finding big-league success while Mel Ott, Frank Frisch, Bob Feller and Al Kaline never played a game in the minors. Such stars as Ted Williams, Hank Greenberg, Bob Feller, Joe DiMaggio, Ralph Kiner and Warren Spahn lost multiple prime seasons to military duty during World War II and the Korean War.

Willie Mays (24) was center stage in 1956, when his New York Giants beat Detroit in the Hall of Fame game at Doubleday Field.

The Hall of Fame is no place for sentimentality

The Baseball Writers' Association of America, the organization that has conducted Hall of Fame elections since 1936, will never be accused of sentimentality. Of the 254 members in baseball's most elite society, only 96 (38 percent) are there because they received the mandatory 75-plus percent of votes needed from the BBWAA for election. The rest have gained Hall of Fame inclusion through various selection committees.

In the charter class of 1936, Ty Cobb was the leading vote-getter at 98.2 percent followed by Honus Wagner and Babe Ruth (95.1), Christy Mathewson (90.7) and Walter Johnson (83.6). Over the years, the writers have honored only 32 more players with first-ballot selection while making 57 others sweat their way through two or more elections. Lou Gehrig, who was dying of amyotrophic lateral sclerosis in 1939, and Roberto Clemente, who died in a 1972 plane crash, were honored in special elections.

Hall of Fame players bypassed by the BBWAA vote, as well as numerous managers, umpires, executives and pioneers, have gained entry through the Committee on Veterans, which has been holding closed-door selection meetings since 1953, and such defunct groups as the Centennial Commission, the Committee of Old-Time Players and Writers, the Committee on Old-Timers and the Special Committee on Negro Leagues.

The 15-member Committee on Veterans will be replaced in future years by a 90-member Veterans Committee, which will vote once every two years on Hall of Fame player candidates not elected by the writers and every four years on non-player candidates. Like the BBWAA vote, 75 percent will be required for election.

Candidates for BBWAA election must have played at least 10 years in the major leagues and be retired for five years, although those requirements have been waived in special cases like Gehrig. Players who do not receive at least 5 percent of the vote fall off the ballot while those who do can remain eligible for 15 years. Non-player candidates have to be retired for five years or be at least six months past their 65th birthday.

Only writers who have covered baseball for 10 years are eligible to vote.

Both World War II and the Korean War took a toll on the career numbers of outfielder/fighter pilot Ted Williams (above). A tragic plane crash struck down Roberto Clemente (left), but not before he got his 3,000th hit.

Physical handicaps couldn't stop Mordecai "Three Finger" Brown, who overcame a childhood accident and won 208 major league games while pitching without two fingers on his throwing hand, and Chick Hafey, who pounded out savage line drives with a bat guided by defective eyes. But tragedy did stop Big Ed Delahanty, Addie Joss, Ross Youngs, Roberto Clemente, Gehrig and Roy Campanella—great players whose careers ended prematurely because of illness or accident.

They're all part of the Hall of Fame fabric that weaves such diverse personalities into a close-knit society—and humanizes their memories for appreciative fans.

It's easy to connect with the contagious smile and "let's play two" enthusiasm of Ernie Banks, difficult to understand the "business, not fun" philosophy that drove Bill Terry and Edd Roush or the controversy that shadowed

The three-story red-brick Hall of Fame museum (above) offers thousands of memories to visitors (top photo) who journey to the Cooperstown, N.Y., shrine.

Rogers Hornsby, Ted Williams and Reggie Jackson.

It's easy to remember such poignant moments as Ruth and Gehrig, standing alone in front of microphones at packed Yankee Stadium, making their tear-jerking exits from the game; it's easy to forget the quiet dignity of Stan Musial, Hank Aaron or Robin Yount.

It's also easy to forget the injustice that kept such Negro League stars as Cool Papa Bell, Josh Gibson, Oscar Charleston, Buck Leonard, John Henry Lloyd and Ray Dandridge from pitting their considerable skills against white major leaguers and the sad reality that many other blacks never got a realistic Hall of Fame opportunity.

Every summer, as surely as the swallows return to Capistrano, the baseball community flocks to Cooperstown, N.Y., for the annual Hall of Fame induction ceremony. Fans arrive with a sense of celebration and pride. They leave with an appreciation for the roots that have been formed with this timeless bastion of baseball history.

Cooperstown, a city of about 2,200 in the lush, rolling hills of central New York, no longer touts itself as the birthplace of baseball, a claim that inspired the building of a Hall of Fame museum that opened there in 1939. But it still is a perfect fit for the National Pastime, the type of rural, scenic community in which the early game must have flourished. With glimmering Lake Otsego providing a beautiful backdrop, streets shaded by giant oak and chestnut trees lead thousands of pilgrims to baseball's shrine.

The three-story, red-brick museum offers interactive exhibits, shows and movies that celebrate baseball history, but the serious fan is more enamored with the gloves, bats, balls, uniforms and hundreds of other mementoes that once belonged to Hall of Fame players or were used in memorable games. This is the "stuff" of legends.

Nearby Doubleday Field, the long-reputed site of baseball's first game in 1839, offers a rustic view of baseball past—a 9,800-seat throwback facility that plays host to the annual Hall of Fame contest between two major league teams. But more than anything else, Hall of Fame weekend is about hob-nobbing with the stars—new inductees and all of the proud Hall of Famers who come back to retrieve fading memories.

For those elected, it's the ultimate rush of pride, the honor that punctuates everything they have worked so hard to achieve.

"Compared with this honor, all others are trifles," Waite Hoyt told a Cooperstown crowd during his 1969 induction speech. "Every ballplayer dreams of being in the Hall of Fame."

Others are more succinct.

"This rounds out my life," a near-tearful Medwick said in 1968.

"This is my happy day," Goose Goslin added. "I will never forget the honor and will take it with me to the grave."

Bill Mazeroski was so emotional at his 2001 induction that he threw aside his 12-page speech, choked out a few thank yous and retired to his seat—as the crowd gave him a standing ovation. Kirby Puckett thrilled those same fans when he looked skyward and thanked someone special.

"Mom's probably looking down right now and thinking about all those spankings she gave me for hitting balls through neighbors' windows and breaking lamps and breaking everything in the house," he said. "I want to tell Mom, well, 'Ma, I hope you can see now that it was worth it. Your little baby is going into the Hall of Fame.'"

The Hall of Fame Library is filled with similar sentiments expressed by players, managers, executives and organizers who, one by one, took their turn at the Cooperstown induction podium—many times with words as eloquent as their play. Brock's 1985 speech epitomized the spirit of baseball and was filled with the almost-reverent passion by which most players are measured.

"While searching the dial of our old Philco radio one night, I came upon a game between the St. Louis Cardinals and the Brooklyn Dodgers," he told a hushed audience, recalling a dream he dared to nourish as a child in Monroe, La. "I thought I had tuned into another world, a world in total contrast to my surroundings.

"During the 1950s, Jim Crow was king in the South and excluded me from the mainstream of society. Baseball fed my fantasies. Identifying with it, I felt free. I believed that there would come a day when I, too, would be out there on the field of play. Whatever it is about baseball that touches a person's soul, it has a magical transforming power."

And a magical connection with its brightest stars.

Carl Yastrzemski's Hall of Fame moment came in 1989 during emotional ceremonies at Cooperstown, N.Y.

HANK AARON

HENRY "HANK" L. AARON
MILWAUKEE N.L., ATLANTA N.L.,
MILWAUKEE A.L., 1954-1976
HIT 755 HOME RUNS IN 23-YEAR CAREER TO
BECOME MAJORS' ALL-TIME HOMER KING. HAD
20 OR MORE FOR 20 CONSECUTIVE YEARS, AT
LEAST 30 IN 15 SEASONS AND 40 OR BETTER
EIGHT TIMES. ALSO SET RECORDS FOR GAMES
PLAYED (3,298), AT-BATS (12,364), LONG HITS
(1,477), TOTAL BASES (6,856), RUNS BATTED
IN (2,297). PACED N.L. IN BATTING TWICE
AND HOMERS, RUNS BATTED IN AND SLUGGING
PCT. FOUR TIMES EACH. WON MOST VALUABLE
PLAYER AWARD IN N.L. IN 1957.

Born: 2-5-34, Mobile, Ala. **Height/Weight:** 6-0/180 **Bats/Throws:** R/R **Primary position:** Outfield **Career statistics:** .305 avg., 3,771 hits, 2,174 runs, 755 HR, 2,297 RBIs, 240 steals **Teams:** Milwaukee Braves 1954-65, Atlanta Braves 1966-74, Brewers 1975-76
Batting champion: N.L., 1956, '59 **HR champion:** N.L., 1957, '63, '66, '67 **Major awards:** N.L. MVP, 1957

He was quiet, unassuming and shy, but no one in the second half century exerted more influence on the record books than Henry Aaron. He mesmerized teammates and fans with a soft-spoken dignity that defined his off-field personality for almost a quarter century while delivering a less-subtle message with the booming bat that helped him find baseball immortality.

That the home run would become Aaron's legacy seemed preposterous when he stepped onto the field as a skinny 6-foot rookie. But no one could have envisioned the unflinching work ethic and competitive fire that would allow Hammerin' Hank to pile up a record 755 home runs over a career that started in 1954 with the Milwaukee Braves and ended 23 seasons later in the same city with the American League's Brewers.

Aaron was a righthanded hitter with a fluid swing

AARON

and lightning reflexes, but his secret was in the wrists — powerful wrists that allowed him to keep his hands back and drive the ball to all fields with tremendous force. The numbers never were spectacular — eight 40-homer seasons, never more than 47; 11 100-RBI seasons, never more than 132 — but the bottom lines were: 3,771 hits (third all-time), 2,174 runs (tied for third), 2,297 RBIs (first), 6,856 total bases (first), a career .305 average with two batting titles and, of course, the homers — 41 more than Babe Ruth's previous record.

Lost in the glare of the home run mountain that Aaron finally scaled in a festive 1974 season was his

> "The best thing you can say about him is, when you walk on the field and you're playing against Hank Aaron, you are in the big leagues." — *Pete Rose*

all-around consistency. He had outstanding speed, good instincts and one of the game's better right-field arms — tools that earned him three Gold Gloves. The man who hit 20-plus homers in 20 straight seasons also appeared in a record-tying 24 All-Star Games.

The power combination of Aaron and Eddie Mathews drove the Braves to consecutive Milwaukee pennants and a World Series victory (1957), but the Braves' Atlanta teams generally were weak. One of Aaron's signature moments came late in his MVP 1957 season — an 11th-inning home run that clinched Milwaukee's first pennant.

Player/Year elected: 1938, 80.9 percent of vote

GROVER ALEXANDER

GROVER CLEVELAND ALEXANDER
GREAT NATIONAL LEAGUE PITCHER
FOR TWO DECADES WITH PHILLIES,
CUBS AND CARDINALS STARTING
IN 1911. WON 1926 WORLD CHAMPIONSHIP
FOR CARDINALS BY STRIKING OUT
LAZZERI WITH BASES FULL IN
FINAL CRISIS AT YANKEE STADIUM.

Born: 2-26-1887, Elba, Neb. **Died:** 11-4-50 **Height/Weight:** 6-1/185 **Bats/Throws:** R/R **Position:** Pitcher **Career statistics:** 373-208, 2.56 ERA, 2,198 strikeouts **Teams:** Phillies 1911-17, 1930; Cubs 1918-26; Cardinals 1926-29

Grover Cleveland Alexander spent 20 major league seasons creating two legends: an on-field master who posted a National League-record-tying 373 career victories, and an off-field drifter who battled alcoholism and other problems to an inglorious end.

The control that so defined his pitching success was notably absent in a demonic vice that defined and overpowered his personal life.

The slim 6-foot-1 Alexander, a Nebraska farm boy, burst upon the big-league scene in 1911 with the greatest rookie performance in history—a 28-13 record and 2.57 ERA for the Philadelphia Phillies. His smooth, effortless, three-quarters and sidearm motions mesmerized opposing hitters and his laser-like fastball and sweeping curves were delivered with pinpoint precision.

"Alex had the most perfect control of any pitcher I ever saw," Hall of Fame outfielder Max Carey once said, and he was a fast worker who operated with unerring instinct and confidence. Alexander's 1915, '16 and '17 seasons were masterpieces. He was 31-10, 33-12 and 30-13; his ERAs were 1.22, 1.55 and

1.83; he led the N.L. in innings and strikeouts all three years; and he posted 36 shutouts, including a still-standing record of 16 in 1916. The 1915 Phillies won the franchise's first pennant and Alex recorded their only World Series win in a five-game loss to Boston.

Alexander's seven-season, 190-victory Philadelphia record, which included 61 of his 90 career shutouts (second all time), was carved out while pitching in the Phillies' tiny Baker Bowl. He followed Philadelphia with 12 less-spectacular but still-productive N.L. seasons in Chicago and St. Louis after spending most of the 1918 campaign on the front line during World War II.

Alexander is best remembered for one dramatic 1926 performance when, at age 39 and reportedly hung over after a night of revelry, he entered the seventh inning of World Series Game 7 with two out and the bases loaded to face New York Yankees slugger Tony Lazzeri. He struck Lazzeri out, preserving the Cardinals' 3-2 lead, and pitched the final two innings to preserve St. Louis' first World Series championship.

> "He made me want to throw my bat away when I went to the plate. He fed me pitches I couldn't hit." —*Johnny Evers*

ALEXANDER

WALTER EMMONS ALSTON

SOFT-SPOKEN, LOW-PROFILE ORGANIZATION MAN WHO MANAGED THE DODGERS FOR 23 YEARS, LEADING TEAM TO ITS ONLY WORLD CHAMPIONSHIP IN BROOKLYN IN 1955 AND TO PENNANT IN 1956 BEFORE TEAM MOVED TO WEST COAST. IN LOS ANGELES HIS CLUBS WON WORLD TITLES IN 1959, 1963 AND 1965 AND PENNANTS IN 1966 AND 1974; AND ONLY JOHN McGRAW, WITH 10, TOPPED ALSTON'S SEVEN N.L. PENNANTS. TEAMS FINISHED IN FIRST DIVISION 18 TIMES, WINNING 2,040 GAMES.

Manager/Year elected: 1983, Committee on Veterans

WALTER ALSTON

Born: 12-1-11, Venice, Ohio **Died:** 10-1-84 **Height/Weight:** 6-2/210 **Teams managed:** Brooklyn Dodgers 1954-57; Los Angeles Dodgers 1958-76 **Career record:** 2,040-1,613, .558 **World Series titles:** 1955, '59, '63, '65

He was the quiet man of Dodgerland, the guru of Brooklyn and Los Angeles baseball for 23 seasons. Nobody epitomized low-key success more than big, slow-talking Walter Alston, a former Ohio school teacher and farmer. The prototypical strong, silent type, "Smokey" guided the National League's glamour franchise to seven pennants and four World Series championships from 1954-76.

Alston, a 13-year minor league player who struck out in his only big-league at-bat for St. Louis in 1936, is best remembered as the man who guided Brooklyn to its only World Series title. That was 1955, his second season after being pulled out of the Dodgers' system as a surprise choice to replace Chuck Dressen. Three years later, the Dodgers were playing on the West Coast and Alston was firmly entrenched as the only manager Los Angeles fans would know for 19 years.

He never said much, but players responded well to his quiet dignity. They also feared the wrath of a 6-foot-2, 210-pound strongman whose occasional tantrums could send everyone scrambling for cover. Alston seldom raised his voice and rarely showed emotion, but players understood his demand for total effort and his obsession for fundamentals.

Like contemporary Casey Stengel, the stoic Alston relied on platooning and his uncanny instincts. He mas-terfully adjusted his managing style to his roster — power in the 1950s, pitching in the '60s, pitching/speed in the 1970s — and the result was spectacular. Alston's Dodgers won pennants in 1955 and '56 in Brooklyn and five more in Los Angeles, three of which led to championships. His masterpiece was 1963, when pitchers Sandy Koufax, Johnny Podres and Don Drysdale held the New York

"Walt has always represented the standard of his profession. He's a man's manager, not too many rules and restrictions. All he ever wanted was your honesty and respect, a full effort." — *Steve Garvey*

Yankees to four runs in a World Series sweep.

When he retired near the end of the 1976 season, Alston's 2,040-1,613 record ranked high on the all-time charts. Only John McGraw won more National League games or pennants and only three managers won more World Series. The man who operated on 23 one-year contracts finished either first or second in 15 of his 23 campaigns.

Manager/Year elected: 2000, Committee on Veterans

SPARKY ANDERSON

GEORGE LEE ANDERSON
"SPARKY"
CINCINNATI, N.L., 1970-1978
DETROIT, A.L., 1979-1995

ONE OF THE GAME'S MOST SUCCESSFUL AND COLORFUL MANAGERS, HIS 2,194 WINS RANK THIRD IN HISTORY BEHIND CONNIE MACK AND JOHN MCGRAW. THE CRANK THAT TURNED THE BIG RED MACHINE. HIS SKILLFUL LEADERSHIP HELPED THOSE CINCINNATI TEAMS DOMINATE IN THE 1970s. REVERED AND TREASURED BY HIS PLAYERS FOR HIS HUMILITY, HUMANITY, ETERNAL OPTIMISM AND KNOWLEDGE OF THE GAME. BASEBALL'S ONLY MANAGER TO WIN A WORLD SERIES IN BOTH LEAGUES AND LEAD TWO FRANCHISES IN VICTORIES. HIS TEAMS WON THREE WORLD SERIES, SEVEN DIVISION TITLES AND FIVE PENNANTS, COMPILING A .619 POST-SEASON WINNING PERCENTAGE.

Born: 2-22-34, Bridgewater, S.D. **Height/Weight:** 5-9/185 **Teams managed:** Reds 1970-78; Tigers 1979-95
Career record: 2,194-1,834, .545 **World Series titles:** 1975, '76, '84 **Major awards:** A.L. Manager of Year, 1984, '87

His movie-screen smile and snow-white hair lit up dugouts for 26 major league seasons. His stream-of-consciousness dialogue entertained reporters and revved up players, who fed off his unwavering optimism and upbeat personality. George "Sparky" Anderson was equal parts manager, motivator and psychologist, talents that translated into 2,194 wins and three World Series championships.

Anderson was like a cool breeze that wafted through Cincinnati and Detroit over two-plus decades. Fans loved his colorful malaprops and bubbly personality, players fed off his unflagging enthusiasm and owners marveled at his ability to inspire top effort. Anderson, a .218-hitting second baseman for the Philadelphia Phillies in his one major league season (1959), batted .545 as a manager, compiling a 2,194-1,834 regular-season record and a 34-21 mark in postseason play.

His most memorable success came as boss of Cincinnati's vaunted Big Red Machine, which rolled to five division titles, four National League pennants and two World Series wins in the 1970s. When the Cincinnati magic wore off, he moved to Detroit and guided the Tigers to two division titles and a 1984 World Series championship over 17 seasons, giving him distinction as the only man to manage fall classic winners in both leagues.

Anderson was blessed with such hitters as Johnny Bench, Joe Morgan, Pete Rose, Tony Perez and George Foster in Cincinnati — the nucleus for one of the most potent lineups ever assembled. His less-talented Tigers needed an astute baseball mind and motivation, which Sparky provided in large doses. Never blessed with great starting pitching, he became known as "Captain Hook" because of his penchant for quick pitching changes.

When he retired in 1995, Anderson ranked behind only John McGraw and Connie Mack on the all-time win list. He also held distinction as a rookie pennant-winner (1970) and the first man to win 600 games in each league. Anderson's 1975-76 Reds were considered one of the greatest teams of all time and his Reds and Tigers posted winning records in 20 of his 26 managerial seasons.

> **"Baseball doesn't need me. I need it."** —*Sparky Anderson*

ANDERSON

Player/Year elected: 1939, Committee of Old-Time Players and Writers

CAP ANSON

ADRIAN CONSTANTINE ANSON
"CAP"

GREATEST HITTER AND GREATEST
NATIONAL LEAGUE PLAYER-MANAGER
OF 19TH CENTURY, STARTED WITH
CHICAGOS IN NATIONAL LEAGUE'S
FIRST YEAR 1876. CHICAGO MANAGER
FROM 1879 TO 1897, WINNING 5 PENNANTS.
WAS .300 CLASS HITTER 20 YEARS,
BATTING CHAMPION 4 TIMES.

Born: 4-11-1852, Marshalltown, Iowa **Died:** 4-14-22 **Height/Weight:** 6-1/225 **Bats/Throws:** R/R **Primary position:** First base
Career statistics: .333 avg., 3,081 hits, 1,722 runs, 1,880 RBIs, 247 steals **Teams played:** Chicago 1876-97
Teams managed (1,296-947): Chicago 1879-97; New York 1898 **Batting champion:** N.L., 1879, '81, '87, '88

Player, manager, pioneer and showman—Adrian "Cap" Anson was to late 19th-century Chicago what Babe Ruth was to New York in the 1920s. Not only did he set baseball's early standards with his "scientific innovations" during a 22-year stay in the Windy City, the man called "Pop" also spread its gospel with a booming bat and colorful, fan-enticing demonstrations. Anson was, in more ways than one, the game's first and most enduring superstar.

As a player, the 6-foot-1, 225-pound Iowan inserted the word "slugger" into baseball's vocabulary. He stood erect in his righthanded stance, heels close together, and waited for his perfect pitch, which he lashed viciously at, over or through intimidated fielders. Anson continued his dead-ball assaults whether facing pitchers at 45 feet, 55 or 60-feet, 6-inches. The four-time batting champ topped the .300 plateau 19 times en route to a career .333 average.

As a manager, Anson took over the White Stockings (forerunners to today's Cubs) in 1879, the National League's fourth season, and led them to

> "**Cap seemingly swallowed from the Fountain of Youth and at times it looked as though he would go on forever. ...**"—*Sportswriter Fred Lieb*

five N.L. pennants before retiring 19 years later. Everything was first class for the N.L.'s showcase team, from hotel accommodations to gaudy parades that delivered players to opposing ballparks. Anson loved grand entrances and often marched his players, military style, onto the field.

Anson the pioneer is credited with such innovations as spring training, the hit-and-run play, use of signals and the pitching rotation. He also was the first player to hit four doubles in one game, belt five home runs in consecutive games and collect 3,000 hits, although his long-accepted 3,081 total has been contested and reduced to 2,995 by some modern-day researchers.

From his 1871 beginning in the National Association to his shocking release in 1897, the aggressive, sometimes-gruff Anson was one of the game's greatest figures. Never a good fielder whether playing third base or first, he ranked among the great hitters of all time while helping to set the game on its successful course.

ANSON

LUIS APARICIO

LUIS ERNESTO APARICIO
CHICAGO A.L. 1956-1962, 1968-1970
BALTIMORE A.L. 1963-1967
BOSTON A.L. 1971-1973
REGULAR SHORTSTOP FOR ALL OF HIS 18 SEASONS. SET MAJOR LEAGUE CAREER RECORDS FOR MOST GAMES (2,581), ASSISTS (8,016), CHANCES ACCEPTED (12,564) AND DOUBLE PLAYS (1,553) BY A SHORTSTOP; AND HAS MOST A.L. PUTOUTS (4,548). LED A.L. IN FIELDING 8 TIMES. TOPPED LEAGUE IN STEALS HIS FIRST 9 SEASONS, BEGINNING STOLEN BASE RENAISSANCE. A.L. ROOKIE OF THE YEAR IN 1956.

Born: 4-29-34, Maracaibo, Venezuela **Height/Weight:** 5-8/155 **Bats/Throws:** R/R **Primary position:** Shortstop **Career statistics:** .262 avg., 2,677 hits, 1,335 runs, 506 steals **Teams:** White Sox 1956-62, 1968-70; Orioles 1963-67; Red Sox 1971-73 **Major awards:** A.L. Rookie of Year, 1956

He zipped, darted and flashed around major league infields for 18 magical seasons, turning sure base hits into outs and tough-minded opponents into gasping admirers. Luis Aparicio, all 5-foot-8 and 155 pounds of him, built a Hall of Fame legacy around speed and defense, earning double-edged distinction as the best-fielding shortstop of his era and the man who resurrected the stolen base as an offensive weapon.

"Little Looie" used quick, sure hands to make the routine play and instant acceleration to range left or right in pursuit of balls other shortstops could only dream of reaching. Former Chicago White Sox coach Don Gutteridge claimed Aparicio made three kinds of plays, "routine, difficult and impossible," and his incredible range and nine Gold Gloves set the standard by which shortstop greats like Ozzie Smith would be judged.

But Aparicio was much more than a fancy glove. The scared kid who couldn't even speak English when he arrived from Maracaibo, Venezuela, evolved into one of the game's most proficient leadoff men and revered leaders. He won Rookie of the Year honors for Chicago in 1956 and began a string of nine straight seasons as the American League stolen base leader. Aparicio teamed with second baseman Nellie Fox for

seven years as one of the game's top double-play combinations.

He was chief instigator when the 1959 "Go-Go Sox" blazed to an A.L. pennant and he later helped the Baltimore Orioles win a 1966 World Series championship. The career .262 hitter wreaked havoc with jittery defenders whenever he reached base and

"That little guy is just about the greatest shortstop I've ever seen. I can't imagine how anybody could possibly be any better, no matter how far back you go." —*Ralph Houk*

blazed a basestealing trail for future speedsters Maury Wills and Lou Brock.

Aparicio, who collected 2,677 hits in 10 seasons with Chicago (1956-62, 1968-70), five with Baltimore (1963-67) and three with Boston (1971-73), was a starter in every one of his 18 big-league seasons. He still holds the major league record for games played at shortstop (2,581) and A.L. marks for assists (8,016), chances (12,564) and putouts (4,548).

LUKE APPLING

LUCIUS BENJAMIN APPLING
CHICAGO A.L. 1930-1950
A.L. BATTING CHAMPION IN 1936 AND 1943.
PLAYED 2,218 GAMES AT SHORTSTOP
FOR MAJOR LEAGUE MARK.
HAD 2,749 HITS.
LIFETIME BATTING AVERAGE OF .310.
LED A.L. IN ASSIST 7 YEARS.
HOLDS A.L. RECORD FOR CHANCES
ACCEPTED BY SHORTSTOP 11,569.

Born: 4-2-07, High Point, N.C. **Died:** 1-3-91 **Height/Weight:** 5-10/183 **Bats/Throws:** R/R **Primary position:** Shortstop

Career statistics: .310 avg., 2,749 hits, 1,319 runs, 1,116 RBIs **Teams:** White Sox 1930-43, 1945-50 **Batting champion:** A.L., 1936, '43

He would amble to the plate, suffering, no doubt, from indigestion, a stiff neck, sore feet, double vision or any one of many afflictions that invariably affected baseball's foremost hypochondriac. Then, as if miraculously cured, Chicago White Sox shortstop Luke Appling would use his natural inside-out swing to stroke another base hit to right field.

Nobody played with a more graceful dodder than "Old Aches and Pains," who anchored the White Sox infield for 20 superlative seasons after his arrival in 1930. Teammates would listen to his litany of ailments, offer proper solace and then watch him perform with Hall of Fame consistency.

Appling was at his best when driving pitchers crazy with his pesky batting style. The righthanded swinger seldom pulled the ball and was a master at fouling off pitches until he got one he could handle. He might lose 10 or 12 balls in one at-bat, a penchant that once prompted Tigers pitcher Dizzy

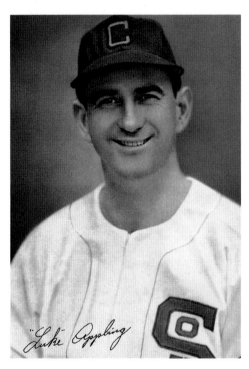

"Luke Appling"

> "I don't know what was the most (balls) I ever fouled off in one trip to the plate. It could have been 13, 14, 15, 16, 17, 18, 19 or something like that." —*Luke Appling*

Trout to throw his glove at Appling and shout, "Here, foul this off, too." Appling was the quintessential singles hitter, collecting 2,162 in a career that produced 2,749 hits.

The seven-time American League All-Star selection and 16-time .300 hitter parlayed that style into a .310 career average and two batting titles. Appling struck out only 25 times while hitting .388 in 1936, a modern-era record for shortstops, and driving in 128 runs on only 44 extra-base hits. He led the A.L. with a .328 mark in 1943 before spending the 1944 season performing military duty in World War II.

A native of High Point, N.C., the ever-smiling Appling spoke with a pronounced Southern drawl and seemed impervious to pressure. The former Oglethorpe University (Atlanta) halfback, one of the most popular players in White Sox history, was a sure-handed shortstop who never played on a White Sox team that finished above third place.

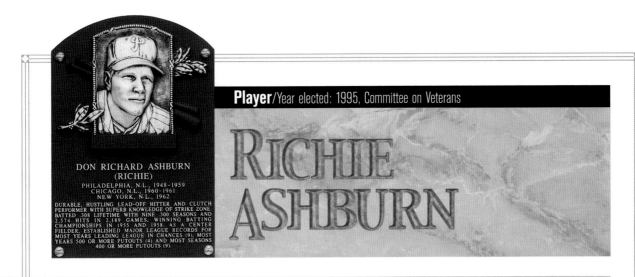

DON RICHARD ASHBURN
(RICHIE)
PHILADELPHIA, N.L., 1948-1959
CHICAGO, N.L., 1960-1961
NEW YORK, N.L., 1962
DURABLE, HUSTLING LEAD-OFF HITTER AND CLUTCH
PERFORMER WITH SUPERB KNOWLEDGE OF STRIKE ZONE.
BATTED .308 LIFETIME WITH NINE .300 SEASONS AND
2,574 HITS IN 2,189 GAMES. WINNING BATTING
CHAMPIONSHIPS IN 1955 AND 1958. AS A CENTER
FIELDER, ESTABLISHED MAJOR LEAGUE RECORDS FOR
MOST YEARS LEADING LEAGUE IN CHANCES (9), MOST
YEARS 500 OR MORE PUTOUTS (4) AND MOST SEASONS
400 OR MORE PUTOUTS (9).

Player/Year elected: 1995, Committee on Veterans

RICHIE ASHBURN

Born: 3-19-27, Tilden, Neb. **Died:** 9-9-97 **Height/Weight:** 5-10/170 **Bats/Throws:** L/R **Primary position:** Center field **Career statistics:** .308 avg., 2,574 hits, 1,322 runs, 234 steals **Teams:** Phillies 1948-59; Cubs 1960-61; Mets 1962 **Batting champion:** N.L., 1955, '58

He was the ultimate pest, a hit-it-where-they-ain't slasher who outran predictions he would never find baseball success as a "singles hitter." Not only did Richie Ashburn defy critics and win over hard-edged Philadelphia fans with his hustling style, he gained Hall of Fame distinction as one of the best leadoff men in history — and a speedy center fielder who covered ground almost as gracefully as contemporaries Willie Mays and Mickey Mantle.

For 12 seasons from 1948-59, Phillies fans watched the lefthanded-swinging Ashburn guide pitches all over the park from his closed stance — legs spread, arms cocked, hands choked well up on his bottle bat. Artistic merit was not a concern for the 5-foot-10, 170-pound instigator, who bounced, sliced, poked, blooped and bunted his way on base, often after foul-ing off numerous pitches.

"The guy is uncanny," said 1951 Cubs manager Frank Frisch, who watched Ashburn force defenders to play shallow with his bunting ability and then consistently slash balls past them. Blond, blue-eyed and popular, "Whitey" supplemented his outstanding on-base percentage by leading the National League in walks four times and he never struck out more than 50 times in any season.

After a .333 debut in 1948, Ashburn became trigger man for Philadelphia's Whiz Kids, who won a pennant on the final day of the 1950 season. It was his memorable ninth-inning throw that nailed Brooklyn's Cal Abrams at the plate, setting the stage for Dick Sisler's pennant-winning home run in the 10th. But team success would be elusive over the remainder of a 15-year career.

The durable Ashburn, a five-time All-Star Game selection, won batting titles in 1955 (.338) and 1958 (.350) en route to a .308 career average, topped 200 hits three times and scored more than 90 runs eight straight seasons. When Ashburn ended his career in 1962 with the expansion New York Mets after a two-year stop with the Cubs, he had 2,574 hits — 29 homers, 2,119 singles.

> "The guy is uncanny. He must follow the pitch with his eye until it hits his bat. And if you watch him closely, you can see him aim his bat in the direction in which he wants the ball to go."
>
> —*Frank Frisch*

EARL AVERILL

HOWARD EARL AVERILL
"ROCK"

CLEVELAND A.L. DETROIT A.L.
BOSTON N.L. 1929-1941
COMPILED .318 CAREER BATTING AVERAGE
AND HIT 238 HOME RUNS. TWICE MADE
MORE THAN 200 HITS IN SEASON, PACING
LEAGUE WITH 232 IN 1936. DROVE IN
100 OR MORE RUNS FIVE TIMES. RAPPED
FOUR HOMERS, THREE CONSECUTIVELY
IN FIRST GAME AND BATTED IN 11 RUNS
IN 1930 TWIN-BILL.

Born: 5-21-02, Snohomish, Wash. **Died:** 8-16-83 **Height/Weight:** 5-9/170 **Bats/Throws:** L/R **Primary position:** Outfield

Career statistics: .318 avg., 2,019 hits, 1,224 runs, 238 HR, 1,164 RBIs **Teams:** Indians 1929-39; Tigers 1939-40; Braves 1941

Earl Averill was a baseball paradox, a 5-foot-9, 170-pound lightweight who traded power punches with such brawny American League contemporaries as Babe Ruth, Lou Gehrig, Jimmie Foxx and Al Simmons. Strong, shy and silent, the Earl of Snohomish let his bat do the talking over a short-but-productive 13-year run as one of the great outfielders in Cleveland history.

Averill, who was born and raised in the small logging community of Snohomish, Wash., became an instant star for a weak Indians team when he homered in his first major league at-bat in 1929, a few weeks short of his 27th birthday. The Indians would never finish higher than third place in his 10 full Cleveland seasons, but Averill, a dead pull left-handed hitter, took aim at League Park's short right field fence and posted some gaudy statistics.

From 1929 through 1938, he was a hitting machine, averaging .323, 22 home runs, 108 RBIs, 115

runs and 189 hits. In 1936, he pounded out 232 hits en route to a .378 average. In 1931, 32 of his 209 hits were homers and he drove in a career-high 143 runs. The dark-haired, durable Averill liked to crowd the plate and look for the inside pitch, a trait that prompted many teams to go into a Ted Williams-like shift.

The hard-hitting Averill played all three outfield positions with grace and efficiency. But he is best remembered for a sharp line drive he hit in the 1937 All-Star Game. The blow fractured the toe of St. Louis Cardinals ace Dizzy Dean and eventually forced him to alter his pitching motion. Dean developed serious arm problems that would force him out of baseball within three years.

Averill's career followed a similar fate. A 1939 back injury resulted in a trade to Detroit, where he played a backup role for the pennant-winning Tigers of 1940. He retired with a .318 average and 2,019 hits in 1941 after eight games with the Boston Braves.

"They used the Ted Williams shift on me long before Williams came into the league. I played five or six seasons before I found out there were three fields to hit the ball to." — *Earl Averill*

A V E R I L L

JOHN FRANKLIN BAKER
PHILADELPHIA A.L. 1908-1914
NEW YORK A.L. 1916-1922
MEMBER OF CONNIE MACK'S FAMOUS
$100,000 INFIELD. LED AMERICAN LEAGUE
IN HOME-RUNS 1911-12-13, TIED IN 1914.
WON TWO WORLD SERIES GAMES FROM
GIANTS IN 1911 WITH HOME-RUNS THUS
GETTING NAME "HOME RUN" BAKER. PLAYED
IN SIX WORLD SERIES 1910-11-13-14-21-22.

Player/Year elected: 1955, Committee on Veterans

FRANK "HOME RUN" BAKER

Born: 3-13-1886, Trappe, Md. **Died:** 6-28-63 **Height/Weight:** 5-11/173 **Bats/Throws:** L/R **Primary position:** Third base **Career statistics:** .307 avg., 1,838 hits, 96 HR, 235 steals **Teams:** Athletics 1908-14; Yankees 1916-19, 1921-22 **HR champion:** A.L., 1911, '12, '13, '14

His real first name was Frank, but baseball remembers him fondly as Home Run Baker. He was a product of the dead-ball era, an almost mythological figure who performed unheard-of longball feats for Connie Mack's Philadelphia Athletics. Before Babe Ruth, before the lively ball and friendly outfield fences, Baker provided a dramatic preview of the game's powerful future.

It seems ludicrous today, but Baker captured or shared American League home run titles from 1911-14 with totals of 11, 10, 12 and nine — and he did it under difficult circumstances, hitting spitters, shiners and tobacco-stained mush balls. His nickname, however, was the result of home runs on consecutive days against the New York Giants in the 1911 World Series — a game-winner off Rube Marquard one day, a game-tying, ninth-inning shot off Christy Mathewson the next — that keyed the A's championship run.

The 5-foot-11 Baker was an unlikely star when Mack discovered him in 1908 — a bow-legged, awkward-

looking third baseman with a powerful body, sure hands, accurate arm and deceptive speed. A lefthanded swinger who clubbed pitches with his 52-ounce bat from a closed stance, Baker hit .305 in his 1909 rookie season and entrenched himself as the A's cleanup man from 1911-14, when he averaged 118 RBIs.

Baker, who did not smoke, drink or use profanity, defying early century baseball stereotypes, was a member of Mack's famed $100,000 infield that included first baseman Stuffy McInnis, second baseman Eddie Collins and shortstop Jack Barry. He also was a five-time .300 hitter for A's teams that won four pennants and three World Series in a five-year span and he batted .363 in six fall classics with three homers and 18 RBIs.

His final two Series came with New York, where Baker played six seasons after Mack sold off his star players in a shocking 1914-15 housecleaning. A solid but unspectacular performer with the Yankees, he retired in 1922 with a .307 career average — and 96 home runs.

> "I could see myself in a big-league uniform. I dreamed of playing before big crowds. I dreamed of being a hero. But never—never, never—did I dream that I would ever be in the Hall of Fame." — *Frank Baker*

Player/Year elected: 1971, Committee on Veterans

DAVID JAMES BANCROFT
"BEAUTY"
PHILADELPHIA N.L., NEW YORK N.L.,
BOSTON N.L., BROOKLYN N.L.
1915-1930
SET MAJOR LEAGUE RECORD FOR CHANCES
HANDLED BY A SHORTSTOP IN A SEASON--984
IN 1922. LED LEAGUE IN PUTOUTS FOR SHORT-
STOPS IN 1918·1920·1921·1922. HIT .319 IN 1921,
.321 IN 1922 AND .304 IN 1923 WITH
NEW YORK GIANTS. HIT .319 IN 1925 AND
.311 IN 1926 WITH BOSTON.
PLAYER-MANAGER OF BRAVES, 1924-1927.

DAVE BANCROFT

Born: 4-20-1891, Sioux City, Iowa **Died:** 10-9-72 **Height/Weight:** 5-9/160 **Bats/Throws:** B/R **Primary position:** Shortstop
Career statistics: .279 avg., 2,004 hits, 1,048 runs **Teams:** Phillies 1915-20; Giants 1920-23, 1930; Braves 1924-27; Dodgers 1928-29

One minute he was prodding teammates, fighting opponents and baiting umpires with his sharp, acerbic tongue. The next he was flashing around the left side of the infield, scooping up short-hop grounders, gunning out runners with his powerful arm and mesmerizing fans with his grace and agility. Little, feisty, energetic Dave Bancroft was a "200 percenter," whether playing shortstop, running the bases or plotting strategy with New York Giants manager and mentor John McGraw.

For 16 major league seasons, the 160-pound lightning rod from Sioux City, Iowa, never stopped battling, a quality that endeared him to fans, teammates and managers. As a rookie in 1915 he was a difference-maker for a Philadelphia team that captured the National League pennant and, after 5 ½ seasons with the Phillies, Bancroft became the glue for McGraw's Giants, who won three straight pennants and two World Series.

Bancroft and McGraw were a natural fit. The man affectionately know as

"**Mechanically, he was almost perfect. It is impossible that he ever had an equal at snatching a half hop or making a cutoff throw from the outfield. ...**"
— *Frank Graham, N.Y. Journal-American*

"Beauty" was an extension of his manager on the field, the defensive captain and team sparkplug. His intensity was contagious, as was the team-first attitude he brought to the game. Bancroft always seemed to be positioned perfectly and he rarely made mental mistakes. A switch-hitter who compiled a respectable .279 career average, he worked pitchers for walks, made consistent contact and hit behind the runner.

The hard-nosed, ever-aggressive "Banny" formed an outstanding double-play combination with young Frank Frisch during a three-year New York stay in which he posted averages of .318, .321 and .304. He also trained his shortstop successor, future Hall of Famer Travis Jackson. With Bancroft slowing down and Jackson ready to step in, a reluctant McGraw traded his star to Boston after the 1923 World Series and he spent the next four years as the Braves' player-manager.

Bancroft retired in 1930 after two final seasons with Brooklyn and 10 games in New York as McGraw's player-coach.

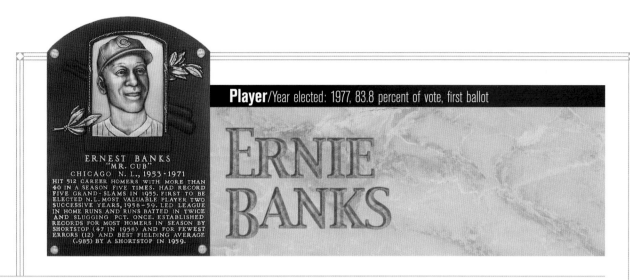

Player/Year elected: 1977, 83.8 percent of vote, first ballot

ERNIE BANKS

ERNEST BANKS
"MR. CUB"
CHICAGO N.L., 1953-1971
HIT 512 CAREER HOMERS WITH MORE THAN
40 IN A SEASON FIVE TIMES. HAD RECORD
FIVE GRAND-SLAMS IN 1955. FIRST TO BE
ELECTED N.L. MOST VALUABLE PLAYER TWO
SUCCESSIVE YEARS, 1958-59. LED LEAGUE
IN HOME RUNS AND RUNS BATTED IN TWICE
AND SLUGGING PCT. ONCE. ESTABLISHED
RECORDS FOR MOST HOMERS IN SEASON BY
SHORTSTOP (47 IN 1958) AND FOR FEWEST
ERRORS (12) AND BEST FIELDING AVERAGE
(.985) BY A SHORTSTOP IN 1959.

Born: 1-31-31, Dallas, Tex. **Height/Weight:** 6-1/180 **Bats/Throws:** R/R **Primary positions:** Shortstop, first base **Career statistics:** .274 avg., 2,583 hits, 1,305 runs, 512 HR, 1,636 RBIs **Teams:** Cubs 1953-71 **HR champion:** N.L., 1958, '60 **Major awards:** N.L. MVP, 1958, '59

His smile lit up Wrigley Field and his quick bat lit up National League scoreboards. Everything about Ernie Banks was contagious, from the boundless enthusiasm he brought to long-suffering Chicago fans to the grace and flair with which he roamed his shortstop and first base positions for 19 major league seasons. Never has an athletic love affair been consummated with more devotion that the one between Mr. Cub and Chicago's North Side fans.

The painfully shy Banks, who was plucked off the roster of the Negro League's Kansas City Monarchs in 1953, injected much-needed hope into a depressed franchise. His movement was quick and agile, his reflexes were magnificent, his eyesight was an exceptional 20/13 and his skinny 6-1, 180-pound frame packed a wallop that would inspire a new legion of "little man" power hitters. The secret was in his wrists and forearms, leading Hall of Fame pitcher Robin Roberts to marvel: "From the elbows down, he's got the muscles of a 230-pounder."

> "I've never seen a man like him. I've known him for 11 years and he hasn't changed since the day I met him. He never says a bad word about anybody." — *Ron Santo*

Banks also used a 31-ounce bat, proving that bat speed, not size, unlocked the secret to power-hitting success. He stood deep in the box, left foot crowding the plate, and stared blankly at the pitcher, fingers drumming rhythmically on the bat handle. Banks didn't swing at the ball; he lashed at it — with a deadly force that yielded spectacular results. Five times he topped 40 home runs en route to a career total of 512. He topped 100 RBIs eight times, played in 13 All-Star Games and captured consecutive MVPs (1958 and '59) with combined two-year totals of 92 home runs and 272 RBIs.

But nothing captures the essence of Banks better than the "let's play two" enthusiasm he always brought to the park, win or lose. He was one of the game's top goodwill ambassadors, a fan favorite who remained upbeat and happy while playing for Cubs teams that seldom posted winning records and never gave him a postseason opportunity that might have added luster to his outstanding career.

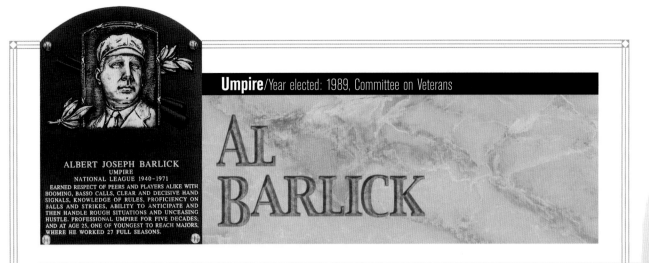

AL BARLICK

ALBERT JOSEPH BARLICK
UMPIRE
NATIONAL LEAGUE 1940-1971
EARNED RESPECT OF PEERS AND PLAYERS ALIKE WITH
BOOMING, BASSO CALLS, CLEAR AND DECISIVE HAND
SIGNALS, KNOWLEDGE OF RULES, PROFICIENCY ON
BALLS AND STRIKES, ABILITY TO ANTICIPATE AND
THEN HANDLE ROUGH SITUATIONS AND UNCEASING
HUSTLE. PROFESSIONAL UMPIRE FOR FIVE DECADES;
AND AT AGE 25, ONE OF YOUNGEST TO REACH MAJORS,
WHERE HE WORKED 27 FULL SEASONS.

Born: 4-2-15, Springfield, Ill. **Died:** 12-27-95 **Height/Weight:** 5-11/195 **Years umpired:** N.L., 1940-43, 1946-55, 1958-71
All-Star Games: 1942, '49, '52, '55, '59 (1), '66, '70 **World Series:** 1946, '50, '51, '54, '58, '62, '67

His booming basso voice penetrated the outer reaches of every ballpark — a foghorn in the light. Al Barlick supplemented his trademark verbal calls with a fisted punching motion delivered with the passion of a Joe Louis uppercut. He was a baseball institution, the loudest, most colorful and most universally respected umpire over a memorable National League career that touched four decades.

The husky 5-foot-11 Barlick was hard to ignore. His powerful voice delivered strike calls with three-syllable force and balls were signaled with a clear yodel-like sound. Barlick's energetic out and safe gyrations left no mistake about his passion for a game he never played. Fans enjoyed his flamboyant style, but players, managers and fellow umpires appreciated his all-out hustle, understanding of the rules and obsession for fairness.

It was Bill Klem, the game's most renowned umpire, who spotted Barlick's potential. Late in the 1940 season, the injured Klem, in need of a substitute, called up his 25-year-old protege from the International League and watched him make his big-league debut. Klem immediately predicted the Illinois-born Barlick would become the best umpire in history, an expectation he spent the next 31 years trying to live up to.

Barlick was good enough to work a record seven All-Star Games and seven World Series, including the 1946 classic when Enos Slaughter made his "Mad Dash" and the 1954 Series when Willie Mays made his

> ## "He's a good umpire mechanically, probably the best on balls and strikes in the league, but what he's really got special is hustle. I'd be happy if all my players hustled like Barlick." — *Chuck Dressen*

over-the-shoulder catch. He was tabbed to work first base during Jackie Robinson's historic debut game in 1947 and he worked the plate in a 1970 All-Star Game that was decided when Pete Rose bowled over catcher Ray Fosse to score the winning run.

Barlick served two years during World War II and missed two seasons while recovering from a heart attack, giving him 27 full years of service. After he retired in 1971, he worked as an N.L. consultant and scout. Barlick was the sixth umpire voted to the Hall of Fame.

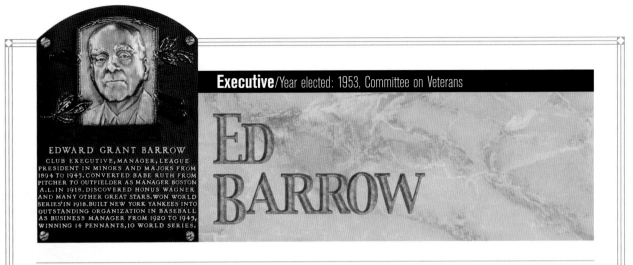

EDWARD GRANT BARROW
CLUB EXECUTIVE, MANAGER, LEAGUE
PRESIDENT IN MINORS AND MAJORS FROM
1894 TO 1945. CONVERTED BABE RUTH FROM
PITCHER TO OUTFIELDER AS MANAGER BOSTON
A.L. IN 1918. DISCOVERED HONUS WAGNER
AND MANY OTHER GREAT STARS. WON WORLD
SERIES IN 1918. BUILT NEW YORK YANKEES INTO
OUTSTANDING ORGANIZATION IN BASEBALL
AS BUSINESS MANAGER FROM 1920 TO 1945,
WINNING 14 PENNANTS, 10 WORLD SERIES.

Executive/Year elected: 1953, Committee on Veterans

ED BARROW

Born: 5-10-1868, Springfield, Ill. **Died:** 12-15-53 **Teams managed (310-320):** Tigers 1903-04; Red Sox 1918-20
Executive career: Business manager and president of Yankees, 1921-45

Baseball oozed from his hulking body and dripped from his thick, black eyebrows. Nobody, on the field or off, knew more about the intricacies of the game than Ed Barrow, who imparted his wisdom with blustery aplomb. "Cousin Ed" was equal parts businessman, talent scout and strategist in his more encompassing role as master builder of the New York Yankees' championship empire.

History will remember Barrow as the creator of a well-oiled Yankees machine that became the scourge of baseball and the standard by which all other franchises would be measured. But it was his bold decision as manager of the 1918 World Series-champion Boston Red Sox that impacted the game beyond anyone's wildest imagination. It was Barrow who converted star left-hander Babe Ruth from the mound to the outfield, literally changing the course of baseball history.

Ruth ushered in the game's "home run era" as the prolific Yankees slugger in 1920 and Barrow followed him to New York later that year, a business manager

responsible for personnel and administrative decisions. Before Barrow's arrival, the Yankees had never won a pennant; when he stepped down as president in 1945, they had won 14 — plus 10 World Series. He was shrewd and ruthless, a conservative who fought against night baseball and other "sideshow frills."

Barrow raided the financially strapped Red Sox to build a foundation for Yankee success and then added players like Lou Gehrig, Tony Lazzeri and Joe DiMaggio with clever signings. He spent owner Jacob Ruppert's money well, made smart trades and hired George Weiss to build an outstanding farm system. "Break up the Yankees" became the 1930s cry of American League owners.

The iron-fisted Barrow, who could intimidate with his deep voice and loud, rumbling laugh, was credited with discovering Honus Wagner while rising through the minor leagues as manager and part-owner of various teams. The memory of Barrow, who never played professional baseball, is honored by a plaque that hangs in Yankee Stadium's Monument Park.

"I think Ed Barrow really was the greatest baseball man, everything considered, in my time. He not only was a judge of players but was a teacher. He knew baseball from all angles." — *Branch Rickey*

Player/Year elected: 1971, Committee on Veterans

JAKE BECKLEY

Born: 8-4-1867, Hannibal, Mo. **Died:** 6-25-18 **Height/Weight:** 5-10/200 **Bats/Throws:** L/L **Primary position:** First base

Career statistics: .308 avg., 2,934 hits, 1,602 runs, 1,577 RBIs, 244 triples, 315 steals **Teams:** Pittsburgh 1888-89, 1891-96; Pittsburgh (P.L.) 1890; New York 1896-97; Cincinnati 1897-1903; Cardinals 1904-07

He was a turn-of-the-century Casey Stengel, a fun-loving, crowd-pleasing first baseman with a sense for the absurd. When Jake Beckley wasn't making fans smile, he was cutting out the heart of opponents with line-drive daggers into the gap. Pioneer, star player and showman, the man from Hannibal, Mo., bridged baseball's formative and modern eras during a two-decade career that produced a .308 average and 2,934 hits.

The 5-foot-10, 200-pound Beckley, with his thick handlebar mustache and confident air, was a dashing figure during major league stops in Pittsburgh, New York, Cincinnati and St. Louis. He also was colorful and unpredictable, the central figure in numerous planned and unplanned bizarre plays. Beckley might flip his bat, grab the fat end and bunt a pitch with the handle. Or he might holler the nonsensical battle cry "Chickazoola!" as he approached the plate.

In a 1904 game, infuriated by an umpire's call, Beckley grabbed the ball and fired it against the screen. Time had not been called. In another game, the scatter-armed St. Louis first baseman made a bad throw on a bunt by Pittsburgh's Tommy Leach, chased the ball down in right field and, rather than risk another throw, raced home and tagged out Leach as he was completing his sprint around the bases.

But opposing pitchers saw the serious side of Beckley, a slashing lefthanded hitter who batted .300 12 times, topped 90 RBIs eight times and rammed out 244 triples, the fourth-highest total in history. Teammates called him "Eagle Eye" because of his ability to make consistent contact and he was a quick, smooth-fielding first baseman—as long as he didn't have to throw.

Beckley never played for a pennant-winner, but that didn't stop him from having fun. He loved pulling the hidden-ball trick, stealthily hiding it under a corner of the base. Although Beckley retired in 1907, he still ranks second only to Eddie Murray in games played at first base (2,380).

"**Beckley's glaring fault was a frightful throwing arm. He had no idea of where the ball was going. ... he was known as the world's worst thrower. Hence the opposition always ran wild when (he) had the ball in his hands.**" —*George Moriarty, former major league player*

BECKLEY

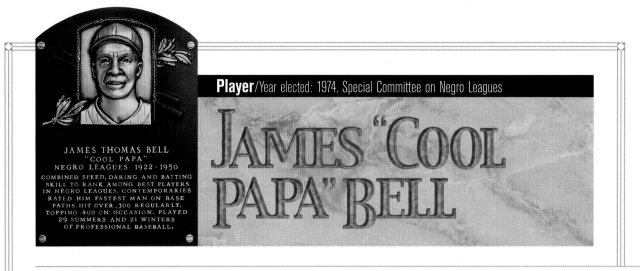

JAMES "COOL PAPA" BELL

JAMES THOMAS BELL
"COOL PAPA"
NEGRO LEAGUES 1922-1950
COMBINED SPEED, DARING AND BATTING
SKILL TO RANK AMONG BEST PLAYERS
IN NEGRO LEAGUES. CONTEMPORARIES
RATED HIM FASTEST MAN ON BASE
PATHS. HIT OVER .300 REGULARLY,
TOPPING .400 ON OCCASION. PLAYED
29 SUMMERS AND 21 WINTERS
OF PROFESSIONAL BASEBALL.

Born: 5-17-03, Starkville, Miss. **Died:** 3-7-91 **Height/Weight:** 6-0/145 **Bats/Throws:** B/L **Primary position:** Center field **Teams (1922-50):** St. Louis Stars; Detroit Wolves; Kansas City Monarchs; Homestead Grays; Pittsburgh Crawfords; Memphis Red Sox; Chicago American Giants

No, Cool Papa Bell could not hit the wall switch and hop into bed before the light went out. And, no, he never hit a ball through the pitcher's legs and got hit by it while sliding into second base. But the point of those exaggerations should not be lost on the modern baseball fan: Bell was fast, very fast; possibly faster than any player in history.

Like fellow Negro League stars Josh Gibson, Buck Leonard and Oscar Charleston, however, Bell never got to show how fast at the major league level. But he did perform in enough barnstorming games against big-league players to make an impression. "He could run like a deer," marveled Frank Frisch. "The smoothest center fielder I've ever seen," said Paul Waner. "He'd steal the pitcher's pants," added an admiring Pie Traynor.

Bell, a stringbean 6-footer who weighed only 145 pounds, wielded his speed like a club over a two-decade-plus career that started in 1922. The switch-hit-

ter slashed and poked balls through the infield and placed bunts as if he had the ball on a string. Legend has it Bell never batted below .308 and most of his averages were in the .350-plus range. But the real damage came after he got on base and the embellishments range from the almost-believable 175 steals in one season to two steals on one pitch.

Bell's aggressive play for such teams as the St. Louis Stars, Pittsburgh Crawfords, Kansas City Monarchs, Chicago American Giants and Homestead Grays belied the laid-back, affable personality that made him one of the most popular players on the Negro League circuit. His baserunning drew comparisons to the reckless daring of Ty Cobb, his hitting style favored Willie Keeler and his shallow-playing, go-get-'em defensive prowess reminded many of Tris Speaker.

Such lofty comparisons helped Bell gain Hall of Fame recognition in 1974 — a recognition he was denied over his outstanding career as a player.

"Cool Papa was one of the most magical players I've ever seen." — *Bill Veeck*

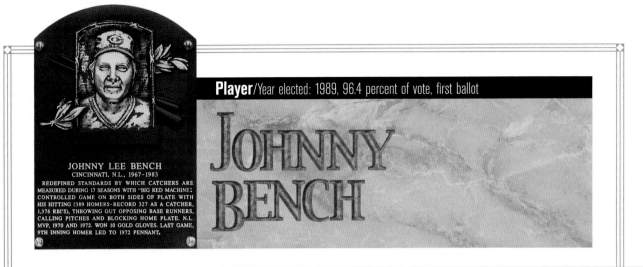

Player/Year elected: 1989, 96.4 percent of vote, first ballot

JOHNNY BENCH

JOHNNY LEE BENCH
CINCINNATI, N.L., 1967-1983
REDEFINED STANDARDS BY WHICH CATCHERS ARE
MEASURED DURING 17 SEASONS WITH "BIG RED MACHINE",
CONTROLLED GAME ON BOTH SIDES OF PLATE WITH
HIS HITTING (389 HOMERS-RECORD 327 AS A CATCHER,
1,376 RBI'S), THROWING OUT OPPOSING BASE RUNNERS,
CALLING PITCHES AND BLOCKING HOME PLATE. N.L.
MVP, 1970 AND 1972. WON 10 GOLD GLOVES. LAST GAME,
9TH INNING HOMER LED TO 1972 PENNANT.

Born: 12-7-47, Oklahoma City, Okla. **Height/Weight:** 6-1/210 **Bats/Throws:** R/R **Primary position:** Catcher **Career statistics:** .267 avg., 2,048 hits, 1,091 runs, 389 HR, 1,376 RBIs **Teams:** Reds 1967-83 **HR champion:** N.L., 1970, '72 **Major awards:** N.L. Rookie of Year, 1968; N.L. MVP, 1970, '72

It might not seem fair, but Johnny Bench is the standard by which catchers will be judged forever. From the rock-solid 210-pound frame that guarded home plate like a stone wall to the cannon-size arm that bewildered baserunners with laser-like throws to second base, Bench gave future generations of catchers a floor plan for Hall of Fame success.

From the first moment of his 1967 debut with the Cincinnati Reds, there was little doubt about the impact he would have on the game. Bench's incredible tools — the arm, the huge hands that could hold seven baseballs at one time, the cat-like quickness — allowed him to play the way no other catcher had dared. Not only did he do everything better than his predecessors, he redefined the position with his one-handed catching style, the one-handed sweep tag that shocked veteran baseball people and the helmet and oversized glove that became part of every catcher's equipment.

Bench could dominate games from behind the plate, where he earned 10 Gold Gloves and set National League records with 9,260 putouts and 10,110 total chances while compiling a .990 fielding

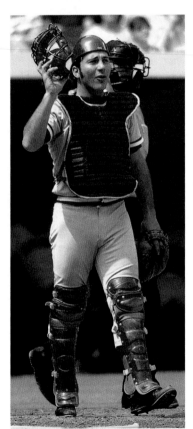

percentage. Or he could dominate with a bat that produced six 100-RBI seasons, three N.L. RBI titles and a pair of home run crowns (45 in 1970, 40 in '72). Of his 389 career homers, 327 came as a catcher — second only to Carlton Fisk on the all-time list.

Bench, the 1968 Rookie of the Year, is best remembered as the power behind a Big Red Machine

> **"Please, don't embarrass any catcher by comparing him with Johnny Bench."** — *Sparky Anderson*

that ran roughshod over the National League in the 1970s, winning four pennants and two World Series. He also captured two MVP awards in the decade while anchoring 1975 and '76 teams that often are ranked among the best in baseball history.

Bench, a proud Oklahoman who played through 10 broken bones in his feet and numerous knee problems throughout his 17-year career, also was fast enough to record double-figure stolen base totals twice. He punctuated his outstanding career with 12 All-Star Game appearances.

CHARLES ALBERT BENDER
"CHIEF"
PHILADELPHIA A.L. 1903 - 1914
PHILADELPHIA N.L. 1916 - 1917
CHICAGO A.L. 1925
FAMOUS CHIPPEWA INDIAN. WON OVER 200
GAMES. PITCHED FOR ATHLETICS IN 1905-
1910 - 1911 - 1913 - 1914 WORLD SERIES.
DEFEATED N.Y. GIANTS 3-0 FOR A'S ONLY
VICTORY IN 1905. FIRST PITCHER IN
WORLD SERIES OF 6 GAMES (1911) TO PITCH
3 COMPLETE GAMES. PITCHED NO-HIT GAME
AGAINST CLEVELAND IN 1910.
HIGHEST A.L. PERCENTAGES IN
1910 - 1911 - 1914.

Player/Year elected: 1953, Committee on Veterans

CHIEF BENDER

Born: 5-5-1884, Crow Wing County, Minn. **Died:** 5-22-54 **Height/Weight:** 6-2/185 **Bats/Throws:** R/R **Position:** Pitcher
Career statistics: 208-111, 2.36 ERA, 1,711 strikeouts **Teams:** Athletics 1903-14; Baltimore (Fed.) 1915; Phillies 1916-17; White Sox 1925

He rose from the obscurity of a Brainerd, Minn., reservation and Carlisle Indian School to 1903 prominence with Connie Mack's Philadelphia Athletics at the tender age of 18. Over the next dozen years, Charles Albert "Chief" Bender toiled as the "money pitcher" for a team that captured five American League pennants and three World Series.

"Bender's the greatest one-game pitcher I ever had," Mack once said, a point supported by his 6-4 record in

> ## "If I needed to win one game, I'd give the ball to the Chief."
> *—Connie Mack*

fall classic matchups against such opponents as Christy Mathewson, Rube Marquard and Dick Rudolph. Bender's success was a product of his durable right arm and an easy-going personality that allowed him to laugh at pressure and ignore discrimination and mean-spirited bench jockeys.

The 6-foot-2, 185-pound part-Chippewa Indian stood erectly on the mound, dissecting batters with darting black eyes, before delivering the ball with a high, classic leg kick. If his outstanding fastball didn't get them, the overhand curve and dreaded "talcum powder" ball would. The talcum pitch, Bender's version of the spitter, dropped unexpectedly and often generated a smug grin.

Bender's pitching arsenal was only half the package. He loved trading banter with opponents whose attempts to get under his bronze skin were greeted by smiles and clever one-liners. Bender was cunning and smart, an intelligent man whose off-field hobbies ranged from gardening and tree care to painting and precious gems.

Often overshadowed by A's teammates Eddie Plank, Rube Waddell and Jack Coombs, Bender usually got Mack's call in times of need. A 23-5 record in 1910 was his masterpiece, but he also posted 21-10, 18-8, 17-5 and 17-3 marks en route to 208 career wins—typically while facing the A.L.'s toughest pitchers. Ironically, his final game with the A's was a one-sided loss to Boston in the opener of the 1914 World Series and his final two full big-league seasons were spent with the cross-town Phillies (1916 and '17) of the National League. In between, he spent one season in the outlaw Federal League.

BENDER

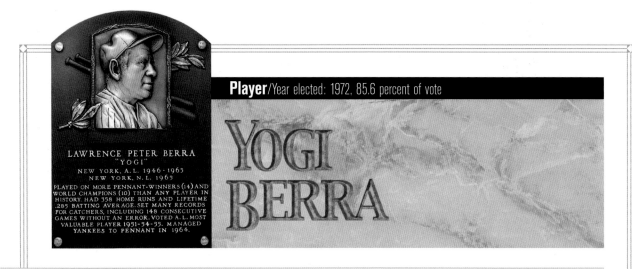

YOGI BERRA

LAWRENCE PETER BERRA
"YOGI"
NEW YORK, A.L. 1946-1963
NEW YORK, N.L. 1965
PLAYED ON MORE PENNANT-WINNERS (14) AND
WORLD CHAMPIONS (10) THAN ANY PLAYER IN
HISTORY. HAD 358 HOME RUNS AND LIFETIME
.285 BATTING AVERAGE. SET MANY RECORDS
FOR CATCHERS, INCLUDING 148 CONSECUTIVE
GAMES WITHOUT AN ERROR. VOTED A.L. MOST
VALUABLE PLAYER 1951-54-55. MANAGED
YANKEES TO PENNANT IN 1964.

Born: 5-12-25, St. Louis, Mo. **Height/Weight:** 5-8/190 **Bats/Throws:** L/R **Primary position:** Catcher **Career statistics:** .285 avg., 2,150 hits, 1,175 runs, 358 HR, 1,430 RBIs **Teams:** Yankees 1946-63; Mets 1965 **Major awards:** A.L. MVP, 1951, '54, '55

The squat, gnome-like body, topped by a face locked in permanent caricature, inspired jokes and friendly barbs. But there was nothing funny about the surprising agility, fast feet and slashing bat that carried Yogi Berra to Hall of Fame heights as the backstop for one of the greatest dynasties in sports history. The lovable, gregarious personality defines Berra the man, but the 14 World Series in which he showcased his talents for the New York Yankees define his baseball legacy.

It was easy to dismiss the 5-foot-8, 190-pound, barrel-chested Berra when

"I hit the bad (pitches) so good that I don't see why I should wait for the good ones." *— Yogi Berra*

he slipped into his baggy No. 8 Yankees uniform for the first time in 1946. But teammates and fans quickly learned to appreciate the boyish enthusiasm with which the knock-kneed youngster moved behind the plate and the desire with which he enhanced his catching skills under the tutelage of fading star Bill Dickey. His quickness was deceptive, his arm was strong if occasionally erratic.

But the bat is what separated Yogi from other big-

league catchers. A left-handed hitter, he stood at the plate with a nervous air of expectancy and used his quick wrists to slash pitches with power to all fields. Berra, a notorious bad-ball hitter who seldom struck out, was tough to pitch to and especially dangerous with the game on the line. Three A.L. MVP awards (1951, 1954, 1955) offer testimony to the respect he earned over a 19-year career that ended in 1965.

Berra is best known for the charming malaprops he delivered with gravelly voiced innocence and endearing honesty, enhancing his image as "the guy next door." But he had a clever baseball mind that enabled him to masterfully handle pitchers, both as a player and later a pennant-winning manager for the Yankees and New York Mets.

Berra played for an incredible 10 World Series champions and retired with fall classic records for games (75), at-bats (259) and hits (71) and top-five rankings with 39 RBIs (second) and 12 home runs (third). He also played in 15 All-Star Games.

BERRA

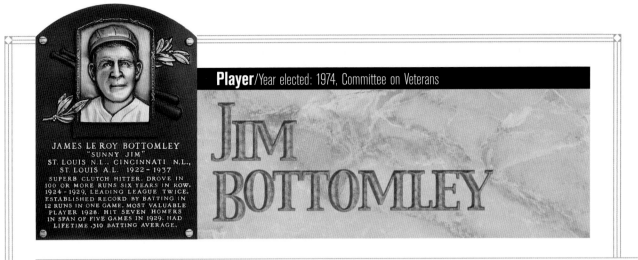

JAMES LE ROY BOTTOMLEY
"SUNNY JIM"
ST. LOUIS N.L., CINCINNATI N.L.,
ST. LOUIS A.L. 1922–1937
SUPERB CLUTCH HITTER. DROVE IN
100 OR MORE RUNS SIX YEARS IN ROW,
1924–1929, LEADING LEAGUE TWICE.
ESTABLISHED RECORD BY BATTING IN
12 RUNS IN ONE GAME. MOST VALUABLE
PLAYER 1928. HIT SEVEN HOMERS
IN SPAN OF FIVE GAMES IN 1929. HAD
LIFETIME .310 BATTING AVERAGE.

Player/Year elected: 1974, Committee on Veterans

JIM BOTTOMLEY

Born: 4-23-00, Oglesby, Ill. **Died:** 12-11-59 **Height/Weight:** 6-0/180 **Bats/Throws:** L/L **Primary position:** First base

Career statistics: .310 avg., 2,313 hits, 1,177 runs, 219 HR, 1,422 RBIs **Teams:** Cardinals 1922-32; Reds 1933-35; Browns 1936-37

HR champion: N.L., 1928, tied **Major awards:** League MVP, 1928

His smile lit up a clubhouse and his booming bat lit up major league scoreboards for 16 memorable seasons. If Jim Bottomley didn't sweep you off your feet with down-home charm, he'd knock you over with a vicious line drive into the gap. Sunny Jim was subtle in life and efficient on the field, a swaggering, smiling, feel-good baseball assassin.

From his natural strut to the cap he cocked over his eye with roguish flair, the handsome 6-footer approached everything with refreshing vitality. The ever-present smile was his trademark and his pleasant nature and disarming drawl cleverly disguised a competitive spirit that helped fuel the St. Louis Cardinals to four National League pennants and two World Series championships.

Bottomley's choked-grip lefthanded swing also had something to do with that. For 11 St. Louis seasons (1922-32), he was a run-producing machine in lineups that included Rogers Hornsby, Chick Hafey, Pepper Martin and Frank Frisch, who called

"Bottomley was a gentleman and he was something else—a winner, a moral man who held together those St. Louis ball clubs." —*Bill Terry*

Bottomley "the greatest clutch hitter I ever saw." Six straight 100-RBI seasons support that notion, as does an MVP (the League Award) 1928 campaign in which Bottomley batted .325, tied for the N.L. lead with 31 home runs and led the league with 20 triples and 136 RBIs while helping the Cardinals win a pennant.

The lefthanded-throwing Bottomley, the son of an Illinois coal miner, also was an outstanding defensive first baseman and nine-time .300 hitter. But for all his accomplishments, he is best remembered for one September afternoon in 1924 at Brooklyn when he exploded for two homers, a double and three singles, driving in 12 runs in a 17-3 St. Louis victory—a major league single-game RBI record that has been tied, but never broken.

Cardinal fans blanched in 1932 when the popular Bottomley was traded to Cincinnati, but he returned to St. Louis three years later as a member of the American League Browns. He retired in 1937 with a .310 career average, 2,313 hits and 1,422 RBIs.

BOTTOMLEY

LOUIS BOUDREAU
CLEVELAND A.L. 1938-1950
BOSTON A.L. 1951-1952

LED A.L. SHORTSTOPS IN FIELDING EIGHT
SEASONS, SET MAJOR LOOP MARK FOR DOUBLE
PLAYS BY SHORTSTOP (134) AND WON BATTING
TITLE, 1944, PACED A.L. IN DOUBLES THREE
TIMES, MOST VALUABLE PLAYER, 1944, WHEN
HE BATTED .355 TO LEAD INDIANS TO PENNANT
AS PLAYER-PILOT. LIFETIME BATTING
AVERAGE .295

Player/Year elected: 1970, 77.3 percent of vote

LOU BOUDREAU

Born: 7-17-17, Harvey, Ill. **Died:** 8-10-2001 **Height/Weight:** 5-11/185 **Bats/Throws:** R/R **Primary position:** Shortstop **Career statistics:** .295 avg., 1,779 hits **Teams played:** Indians 1938-50; Red Sox 1951-52 **Batting champion:** A.L., 1944 **Major awards:** A.L. MVP, 1948 **Teams managed (1,162-1,224):** Indians 1942-50; Red Sox 1952-54; Athletics 1955-57; Cubs 1960 **World Series title:** 1948

Slow, stocky, slouching Lou Boudreau was not your typical, athletically gifted poster boy. But no player since Babe Ruth has more thoroughly captured the affection of a community than the talented shortstop from Harvey, Ill. From 1942 through 1950, the likeable, easygoing Boudreau was a Cleveland icon—the boy-wonder manager who led the Indians to baseball heaven with his sharp mind, steady glove and booming bat.

Everything about Boudreau seemed unlikely. He was a 5-foot-11 University of Illinois baseball and basketball All-American who played one professional season with the old National Basketball League before settling on a baseball career that started full time in 1939. By the start of the 1942 season, he was the youngest manager ever to open a season (age 24) and one of the most respected shortstops in the game.

There was nothing flashy about the seven-time All-Star selection, who always seemed to know where the ball would be hit and led the A.L. in fielding percentage

eight times. His righthanded swing could be lethal, especially with a game on the line, and he was the master of fundamental hitting and line drives into the gap. Kids everywhere copied his crouching stance and other managers copied his innovative infield shift against Boston slugger Ted Williams.

The Indians never finished higher than third during Boudreau's first six managerial seasons, but when word leaked out in 1947 that new owner Bill Veeck was trying to trade him, Cleveland fans revolted. Veeck relented and Boudreau led the 1948 Indians to a first-place tie with Boston, hit two homers in a dramatic pennant-playoff win over the Red Sox and delivered Cleveland's first World Series championship since 1920 with a six-game win over the Boston Braves. Boudreau, a .355 hitter with 18 homers and 106 RBIs, won A.L. MVP honors.

The Cleveland honeymoon lasted through 1950, at which time the .295 career hitter and 1944 batting champion (.327) moved to Boston for two more seasons, his last as player-manager of the Red Sox.

"It is uncanny the way he can call plays and actually outguesses the opposition. ... Boudreau's ability to guess where the ball will be hit amounts almost to a sixth sense. It is bewildering."—*Eddie Sawyer*

B
O
U
D
R
E
A
U

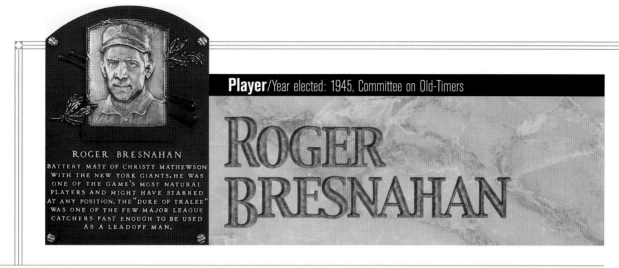

ROGER BRESNAHAN

BATTERY MATE OF CHRISTY MATHEWSON
WITH THE NEW YORK GIANTS, HE WAS
ONE OF THE GAME'S MOST NATURAL
PLAYERS AND MIGHT HAVE STARRED
AT ANY POSITION. THE "DUKE OF TRALEE"
WAS ONE OF THE FEW MAJOR LEAGUE
CATCHERS FAST ENOUGH TO BE USED
AS A LEADOFF MAN.

Player/Year elected: 1945, Committee on Old-Timers

ROGER BRESNAHAN

Born: 6-11-1879, Toledo, Ohio **Died:** 12-4-44 **Height/Weight:** 5-8/200 **Bats/Throws:** R/R **Primary position:** Catcher **Career statistics:** .279 avg., 1,252 hits **Teams:** Washington 1897; Chicago 1900; Baltimore (A.L.) 1901-02; Giants 1902-08; Cardinals 1909-12; Cubs 1913-15

He was a fiery, two-fisted Irishman with thick bottle legs, a protruding chest and a powerful jaw that suggested stubborn confidence. If Roger Bresnahan wasn't the perfect fit for the rugged turn-of-the-century managing style of John McGraw, he at least was cut from the right mold. Tough, fast, smart and versatile, the "Duke of Tralee" traveled a colorful path to Hall of Fame glory.

Tralee, a city in Ireland, was the long-reported birthplace of the 5-foot-8 Bresnahan, who never discouraged the nickname and spoke with a strong Irish brogue. Born in the less-glamorous setting of Toledo, O., he enjoyed his little joke almost as much as showing off his many talents on the field.

Bresnahan was 4-0 as an 18-year-old pitcher for the 1897 Washington team of the old National League and he played all nine positions at various points of his career. But he made his greatest impact as a catcher for McGraw, first at Baltimore of the new American League in 1901 and then for the New York Giants from 1902-08. Even after Bresnahan had settled in as McGraw's catcher and savvy field general, it was not uncommon to see him chasing down fly balls in center field.

He had that kind of speed and his daring baserunning style appealed to McGraw, who used him as his leadoff man. A choke hitter with bat control, Bresnahan batted .350 in 1903 and helped the Giants win pennants in 1904 and '05. "Christy Mathewson's catcher" was behind the plate for all three of Matty's shutout wins in the 1905 World Series victory over Philadelphia.

Bresnahan, who spent four years as player-manager of the St. Louis Cardinals and later performed the same function for the Chicago Cubs, is best remembered

> "Bresnahan was as close to McGraw as any man ever got. ... Raised at McGraw's knee, he had McGraw's implacable hatred of umpires and McGraw's incomparably pungent gift of expression. He gave both free rein. ..."
>
> —*Red Smith, New York Times*

as the man who invented shinguards. He first donned his homemade leg protectors in 1907, to the amusement of fans and jeering Pittsburgh players, and he also experimented with a batting helmet after several serious beanings.

GEORGE HOWARD BRETT
KANSAS CITY, A.L., 1973 – 1993

PLAYED EACH GAME WITH CEASELESS INTENSITY AND UNBRIDLED
PASSION. LIFETIME MARKS INCLUDE .305 BA, 317 HR, 1,595 RBI AND
3,154 HITS. ELEVEN .300 SEASONS. A 13-TIME ALL-STAR AND THE
FIRST PLAYER TO WIN BATTING TITLES IN THREE DECADES (1976,
'80, '90). HIT .390 IN 1980 MVP SEASON AND LED ROYALS TO FIRST
WORLD SERIES TITLE IN 1985. RANKS AMONG ALL-TIME LEADERS IN
HITS, DOUBLES, LONG HITS AND TOTAL BASES. A.L. CAREER RECORD,
MOST INTENTIONAL WALKS. A CLUTCH HITTER WHOSE PROFOUND
RESPECT FOR THE GAME LED TO UNIVERSAL REVERENCE.

GEORGE BRETT

BRETT

"When I think of how hard I've worked at hitting and how many hours I've put into it and then look at Brett making it look so easy, I'm amazed. Yes, he makes hitting look easy." —*Carl Yastrzemski*

Born: 5-15-53, Glen Dale, W. Va. **Height/Weight:** 6-0/200
Bats/Throws: L/R **Primary position:** Third base **Career statistics:** .305 avg., 3,154 hits, 1,583 runs, 317 HR, 1,595 RBIs
Teams: Royals 1973-93 **Batting champion:** A.L., 1976, '80, '90
Major awards: A.L. MVP, 1980

The first thing pitchers noticed about George Brett was the concentration, the intense eye contact that suggested he was up for any challenge. The second was one of his line drives plugging the gap or nestling into either corner, a likely occurrence with a game on the line. Brett was known for many magical moments during his 21-season run with the Kansas City Royals, but his reputation as one of the most feared clutch hitters in history is his baseball legacy.

He broke into the major leagues in 1973 as a sure-handed but scatter-armed third baseman and finished his career 3,154 hits later as a first baseman. The sandy-haired, free-spirited Californian credited his offensive prowess, which produced 1,119 extra-base hits and American League batting titles in three different decades, to hitting guru Charley Lau, who changed him from a Carl Yastrzemski-type free swinger into a controlled, weight-shifting machine.

The sight of the lefthanded-hitting Brett crouching, weight shifted to the back leg and bat resting comfortably on his shoulder, suggested confidence and relaxed control. His focus was unbreakable, his swing was picture-perfect and he always was a step ahead of the pitcher. He could drive the ball with power to any section of the park and his flair for dramatics was uncanny.

Numerous big-game home runs and his postseason passion attest to that. So does an MVP-winning 1980 season in which Brett batted .390 and drove in 118 runs in 117 games. He also is remembered for his A.L. Championship Series heroics against the New York Yankees — a dramatic Game 5 home run in 1976, a three-homer game in 1978, a pennant-securing homer in 1980 — as well as the infamous 1983 "Pine Tar" homer he belted at Yankee Stadium.

Brett, a .373 hitter in two World Series and a 10-time All-Star Game participant, could have posted even better numbers if not for a series of nagging injuries, the product of the aggressive, hustling intensity he always brought to the field.

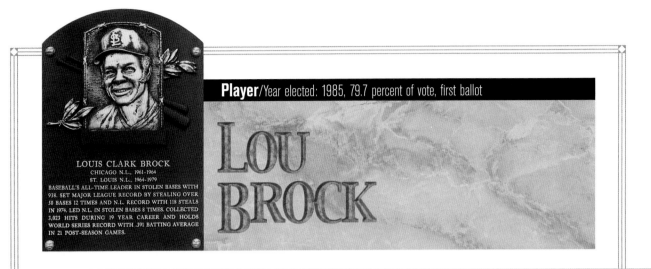

LOU BROCK

LOUIS CLARK BROCK
CHICAGO N.L., 1961-1964
ST. LOUIS N.L., 1964-1979
BASEBALL'S ALL-TIME LEADER IN STOLEN BASES WITH
938. SET MAJOR LEAGUE RECORD BY STEALING OVER
50 BASES 12 TIMES AND N.L. RECORD WITH 118 STEALS
IN 1974. LED N.L. IN STOLEN BASES 8 TIMES. COLLECTED
3,023 HITS DURING 19 YEAR CAREER AND HOLDS
WORLD SERIES RECORD WITH .391 BATTING AVERAGE
IN 21 POST-SEASON GAMES.

Born: 6-18-39, El Dorado, Ark. **Height/Weight:** 5-11/170 **Bats/Throws:** L/L **Primary position:** Left field
Career statistics: .293 avg., 3,023 hits, 1,610 runs, 938 steals **Teams:** Cubs 1961-64; Cardinals 1964-79

His big smile, soft voice and slow, graceful movements belied the thievery in Lou Brock's heart. His thoughtful, analytical mind meticulously planned the controlled mayhem he would perpetrate on helpless pitchers and defenders. The stolen base was Brock's weapon and he dominated games throughout the 1960s and '70s without even touching a bat, ball or glove.

Brock, a reliable left fielder with good range, was the ultimate leadoff man and driving force for the St. Louis Cardinals in an era that featured longball hitters, one-base-at-a-time strategy and dominant pitchers. He was a dangerous lefthanded batter who slashed out 3,023 hits, but the real damage Brock inflicted came after he had reached base. Using his outstanding speed like a club, he pounded away at distracted pitchers while setting a new course for baseball strategy.

If the stolen base was Brock's artform, then the 1974 season was his masterpiece. His .306 average and 194 hits set the tone for a startling 118-stolen base performance — 14 steals better than the record-setting Maury Wills total of 1962. Brock taking a short lead, sprinting for second and arriving safely with a quick pop-up slide was a familiar sight throughout National League cities.

It wasn't as easy as it looked. Brock spent hours studying pitchers, timing their deliveries and moves to first base. He approached hitting in the same meticulous manner and his work ethic paid dividends. Eight times he batted .300 and four times he reached the 200-hit plateau. Brock, a trade acquisition from the Chicago Cubs in 1964, scored 90 or more runs 10 times — in close correlation to his eight stolen base titles.

A five-time All-Star Game performer who sparked the Cardinals to three pennants and two World Series titles in the 1960s, Brock batted .391 with 34 hits and 13 RBIs in fall classic play. His final signature on a Hall of Fame career came in 1979 when he became baseball's all-time leading basestealer — a plateau he reached with then record-setting steal No. 938.

"When he didn't get on base or play well, we didn't win." —*Bob Gibson*

BROCK

DAN BROUTHERS

DAN BROUTHERS

HARD-HITTING FIRST BASEMAN OF
EIGHT MAJOR LEAGUE CLUBS, HE WAS
PART OF ORIGINAL "BIG FOUR" OF BUFFALO.
TRADED WITH OTHER MEMBERS OF
THAT COMBINATION TO DETROIT, HE HIT
.419 AS CITY WON ITS ONLY NATIONAL
LEAGUE CHAMPIONSHIP IN 1887.

Born: 5-8-1858, Sylvan Lake, N.Y. **Died:** 8-2-32 **Height/Weight:** 6-2/210 **Bats/Throws:** L/L **Primary position:** First base **Career statistics:** .349 avg., 2,367 hits, 1,523 runs, 106 HR **Teams:** Troy 1879-80; Buffalo 1881-85; Detroit 1886-88; Boston 1889; Boston (P.L.) 1890; Boston (A.A.) 1891; Brooklyn 1892-93; Balt. 1894-95; Louisville 1895; Phil. 1896; Giants 1904 **Batting champion:** N.L., 1882, '83, '89, '91, '92

The first thing fans noticed about Dan Brouthers was his formidable bulk, a 6-foot-2, 210-pound mass of muscle chiseled expertly out of human flesh. The second was a bushy mustache that twitched with delight in that instant before Big Dan crushed another ball with another thunderous lefthanded swing. Consummate hitter, dangerous slasher and solid first baseman, Brouthers also was the 19th-century master of the tape-measure home run.

One ball he hit while playing for Detroit in 1886 sailed over the distant center field fence at Washington's Capitol Park and became the standard by which all prodigious home runs of the dead-ball era were measured. Another memorable 1886 blast at Boston hit a distant wooden tower beyond the left field fence. Brouthers won only two National League homer titles (with totals of 8 and 11), but fans flocked to parks hoping to see one of his moonshots.

What they were more likely to see was a flurry of hits, usually well-aimed drives over the infield or into the gaps. Brouthers, who seldom struck out, was a hitting machine who won five batting titles, topped 100 RBIs

five times and led the N.L. at one time or another in virtually every offensive category. Not surprisingly, he was a seven-time leader in slugging percentage.

The New York-born slugger was the most feared member of a 19th-century Murderer's Row that included Hardy Richardson, Jack Rowe and Deacon White. Detroit won an N.L. pennant in 1887 with its "Big Four" and Brouthers later played on pennant-winners with Baltimore and different Boston teams in the outlaw Players League and American Association.

Over 19 big-league seasons, Brouthers played for nine N.L. teams and two in the outlaw leagues. A failure as an early career pitcher, he found fame as a .349 hitter, the fourth-highest average of all time, and the first man to win consecutive batting titles (1882 and '83). Most of his 106 homers were worth the price of admission.

"Big Dan might be described as the Babe Ruth of his day. ... When Big Dan went to bat, the stands went into an uproar and the outfielders moved back." —*Guy McI.Smith, baseball historian*

Player/Year elected: 1949, Committee on Old-Timers

MORDECAI BROWN

Born: 10-19-1876, Nyesville, Ind. **Died:** 2-14-48 **Height/Weight:** 5-10/175 **Bats/Throws:** B/R **Position:** Pitcher **Career statistics:** 208-111, 1.93 ERA, 1,375 strikeouts **Teams:** Cardinals 1903; Cubs 1904-12, 1916; Reds 1913; St. Louis (Fed.) 1914; Brooklyn (Fed.) 1914; Chicago (Fed.) 1915

He is listed officially as Mordecai Peter Centennial Brown, the third name a tribute to his 1876 date of birth. But baseball remembers him more fondly as "Three Finger" Brown because of the missing digit on his pitching hand. From a childhood handicap and the coal mines of Indiana, the determined righthander rose to Hall of Fame recognition alongside such contemporaries as Christy Mathewson and Cy Young.

There was nothing unusual about the 5-foot-10, round-faced Chicago Cubs workhorse until you examined a disfigured right hand with an oversized knot on the stub of what had been an index finger. Brown lost the finger at age 5 when he stuck his hand into a running feed-cutter machine. Unable to get zip on his fastball because of the missing digit, "Brownie" soon discovered he could get extra spin on his curve, which would dart down and away from righthanded hitters.

That became his signature pitch and he used a moderate fastball, occasional screwball and outstanding control to carve up confused hitters over 12 major league seasons. He made a mediocre debut in 1903 with the St. Louis Cardinals but it was his 1904-12 run with the Cubs that vaulted him to national prominence. Compiling such records as 26-6, 29-9, 27-9 and 20-6, Brown became the ace of a Chicago powerhouse that won four National League pennants and consecutive World Series championships in 1907 and '08.

The quiet Brown, one of the premier defensive pitchers of all time, was most remembered for his classic duels with New York Giants ace Mathewson. Brown relished those matchups, once recording nine straight wins over his celebrated rival—including a 1908 pennant-deciding victory in the replay of the now-classic "Merkle's Boner" game.

Brown was traded to Cincinnati after the 1912 season and jumped a year later to the outlaw Federal League, where he posted 31 wins over two seasons. He returned to the Cubs for 12 games in 1916 before dropping from sight with a 208-111 career record.

"I don't doubt that the hand injury gave me an advantage in throwing the curve. The stub gave support to the ball and with the rest of the finger gone, I was able to get more spin on the ball." — *Mordecai Brown*

Executive/Year elected: 1937, Centennial Commission

MORGAN BULKELEY

HON. MORGAN G. BULKELEY

FIRST PRESIDENT OF THE NATIONAL LEAGUE AND A LEADER IN ITS ORGANIZATION IN 1876 WHICH LAID THE FOUNDATION OF THE NATIONAL GAME FOR POSTERITY.

Born: 12-26-1837, East Haddam, Conn. **Died:** 11-6-22 **Executive career:** First president of National League, 1876

He was a baseball figurehead, a man of stature who brought much-needed respect to a sport on the rise. Morgan Bulkeley will never be mistaken as one of the game's prime movers, but it's hard to deny the dignity he brought to his role as the National League's first president. Banker, businessman, politician and family man — Bulkeley was an influential advertisement for the future National Pastime in 1876.

The man with the perfectly trimmed handlebar mustache and three-piece suits was son of Eliphalet Bulkeley, founder of Aetna Life Insurance Company. Morgan also was organizer of the United States Bank in Hartford, Conn., and backer of the local professional baseball team. The Hartford Dark Blues were merely a hobby for Bulkeley and they played in the struggling National Association.

When Chicagoan William Hulbert and star pitcher Albert Spalding called a New York meeting in the winter of 1875 to present the constitution for a proposed new league, Bulkeley attended and was surprised when Hulbert nominated him for president. He graciously accepted the honor, warning he probably would not serve more than one year.

He was true to his word. Bulkeley didn't even attend the 1876 meeting in which Hulbert assumed the N.L. presidency. But the crafty Hulbert had achieved his goal. His new league had garnered respectability from Bulkeley's association and it had established an important foothold on the East Coast. Bulkeley remained president of the Hartford club until 1877, when the franchise shifted to Brooklyn. He never again would be associated with baseball.

Bulkeley's career prospered in other directions. In 1879, he became president of Aetna, a job he held until his death in 1922. He later became alderman and mayor of Hartford, governor of Connecticut, a delegate to the Republican National Convention that nominated future president William McKinley and a United States senator. Along with American League founder and first president Ban Johnson, Bulkeley was enshrined in the Hall of Fame in 1937.

"Mr. Bulkeley's ability as a presiding officer and his zeal for the new organization so impressed the delegates that he was chosen as first president of the National League. ..." —*Francis C. Richter, The Sporting News, 1922*

Player/Year elected: 1996, Committee on Veterans

JIM BUNNING

JAMES PAUL DAVID BUNNING
DETROIT, A.L. 1955-1963
PHILADELPHIA, N.L. 1964-1967, 1970-1971
PITTSBURGH, N.L. 1968-1969
LOS ANGELES, N.L. 1969
MAINTAINED DEDICATION AND CONSISTENCY
THROUGHOUT 17 SEASONS WHILE POSTING CAREER
RECORD OF 224-184 WITH 3.27 ERA. INTIMIDATING
RIGHT-HANDED SIDEARMER WON 100 GAMES, PITCHED
NO-HITTER AND STRUCK OUT 1,000 IN BOTH LEAGUES.
1964 PERFECT GAME WAS FIRST IN N.L. IN 20TH
CENTURY. SECOND ALL-TIME IN STRIKEOUTS (2,855).
UPON RETIREMENT IN 1971, ENJOYED SECOND CAREER
AS MULTI-TERM U.S. CONGRESSMAN

Born: 10-23-31, Southgate, Ky. **Height/Weight:** 6-3/200 **Bats/Throws:** R/R **Position:** Pitcher **Career statistics:** 224-184, 3.27 ERA, 2,855 strikeouts **Teams:** Tigers 1955-63; Phillies 1964-67, 1970-71; Pirates 1968-69; Dodgers 1969

His long right arm came at you from the side, whipping the ball menacingly homeward with manhood-challenging force. Every Jim Bunning pitch was delivered with maximum effort from a delivery that flung his body awkwardly toward first base. If the flailing sidearm motion didn't get you, then the hopping fastballs, sharp-breaking sliders and multiple-speed curveballs, all thrown with pinpoint control, probably would.

"He's 200 pounds of pride," former Philadelphia Phillies manager Gene Mauch said about his staff ace from 1964-67. The 6-foot-3 Bunning also was one of the more intellectual pitchers in baseball history, an Xavier University graduate and future U.S. senator from Kentucky who studied hitters and kept detailed notes, both on paper and in his head. When the lanky righthander stood confidently on the mound, everybody knew something momentous could happen.

That became apparent in 1957, when the 25-year-old Bunning carved out a 20-8 record in his first full season with Detroit after seven minor league campaigns. A year later, he fired a no-hitter against the Boston Red Sox. In 1964, his first season after being traded to Philadelphia because the Tigers thought he was nearing the end of the line, Bunning retired all 27 New York Mets batters he faced in a perfect game — the signature performance of three straight 19-win seasons for the Phillies.

Talent, brains and pride all contributed to

Bunning's 224-184 success story over 17 major league seasons that included brief stints in Pittsburgh and Los Angeles. But most of his contemporaries point to the competitive fire and never-give-an-inch mentality he brought to every pitch. A conditioning buff who averaged 298 innings from 1964-67, Bunning would knock hitters down with one

"He's 200 pounds of pride. He takes care of himself, likes money, loves his family, has a great arm and a great delivery." — *Gene Mauch*

pitch, cut them down with a tantalizing slow curve on the next.

When Bunning retired after the 1971 season with a 3.27 earned-run average and 2,855 strikeouts, he was one of two pitchers (joining Cy Young) with 100-plus wins in both leagues. But the seven-time All-Star Game performer never pitched in the postseason.

JESSE BURKETT

JESSE C. BURKETT
BATTING STAR WHO PLAYED OUTFIELD FOR THE NEW YORK, CLEVELAND AND ST.LOUIS N.L.TEAMS AND THE ST.LOUIS AND BOSTON A.L.TEAMS. SHARES WITH ROGERS HORNSBY AND TY COBB THE RECORD OF HITTING .400 OR BETTER THE MOST TIMES. ACCOMPLISHED THIS ON THREE OCCASIONS. TOPPED THE N.L.IN HITTING THREE TIMES, BATTING OVER .400 TO GAIN THE CHAMPIONSHIP IN 1895 AND 1896.

Born: 12-4-1868, Wheeling, W. Va. **Died:** 5-27-53 **Height/Weight:** 5-8/155 **Bats/Throws:** L/L **Primary position:** Outfield
Career statistics: .338 avg., 2,850 hits, 1,720 runs, 389 steals **Teams:** New York 1890; Cleveland 1892-98; St. Louis 1899-1901; Browns 1902-04; Red Sox 1905 **Batting champion:** N.L., 1895, '96, 1901

Teammates called Jesse Burkett "Crab" because of his testy disposition, but opponents, umpires and heckling fans preferred more disparaging nicknames. Love him or hate him, there was no denying the 5-foot-8, 155-pound Burkett's role as a turn-of-the-century baseball giant. Scratch, claw, fight, hit — the kid from Wheeling, W. Va., could decide games with fiery inspiration as well as his lethal bat.

What Burkett lacked in size and speed he more than made up for with attitude and a win-at-all-costs mentality. He was a key figure on the rough-and-tumble Cleveland Spiders teams that battled the Baltimore Orioles for baseball supremacy in the 1890s-era National League. A quiet, patient ice cream lover who did not smoke, drink or chew tobacco, Burkett transformed into a snarling, aggressive, umpire-baiting wildcat when he stepped onto the field.

In temperament, the talented left fielder resembled the immortal Ty Cobb. In playing style, he mirrored contemporary Wee Willie Keeler — a lefthanded batter who would foul off pitch after pitch before finally "hitting it where they ain't." An accomplished bunter and punishing baserunner, Burkett hit .300 or better 11 times, .400 or better twice and won three batting titles, one during an 1896 season in which he batted .410,

collected 240 hits and scored 160 runs.

In his best West Virginia drawl, Burkett would credit his success to "the ol' confeedience" and brag that he could "bunt .300." And based on a five-year stretch from 1895-99 that produced 1,097 hits and a .387 average, it was hard to argue the point. Over a 16-year career that Burkett started in New York as a lefthanded pitcher, he batted .338 and collected 2,850 hits in 2,067 games.

Eleven of those seasons were spent with the Spiders franchise — eight in Cleveland, three in St. Louis after it relocated following the 1898 campaign. Burkett jumped to the American League's St. Louis Browns in 1902 and finished his career in 1905 with the Boston Red Sox.

> "Burkett's real value to a baseball team was his constant desire to win. He always went into a game with but one thought in mind — to win the game — and he never stopped fighting until the game was over."
>
> — *The Wheeling (W. Va.) News-Register, 1938*

B U R K E T T

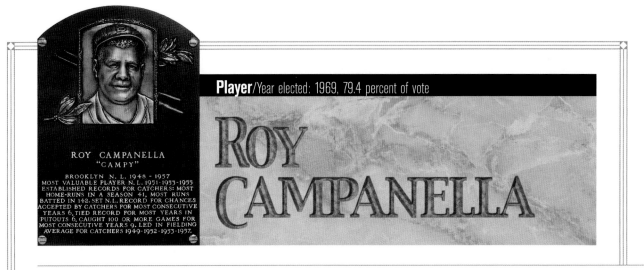

ROY CAMPANELLA

ROY CAMPANELLA
"CAMPY"
BROOKLYN N. L. 1948 - 1957
MOST VALUABLE PLAYER N. L. 1951-1953-1955
ESTABLISHED RECORDS FOR CATCHERS: MOST
HOME-RUNS IN A SEASON 41, MOST RUNS
BATTED IN 142. SET N.L. RECORD FOR CHANCES
ACCEPTED BY CATCHERS FOR MOST CONSECUTIVE
YEARS 6. TIED RECORD FOR MOST YEARS IN
PUTOUTS 6, CAUGHT 100 OR MORE GAMES FOR
MOST CONSECUTIVE YEARS 9. LED IN FIELDING
AVERAGE FOR CATCHERS 1949-1952-1953-1957.

Born: 11-19-21, Philadelphia, Pa. **Died:** 6-26-93. **Height/Weight:** 5-8/200 **Bats/Throws:** R/R **Primary position:** Catcher **Career statistics:** .276 avg., 1,161 hits, 242 HR, 856 RBIs **Teams:** Dodgers 1948-57 **Major awards:** N.L. MVP, 1951, '53, '55

On one hand, the boyish enthusiasm that gushed from catcher Roy Campanella embodied the exciting, crazy Dodgers of the 1950s, Brooklyn's Boys of Summer. On the other hand, the same Campanella became the tragic symbol for a city's divorce from the team it had loved unconditionally for more than half a century. For 10 glorious seasons, Campy ruled the baseball world from his crouch behind home plate. Then he spent the rest of his life in a wheelchair, the result of a crippling 1958 automobile accident.

The Campanella story is one of indomitable spirit. Following in the trail-blazing footsteps of Dodgers teammate Jackie Robinson, Campanella, who had started his professional career as a Negro League catcher at age 15, reported for major league duty in 1948 and quickly won over baseball-crazy Brooklyn fans. The combination of Campy's thick-necked, roly-poly build (5-foot-8, 200 pounds) and happy-go-lucky outlook was too much to resist.

So was the hustle, agility and cannon arm he displayed while challenging New York Yankees contemporary Yogi Berra for status as baseball's best catcher. Campanella was an adept handler of pitchers, agile and durable, a rock who could steady a sometimes erratic staff. And his quick, compact righthanded swing consistently muscled errant pitches into the left field stands at Ebbets Field.

How good was Campy? Three times in a five-year period he walked away with National League MVP awards, one following an incredible .312, 41-homer, 142-RBI 1953 campaign. His Dodgers claimed five pennants and brought Brooklyn its first World Series crown; he played in seven All-Star Games.

Campanella, whose easy-going personality was a perfect fit for a difficult racial period, suffered a broken neck and paralysis in a January 1958 car accident—the offseason before the Dodgers jilted Brooklyn fans with their cross-country move to Los Angeles. The wheelchair-confined Campy was elected to the Hall of Fame in 1969 and remained one of baseball's most gracious ambassadors until his death in 1993.

"Go ahead, just try to name a better catcher. Sometimes I'd go five or six games without shaking him off." — *Don Newcombe*

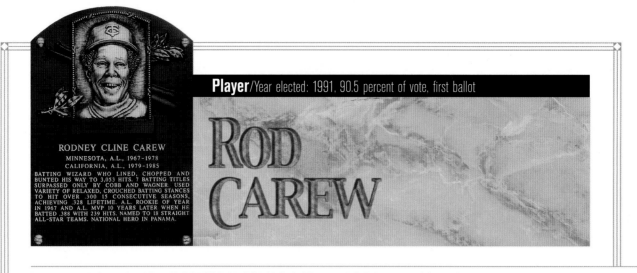

RODNEY CLINE CAREW
MINNESOTA, A.L., 1967-1978
CALIFORNIA, A.L., 1979-1985
BATTING WIZARD WHO LINED, CHOPPED AND
BUNTED HIS WAY TO 3,053 HITS. 7 BATTING TITLES
SURPASSED ONLY BY COBB AND WAGNER. USED
VARIETY OF RELAXED, CROUCHED BATTING STANCES
TO HIT OVER .300 15 CONSECUTIVE SEASONS,
ACHIEVING .328 LIFETIME. A.L. ROOKIE OF YEAR
IN 1967 AND A.L. MVP 10 YEARS LATER WHEN HE
BATTED .388 WITH 239 HITS. NAMED TO 18 STRAIGHT
ALL-STAR TEAMS. NATIONAL HERO IN PANAMA.

Player/Year elected: 1991, 90.5 percent of vote, first ballot

ROD CAREW

Born: 10-1-45, Gatun, Canal Zone **Height/Weight:** 6-0/182 **Bats/Throws:** L/R **Primary positions:** Second base, first base
Career statistics: .328 avg., 3,053 hits, 1,424 runs, 1,015 RBIs, 353 steals **Teams:** Twins 1967-78; Angels 1979-85
Batting champion: A.L., 1969, '72, '73, '74, '75, '77, '78 **Major awards:** A.L. Rookie of Year, 1967; A.L. MVP, 1977

He handled the bat with the same efficiency Merlin coaxed from his wand. Rod Carew was a baseball magician with the power to make well-placed pitches disappear into every conceivable outfield gap. Carew was to the 1970s what Ty Cobb was to the 1910s and Rogers Hornsby to the 1920s—a bat-control artist, the keeper of batting titles and an annual threat to hit .400.

Carew performed his magic from an exaggerated crouch with a 32-ounce bat and a natural inside-out lefthanded swing that allowed him to stay back until the last possible second and spray line drives to all fields. He was selective and smart, an outstanding two-strike hitter with the speed to beat out infield hits and steal bases. Former manager Billy Martin marveled at Carew's bat-handling abilities ("he could bunt .330 if he tried") and instinctive baserunning after watching him swipe home seven times in an inspiring 1969 performance.

Such efficiency allowed him to win seven batting

titles in 12 seasons with the Minnesota Twins—the first in his third big-league season (1969) and the other six in a seven-year period beginning in 1972. Carew, a career .328 hitter, never quite reached the .400 plateau that many predicted, but he did pull off a .388, 239-hit 1977 performance that earned him American League MVP honors. The slender Panamanian topped .300 15 times and .330 nine times while posting four 200-hit seasons.

Carew, young and unsure of his sudden celebrity, was a moody, sometimes-difficult locker room loner when he captured Rookie of the Year honors as an erratic Twins second baseman in 1967. But he was a well-respected veteran first baseman when he collected his 3,000th career hit in 1985, his seventh and final season with the California Angels.

The only thing missing from Carew's Hall of Fame ledger was a World Series appearance, although he did play in four A.L. Championship Series—two each with the Twins and Angels—and 15 All-Star Games.

"I could always hit a baseball. I remember when I was a youngster telling myself, 'You can't get me out. I'm the best hitter.'"—*Rod Carew*

Umpire/Year elected: 1999, Committee on Veterans

NESTOR CHYLAK

Born: 5-11-22, Olyphant, Pa. **Died:** 2-17-82 **Height/Weight:** 6-0/195 **Years umpired:** A.L., 1954-78 **All-Star Games:** 1957, '60 (1), '60 (2), '64, '73, '78 **World Series:** 1957, '60, '66, '71, '77

From war hero to dean of American League umpires, Nestor Chylak lived life as a man of vision. He survived a sight-threatening shrapnel injury during World War II and became baseball's model arbiter of the post-war era. Honesty, dignity and respect were adjectives used often to describe the husky Pennsylvanian, who never lost his infectious enthusiasm for the game over a 25-year career that ended in 1978.

A round-faced man with a friendly smile, crooked nose and penetrating blue eyes, Chylak lacked the color of such contemporaries as Jocko Conlan and Al Barlick. But nobody could match his near-perfect technical abilities and unwavering patience, both on the field and as a late-career mentor for young umpires. Chylak took great pride in his craft and always was prepared — a 24/7 "man in blue."

Ironically, he had never seen a major league game when he got a call to report for spring training in 1954, after six years in the minors. Chylak, who had received the presti-gious Silver Star and a Purple Heart for his valor in the Battle of the Bulge, held a degree in mechani-cal engineering. But he would get more use out of his people skills, which included an even temperament, a good sense of humor and an authoritative decisiveness that com-manded the respect of players and managers.

Chylak, a longtime crew chief, was center stage in baseball's prestigious events. He worked three A.L. Championship Series and five World Series, including a 1960 classic that ended when Pittsburgh's Bill Mazeroski shocked the New York Yankees with a Game 7 home run. Chylak also was at Yankee Stadium in 1977 when Reggie Jackson's three-homer Game 6 explosion sent the Los Angeles Dodgers to defeat.

Chylak, who also worked six All-Star Games, retired after the 1978 season, ending a quarter century of A.L. service. He worked as assistant supervisor of umpires before dying at age 59 in 1982. Chylak was the eighth umpire inducted into the Hall of Fame.

> "If I didn't like my job, if I didn't go into each season with enthusiasm, I figure it would be time to quit. Why, I actually get psyched every spring."
> —*Nestor Chylak*

FRED CLARKE

THE FIRST OF THE SUCCESSFUL
"BOY MANAGERS," AT TWENTY-FOUR HE
PILOTED LOUISVILLE'S COLONELS IN
THE NATIONAL LEAGUE. WON 4 PENNANTS
FOR PITTSBURGH AND A WORLD
CHAMPIONSHIP IN 1909. STARRED AS
AN OUTFIELDER FOR 22 SEASONS.

Player/Year elected: 1945, Committee on Old-Timers

FRED CLARKE

Born: 10-3-1872, Winterset, Iowa **Died:** 8-14-60 **Height/Weight:** 5-10/165 **Bats/Throws:** L/R **Primary position:** Outfield

Career statistics: .312 avg., 2,678 hits, 1,622 runs, 1,015 RBIs, 509 steals **Teams played:** Louisville 1894-99; Pirates 1900-15

Teams managed (1,602-1,180): Louisville 1897-99; Pirates 1900-15 **World Series title:** 1909

He was a 5-foot-10, 165-pound wildcat, a fire-and-brimstone competitor with flying feet, flailing elbows and exceptional instincts. Fred Clarke could beat you physically with his efficient bat, dazzling outfield speed and rugged baserunning, or he could outsmart you in his role as baseball's original "Boy Manager." Clarke showcased his special combination of talent and guile over 21 seasons, most of them with the early-century Pittsburgh Pirates.

Well before Ty Cobb, Clarke was slashing base hits around major league parks with his lefthanded swing and drawing raves as one of the speediest left fielders in the game. He also was terrorizing defenders with his spikes-high slides and prodding elbows, turn-of-the-century tactics that defined the dead-ball era. Clarke was a 110 percenter who would do anything to reach base and fielders who didn't pay close attention often paid a price.

A no-nonsense Iowa farm boy, Clarke made a big impression on Louisville owner Barney Dreyfuss in 1894 when he banged out five hits in his first N.L. game. By 1897, he was a 24-year-old manager and he batted a lofty .390 in his first season in that role. When Louisville disbanded and Dreyfuss took over operation of the new Pittsburgh team in 1900, Clarke was his player-manager and Honus Wagner his star shortstop.

That was a winning combination. The Pirates captured N.L. pennants in 1901, '02 and '03 — capping the latter by losing to Boston in baseball's first World Series.

"Fearless Fred" led the Pirates to 110 wins and another pennant in 1909 and hit two World Series home runs as the franchise won its first championship after a seven-

game battle with Cobb's Detroit Tigers.

Clarke managed Pittsburgh through its first 16 N.L. seasons and was a regular player in 12 of them. When the 10-time .300 hitter retired in 1915 with a .312 average, 2,678 hits and a 1,602-1,180 managerial record, he was honored with a "Fred Clarke Day" at Forbes Field — an unusual gesture in pre-World War I baseball.

"You can put this down, and it's every bit as true now as then. The fellows who work the hardest last the longest." —*Fred Clarke*

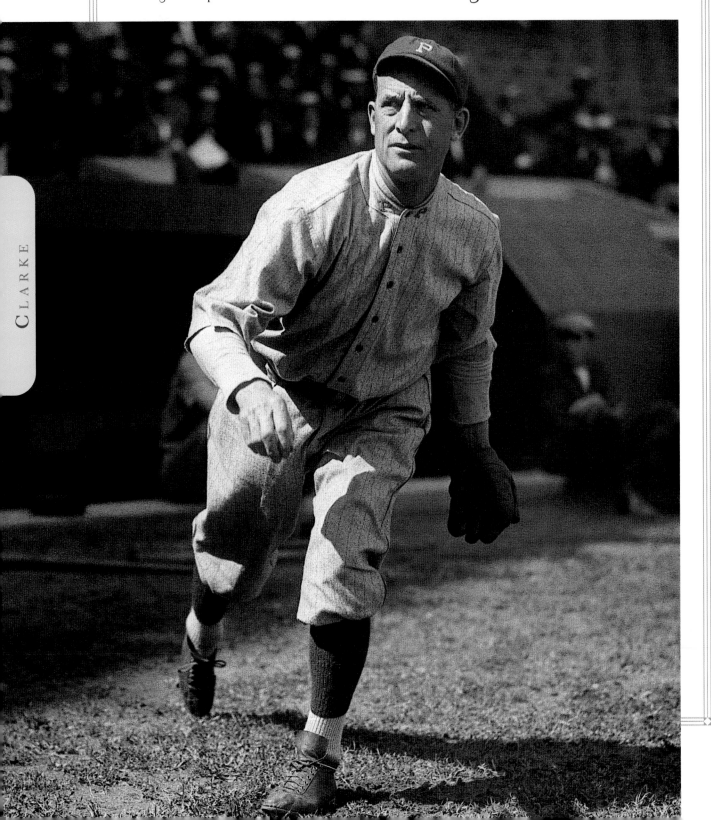

JOHN CLARKSON

JOHN GIBSON CLARKSON
WORCESTER, N.L. 1882
CHICAGO, N.L. 1884-87
BOSTON, N.L. 1888-92
CLEVELAND, N.L. 1892-94
PITCHED 4 TO 0 NO-HIT GAME AGAINST
PROVIDENCE IN 1885. WON 328 LOST 175
PCT. 652 LED LEAGUE WITH 53 VICTORIES
IN 1885 (INCLUDING 10 SHUTOUTS) 38 IN
1887, 49 IN 1888 AND 49 IN 1889. HAD
2013 STRIKEOUTS IN 4514 INNINGS.

Born: 7-1-1861, Cambridge, Mass. **Died:** 2-4-09 **Height/Weight:** 5-10/155 **Bats/Throws:** R/R **Position:** Pitcher **Career statistics:** 328-178, 2.81 ERA, 1,978 strikeouts **Teams:** Worcester 1882; Chicago 1884-87; Boston 1888-92; Cleveland 1892-94

He was a master of the 50-foot pitching box, a pioneering 19th-century curveballer with a rubber arm and unusual instinct for the game. John Clarkson carved up hitters with the most diverse pitching repertoire of his era and broke their spirit with his bulldog intensity and stamina. He was, literally, a pitching machine in a short-but-sweet 12-year career that produced 328 wins and an amazing 485 complete games in 518 starts.

The handsome, dark-complected righthander threw an above-average fastball, but he much preferred to tantalize hitters with a variety of curves and an outstanding change of pace. Clarkson's best pitch was a drop-curve, an early version of today's sinker, and he used his photographic memory to process the strengths and weaknesses of opponents — a scientific approach that separated him from other 1880s hurlers.

At 5-foot-10 and 155 pounds, the Cambridge, Mass., product looked anything but durable. But in 1885, pitching his second full season for Cap Anson's Chicago White Stockings, he worked an incredible 623 innings, completing 68 of 70 starts, and struck out 308 hitters while walking only 97 and compiling a 53-16 record. Chicago won the first of consecutive National League pennants.

From 1885 to 1892, Clarkson never won fewer than 25 games or pitched fewer than 383 innings. He worked 620 innings and won 49 times for Boston in 1889 and he combined with Kid Nichols to post 63 victories for the pennant-winning Beaneaters in 1891. In an unusual 1892 campaign that featured a split-season schedule, Clarkson won eight games for first-half winner Boston and 17 for second-half champion Cleveland.

If the quiet Clarkson had a weakness, it was a nervous disposition that required constant encouragement and praise. The slightest criticism could put him in a funk that might last a week. But when properly inspired, he could pitch five or six days in a row. When the pitching distance was extended to 60-feet, 6-inches in 1893, Clarkson's career faded quickly. He finished 16-17 that season for Cleveland and 8-10 the next, after which he retired.

> "John Clarkson was one of the greatest pitchers of all time. ... Scold him, find fault with him, and he could not pitch at all. Praise him, and he was unbeatable. ..." —*Cap Anson*

CLARKSON

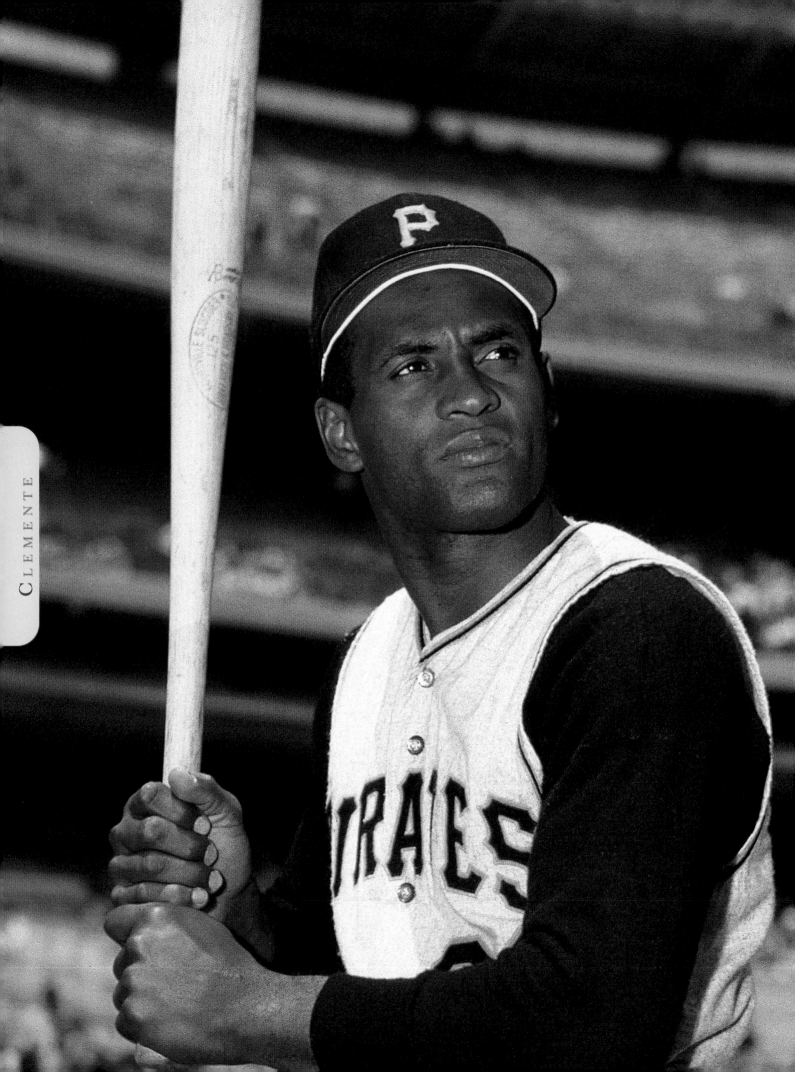

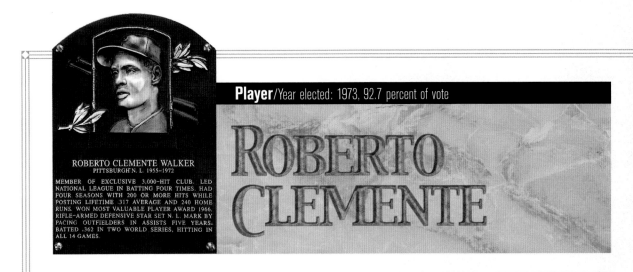

ROBERTO CLEMENTE

ROBERTO CLEMENTE WALKER
PITTSBURGH N. L. 1955-1972

MEMBER OF EXCLUSIVE 3,000-HIT CLUB. LED NATIONAL LEAGUE IN BATTING FOUR TIMES. HAD FOUR SEASONS WITH 200 OR MORE HITS WHILE POSTING LIFETIME .317 AVERAGE AND 240 HOME RUNS. WON MOST VALUABLE PLAYER AWARD 1966. RIFLE-ARMED DEFENSIVE STAR SET N. L. MARK BY PACING OUTFIELDERS IN ASSISTS FIVE YEARS. BATTED .362 IN TWO WORLD SERIES, HITTING IN ALL 14 GAMES.

Born: 8-18-34, Carolina, P. R. **Died:** 12-31-72 **Height/Weight:** 5-11/180 **Bats/Throws:** R/R **Primary position:** Right field
Career statistics: .317 avg., 3,000 hits, 1,416 runs, 240 HR, 1,305 RBIs **Teams:** Pirates 1955-72 **Batting champion:** N.L., 1961, '64, '65, '67 **Major awards:** N.L. MVP, 1966

He strutted through 18 major league seasons like a high-strung thoroughbred and gained baseball immortality in a tragic career-ending death while acting as a life-sustaining humanitarian. Proud, honest, intense, sensitive and incredibly talented: Adjectives simply oozed from the sometimes-complicated persona of Roberto Clemente.

The Pittsburgh Pirates great, who learned the game on the sandlots of his native Puerto Rico, was baseball's prototypical right fielder from 1955-72 — a defensive machine built around speed, razor-sharp instincts and an arm that terrorized baserunners throughout the National League. He patrolled the vast right field pasture at Forbes Field for most of his career, defiantly staking his claim to greatness with 12 Gold Gloves and defensive comparisons to outfield contemporary Willie Mays.

Clemente's hitting style was unorthodox, but effective enough to produce four batting titles, an MVP award and 15 All-Star Game invitations. A 5-foot-11,180-pound specimen with chiseled features and quick wrists, he stood away from the plate and kept hands and bat

> "He's one of the very few who is a complete player with a great arm, great glove and great bat, an excellent runner and hustler." — *Harry Walker*

cocked until the last possible second, seemingly pulling line drives right out of the catcher's mitt with an inside-out swing. He was a notorious bad-ball hitter who posted a .317 career average while leading the Pirates to two World Series titles.

Clemente, a chronic complainer about aches and pains that never seemed to affect his play, batted .317 with 29 homers and 119 RBIs in his MVP 1966 season and won batting titles with such averages as .329, .339, .351 and .357. But Pittsburgh fans best remember Clemente's 12-hit, two-homer, .414 flourish that drove the team to a 1971 World Series win over Baltimore.

Clemente never forgot his roots and was revered in Puerto Rico as a national hero. He was part of a team flying relief supplies to earthquake-ravaged Nicaragua on December 31, 1972, when the small aircraft exploded and crashed into the ocean. His death came only a few months after he had recorded his 3,000th career hit and prompted a special election that gave him distinction as baseball's first Hispanic Hall of Famer.

C L E M E N T E

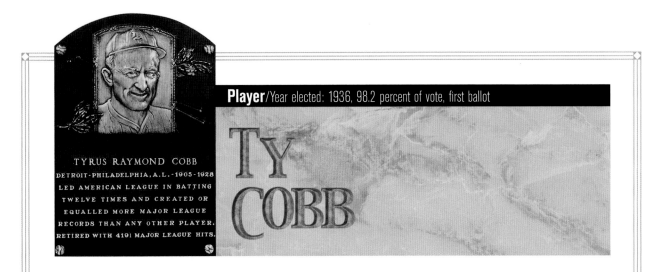

TY COBB

TYRUS RAYMOND COBB
DETROIT-PHILADELPHIA, A.L.·1905-1928
LED AMERICAN LEAGUE IN BATTING
TWELVE TIMES AND CREATED OR
EQUALLED MORE MAJOR LEAGUE
RECORDS THAN ANY OTHER PLAYER.
RETIRED WITH 4191 MAJOR LEAGUE HITS.

Born: 12-18-1886, Narrows, Ga. **Died:** 7-17-61 **Height/Weight:** 6-1/175 **Bats/Throws:** L/R **Primary position:** Outfield **Career statistics:** .366 avg., 4,191 hits, 2,245 runs, 117 HR, 1,938 RBIs, 892 steals **Teams:** Tigers 1905-26; Athletics 1927-28 **Batting champion:** A.L., 1907, '08, '09, '10, '11, '12, '13, '14, '15, '17, '18, '19 **HR champion:** A.L., 1909 **Major awards:** Chalmers MVP, 1911

No player in history generated more emotion, created more havoc, bruised more egos and left more battlescars than Tyrus Raymond Cobb, a snarling wildcat who cut a bloody path to baseball immortality with a take-no-prisoners style, razor-sharp spikes, iron fists and a tongue that spared nobody, friend or foe.

Exactly what motivated the 6-foot-1, 175-pound Georgia Peach remains a dark mystery. But his incredible talents were fueled by equal parts anger, intensity, cunning, intimidation and a mean-spirited, win-at-all-costs drive that never wavered over an incredible 22 seasons with the Detroit Tigers and two with the Philadelphia Athletics. Cobb was a bully and a brawler, but he also was the dominant player of the dead-ball era and his near-legendary feats have withstood the test of time.

Cobb was to bat control

COBB

> ## "He could do everything better than any player I ever saw." — *Walter Johnson*

what Babe Ruth was later to the home run. A lefthanded hitter, he choked up on the bat with a split grip and drove the ball anywhere he wanted. If muscle was required, Cobb could supply it, and he was a master bunter. But he was most dangerous on the bases, where he used his speed to dominate and his spikes to deliver bloody messages.

Love him or hate him, this was no ordinary demon. When Cobb retired in 1928 at age 42, he owned an incredible 90 all-time records. His 12 American League batting titles (nine in succession) and .366 career average still top the all-time charts. His career records of 892 stolen bases, 2,245 runs scored and 4,191 hits have been broken, but not erased from baseball lore. Cobb, a three-time .400 hitter who helped the Tigers to three straight pennants (1907-09) but never played on a World Series winner, also was an accomplished outfielder with speed and an above-average arm.

Unpopular and feared, Cobb still earned grudging respect from the baseball world with his inspired play. When the first class of Hall of Fame players was elected in 1936, he garnered 98.2 percent of the vote — easily topping the second-place total of 95.1 shared by Babe Ruth and Honus Wagner.

Player/Year elected: 1947, 79.5 percent of vote

MICKEY COCHRANE

Born: 4-6-03, Bridgewater, Mass. **Died:** 6-28-62 **Height/Weight:** 5-11/180 **Bats/Throws:** L/R **Primary position:** Catcher **Career statistics:** .320 avg., 1,652 hits, 1,041 runs **Teams:** Athletics 1925-33; Tigers 1934-37 **Major awards:** League MVP, 1928; A.L. MVP, 1934

The first thing you noticed about Mickey Cochrane was his ears, ham-size protrusions with funny little points that had to tempt baseball's hard-core bench jockeys. The second was the respect he commanded — ears and all — as one of the grittiest and smartest leaders the game has produced. Cochrane was equal parts fascinating, contradictory and puzzling in his never-wavering dedication to — and obsession for — winning.

History remembers him as one of the best Depression-era catchers, the heart and soul of a Connie Mack Philadelphia Athletics machine that captured three straight American League pennants and consecutive World Series titles from 1929-31. Others recall the intense, driven player/manager of a Detroit team that won two straight pennants and one World Series in 1934 and '35.

Cochrane, both player and manager, was a whirling dervish, a savvy student who never stopped looking for an edge that could mean the difference between winning and losing. Nobody took defeat harder and that was reflect-

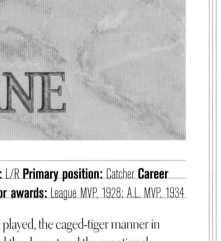

ed by the way he played, the caged-tiger manner in which he prowled the dugout and the emotional demands he made on teammates.

The man Mack credited as the driving force behind his Philadelphia champions was an agile, take-charge catcher who could change the course of games with his powerful arm or a lefthanded swing that sprayed line drives to every section of the park. Cochrane, a selective hitter who seldom struck out, topped .300 eight times en route to a .320 career average and he won two MVPs — the League award in 1928 and the baseball writers' honor six years later.

The emotional peaks and valleys took their toll on Cochrane in 1936 when, two years after winning his second MVP, he suffered a midseason nervous breakdown. The following spring, a pitch from New York's Bump Hadley beaned Cochrane, fracturing his skull in three places and prematurely ending his playing career in its 13th season. Cochrane's on-field association ended in August 1938 when he was replaced as manager.

"**More than any other player, Mickey Cochrane was responsible for the three pennants (the Athletics) won in 1929, 1930 and 1931. ... He was Ty Cobb wearing a mask.**" —*Connie Mack*

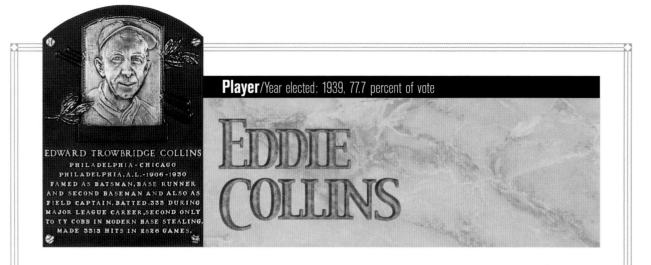

EDDIE COLLINS

EDWARD TROWBRIDGE COLLINS
PHILADELPHIA - CHICAGO
PHILADELPHIA, A.L.-1906-1930
FAMED AS BATSMAN, BASE RUNNER
AND SECOND BASEMAN AND ALSO AS
FIELD CAPTAIN. BATTED .333 DURING
MAJOR LEAGUE CAREER, SECOND ONLY
TO TY COBB IN MODERN BASE STEALING.
MADE 3313 HITS IN 2826 GAMES.

Born: 5-2-1887, Millerton, N.Y. **Died:** 3-25-51 **Height/Weight:** 5-9/175 **Bats/Throws:** L/R **Primary position:** Second base **Career statistics:** .333 avg., 3,315 hits, 1,821 runs, 1,300 RBIs, 745 steals **Teams:** Athletics 1906-14, 1927-30; White Sox 1915-26 **Major awards:** Chalmers MVP, 1914

Pound for pound, Eddie Collins might have been the best player in baseball history. Ty Cobb thought he was; so did Collins' former Philadelphia Athletics manager, the esteemed Connie Mack. The 5-foot-9, 175-pound Collins, a graduate of Columbia University, certainly was one of the most cerebral players during his quarter-century reign as the game's best all-around second baseman.

Collins, who began his career in 1906 with Mack's Athletics, covered more ground than early-century contemporary Nap Lajoie, made the double-play pivot more gracefully than late-career rival Rogers Hornsby and was especially adept at retreating into the outfield to pick off potential bloop hits. More than seven decades after his retirement, Collins still owns second base career records for total chances and assists.

The slashing lefthanded hitter was a perfect fit for the dead-ball era in which he spent most of his career and learned to play the game. Collins seldom struck out,

"For a man who could do anything—hit, field, run bases and play inside and brainy baseball—Collins stands at the top."

—Ty Cobb

posted an impressive .333 average (10 times over .340) and scored lots of runs—1,821 over a career that also produced 3,315 hits. The only reason Collins never won an A.L. batting title was because his career spanned the same period as Cobb.

The speedy Collins, an outstanding bunter and consummate team player, might have been most dangerous on the basepaths. He stole 67 bases in 1909 and 81 a year later en route to a career total of 745, but he is best remembered for his daring dash to the plate in Game 6 of the 1917 World Series with the run that secured a championship for the Chicago White Sox.

Collins also is remembered for other things. He was an innocent member of the 1919 Black Sox team that conspired to throw the World Series; he was a member of Philadelphia's famed $100,000 infield (Stuffy McInnis at first, Collins at second, Jack Barry at shortstop and Home Run Baker at third) in 1913-14; he was a key member of Philadelphia World Series winners in 1910, '11 and '13; and he batted .328 in six fall classics with 42 hits.

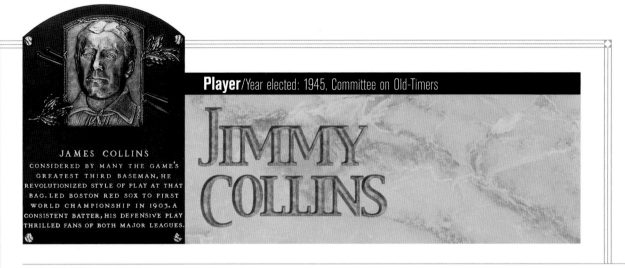

Player/Year elected: 1945, Committee on Old-Timers

JIMMY COLLINS

JAMES COLLINS

CONSIDERED BY MANY THE GAME'S GREATEST THIRD BASEMAN, HE REVOLUTIONIZED STYLE OF PLAY AT THAT BAG. LED BOSTON RED SOX TO FIRST WORLD CHAMPIONSHIP IN 1903. A CONSISTENT BATTER, HIS DEFENSIVE PLAY THRILLED FANS OF BOTH MAJOR LEAGUES.

Born: 1-16-1870, Buffalo, N.Y. **Died:** 3-6-43 **Height/Weight:** 5-9/175 **Bats/Throws:** R/R **Primary position:** Third base
Career statistics: .294 avg., 1,999 hits, 1,055 runs **Teams:** Boston 1895, 1896-1900; Louisville 1895; Red Sox 1901-07; Athletics 1907-08 **HR champion:** N.L., 1898

John McGraw knew. So did Willie Keeler, Jesse Burkett, Billy Hamilton and all the other great players who used the bunt as an important offensive weapon in 19th century baseball. Jimmy Collins, a rookie for Louisville in 1895, was a threat to their livelihood—a cat-quick, unorthodox, electrifying third baseman who would change the way the position—and the game—was played.

One by one, the great bunters of the era tested Collins and, one by one, they discovered a hard truth—the 5-foot-9, 175-pounder could dart in, barehand the ball and make an accurate, single-motion, underhand throw to first base and cut them down. His technique was unprecedented. So was the way he played well off the third base bag and ranged left and right, creeping forward in bunt situations. He was the prototype by which future generations of third basemen would be judged.

Collins also was a clutch righthanded hitter who topped .300 five times in his 14-year career and he'll always be remembered as the player-manager who led

> "They say I was the greatest third baseman and I would like to believe it. But I don't know. There were many great third basemen in my day." —*Jimmy Collins*

the Boston Red Sox to consecutive pennants in the fledgling American League and the first World Series championship—an eight-game upset of National League-champion Pittsburgh in 1903. But Collins' enormous reputation and popularity was built around his glove.

Combining with first baseman Fred Tenney, second baseman Bobby Lowe and shortstop Herman Long in the most heralded infield of the 19th century, he helped Boston win N.L. pennants in 1897 and 1898—batting .328 and leading the league with a then-remarkable total of 15 home runs in the latter campaign. Beaneaters fans were shocked when he jumped to the A.L. Boston team in 1901 and Red Sox fans were equally appalled when a 1907 trade sent the popular Collins to Philadelphia, where he finished his career a year later with the Athletics.

Collins retired with a .294 average and his totals of 601 chances in 1899 and 252 putouts in 1900 are still-standing N.L. defensive records.

COLLINS

Horner
Photo

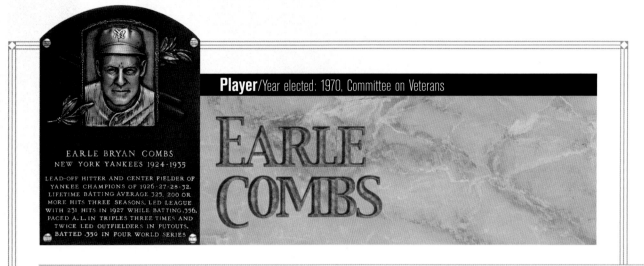

Player/Year elected: 1970, Committee on Veterans

EARLE COMBS

EARLE BRYAN COMBS
NEW YORK YANKEES 1924-1935

LEAD-OFF HITTER AND CENTER FIELDER OF
YANKEE CHAMPIONS OF 1926·27·28·32.
LIFETIME BATTING AVERAGE .325. 200 OR
MORE HITS THREE SEASONS. LED LEAGUE
WITH 231 HITS IN 1927 WHILE BATTING .356.
PACED A.L. IN TRIPLES THREE TIMES AND
TWICE LED OUTFIELDERS IN PUTOUTS.
BATTED .350 IN FOUR WORLD SERIES

Born: 5-14-1899, Pebworth, Ky. **Died:** 7-21-76 **Height/Weight:** 6-0/185 **Bats/Throws:** L/R **Primary position:** Center field
Career statistics: .325 avg., 1,866 hits, 1,186 runs **Teams:** Yankees 1924-35

He was the table setter for Babe Ruth and Lou Gehrig, the spark for one of the most prolific offenses in baseball history. An Earle Combs line drive toward the gap at Yankee Stadium was a typical appetizer for the devastation that inevitably followed. "Murderer's Row" baseball might have been defined by the booming bats of Ruth, Gehrig and Bob Meusel, but it was choreographed by the graceful style of New York's efficient leadoff man and center fielder.

The speedy Kentuckian, who played in the massive shadow of his more spectacular teammates, never had a bad year. In 12 Yankee seasons beginning in 1924, he batted .300 or better 10 times, scored more than 100 runs eight times, collected 190 or more hits five times and led the American League in triples on three occasions. "The Colonel," a .350 hitter in four World Series, batted .356 and scored 137 runs in 1927, the year Ruth hit 60 homers, Gehrig drove in 175 runs and the powerful Yanks won 110 games and swept to a Series championship.

Fans and teammates marveled at the consistency Combs displayed at the plate with his surgical lefthanded swing and on defense with his ability to range far into right field to cover up for the slow-footed Ruth. His only flaw was a weak arm and his greatest asset was speed, which he throttled back on the bases because of the powerful Yankees lineup.

Ironically, the 6-foot Combs was an interesting contrast to Ruth. The Babe was loud, profane and colorful with a huge appetite for food, drink and women. Combs was a quiet, modest college graduate (Eastern Kentucky State Teachers College) — a suave, dignified, prematurely-gray man who didn't smoke or drink.

Combs, a .325 career hitter, crashed into a wall chasing a fly ball during a 1934 game at St. Louis, breaking a shoulder and fracturing his skull, but he returned to play 89 games in 1935 before retiring. In 1936, he coached a young center field prospect named Joe DiMaggio.

> "He was a smashing hitter, a fleet and sure catch in the outfield and an unerring judge of fly balls. I think he was the best leadoff hitter of all time. ..." —*Ed Barrow*

COMBS

CHARLES COMISKEY

CHARLES A. COMISKEY
"THE OLD ROMAN"
STARTED 50 YEARS OF BASEBALL AS
ST. LOUIS BROWNS FIRST-BASEMAN IN 1882
AND WAS FIRST MAN AT THIS POSITION TO
PLAY AWAY FROM THE BAG FOR BATTERS. AS
BROWNS' MANAGER-CAPTAIN-PLAYER WON
4 STRAIGHT AMERICAN ASSOCIATION
PENNANTS STARTING 1885, WORLD CHAMPIONS
FIRST 2 YEARS. OWNER AND PRESIDENT
CHICAGO WHITE SOX 1900 TO 1931.

Born: 8-15-1859, Chicago, Ill. **Died:** 10-26-31 **Height/Weight:** 6-0/180 **Bats/Throws:** R/R **Primary position:** First base **Career statistics:** .267 avg., 1,556 hits **Teams played:** St. Louis (A.A.) 1882-89, 1891; Chicago (P.L.) 1890; Cincinnati 1892-94 **Teams managed (838-541):** St. Louis (A.A.) 1883-89, 1891; Chicago (P.L.) 1890; Cincinnati 1892-94 **Executive career:** Founder/owner White Sox, 1901-31

He was the only man to reach the championship pinnacle as a player, manager and owner. But Charles Comiskey's legacy cuts much deeper than that. "The Old Roman" also was a key figure in the founding and success of the American League and a powerful behind-the-scenes baseball force for the next three decades as sole owner of the Chicago White Sox.

Comiskey is remembered as the prominent bow-tied Chicago gentleman, smiling at the world from beneath his roguishly cocked fedora. But long before that he was the innovative first baseman and manager of a St. Louis Browns team that won four straight American Association pennants from 1885-88. A .267 career hitter over 13 seasons, Comiskey was the first man to position himself well off the bag, requiring the pitcher to cover first on ground balls to the right side.

It was the stature Comiskey gained as player and manager at St. Louis and Cincinnati that helped close friend Ban Johnson gain a baseball foothold as head of the Western League in 1895. Together they took that minor league circuit to major league status and successfully challenged the monopoly of the National League in 1901 — Johnson positioned as "American League" president and Comiskey as owner of a key franchise in his hometown Chicago.

As baseball grew and prospered, so did Comiskey. Nothing of importance happened without his approval and Comiskey Park became the game's showcase ballpark when it opened in 1910. The lovable "Commy," a dashing figure, watched his White Sox win the first A.L. pennant in 1901, World Series championships in 1906 and 1917 and a final pennant in 1919.

"He was a wonderful figure in baseball. He was one of the real strong men of the league. Comiskey was the power behind the throne. His judgment was always the best."

—Frank Navin

It was in 1919, a season that should have generated great joy, that Comiskey's baseball world collapsed. The "Black Sox" scandal, combined with accusations of his "cheapskate" responsibility, tortured him for the rest of his life, as did a feud with Johnson and the tattered condition of his team. An embittered Comiskey died in 1931, longing for one more pennant to erase the stigma of 1919.

JOCKO CONLAN

JOHN BERTRAND CONLAN
"JOCKO"
UMPIRE
NATIONAL LEAGUE 1941-1965
SUNNY DISPOSITION, ACCURACY AND
HUSTLE EARNED HIM RATING AS STANDOUT
UMPIRE AND HE WON RESPECT OF
PLAYERS AND MANAGERS WITH HIS
FAIRNESS. ONLY ARBITER TO WORK IN
EACH OF FIRST FOUR N.L. PENNANT
PLAYOFFS. CHOSEN FOR SIX WORLD SERIES
AND SIX ALL-STAR GAMES.

Born: 12-6-02, Chicago, Ill. **Died:** 4-16-89 **Height/Weight:** 5-7/160 **Years umpired:** N.L., 1941-65

All-Star Games: 1943, '47, '50, '53, '58, '62 (2) **World Series:** 1945, '50, '54, '57, '61

One writer called him "James Cagney without the swagger," a tribute to Jocko Conlan's ability to be tough and funny at the same time. Managers and players used such adjectives as "accurate," "fair" and "devoted" to describe the 5-foot-7 umpire with the 160-pound heart. Generally liked and universally respected, the little big man of baseball's peacekeeping fraternity ruled over the sport with unquestioned integrity and colorful enthusiasm for a quarter century.

Off the field, Conlan was fun and gregarious, a delightful companion who could charm with his fine tenor voice and quick Irish wit. His diminutive body was topped by what *New York Times* columnist Arthur Daley called "a map-of-Ireland face" and his ever-present grin camouflaged a bantam-rooster feistiness.

On the field, he was in total command — the umpiring style he picked up from mentor Bill Klem. Tolerant when appropriate and quick to diffuse trouble with his ready one-liners, Conlan came down hard on anyone who cursed or stepped over his well-established line. He went face-to-face with the most belligerent managers and once engaged in a celebrated shin-kicking battle with longtime nemesis Leo Durocher.

Conlan, a 14-year minor league outfielder who got a cup of coffee with his hometown Chicago White Sox in 1934 and '35, discovered his umpiring abilities by accident. Out of the lineup because of an injury, he filled in on the bases when Red Ormsby was overcome by heat during a 1935 doubleheader at St. Louis. By 1936, he was a $300-per-month arbiter in the New York-Penn League; by 1941, he was a National League rookie under Klem's supervision.

Conlan, easy to spot with his trademark bow tie, balloon protector and unusual lefthanded signals, developed into the game's most respected and popular umpire. He earned assignments in four pennant-deciding playoff games, six All-Star Games and five World Series before leg problems forced a 1964 retirement. He returned in 1965 as a substitute, bringing his length of service to 25 years.

"We had our battles on the field, but we were good friends off the field. He was a fine umpire and a fine man." —*Leo Durocher*

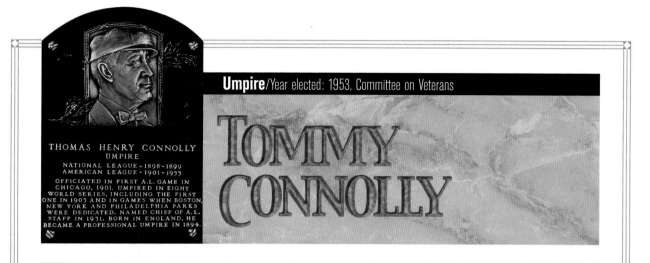

TOMMY CONNOLLY

THOMAS HENRY CONNOLLY
UMPIRE
NATIONAL LEAGUE · 1898-1899
AMERICAN LEAGUE · 1901-1953
OFFICIATED IN FIRST A.L. GAME IN
CHICAGO, 1901. UMPIRED IN EIGHT
WORLD SERIES, INCLUDING THE FIRST
ONE IN 1903 AND IN GAMES WHEN BOSTON,
NEW YORK AND PHILADELPHIA PARKS
WERE DEDICATED. NAMED CHIEF OF A.L.
STAFF IN 1931. BORN IN ENGLAND, HE
BECAME A PROFESSIONAL UMPIRE IN 1894.

Born: 12-31-1870, Manchester, England **Died:** 4-28-61 **Height/Weight:** 5-7/135 **Years umpired:** N.L., 1898-1900; A.L., 1901-31; Supervisor of A.L. umpires, 1932-54 **World Series:** 1903, '08, '10, '11, '13, '16, '20, '24

He delivered rulings in an Irish brogue to players who often towered over him. Size never mattered to Tommy Connolly, a 5-foot-7, 135-pound giant who helped bring pride and dignity to turn-of-the-century umpiring. Quietly forceful, patiently respectful and unwaveringly fair, Connolly spent 33 seasons as the prototypical Ban Johnson arbiter — always the "boss of the game" and "honorable representative of his league."

Connolly was to American League umpiring what Bill Klem was to the National League. But unlike Klem, who was loud, funny and temperamental, Connolly was quiet and dignified, disdainful of crowd-pleasing flourishes. He wore high, hard collars that propped up his proud chin and a stern countenance that discouraged would-be protestors. His balloon chest protector became the trademark of A.L. umpires.

Born in England and raised from age 13 in Natick, Mass., Connolly became enamored with the rules of the popular game sweeping the land in the 1880s. By 1894 he was a professional umpire in the New

"You can go so far with Connolly, but when you see his neck get red, it's time to lay off him." — *Ty Cobb*

England League, four years later he was working in the rough-and-tumble N.L. and in 1901 he worked the first game in A.L. history at Chicago. It was under the strict disciplinary arm of A.L. president Johnson that Connolly's stature grew.

A master of the rule book and its interpretation, he survived the boisterous, one-umpire era as "Mr. Connolly," the respected man in blue. Connolly took pride in his ability to quell potential uprisings, but drew a line that even superstars like Babe Ruth and Ty Cobb refused to cross. He proudly worked one 10-year stretch without an ejection.

Connolly holds the distinction of working eight World Series, including the first in history (1903). He also worked inaugural games at Chicago's Comiskey Park, Boston's Fenway Park, Philadelphia's Shibe Park and New York's Hilltop Park and Yankee Stadium. He retired from field duty in 1931 and spent 23 more years as the A.L.'s supervisor of umpires, retiring in 1954 at age 83.

CONNOLLY

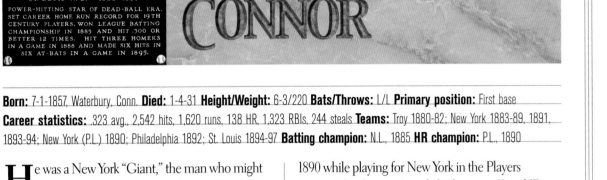

ROGER CONNOR

ROGER CONNOR
TROY N.L., NEW YORK N.L.,
NEW YORK P.L., PHILADELPHIA N.L.,
ST. LOUIS N.L. 1880-1897
POWER-HITTING STAR OF DEAD-BALL ERA.
SET CAREER HOME RUN RECORD FOR 19TH
CENTURY PLAYERS. WON LEAGUE BATTING
CHAMPIONSHIP IN 1885 AND HIT .300 OR
BETTER 12 TIMES. HIT THREE HOMERS
IN A GAME IN 1888 AND MADE SIX HITS IN
SIX AT-BATS IN A GAME IN 1895.

Born: 7-1-1857, Waterbury, Conn. **Died:** 1-4-31 **Height/Weight:** 6-3/220 **Bats/Throws:** L/L **Primary position:** First base
Career statistics: .323 avg., 2,542 hits, 1,620 runs, 138 HR, 1,323 RBIs, 244 steals **Teams:** Troy 1880-82; New York 1883-89, 1891, 1893-94; New York (P.L.) 1890; Philadelphia 1892; St. Louis 1894-97 **Batting champion:** N.L., 1885 **HR champion:** P.L., 1890

He was a New York "Giant," the man who might have inspired the nickname of one of baseball's premier franchises. At 6-foot-3 and 220 pounds, Roger Connor stood tall and loomed large in the minds of 19th-century Big Apple fans. Long before Babe Ruth, back when balls were dead and the hit-and-run was the weapon of choice, Connor was the king of clout, the most prolific home run hitter of the game's formative era.

A tall, dashing gentleman who could light up a room with a hearty laugh and a twitch of his broad, handlebar mustache, Connor lit up major league ballparks with a long, free, lefthanded swing that terrorized pitchers for 18 seasons. Like contemporary Dan Brouthers, Connor amazed fans with prodigious blows that one writer said would either "break the back fences or clear them."

The Waterbury, Conn., product "cleared them" 138 times from 1880 to 1897, a record that stood until 1921 when Ruth sped past him during a 59-homer barrage. Curiously, Connor won only one homer title (14 in

1890 while playing for New York in the Players League), but he consistently hit between 11 and 17 from 1887-93, high numbers for the period.

The soft-spoken first baseman was anything but one-dimensional. He walked with a peculiar, confident gait and ran with surprising, disruptive speed. Connor could steal a base or wreak havoc with his powerful slides. He was known for home runs, but his 233 career triples rank fifth on the all-time list and he was a 12-time .300 hitter who won one batting title (.371 in 1885), topped 100 RBIs four times and scored 100 or more runs on eight occasions.

The popular Irishman, known affectionately as "Dear old Roger," began his career with Troy, remained with the franchise when it moved to New York in 1883 and helped the Giants secure National League pennants in 1888 and 1889. Connor, who led N.L. first basemen in fielding average four times, ended his career at St. Louis in 1897 with a .323 average, 2,542 hits and 1,620 runs.

"With his benignant air and rolling gait, Connor seemed to be more of a country squire than a professional ball player, and ... he was a never-ending surprise, because of his agility and nimbleness." —*The Sporting News, 1931*

CONNOR

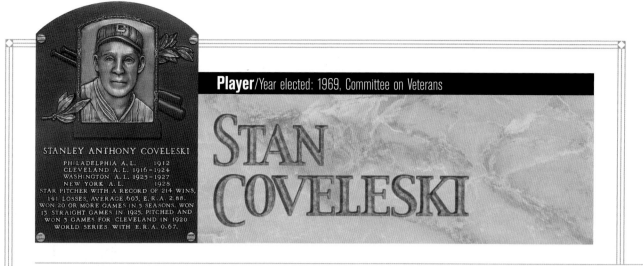

Player/Year elected: 1969, Committee on Veterans

STAN COVELESKI

STANLEY ANTHONY COVELESKI
PHILADELPHIA A.L. 1912
CLEVELAND A.L. 1916–1924
WASHINGTON A.L. 1925–1927
NEW YORK A.L. 1928
STAR PITCHER WITH A RECORD OF 214 WINS,
141 LOSSES, AVERAGE .603, E.R.A. 2.88.
WON 20 OR MORE GAMES IN 5 SEASONS. WON
13 STRAIGHT GAMES IN 1925. PITCHED AND
WON 3 GAMES FOR CLEVELAND IN 1920
WORLD SERIES WITH E.R.A. 0.67.

Born: 7-13-1889, Shamokin, Pa. **Died:** 3-20-84 **Height/Weight:** 5-11/166 **Bats/Throws:** R/R **Position:** Pitcher
Career statistics: 215-142, 2.89 ERA, 981 strikeouts **Teams:** Athletics 1912; Indians 1916-24; Senators 1925-27; Yankees 1928

The ball fluttered homeward, faster than a knuckleball but similar in appearance and spin. Then, only a split second before it reached the plate, the ball dipped downward or broke sideways, always in accordance with the dictates of Cleveland righthander Stan Coveleski. He was the master of frustration, the slippery-elm artist who enjoyed success as one of the game's last legal spitballers.

Coveleski, the brother of contemporary major league lefthander Harry Coveleski and son of a Pennsylvania coal miner, put his special pitch to good use over a 14-year career that produced 215 victories and a 2.89 ERA. A thin sliver of slippery elm wood, which he chewed throughout the game, generated juice for the spitball he threw with surprising accuracy and he mixed it with a good fastball, curve and pinpoint control to shut down most of the American League's biggest hitters.

Control was Coveleski's secret. He would wind up, glove hiding his face, and deliver strike after strike to perfect spots, seldom letting hitters get solid wood on the

"Elm would make the ball as slippery as ice. It would react like a knuckleball and wouldn't spin. I could throw it much faster than pitchers can the knuckler. And I could control its break."

— *Stan Coveleski*

ball. Because the 5-foot-11, 166-pounder seldom walked batters, they went to the plate swinging and his typical complete-game performance would be under 100 pitches. He worked fast and deep into games, never pitching fewer than 228 innings from 1916-26.

A 15-game winner in 1916 after eight frustrating minor league seasons, Coveleski won 19 in 1917 and topped 20 wins in each of his next four campaigns. The 1920 season was his masterpiece, a 24-14 effort that helped Cleveland win the pennant. Coveleski posted three victories in the Indians' World Series win over Brooklyn—all complete-game five-hitters with pitch counts of 72, 78 and 82.

It also was in 1920 that baseball outlawed the spitball, granting 17 current practitioners the right to continue throwing it. Coveleski did with great success until 1923 and '24, when he slid to 13-14 and 15-16 records. The Indians shipped him to Washington where he bounced back for one more big season— a 20-5 effort in 1925 for the pennant-winning Senators.

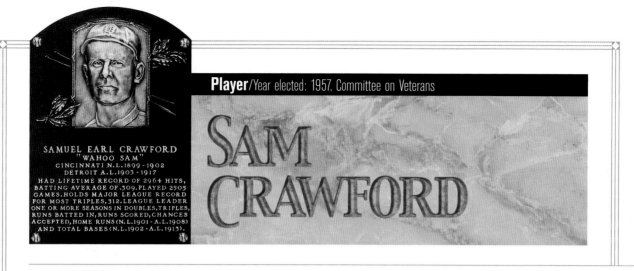

SAMUEL EARL CRAWFORD
"WAHOO SAM"
CINCINNATI N.L. 1899-1902
DETROIT A.L. 1903-1917
HAD LIFETIME RECORD OF 2964 HITS,
BATTING AVERAGE OF .309. PLAYED 2505
GAMES. HOLDS MAJOR LEAGUE RECORD
FOR MOST TRIPLES, 312. LEAGUE LEADER
ONE OR MORE SEASONS IN DOUBLES, TRIPLES,
RUNS BATTED IN, RUNS SCORED, CHANCES
ACCEPTED, HOME RUNS (N.L. 1901 - A.L. 1908)
AND TOTAL BASES (N.L. 1902 - A.L. 1913).

SAM CRAWFORD

Born: 4-18-1880, Wahoo, Neb. **Died:** 6-15-68 **Height/Weight:** 6-0/190 **Bats/Throws:** L/L **Primary position:** Outfield **Career statistics:** .309 avg., 2,961 hits, 1,391 runs, 97 HR, 1,525 RBIs, 366 steals **Teams:** Cincinnati 1899-1902, Tigers 1903-17 **HR champion:** N.L., 1901; A.L., 1908

Sam Crawford stood out like a sore thumb. The enormous shoulders, the muscular, well-conditioned body and the hard, menacing swing were futuristic illusions in a turn-of-the-century era that glorified its speedy contact hitters. Wahoo Sam (he was born and raised in Wahoo, Neb.) was more typical of the sluggers who would thrive after the 1920s and his contemporaries claimed he could have posted Babe Ruth-like home run totals if he had been born 20 years later.

So Crawford had to settle for a reputation as the hardest hitter of the dead-ball era. He stood erect in his lefthanded stance, feet spread, and whaled away at the offerings of pitchers he often intimidated. Many of his vicious line drives ended up in outfielders' gloves just short of the fence, but many others whistled into the gaps—and beyond.

Crawford, who began his career in 1899 with Cincinnati, holds distinction as the first player to lead both leagues in home runs—16 in 1901 with the Reds; seven in 1908 with the Tigers. But Crawford, who was not considered fast, is even better known for another kind of extra-base hit. He led his league six times in triples (he had at least 10 in every full season he played) and still holds

the all-time record for three-base hits with 309, 14 more than longtime Detroit teammate Ty Cobb.

Crawford and Cobb, who worked side-by-side in Detroit's outfield for 13 years, formed a formidable combination that fueled the Tigers to three straight American League pennants from 1907-09. But Crawford, the cleanup man, was overshadowed for most of his career by the fiery Cobb, who in turn

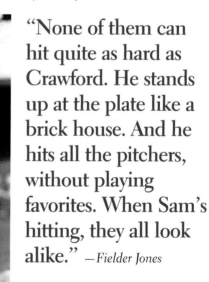

> "None of them can hit quite as hard as Crawford. He stands up at the plate like a brick house. And he hits all the pitchers, without playing favorites. When Sam's hitting, they all look alike." —*Fielder Jones*

resented Crawford's emotional connection with the fans of Detroit. Still they performed well in tendem, Cobb as the instigator and Crawford as one of the most dangerous clutch hitters in the game, until 1917 when Crawford ended his 19-year career with a .309 average.

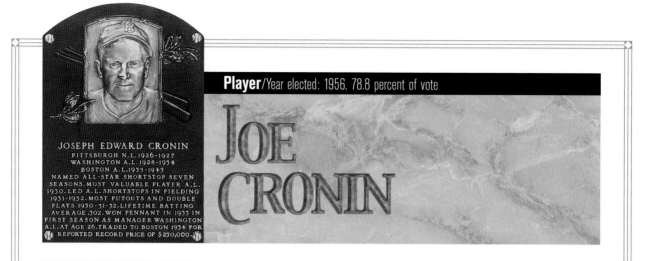

JOE CRONIN

JOSEPH EDWARD CRONIN
PITTSBURGH N.L.1926-1927
WASHINGTON A.L.1928-1934
BOSTON A.L.1935-1945
NAMED ALL-STAR SHORTSTOP SEVEN
SEASONS. MOST VALUABLE PLAYER A.L.
1930. LED A.L.SHORTSTOPS IN FIELDING
1931-1932. MOST PUTOUTS AND DOUBLE
PLAYS 1930-31-32. LIFETIME BATTING
AVERAGE .302. WON PENNANT IN 1933 IN
FIRST SEASON AS MANAGER WASHINGTON
A.L. AT AGE 26. TRADED TO BOSTON 1934 FOR
REPORTED RECORD PRICE OF $250,000.

Born: 10-12-06, San Francisco, Calif. **Died:** 9-7-84 **Height/Weight:** 6-0/180 **Bats/Throws:** R/R **Primary position:** Shortstop **Career statistics:** .301 avg., 2,285 hits, 1,233 runs, 1,424 RBIs **Teams played:** Pirates 1926-27; Senators 1928-34; Red Sox 1935-45 **Teams managed (1,236-1,055):** Senators 1933-34; Red Sox 1935-47 **Executive career:** G.M. Red Sox, 1948-58; A.L. president, 1959-73

Connie Mack called him the greatest clutch hitter he had ever seen. Others called him the greatest shortstop of his era — maybe even of all time. Everyone might have been understated in their praise. No man in history combined playing talent, brains and business acumen more impressively than Joe Cronin in a career that spanned almost a half century in the roles of player, manager, executive and American League president.

Cronin, the son of Irish immigrants who settled in San Francisco, was an unusually big shortstop (6-foot, 180 pounds) who frustrated hitters with his steady glove and pounded pitchers with his lethal bat over a 20-year career. He also was one of the youngest player-managers of all time, a still-rising star when he drove the Washington Senators to an A.L. pennant as a rookie boss in 1933.

The strong-jawed, always-charming Cronin was nothing if not interesting. He was a hard-working righthanded hitter who taught himself to lash the ball to all fields, a batting style that produced a .301 career

average, 2,285 hits and eight 100-RBI seasons. Hard-hitting shortstops didn't exist until Cronin became a Senators regular in 1929 and his .346, 126-RBI 1930 performance opened eyes.

So did his relationship with Senators owner Clark Griffith, a future father-in-law who asked Cronin to replace Walter Johnson as manager in 1933 and then traded him to Boston for shortstop Lyn Lary and $250,000 after the 1934 season. Cronin, who played in seven All-Star Games, continued his assault on big-league pitchers as player-manager of the Red Sox through 1945 and then spent two more seasons as a bench manager, bringing Boston a pennant in 1946.

Cronin's clutch-hitting abilities were amplified in his late-career role as a pinch-hitter. He hit a record five pinch home runs in 1943 and seemed to relish every pressure at-bat. After retiring with 1,236 career managerial wins in 1947, he served as Boston's general manager until becoming A.L. president from 1959-73.

> "Baseball is a game of disappointments. The .300 hitter is a man who is disappointed seven times out of 10." — *Joe Cronin*

W. A. "CANDY" CUMMINGS

PITCHED FIRST CURVE BALL IN BASEBALL
HISTORY. INVENTED CURVE AS AMATEUR
ACE OF BROOKLYN STARS IN 1867. ENDED
LONG CAREER AS HARTFORD PITCHER IN
NATIONAL LEAGUE'S FIRST YEAR 1876.

Player/Year elected: 1939, Committee of Old-Time Players and Writers

CANDY CUMMINGS

Born: 10-18-1848, Ware, Mass. **Died:** 5-16-24 **Height/Weight:** 5-9/120 **Bats/Throws:** R/R **Position:** Pitcher
Career statistics: 21-22, 2.78 ERA **Teams:** Hartford 1876; Cincinnati 1877

He was a wisp of a man, a 120-pound weakling who seemed more suited for a library than a baseball uniform. But Arthur "Candy" Cummings had a trick up his sleeve, some special sleight-of-wrist magic that would change the course of the young sport's history. With a snappy twist, he could make a pitch veer suddenly off its directed course, away from startled hitters. Cummings was, according to Hall of Fame lore, the game's first "curveballer."

Other 1870s-era pitchers claimed the invention, but Cummings was endorsed by Henry Chadwick, the long-acknowledged "Father of Baseball." Cummings liked to tell about throwing clam shells as a child while walking the beach in Brooklyn, wondering what made them sail erratically. He spent his teen years experimenting with baseballs, trying to make them defy the laws of physics.

Cummings claimed to have thrown his first curveball in 1864, but he didn't unveil his pitch for the general public until 1867, when

Cummings, at right

he traveled with the Excelsiors of Brooklyn team to New England for a game against the Harvards of Cambridge. Pitching against the wind, which seemed to help his curve, the 18-year-old righthander baffled the hitters and news quickly spread about the revolutionary pitch.

Candy, a nickname denoting admiration in the 1860s, joined the celebrated Stars of Brooklyn in 1868 and eventually found his way to the National Association, forerunner to the National League. Pitching from 45 feet with an underhand motion, Cummings posted a 33-20 record for the 1872 New York Mutuals and worked 497 innings.

He pitched for Baltimore, Philadelphia and Hartford over the next three seasons, with win totals of 28, 28 and 35. By 1876, when Cummings made his N.L. debut for Hartford, overwork was taking a toll and the curveball was in common use. He made history that season by becoming the first pitcher to work and win both ends of a doubleheader, but his record was only 16-8. He was 5-14 the next season for Cincinnati before drifting away from the game.

"Candy was slender of build, short and downright frail. But he possessed a pair of long and sinewy wrists and had a trick of holding the ball near his finger ends, releasing it with a peculiar wrist joint motion which imparted a spin." —*The Sporting News, 1942*

KIKI CUYLER

HAZEN SHIRLEY CUYLER
"KIKI"

PITTSBURGH N.L. 1921 TO 1927
CHICAGO N.L. 1928 TO 1935
CINCINNATI N.L. 1935 TO 1937
BROOKLYN N.L. 1938

LED N.L. IN STOLEN BASES 1926, 1928,
1929, 1930. BATTED .354 IN 1924,
.357 IN 1925, .360 IN 1929, .355 IN 1930.
LIFETIME TOTAL 2299 HITS,
BATTING AVERAGE .321.
NAMED TO ALL STAR TEAM IN 1925.

Born: 8-30-1898, Harrisville, Mich. **Died:** 2-11-50 **Height/Weight:** 5-11/185 **Bats/Throws:** R/R **Primary position:** Right field **Career statistics:** .321 avg., 2,299 hits, 1,305 runs, 1,065 RBIs, 328 steals **Teams:** Pirates 1921-27; Cubs 1928-35; Reds 1935-37; Dodgers 1938

Hailed as "the new Ty Cobb" when he began his first full major league season with Pittsburgh in 1924, Hazen "Kiki" Cuyler failed to scale that lofty plateau. He simply was too nice. But that didn't stop the five-tool star from carving out his own special niche over a 16-year career that included four pennant-winning seasons with the Pirates and Chicago Cubs.

The 5-foot-11, 185-pound kid from Harrisville, Mich., appeared to be a gift from the baseball gods when he took over right field for the 1924 Pirates and batted .354 with 85 RBIs in 117 games. He could run, throw and hit with anybody and he enamored fans with his no-smoke, no-drink All-American image. A .357, 18-homer, 102-RBI 1925 season only added to the mystique and he capped that storybook campaign

"Cobb was ornery and fierce, and that's where Cuyler didn't match him. But he was virtually a carbon copy in other respects." —*Jack Doyle*

with a World Series-winning Game 7 double off Washington pitcher Walter Johnson.

The soft-spoken, sensitive Cuyler might have lacked Cobb's intensity, but he still whipped line drives all over the park with his long righthanded swing and relished his role as premier run-producer. Tutored by early-career teammate Max Carey, he also led the National League in stolen bases four times and his fly-chasing abilities, either in center field or right, were second to none.

Given Cuyler's affable personality, it was hard for Pittsburgh fans to understand why he suddenly fell into disfavor with Pirates manager Donie Bush in the 1927 pennant-winning season. But, without explanation, he was benched down the stretch, ignored while his team was being swept in the World Series by the New York Yankees and traded to Chicago a month later. His .360 average and 102 RBIs sparked a Cubs pennant run in 1929 and he batted .355, drove in 134 runs and scored 155 a year later when teammate Hack Wilson set a still-standing RBI mark with 191.

That was the last of Cuyler's elite seasons, although he did contribute to another Cubs pennant run in 1932. He retired in 1938 with a .321 average, 2,299 hits and 1,065 RBIs.

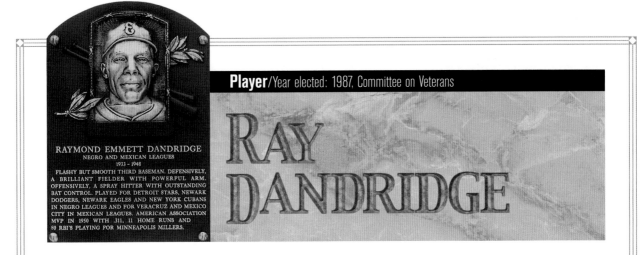

RAYMOND EMMETT DANDRIDGE
NEGRO AND MEXICAN LEAGUES
1933 - 1948
FLASHY BUT SMOOTH THIRD BASEMAN. DEFENSIVELY,
A BRILLIANT FIELDER WITH POWERFUL ARM.
OFFENSIVELY, A SPRAY HITTER WITH OUTSTANDING
BAT CONTROL. PLAYED FOR DETROIT STARS, NEWARK
DODGERS, NEWARK EAGLES AND NEW YORK CUBANS
IN NEGRO LEAGUES AND FOR VERACRUZ AND MEXICO
CITY IN MEXICAN LEAGUES. AMERICAN ASSOCIATION
MVP IN 1950 WITH .311, 11 HOME RUNS AND
90 RBI'S PLAYING FOR MINNEAPOLIS MILLERS.

RAY DANDRIDGE

Born: 8-31-13, Richmond, Va. **Died:** 2-12-94 **Height/Weight:** 5-7/170 **Bats/Throws:** R/R **Primary position:** Third base **Teams (1933-53):** Detroit Stars; Nashville Elite Giants; Newark Dodgers; Newark Eagles; New York Cubans; Minneapolis (A.A.); Sacramento (PCL); Oakland (PCL)

It was an inviting target, legs bowed in a horseshoe-shaped arc that players swore they could have driven a train through, but not a ball—at least none that anybody can remember in the Negro League career of Ray Dandridge. One writer called him "a defensive Houdini" while friends and foes merely insisted he was the best third baseman in baseball history, bar none.

Nobody will ever know for sure because Dandridge was never given the opportunity to play in the major leagues. But stories of his soft hands, lightning-quick instincts, powerful arm and outstanding range have been passed through the generations, tales that describe Pie Traynor and Brooks Robinson-like defensive feats during a career that stretched from 1933-53.

The proud Dandridge, a serious-minded, hard-working Virginian, was almost as accomplished with his 37-ounce bat as he was with his oversized glove. The 5-foot-7, 170-pound righthander went with the pitch, seldom struck out and sprayed line drives all over the field. He was an outstanding hit-and-run man, a consistent .300 hitter who ran the bases aggressively, bandy legs notwithstanding.

Dandridge's reputation was etched into the minds of

"He was fantastic, the best I've ever seen at third. I saw all the greats ... but I've never seen a better third baseman than Dandridge."

—*Monte Irvin,*
The Negro Leagues Book

Negro League fans in the late 1930s, when he became part of the Newark Eagles' "million-dollar infield" with shortstop Willie Wells, second baseman Dick Seay and first baseman Mule Suttles. Dandridge spent most of the 1940s playing in the Mexican League, where he enjoyed the adulation he never would get in the United States. He was a year-round performer who also gained hero status in Venezuela, Puerto Rico and Cuba.

In 1949, after Jackie Robinson had broken baseball's color barrier, Dandridge, at age 35, was signed by the New York Giants and assigned to their Class AAA club at Minneapolis. He posted batting marks of .362, .311 and .324 and won the 1950 American Association MVP while leading the Millers to a pennant. But the Giants refused to promote him or sell his contract and he finally retired in 1953.

Player/Year elected: 1998, Committee on Veterans

GEORGE DAVIS

GEORGE STACEY DAVIS
CLEVELAND, N.L., 1890-1892
NEW YORK, N.L., 1893-1901, 1903
CHICAGO, A.L., 1902, 1904-1909
A SHORTSTOP OF SHINING PROMINENCE WHOSE OFFENSIVE PROWESS GREATLY SURPASSED HIS PEERS IN THE DEAD BALL ERA. A PROLIFIC SWITCH-HITTER, HIS IMPRESSIVE CAREER TOTALS INCLUDE A .295 BATTING AVERAGE, 2,660 HITS, 451 DOUBLES, 1437 RBI, 616 STOLEN BASES AND 163 TRIPLES. A RECORD AMONG SWITCH-HITTERS. HIT .300 OR BETTER NINE TIMES AND HIS 136 RBI IN 1897 LED THE NATIONAL LEAGUE. PACED THE 1906 CHICAGO "HITLESS WONDERS" TO A WORLD SERIES CHAMPIONSHIP SERVED AS PLAYER-MANAGER FOR THE 1898, 1900 AND 1901 GIANTS.

Born: 8-23-1870, Cohoes, N.Y. **Died:** 10-17-40 **Height/Weight:** 5-9/180 **Bats/Throws:** B/R **Primary position:** Shortstop **Career statistics:** .295 avg., 2,665 hits, 1,545 runs, 1,439 RBIs **Teams:** Cleveland 1890-92; N.Y. 1893-1901, 1903; White Sox 1902, 1904-09

He stood strong and erect in the batter's box, a slashing switch-hitter with a run-producing flair. George Davis also ranked among the game's smoothest turn-of-the-century shortstops. But baseball became a sidescript in the career of the talented New Yorker, who is best remembered for an ugly 1903 courtroom battle that almost wrecked a precarious peace between the American and National leagues.

Davis was one of the game's premier performers when he made his challenge to baseball's reserve clause. A former New York Giants player and manager who had jumped to the A.L.'s Chicago White Sox in 1902, Davis tried to return to New York when the two leagues made peace a year later. When he was ordered to stay in Chicago, he hired attorney John Montgomery Ward and went to court, a case he eventually lost—with long-term repercussions.

For years, Davis was passed over for Hall of Fame consideration, a slight many historians trace to resentment over his controversial court case. It's hard to deny his qualifications based on numbers he posted over an outstanding 20-year career that stretched from 1890-1909 in Cleveland, New York and Chicago.

From 1893-1901, a nine-year stretch with the Giants, Davis topped .300 and posted such marks as .355, .353 and .352. He led the National League with 136 RBIs in 1897, one of six seasons above 90, and he led league shortstops in fielding percentage four times—twice in the N.L., twice in the A.L. A member of the Hitless Wonder White Sox who captured baseball's third World Series in 1906, Davis finished his career with a .295 average, 2,665 hits, 1,439 RBIs and 619 stolen bases.

The 5-foot-9, 180-pound Davis didn't discover his shortstop prowess until 1897—his eighth big-league season. He was a solid outfielder and third baseman in his early years with the Cleveland Spiders and Giants. After years of being ignored, Davis finally was voted into the Hall of Fame in 1998 by baseball's Veterans Committee.

> **"The Davis case was as famous in its day as the Sisler case, Scott Perry case and Feller case of later eras. It almost wrecked the precarious peace made by the two majors in 1903. ..."** —*Lee Allen, Hall of Fame historian*

DAVIS

LEON DAY

LEON DAY
NEGRO LEAGUES 1934-1949
USED DECEPTIVE, NO-WIND UP, SHORT-ARM DELIVERY
TO COMPILE IMPRESSIVE SINGLE-SEASON AND
CAREER STATISTICS DURING 10 YEARS IN NEGRO
LEAGUES. ALSO PLAYED BALL IN PUERTO RICO,
CUBA, VENEZUELA, MEXICO AND CANADA. SET NEGRO
NATIONAL LEAGUE RECORD IN 1942 WITH 18 STRIKEOUTS
IN GAME. HURLED NO-HITTER ON OPENING DAY 1946
FOR NEWARK EAGLES VS. PHILADELPHIA STARS. PITCHED
IN RECORD 7 NEGRO LEAGUE ALL-STAR GAMES.

Born: 10-30-16, Alexandria, Va. **Died:** 3-13-95 **Height/Weight:** 5-7/150 **Bats/Throws:** R/R **Primary positions:** Pitcher, second base, outfield **Teams (1934-52):** Baltimore Black Sox; Brooklyn Eagles; Baltimore Elite Giants; Toronto (International); Scranton (Eastern)

They called him a "pitcher," but Leon Day was so much more than that. He was a well-armed, superbly constructed "athlete" disguised in a 5-foot-7, 150-pound body. Little Leon was a big man in the 1930s and '40s-era Negro National League — black baseball's most accomplished strikeout ace one day, a hard-hitting, smooth-fielding second baseman or outfielder the next.

Contemporaries compared Day to the versatile Martin Dihigo, faster but with less power. A righthanded contact hitter, Day could hit for average, move runners and charge around the bases. He also could play any position but catcher, although he is best remembered for his graceful double-play pivots and extensive range around second.

Day, however, took most delight in his ability to throw pitches past overmatched hitters. He was unorthodox — a no-windup righthander who delivered 95-mph fastballs like he was throwing darts. Day cocked his arm at his ear and simply jerked the ball homeward, getting amazing velocity without

"I didn't see anybody in the major leagues that was better than Leon Day. If you want to compare him with Bob Gibson stuff-wise, Day had just as good stuff. ..."

— Larry Doby, from the book Blackball Stars

benefit of full extension. His "short-arm" style, the result of an early career shoulder injury, was deceptive and he further puzzled hitters with a sharp-breaking curve and changeup.

Day, born in Virginia and raised in Baltimore, was most renowned as a strikeout artist over his eight seasons with the Newark Eagles. He fanned a Negro National League-record 18 batters in a one-hit 1942 win over the Baltimore Elite Giants and a Puerto Rican League-record 19 in a 1941 extra-inning winter league contest. He also turned in several outstanding strikeout efforts in the seven East-West All-Star Games in which he appeared.

Day was a silent, workmanlike competitor who was well-liked by teammates. His career, which stretched from 1934-52 and included winter and summer seasons in Venezuela, Mexico and Canada, was interrupted by two years of military service during World War II. In his first game back in 1946 for the pennant-bound Eagles, Day fired a no-hitter against the Philadelphia Stars.

DIZZY DEAN

JAY HANNA (DIZZY) DEAN
ST. LOUIS (N.L.) 1932-1937
CHICAGO (N.L.) 1938-1941
ONE OF FOUR N.L. PITCHERS TO WIN 30 OR
MORE GAMES UNDER MODERN REGULATIONS.
PITCHED IN 1934 (ST.L.) 1938 (CHICAGO)
WORLD SERIES. LED LEAGUE IN STRIKEOUTS
1932-33-34-35. SINGLE GAME RECORD WITH
17, JULY 30, 1933. FIRST PITCHER TO MAKE
TWO HITS IN ONE INNING IN WORLD SERIES.
MOST VALUABLE N.L. PLAYER IN 1934.

Born: 1-16-10, Lucas, Ark. **Died:** 7-17-74 **Height/Weight:** 6-2/182 **Bats/Throws:** R/R
Position: Pitcher **Career statistics:** 150-83, 3.02 ERA, 1,163 strikeouts **Teams:** Cardinals
1930-37; Cubs 1938-41; Browns 1947 **Major awards:** N.L. MVP, 1934

He was the lovable, colorful, cornpone-spewing righthander who helped fuel the success of St. Louis' Gashouse Gang in the Depression-wracked 1930s. Dizzy Dean had the stuff of which legends are made, whether dazzling National League hitters with his powerful arm or sportswriters, teammates and fans with his braggadocio and glib tongue. Dean's supreme confidence could be annoying, but he backed up his boasts in a short-but-sweet career that ended all too prematurely because of an arm injury.

Ol' Diz, the self-ascribed moniker that reflected his poor Arkansas roots, was a baseball character. But he also was a 6-foot-2, strong-armed strikeout pitcher with a blazing fastball, a good curve and a nasty changeup. The always-smiling Dean fired his pitches with the same fluid delivery with which he fired barbs at hitters who let the good-natured ribbing add to their frustration.

Dean was the class of the N.L. from 1932, his first full big-league season, through 1936, a five-year stretch in which he won 120 games and led the league in strikeouts four times. He was a magnificent 30-7 in an MVP 1934 season in which he combined with brother Paul, a 19-game winner, to lead the Cardinals to a pennant and World Series victory over Detroit. The "Me 'n' Paul" Dean combination won four games in the World Series and Dizzy remained baseball's last 30-game winner for

DEAN

34 years.

Dean, who added 28 wins in 1935 and 24 more in '36, saw his career turn dramatically in the 1937 All-Star Game when he was hit on the foot by an Earl Averill line drive. Trying to pitch with a broken toe, Dean altered his delivery and suffered an arm injury that limited him to 29 wins over his final six major league seasons—five with the Chicago Cubs and one with the St. Louis Browns.

"He was one terrific ballplayer. Of course, he was always driving me nuts, but I was willing to put up with that as long as he'd win 30 games a year." —*Frank Frisch*

Out of work at age 31, Dean went on to wow a second generation of fans with the distinctive, fractured rhetoric he unleashed from the broadcast booth as a colorful baseball analyst.

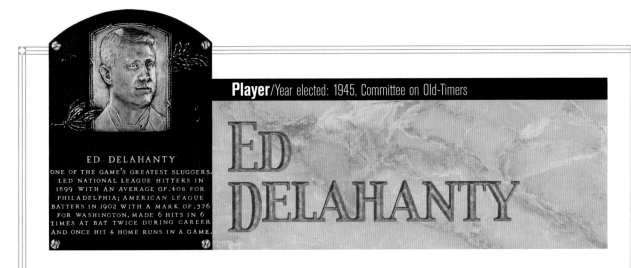

ED DELAHANTY

ED DELAHANTY
ONE OF THE GAME'S GREATEST SLUGGERS.
LED NATIONAL LEAGUE HITTERS IN
1899 WITH AN AVERAGE OF .408 FOR
PHILADELPHIA; AMERICAN LEAGUE
BATTERS IN 1902 WITH A MARK OF .376
FOR WASHINGTON. MADE 6 HITS IN 6
TIMES AT BAT TWICE DURING CAREER
AND ONCE HIT 4 HOME RUNS IN A GAME.

Born: 10-30-1867, Cleveland, Ohio **Died:** 7-2-03 **Height/Weight:** 6-1/170 **Bats/Throws:** R/R **Primary position:** Outfield
Career statistics: .346 avg., 2,597 hits, 1,600 runs, 1,466 RBIs, 455 steals **Teams:** Philadelphia 1888-89, 1891-1901; Cleveland (P.L.) 1890; Senators 1902-03 **Batting champion:** N.L., 1899; A.L., 1902 **HR champion:** N.L., 1893, '96

He was a wild-swinging, boisterous and temperamental hitting machine for the 1890s-era Philadelphia Phillies. And when Ed Delahanty finished at the ballpark, he attacked the city's nightlife with equal energy and enthusiasm. Big Ed knew no limits as either a player or carouser whose life was cut short by a tragic and mystery-shrouded accident.

The 6-foot-1 Delahanty, the oldest of five brothers who played major league baseball, was not a finesse hitter. Every pitch — high, low, inside or outside — was fair game for his savage swing and there was little comfort zone for fielders when he stepped to the plate. In the era of dead balls and contact hitters, the righthanded-swinging Delahanty was a run-producer-extraordinaire.

Amazingly, many of the numbers he posted in 13 Philadelphia seasons still rank at or near the top of all-time Phillies lists. Delahanty is first in doubles (442) and triples (158), second in average (.348), stolen bases (411), runs (1,368), total bases (3,233) and

"His drop, though it caused grief among his intimates and sorrow among his fans, gave a stern lesson to ballplayers to avoid the shining bar and brass footrail."

—*Boston Herald, 1903*

RBIs (1,288). A three-time .400 hitter, Big Ed also was a speedy runner who played in the same outfield with fellow Hall of Famers Billy Hamilton and Sam Thompson.

The popular Delahanty seldom did anything with moderation. He was the first player to go 6-for-6 in a game twice and the second to hit four home runs — a feat he performed in 1896 at Chicago. He also was the first to win batting titles in both leagues — .410 for the Phillies in 1899 and .376 in 1902 after jumping to Washington of the American League. Delahanty topped 100 RBIs seven times and twice led the N.L. in homers en route to a .346 career average.

Big Ed, 35, met a tragic end in 1903, midway through his second Washington season. Suspended by manager Tom Loftus and drinking heavily, a rowdy Delahanty was put off a train at Fort Erie, Ontario, and, according to reports, stumbled blindly onto the International Bridge over the Niagara River. His mangled body was found below Niagara Falls a week later.

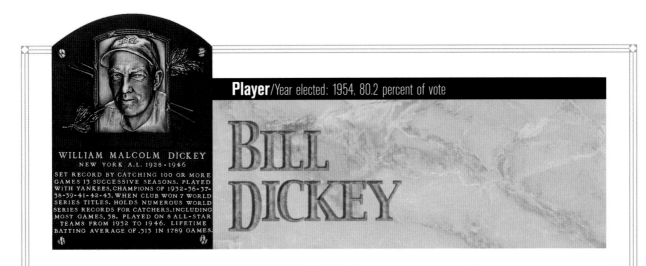

Player/Year elected: 1954, 80.2 percent of vote

BILL DICKEY

Born: 6-6-07, Bastrop, La. **Died:** 11-12-93 **Height/Weight:** 6-1/185 **Bats/Throws:** L/R **Primary position:** Catcher

Career statistics: .313 avg., 1,969 hits, 202 HR, 1,209 RBIs **Teams:** Yankees 1928-43, 1946

He fit into his catching gear as naturally as a turtle into its shell. When Bill Dickey crouched behind the plate, all was right in Yankeeland and pennant-crazy New York fans could thank the baseball gods that their pitching staff was in good hands. Dickey lived up to his part of that bond for 17 major league seasons as a link between the Ruth/Gehrig/Lazzeri champions of the late 1920s and the DiMaggio/Keller/Gordon winning machines of the late 1930s and early '40s.

Before heading off to war in 1944, Dickey back-stopped eight New York pennant winners and seven World Series champs, a legacy he passed on in 1946 to rookie Yogi Berra, who would catch 14 pennant-winners and 10 champions of his own. The stately Dickey provided an interesting contrast as tutor to the roly-poly Berra, but both men moved around behind the plate with similar cat-like quickness, authority and agility. No one, however, could match Dickey's tactical genius and ability to keep pitchers on an even keel.

"I never shake Dickey off. I just let him pitch my game for me."—*Tiny Bonham*

Few catchers, before or since, have been able to match Dickey's dangerous bat, either. A 10-time .300 hitter who sprayed hits all over the park from his upright lefthanded stance, he was especially dangerous in the clutch. Not surprisingly, the four consecutive 100-RBI seasons he strung together from 1936-39 coincided with four straight Yankees World Series wins, a then-unprecedented achievement. Dickey's signature fall classic moment came in 1943, when he decided the Game 5 finale against St. Louis with a two-run homer.

But Dickey, who played in eight All-Star Games, is best remembered for a rugged durability that allowed him to catch 100-plus games in 13 straight seasons and a surprising 1932 incident in which the quiet, mild-mannered catcher delivered a one-punch knockout to Washington's Carl Reynolds after a home-plate collision, breaking his jaw and drawing a 30-day suspension. More significant was his introduction of a smaller, lightweight catcher's mitt that helped revolutionize the position.

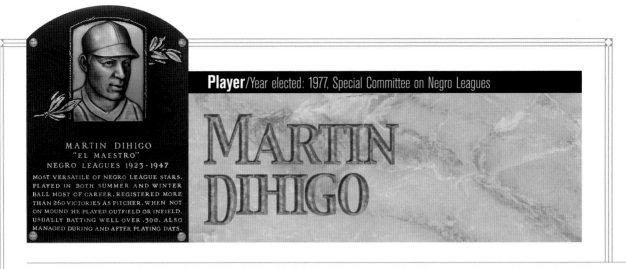

MARTIN DIHIGO
"EL MAESTRO"
NEGRO LEAGUES 1923-1947
MOST VERSATILE OF NEGRO LEAGUE STARS.
PLAYED IN BOTH SUMMER AND WINTER
BALL MOST OF CAREER. REGISTERED MORE
THAN 260 VICTORIES AS PITCHER. WHEN NOT
ON MOUND HE PLAYED OUTFIELD OR INFIELD,
USUALLY BATTING WELL OVER .300. ALSO
MANAGED DURING AND AFTER PLAYING DAYS.

Player/Year elected: 1977, Special Committee on Negro Leagues

MARTIN DIHIGO

Born: 5-25-05, Matanzas, Cuba **Died:** 5-20-71 **Height/Weight:** 6-3/200 **Bats/Throws:** B/R **Primary positions:** Pitcher, infield, outfield

Teams (1923-45): Cuban Stars (East); Homestead Grays; Hilldale Daisies; Baltimore Black Sox; Stars of Cuba; New York Cubans

They called him El Maestro, a tribute to his incredible versatility. And, indeed, Martin Dihigo was the master of baseball disguises — a lanky, smooth-fielding second baseman one day, a gliding right fielder or power pitcher the next. Dihigo might not rank among the all-time best players at any one position, but nobody in history could match his uncanny ability to play all of them.

That Dihigo never got to showcase those talents for major league fans was sad, but it didn't stop him from carving out a proud legacy in the Negro Leagues and throughout Mexico and Latin America. The 6-foot-3, 200-pound Dihigo, a friendly, fun-loving kid who was popular wherever he played, is the only man to be elected to a baseball Hall of Fame in three countries — the United States, Mexico and his native Cuba.

Dihigo was a graceful, far-ranging outfielder with a loping stride like Joe DiMaggio and a cannon arm like Roberto Clemente. That arm was always on display,

"He was the greatest all-round player I know. I say he was the best ballplayer of all time, black or white. He could do it all. ..."

—*Buck Leonard, from the book Blackball Stars*

whether he was fielding smashes at third, going into the hole at shortstop or making a double-play pivot. Dihigo, who baffled hitters with a powerful fastball that he threw from either an overhand or sidearm motion, could have been a great pitcher if he had concentrated on that position.

But he was too good with the bat to do that. Dihigo was a free-swinging switch-hitter who seldom batted under .300 and typically contended for league home run honors. In 1938, he bewitched Mexican League fans by compiling an 18-2 record, carving out a 0.90 ERA and winning a batting title with a .387 average. He was that good.

Dihigo spent most of his early career (1923-36) in the Negro Leagues, where he was known for his hitting, and his later career (1937-45) in Mexico, where he primarily pitched. Dihigo, whose Negro League teams included Homestead, Hilldale and the New York Cubans, played 24 winter seasons in Cuba, where he was a national hero with a 115-60 lifetime record.

Player/Year elected: 1955, 88.8 percent of vote

JOE DIMAGGIO

Born: 11-25-14, Martinez, Calif. **Died:** 3-8-99 **Height/Weight:** 6-2/193 **Bats/Throws:** R/R **Primary position:** Center field

Career statistics: .325 avg., 2,214 hits, 1,390 runs, 361 HR, 1,537 RBIs **Teams:** Yankees 1936-42, 1946-51

Batting champion: A.L., 1939, '40 **HR champion:** A.L., 1937, '48 **Major awards:** A.L. MVP, 1939, '41, '47

Aloof and mysterious, graceful and dignified, the very essence of Joe DiMaggio defied his status as an American icon. But years after he retired from a Hall of Fame career, years after his marriage to movie star Marilyn Monroe had ended, years after his name had been immortalized in song by Simon and Garfunkel and in television lore by Mr. Coffee commercials, DiMaggio maintained his status as a genuine hero.

That unwanted superstardom was thrust upon a 21-year-old do-everything center fielder when he made a spectacular 1936 debut with the New York Yankees, batting .323 with 29 home runs, 125 RBIs and an A.L. rookie-record 132 runs scored. It was love at first sight for New York fans, who immediately accorded DiMaggio the hero status passed down from Babe Ruth and Lou Gehrig. Over a 13-season career interrupted by three years of military service, "Joltin' Joe" reciprocated by leading the Yankees to 10 American League pennants and nine World Series championships.

Everything about the 6-foot-2 Californian suggested

> "He only struck out 13 times in 1941. That's amazing. He's the best player I've ever seen."
>
> — *Bobby Doerr*

class. DiMaggio roamed the expansive center field pasture at Yankee Stadium like a gazelle, fearlessly attacked pitchers with his lashing righthanded swing and quietly personified the team-first philosophy of the Yankees. Even his stance — feet spread wide, bat held straight and motionless — was distinctive and everybody marveled at his instinctive baserunning ability.

DiMaggio, a national symbol for Italian-American success, handled his superstar burden with quiet dignity. He fought through numerous injuries to compile a .325 career average, win two batting titles and top 100 RBIs nine times. His 1941 record 56-game hitting streak is a legendary feat and he shares the A.L. record for MVP awards with three. Amazingly, the two-time home run champion posted almost as many career homers (361) as strikeouts (369).

DiMaggio, who was selected to play for the A.L. All-Star team in each of his 13 seasons, passed on his center field aura to Mickey Mantle after his 1951 retirement. That aura lives on today, like the Yankee World Series dynasty he helped create.

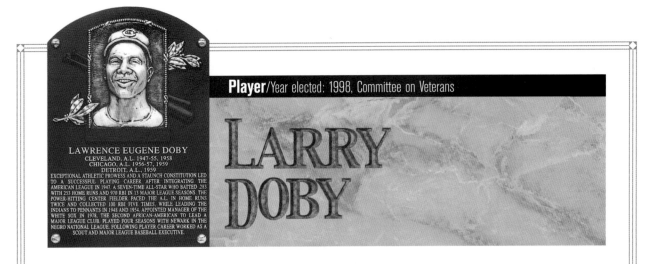

Player/Year elected: 1998, Committee on Veterans

LARRY DOBY

LAWRENCE EUGENE DOBY
CLEVELAND, A.L. 1947-55, 1958
CHICAGO, A.L. 1956-57, 1959
DETROIT, A.L. 1959
EXCEPTIONAL ATHLETIC PROWESS AND A STAUNCH CONSTITUTION LED TO A SUCCESSFUL PLAYING CAREER AFTER INTEGRATING THE AMERICAN LEAGUE IN 1947, A SEVEN-TIME ALL-STAR WHO BATTED .283 WITH 253 HOME RUNS AND 970 RBI IN 13 MAJOR LEAGUE SEASONS. THE POWER-HITTING CENTER FIELDER PACED THE A.L. IN HOME RUNS TWICE AND COLLECTED 100 RBI FIVE TIMES, WHILE LEADING THE INDIANS TO PENNANTS IN 1948 AND 1954. APPOINTED MANAGER OF THE WHITE SOX IN 1978, THE SECOND AFRICAN-AMERICAN TO LEAD A MAJOR LEAGUE CLUB. PLAYED FOUR SEASONS WITH NEWARK IN THE NEGRO NATIONAL LEAGUE. FOLLOWING PLAYER CAREER WORKED AS A SCOUT AND MAJOR LEAGUE BASEBALL EXECUTIVE.

Born: 12-13-23, Camden, S.C. **Height/Weight:** 6-1/185 **Bats/Throws:** L/R **Primary position:** Center field **Career statistics:** .283 avg., 1,515 hits, 253 HR, 970 RBIs **Teams:** Indians 1947-55, 1958; White Sox 1956-57, 1959; Tigers 1959 **HR champion:** A.L. 1952, '54

He was young, proud and unprepared for the daunting task laid before him. When Larry Doby became the first black player in American League history in 1947, he was a shy, overwhelmed 23-year-old prospect, both shielded and exposed by the spotlight on Jackie Robinson, his pioneering predecessor. From the obscurity of Negro League baseball to major league prominence with the Cleveland Indians, there was nowhere to hide.

Thirteen years later, Doby could look back on a solid major league career that produced a .283 average, 253 home runs, 1,515 hits and two World Series appearances with the Indians. That was a proud legacy while dealing with the racial slurs, threats, name-calling, dirty play and other cruel innuendoes he endured while ushering in an era of opportunity for black players—always in the massive shadow of Brooklyn's Robinson.

Doby was a 6-foot-1, 185-pound second baseman when he was plucked off the roster of the Newark Eagles by Cleveland owner Bill Veeck. Unlike Robinson, Doby was not groomed for his ground-

"He reminds me of a young panther, with his lithe, supple, well coordinated movements. I wish we had him on our club and I'd give a lot to get him." —*Frank Lane, White Sox G.M.*

breaking role and made his major league debut July 5, 1947, at Chicago, a scared rookie who clearly needed minor league preparation. But one thing was clear: Doby had five-tool talents that eventually would surface.

The Indians moved him to center field, where he developed into a defensive stopper for the 1948 World Series champions. The long-striding Doby, who always attacked pitches with a lusty swing, emerged offensively in 1950 when he batted .326 with 25 home runs and 102 RBIs and his A.L.-leading totals of 32 homers and 126 RBIs fueled a 1954 Indians pennant run that produced an A.L.-record 111 wins.

Doby, who appeared in six All-Star Games and won two A.L. homer crowns while playing for Cleveland, Chicago and Detroit, overcame self-doubts that often left him sullen, moody and withdrawn from teammates during his early years. The kid from Camden, S.C., remained in baseball long after his retirement and briefly served as field boss of the White Sox in 1978—baseball's second black manager.

DOBY

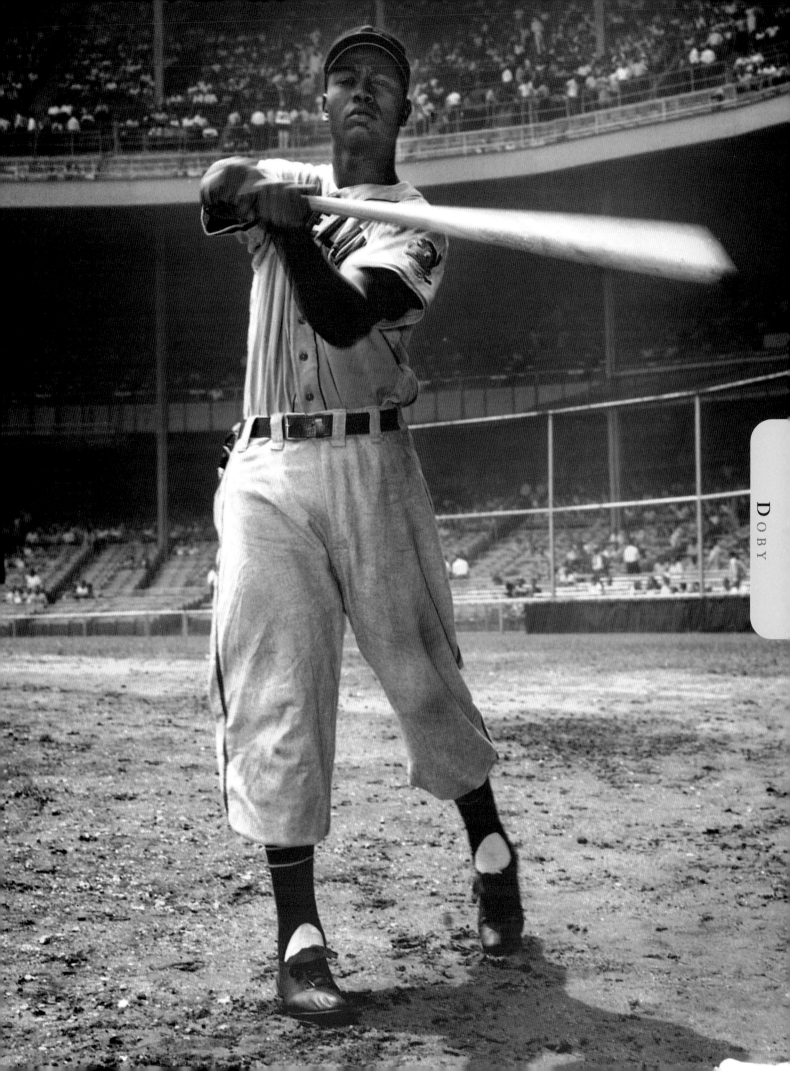

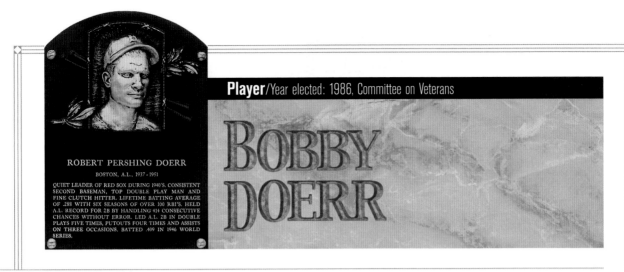

BOBBY DOERR

ROBERT PERSHING DOERR

BOSTON, A.L., 1937 - 1951

QUIET LEADER OF RED SOX DURING 1940'S. CONSISTENT SECOND BASEMAN, TOP DOUBLE PLAY MAN AND FINE CLUTCH HITTER. LIFETIME BATTING AVERAGE OF .288 WITH SIX SEASONS OF OVER 100 RBI'S. HELD A.L. RECORD FOR 2B BY HANDLING 414 CONSECUTIVE CHANCES WITHOUT ERROR. LED A.L. 2B IN DOUBLE PLAYS FIVE TIMES, PUTOUTS FOUR TIMES AND ASSISTS ON THREE OCCASIONS. BATTED .409 IN 1946 WORLD SERIES.

Born: 4-7-18, Los Angeles, Calif. **Height/Weight:** 5-11/175 **Bats/Throws:** R/R **Primary position:** Second base

Career statistics: .288 avg., 2,042 hits, 1,094 runs, 1,247 RBIs **Teams:** Red Sox 1937-44, 1946-51

Slowly and surely, with quiet efficiency and confidence, Bobby Doerr captured the eternal affection of always-demanding Boston fans. From 1937 through 1951, Jimmie Foxx and Ted Williams were the heart of a potent offense, but Doerr was the soul of a city that suffered and celebrated with every Red Sox strikeout and home run. Mr. Consistency, Mr. Reliable, Mr. Nice Guy—by any name, the talented second baseman was always on the job.

There was nothing flashy about the 5-foot-11, 175-pound Californian, who would glide left and right to throw out batters or make the double-play pivot with effortless ease. It wasn't a matter of range for the soft-spoken Doerr, who studied the tendencies of every opponent and instinctively positioned himself in the perfect spot. He seldom mishandled a ball and topped the American League four times in fielding percentage.

When Doerr made his major league debut at age 19, it didn't take long to discover the key to offensive success at

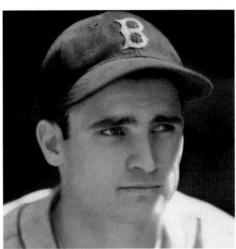

> "I thought while managing the Yankees that Joe Gordon was as valuable a second sacker as I ever saw, but I couldn't pick him over Doerr after what Bobby showed me during my stay with the Sox."
>
> —*Joe McCarthy*

Fenway Park. He tailored his righthanded swing to exploit the short left field wall and spent most of his career bouncing shots off the Green Monster. Three times he topped .300, but his value as a clutch hitter was reflected by six 100-RBI seasons.

With Doerr stationed at second, the Red Sox battled consistently for league honors but often fell short of the powerful New York Yankees. That wasn't the case in 1946, when Doerr returned from a year in World War II and helped the Sox capture a pennant. He batted .409 in the World Series, which ended with a heart-breaking seven-game loss to St. Louis.

Doerr, who played in eight All-Star Games, retired at age 33 because of a bad back, leaving after the 1951 season with a .288 average, 223 home runs, 1,247 RBIs and 2,042 hits. Always the gentleman, Doerr thanked Boston fans and writers and retired to the forests of Oregon, leaving a major void that took many years for the Red Sox organization to fill.

DOERR

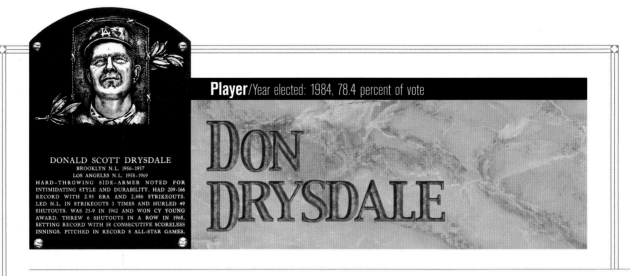

DON DRYSDALE

DONALD SCOTT DRYSDALE
BROOKLYN N.L. 1956-1957
LOS ANGELES N.L. 1958-1969
HARD-THROWING SIDE-ARMER NOTED FOR
INTIMIDATING STYLE AND DURABILITY. HAD 209-166
RECORD WITH 2.95 ERA AND 2,486 STRIKEOUTS.
LED N.L. IN STRIKEOUTS 3 TIMES AND HURLED 49
SHUTOUTS. WAS 25-9 IN 1962 AND WON CY YOUNG
AWARD. THREW 6 SHUTOUTS IN A ROW IN 1968,
SETTING RECORD WITH 58 CONSECUTIVE SCORELESS
INNINGS. PITCHED IN RECORD 8 ALL-STAR GAMES.

Born: 7-23-36, Van Nuys, Calif. **Died:** 7-3-93 **Height/Weight:** 6-6/215 **Bats/Throws:** R/R **Position:** Pitcher **Career statistics:** 209-166, 2.95 ERA, 2,486 strikeouts **Teams:** Brooklyn Dodgers 1956-57; Los Angeles Dodgers 1958-69 **Major awards:** M.L. Cy Young, 1962

Hitters remember him as mean, temperamental and nasty, a 6-foot-6, 215-pound enforcer with a 90-mph fastball and sweeping sidearm delivery. Don Drysdale gave new meaning to the term "power pitcher." Equal parts intimidator and psychologist, he never backed down while battling his way through 14 exciting seasons with the Brooklyn and Los Angeles Dodgers.

Only the most fearless of hitters enjoyed facing the big righthander, who considered the knockdown pitch as vital to success as his sinking fastball. Hitters who dug in became instant targets, as did batters who crowded the plate or disrespected "Big D" in the slightest way. Anybody with a complaint was invited to discuss it with Drysdale, who fearlessly welcomed those who accepted.

Intimidation was an art Drysdale learned from Brooklyn teammate Sal Maglie when he made his 1956 debut and he took it to a new level, enhanced by the buggy-whip sidearm motion that made his pitches look like they were coming from third base. He hit a modern N.L.-record 154 batters and sent countless others

"I've never seen a pitcher so unafraid of the batters." —*Walter Alston*

sprawling, but he also struck out 2,486, leading the National League three times.

The handsome Californian was a 1960s workhorse who teamed for 11 seasons with lefthander Sandy Koufax to give the Dodgers baseball's most prolific 1-2 pitching punch. He was 25-9 with a 2.83 ERA in his Cy Young 1962 season, and he recorded six straight shutouts and 58 consecutive scoreless innings in 1968—records that stood until 1988. Koufax and Drysdale, who once held out in tandem for higher salaries, combined for win totals of 44, 49 and 40 in 1963, '65 and '66, seasons in which the Dodgers won pennants and two World Series.

The articulate, charming Drysdale was as gentlemanly off the field as he was fearsome on it, qualities that helped him in his second career as a broadcaster. He also was a fearless hitter who survived retaliatory beanballs and hit 29 home runs before a shoulder injury ended his career prematurely in 1969. Drysdale, who pitched in eight All-Star Games, retired with a 209-166 record, 2.95 ERA and 3-3 mark in five World Series.

DRYSDALE

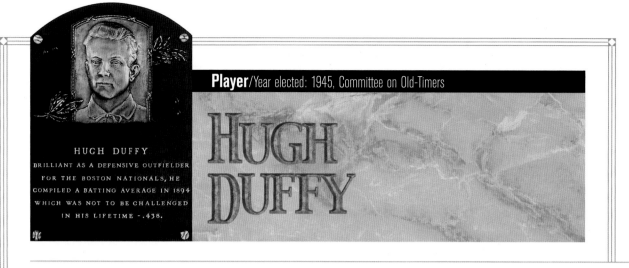

Player/Year elected: 1945, Committee on Old-Timers

HUGH DUFFY

HUGH DUFFY
BRILLIANT AS A DEFENSIVE OUTFIELDER
FOR THE BOSTON NATIONALS, HE
COMPILED A BATTING AVERAGE IN 1894
WHICH WAS NOT TO BE CHALLENGED
IN HIS LIFETIME -.438.

Born: 11-26-1866, Cranston, R.I. **Died** 10-19-54 **Height/Weight:** 5-7/165 **Bats/Throws:** R/R **Primary position:** Center field **Career statistics:** .324 avg., 2,283 hits, 1,554 runs, 1,302 RBIs, 574 steals **Teams:** Chicago 1888-89; Chicago (P.L.) 1890; Boston (A.A.) 1891; Boston 1892-1900; Milwaukee (A.L.) 1901; Phillies 1904-06 **Batting champion:** N.L., 1893, '94 **HR champion:** N.L., 1894, '97

"Where's the rest of you?" asked Chicago manager Cap Anson when he got his first look at 5-foot-7 newcomer Hugh Duffy in 1888. Thus began a 17-year major league journey that would take the 165-pound baseball gnome from wisecracks and disbelief to acceptance as one of the great players of the dead-ball era. Size never was an obstacle for the Rhode Island prodigy who always walked softly and carried a big stick.

What Duffy lacked in size he more than made up for with heart and his ability to patrol center field. True to the batting style of his era, Duffy sprayed hits all over the field from a leg-kicking righthanded stance and ran the bases with reckless abandon. But unlike many hitters of the 1890s, the little guy could flick his powerful wrists and hit mistake pitches out of the park.

Duffy didn't gain baseball prominence until 1892, when he began a nine-year stint with the Boston Beaneaters and posted the first of six straight .300-plus seasons. Duffy's masterpiece was 1894, when he posted a .440 average with N.L.-leading totals of 237 hits, 51 doubles, 18 home runs, 145 RBIs and 374 total bases. His average remains the highest since 1887, when the pitching distance was still 50 feet and walks were counted as hits.

Duffy combined with 5-7 outfield mate Tommy McCarthy to form Boston's "Heavenly Twins" from 1892-95. It was a dynamic pairing of pesky instigators who baffled opponents with their hit-and-run magic and creative double steals, virtually sealed off the right side of the outfield and led the Beaneaters to two of five N.L. pennants they would win in the decade.

By 1900, the clean-living Duffy had become the most popular athlete in Boston and Milwaukee fans matched that affection in 1901 when he took the managerial reins for a one-season franchise in the new American League. Duffy retired after three years as player-manager for the Philadelphia Phillies with 2,283 hits, a .324 average and 574 stolen bases.

> "Hughie was a through-the-middle man. He'd tell our ballplayers, 'Aim at the pitcher! Aim that ball up the middle. Do that and if the pitch is inside, it'll go to left. If it is outside, it'll go to right.' " —*Joe Cronin*

DUFFY

Manager/Year elected: 1994, Committee on Veterans

LEO DUROCHER

LEO ERNEST DUROCHER
"THE LIP"
BROOKLYN, N.L., 1939-1946, 1948
NEW YORK, N.L., 1948-1955
CHICAGO, N.L., 1966-1972
HOUSTON, N.L., 1972-1973
COLORFUL, CONTROVERSIAL MANAGER FOR 24 SEASONS,
WINNING 2,008 GAMES. 7TH ON ALL-TIME LIST.
COMBATIVE, SWASHBUCKLING STYLE A CARRY-OVER
FROM 17 YEARS AS STRONG FIELDING SHORTSTOP FOR
MURDERERS ROW YANKS, GASHOUSE GANG CARDS, REDS
AND DODGERS. MANAGED CLUBS TO PENNANTS IN 1941
AND 1951 AND TO WORLD SERIES WIN IN 1954. 3-TIME
SPORTING NEWS MANAGER OF THE YEAR.

Born: 7-27-05, West Springfield, Mass. **Died:** 10-7-91 **Height/Weight:** 5-9/160 **B/T:** R/R **Primary position:** Shortstop
Career statistics: .247 avg. **Teams played:** Yankees 1925, 1928-29; Reds 1930-33; Cardinals 1933-37; Dodgers 1938-41, 1943, 1945
Teams managed (2,008-1,709): Dodgers 1939-46, 1948; Giants 1948-55; Cubs 1966-72; Astros 1972-73 **World Series titles:** 1954

He rankled the baseball establishment for almost half a century, an irritating itch that moved around but wouldn't go away. Loud, abrasive, combative and flamboyant, Leo Durocher carved out his Hall of Fame niche both as a fiery shortstop and volatile manager. "Leo the Lip" was edgy and colorful, a relentless battler who lived by his self-coined philosophy that "nice guys finish last."

The 5-foot-9, 160-pound Massachusetts product is best remembered as the umpire-baiting manager who earned folk hero status with rowdy Brooklyn fans, married actress Laraine Day, drew a one-year suspension because of his association with gamblers and led teams to three National League pennants and one World Series title. But he also was a fine-field, no-hit shortstop for 17 seasons, five as kindred spirit for St. Louis' 1930s-era Gashouse Gang.

Durocher's abrasive personality and win-at-all-costs mentality was center stage from his 1925 debut with the New York Yankees through stops with the Cincinnati Reds, Cardinals and Dodgers. It was the equally stormy Larry MacPhail

who tabbed Durocher to manage the Dodgers in 1939, a love-hate association that produced heated arguments and frequent Durocher "firings" as well as a 1941 pennant, the team's first in 21 years.

The baseball-savvy, intimidation-preaching Durocher managed the Dodgers eight seasons, then watched, under suspension, as Jackie Robinson broke baseball's color barrier in 1947 and the Dodgers won the pennant. Durocher returned in 1948 but shocked Dodger fans by bolting at midseason to manage the hated Giants. Three years later, Durocher's Giants prevailed in the most dramatic pennant race ever staged, beating the Dodgers on Bobby Thomson's playoff home run.

Durocher's only World Series win was a shocker, a four-game Giants sweep over the powerful Cleveland Indians in 1954. He managed one more year in New York, returned to the (Los Angeles) Dodgers as coach under Walter Alston and resurfaced as manager of the Chicago Cubs and Houston Astros from 1966-73. He retired with a 2,008-1,709 record—the seventh-highest win total in managerial history.

> **"In the '40s and '50s, I thought he was the best manager in baseball. He plotted every move like a chess game and there was nobody sharper."**
>
> —*Ralph Branca*

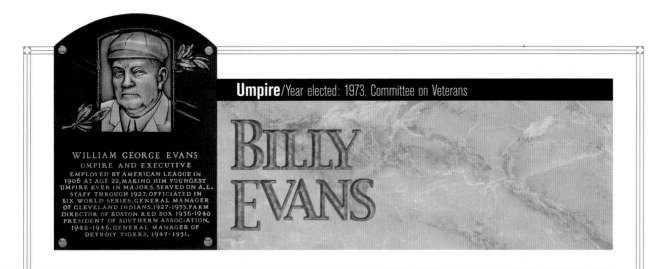

BILLY EVANS

WILLIAM GEORGE EVANS
UMPIRE AND EXECUTIVE
EMPLOYED BY AMERICAN LEAGUE IN
1906 AT AGE 22, MAKING HIM YOUNGEST
UMPIRE EVER IN MAJORS. SERVED ON A.L.
STAFF THROUGH 1927. OFFICIATED IN
SIX WORLD SERIES. GENERAL MANAGER
OF CLEVELAND INDIANS, 1927·1935. FARM
DIRECTOR OF BOSTON RED SOX 1936·1940
PRESIDENT OF SOUTHERN ASSOCIATION,
1942·1946. GENERAL MANAGER OF
DETROIT TIGERS, 1947·1951.

Born: 2-10-1884, Chicago, Ill. **Died:** 1-23-56 **Height/Weight:** 6-0/190 **Years umpired:** A.L., 1906-27 **World Series:** 1909, '12, '15, '17, '19, '23 **Executive career:** G.M. Indians, 1927-35; farm director Red Sox, 1936-40; president Southern Assoc., 1942-46; G.M. Tigers, 1946-51

He was a study in contrasts, a rose in baseball's early century rock garden. Young, trim, educated, well-groomed and unflappably patient, Billy Evans brought dignity and spirit to an umpiring profession that was frighteningly short of both. A 1906 curiosity when he umpired his first American League game at age 22, he won acclaim over the next 45 years as the "gentleman arbiter," a nationally recognized writer and skilled front-office executive.

The baseball world was not ready for the brash 6-footer when he jumped from the Class C Ohio-Pennsylvania League to become one of A.L. president Ban Johnson's new-breed umpires. Evans was a fastidious dresser who wore tailored umpire suits and a friendly smile that quelled many arguments before they even started. As a former Cornell University student and athlete, he was fit, smart and willing to do little things that set him apart.

Evans raised eyebrows by sprinting from home to first to make calls on infield grounders. He was articulate, fair and diplomatic, a man who enjoyed joking with players and letting them have their say on disputes before cutting off discussion with a signature glare. When provoked, Evans was a battler who once engaged in a legendary fight with Ty Cobb under the grandstands at Washington.

But umpiring was only part of the Evans story. The former Youngstown, O., sportswriter started a baseball column in 1910 that became syndicated to more than 100 newspapers across the country. From 1920-27, he wrote his "Billy Evans Says" daily column for the Newspaper Enterprise Association as well as magazine articles and books. He had plenty to write about, including his work in the infamous 1919 World Series and five other fall classics.

Evans, a master of the rules book and one of the game's most respected balls-and-strikes arbiters, left the field in 1927 to become general manager of the Cleveland Indians. He later performed executive duties for Detroit and Boston and served as president of the Southern Association.

"I thought I was a pretty good fighter, but I believe Cobb could have been a champion in the ring as well as on the playing field." —*Billy Evans*

E V A N S

Player/Year elected: 1946, Committee on Old-Timers

JOHNNY EVERS

Born: 7-21-1881, Troy, N.Y. **Died:** 3-28-47 **Height/Weight:** 5-9/125 **B/T:** L/R **Primary position:** Second base **Career statistics:** .270 avg., 1,659 hits, 324 steals **Teams:** Cubs, 1902-13; Braves 1914-17, 1929; Phillies 1917; White Sox 1922 **Major awards:** Chalmers MVP, 1914

At first glance, Johnny Evers was a 5-foot-9, 125-pound weakling, a frail-looking man with narrow shoulders and chest, spindly arms and legs. But the hungry, blazing eyes and a square jaw that protruded from an unsmiling, weather-beaten face revealed something else—a burning intensity and fighting spirit that coursed through the veins of a baseball demon.

The diminutive Evers, who reportedly weighed 95 pounds when he played his first game for the Chicago Cubs in 1902, was an unyielding battler who would scratch, claw, bicker and snarl his way through games. Umpires hated "The Crab" for his constant chirping and opponents were angered by a foghorn-like voice that delivered his biting taunts. Teammates were annoyed by his prodding and criticism but inspired by his insatiable desire to win.

History remembers Evers fondly. He was the middle man for the Joe Tinker-to-Evers-to-Frank Chance double-play combination that was immortalized in verse

while helping the Cubs win three pennants and 530 games over a five-year span from 1906-10. And in 1914, he captained the Boston Braves when they performed their pennant and World Series-winning "Miracle." But you can't think of Evers without recalling a 1908 game against the New York Giants.

It was Evers, a clever strategist and a rules fanatic, who stole a pennant by calling for the ball and touching second base on an apparent game-winning single by New York's Al Bridwell, claiming first base runner Fred Merkle left the field without touching the bag.

The appeal was upheld and the Cubs won a replay that vaulted them into the World Series—the last the franchise would win in the century.

Evers, a lefthanded batter who mastered the bunt-and-slash hitting style of the era, compiled a respectable .270 average over 16 seasons. But the kid from Troy, N.Y., was most respected for his defensive excellence and the fire-and-brimstone intangibles he brought to the field—every minute of every game.

> "I never learned to shut the clubhouse door on a lost ball game. I took it home with me and played it over again all night."—*Johnny Evers*

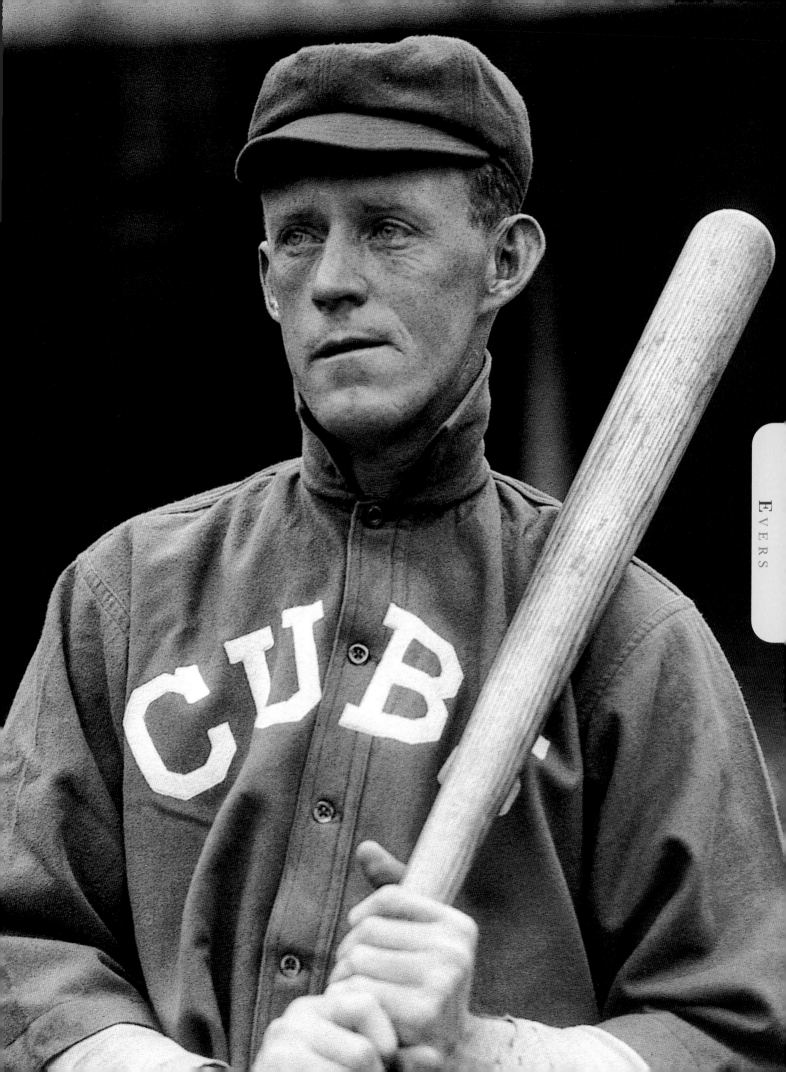

WM. B. "BUCK" EWING
GREATEST 19TH CENTURY CATCHER. GIANT
IN STATURE AND GIANT CAPTAIN OF
NEW YORK'S FIRST NATIONAL LEAGUE
CHAMPIONS 1888 AND 1889. WAS GENIUS
AS FIELD LEADER, UNSURPASSED IN
THROWING TO BASES. GREAT LONG-RANGE
HITTER. NATIONAL LEAGUE CAREER
1881 TO 1899 TROY, N.Y. GIANTS AND
CLEVELAND; CINCINNATI MANAGER.

Player/Year elected: 1939, Committee of Old-Time Players and Writers

BUCK EWING

Born: 10-17-1859, Hoagland, Ohio **Died:** 10-20-06 **Height/Weight:** 5-10/188 **Bats/Throws:** R/R **Primary position:** Catcher
Career statistics: .307 avg., 1,655 hits, 1,129 runs, 354 steals **Teams:** Troy 1880-82; New York 1883-89, 1891-92;
New York (P.L.) 1890; Cleveland 1893-94; Cincinnati 1895-97 **HR champion:** N.L., 1883

It didn't take long to fall under the base-ball spell of William "Buck" Ewing, who could charm the most disagreeable umpire, coddle the most sensitive pitcher, fire up fans, inspire teammates and intimidate the most daring baserunners of the dead-ball era. New York teammate Mickey Welch once described him as a real "thinking man's player," equal parts catcher, psychologist and all-around athlete. To Connie Mack, Ewing was a 20th-century player in a 19th-century uniform.

During the 18-year span from 1880-97, Ewing revolutionized the catcher's position while showing that brains and brawn could form a powerful union on the field. The man who introduced the "pillow-style" padded mitt also was one of the first players to study opponents' weaknesses, knowledge he passed on to his pitchers, and organize pregame strategy meetings. Behind the plate, the affable Ewing praised and cajoled umpires who reciprocated occasionally with generous calls.

Opponents remembered the mustachioed 5-foot-10, 188-pound Ohioan for his quickness and powerful arm. Ewing could deliver laser-like throws to any base without leaving his crouch, a style he mastered

"I have never seen anyone throw like him since I have been in baseball."

—Tom Loftus, 1889, Cleveland manager

because of muscular forearms that allowed him to snap the ball without a full overhand extension. He was amazingly accurate and runners had to be ever alert and cautious.

Primarily a catcher, Ewing was versatile enough to play all nine positions, which he did, and fast enough to steal 354 bases. A righthanded hitter who frequently was used in the leadoff spot, the 10-time .300 hitter led the National League in home runs (10 in 1883) and triples (20 in 1884) while seldom striking out and playing the game with a scientific precision.

Ewing, an original "Giant" when the team moved from Troy to New York in 1883, contributed to Giants pennants in 1888 and 1889 and spent 10 seasons in New York, one as a player-manager in the outlaw Players League. The .307 career hitter retired as an active player in 1897, after completing his third season as player-manager at Cincinnati.

EWING

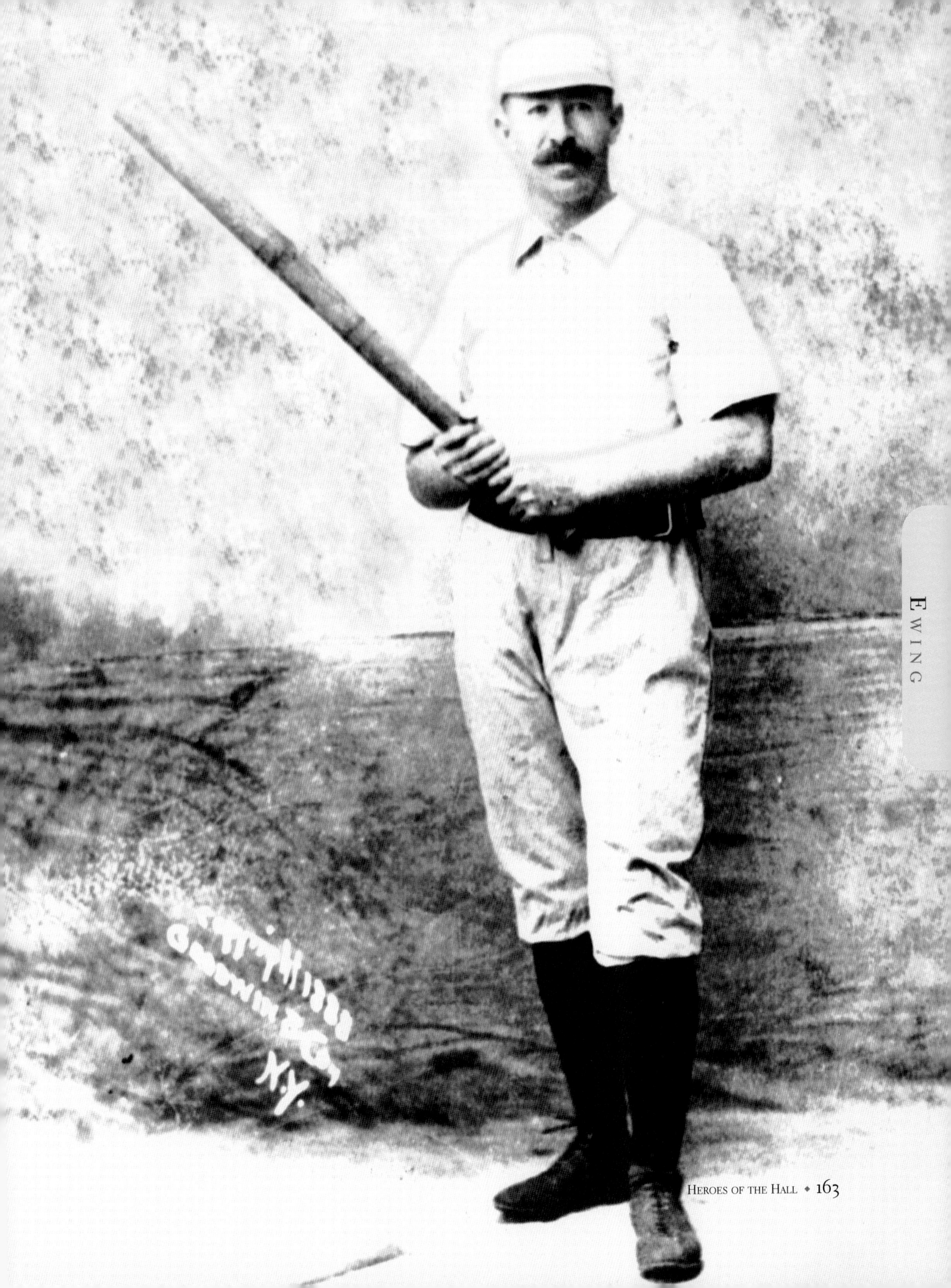

Ewing

URBAN CLARENCE FABER
CHICAGO A. L. 1914-1933
DURABLE RIGHTHANDER WHO WON 253,
LOST 211, E.R.A. 3.13 GAMES IN TWO DECADES
WITH WHITE SOX. VICTOR IN 3 GAMES
OF 1917 WORLD'S SERIES AGAINST GIANTS.
WON 20 OR MORE GAMES IN SEASON
FOUR TIMES, THREE IN SUCCESSION.

RED FABER

Born: 9-6-1888, Cascade, Iowa **Died:** 9-25-76 **Height/Weight:** 6-2/180 **Bats/Throws:** B/R **Position:** Pitcher
Career statistics: 254-213, 3.15 ERA, 1,471 **Teams:** White Sox 1914-33

He was one of baseball's last legal spitballers, a 6-foot-2 Iowa farmboy who survived a world war and the stigma of the game's most nefarious scandal to post 254 career victories over 20 major league seasons, all with the Chicago White Sox. From 1914 through 1933, Urban "Red" Faber dazzled hitters like Babe Ruth, Ty Cobb and Lou Gehrig with his two-pitch repertoire and a bulldog-like determination to succeed for generally weak teams.

Fastball and spitter — everybody knew what to expect from the red-headed righthander. Every pitch was thrown after Faber had gone to his mouth and the constant fear of his darting spitter made the fastball more effective. Faber, who doctored balls with a combination of tobacco and gum juice, applied it with the tips of his fingers and had masterful control of the pitch, which he threw from sidearm, overhand and underhand motions.

Faber, who thrived when overanxious batters pounded his spitter into the ground, rode that

"Red wouldn't throw more than four or five spitters in some games. In fact, his best pitch was his fastball. He'd just keep the batters guessing." — *Ray Schalk*

pitch to Hall of Fame success while recording four 20-win seasons, winning two earned-run average titles and gaining distinction as a World Series hero. After posting a 1.92 ERA in the 1917 regular season, he won three times for the champion White Sox in the fall classic and two years later he watched from the bench while nursing an injury as his teammates lost the World Series to Cincinnati, triggering the infamous Black Sox scandal.

From 1921 through Faber's final season, the White Sox never finished above fifth place. "Red would have won more than 300 games if we hadn't been so bad," said former Sox catcher Ray Schalk. But Faber never wavered, posting back-to-back 25-15 and 21-17 marks in 1921 and '22 with A.L.-best ERAs of 2.48 and 2.81.

Faber, one of 17 pitchers who were allowed to continue using the spitter after it was outlawed in 1920, retired at age 45, one year before Burleigh Grimes, the last of the spitballers. In 4,087 innings, he surrendered only 111 home runs.

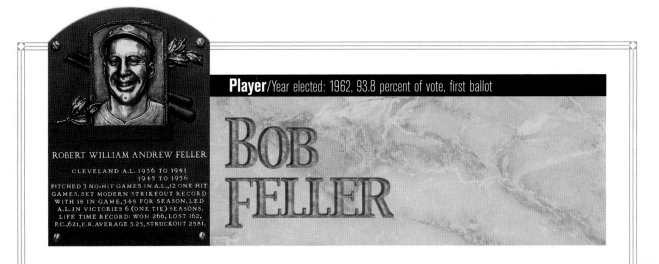

ROBERT WILLIAM ANDREW FELLER

CLEVELAND A.L. 1936 TO 1941
1945 TO 1956
PITCHED 3 NO-HIT GAMES IN A.L., 12 ONE HIT
GAMES, SET MODERN STRIKEOUT RECORD
WITH 18 IN GAME, 348 FOR SEASON. LED
A.L. IN VICTORIES 6 (ONE TIE) SEASONS.
LIFE TIME RECORD: WON 266, LOST 162,
P.C., 621, E.R. AVERAGE 3.25, STRUCKOUT 2581.

BOB FELLER

Born: 11-3-18, Van Meter, Iowa **Height/Weight:** 6-0/185 **Bats/Throws:** R/R **Position:** Pitcher **Career statistics:** 266-162, 3.25 ERA, 2,581 strikeouts **Teams:** Indians 1936-41, 1945-56

He whirled into major league prominence in 1936 as a naive 17-year-old farmboy and retired two decades later as one of the most sophisticated strikeout machines in baseball history. Through most of his 18 seasons with the Cleveland Indians, Bob Feller must have seemed like a white blur to hitters trying to catch up with his 98-plus mph fastballs.

Feller, a 6-foot, high-kicking righthander who never played a minor league game, stepped off the Van Meter, Iowa, farm and struck out 15 St. Louis Browns in his first big-league start. Three weeks later, he tied Dizzy Dean's major league record with 17 strikeouts in a two-hit win over the Philadelpha Athletics. When his short rookie season ended, Feller returned home and finished high school.

Feller's pitching ledger is filled with strikeouts (2,581), no-hitters (3), one-hitters (12) and 20-win seasons (6). But those numbers and his 266-162 career record could have been a lot higher if not for the three-plus seasons he spent winning battle stars for the

"Feller was the fastest pitcher I've ever seen, and he had the best curveball I've ever seen." —*Jim Hegan*

Navy during World War II. Baseball's All-American boy, who could have avoided military duty because his father was dying of cancer, chose instead to serve his country at age 23—after three straight 20-win seasons.

That was typical Feller, who once insisted on taking a pay cut after what he considered a bad season. He was proud, outspoken, opinionated and self-promoting—but the strutting arrogance he displayed on the mound did not draw criticism from the hitters he dominated. Feller's premier season was 1940, when, at age 21, he pitched an opening-day no-hitter and went on to compile a 27-11 record with a 2.61 ERA and 261 strikeouts.

He was 26-15 in 1946 with a career-high 348 strikeouts and career-low 2.18 ERA.

The biggest void in Feller's career was his inability to record a postseason victory. The five-time All-Star Game performer was 0-2 in Cleveland's 1948 World Series win and, surprisingly, he did not pitch as the Indians were swept in the 1954 fall classic by the New York Giants.

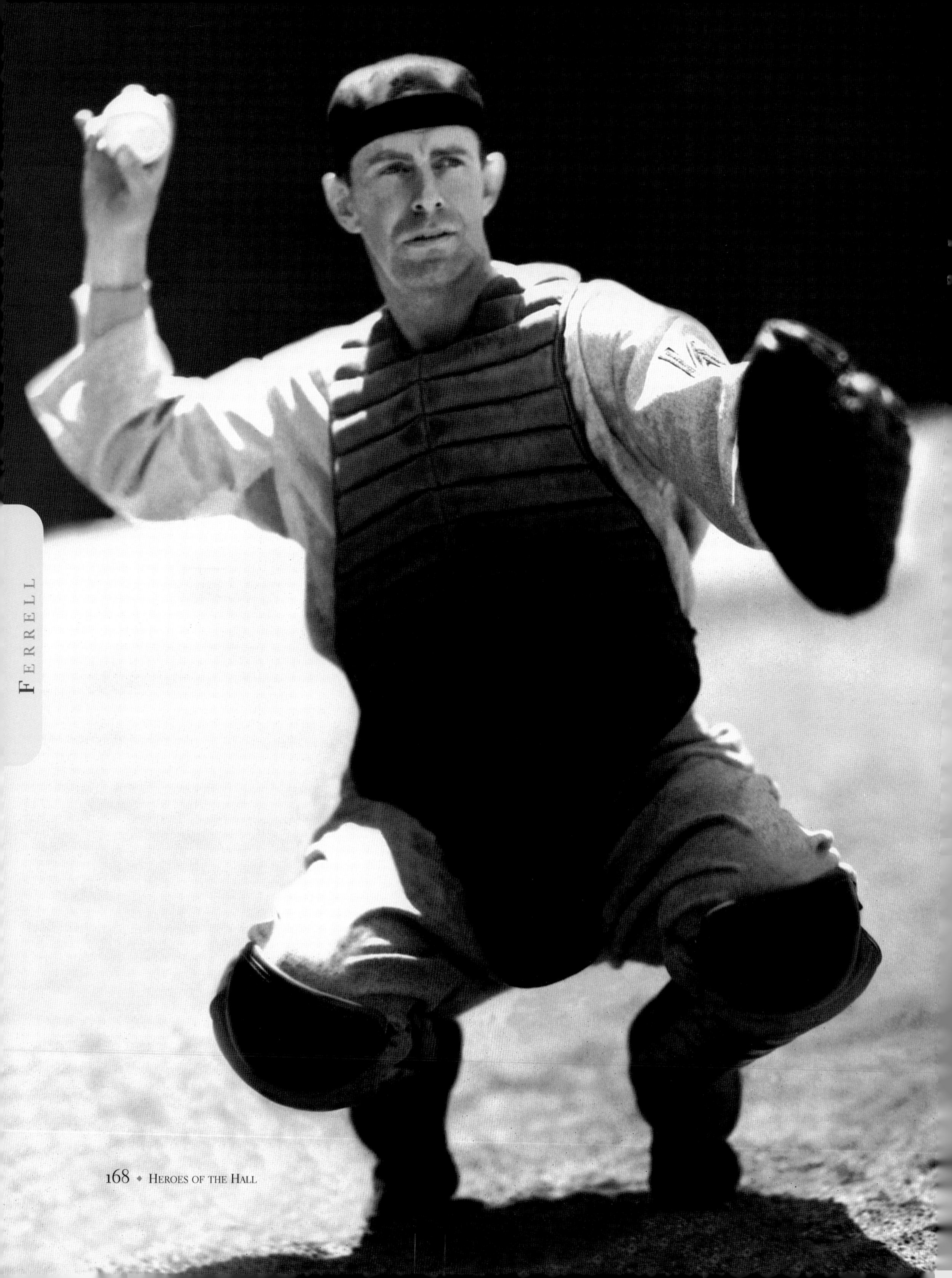

RICK FERRELL

RICHARD BENJAMIN FERRELL
ST. LOUIS A.L. 1929-1933, 1941-1943
BOSTON A.L. 1933-1937
WASHINGTON A.L. 1937-1941, 1944-1947
CAUGHT MORE GAMES (1,806) THAN ANY OTHER
AMERICAN LEAGUER. DURABLE DEFENSIVE STAND-OUT
WITH FINE ARM. EXPERT AT HANDLING PITCHERS.
MET CHALLENGE OF 4 KNUCKLE-BALLERS IN SENATORS'
STARTING ROTATION. OFTEN FORMED BATTERY WITH
BROTHER, WES. HIT OVER .300 4 TIMES. SECOND
ONLY TO DICKEY IN A.L. CAREER PUTOUTS AT
RETIREMENT.

Born: 10-12-05, Durham, N.C. **Died:** 7-27-95 **Height/Weight:** 5-10/160 **Bats/Throws:** R/R **Primary position:** Catcher
Career statistics: .281 avg., 1,692 hits **Teams:** Browns, 1929-33, 1941-43; Red Sox 1933-37; Senators 1937-41, 1944-45, 1947

He squatted and bounded behind the plate for 18 grueling seasons, a testament to physical endurance and a blue-collar work ethic. Rick Ferrell might have looked like a well-oiled machine to the many fans who watched him play, but he was a tireless mechanic and hard-working craftsman to the grateful pitchers he handled. Quiet, soft-spoken and even-tempered, Ferrell helped turn catching into a baseball artform.

Some catchers could hit better and others could outrun him, but Ferrell's mechanics were as good as it gets. He looked effortless as he worked the strike zone, blocked errant throws and threw out base-stealers with a strong, accurate arm. Ferrell turned mediocre hurlers into winners with his masterful pitch selection and he caught 1,806 career games like a man sitting in a rocking chair.

But Ferrell was more than just another pretty catcher. A righthanded batter without much power, he managed four .300 seasons while striking out only 277 times as a contact hitter for the St. Louis Browns,

"My biggest thrill? No question about it, playing in the first major league All-Star Game in 1933. Not only playing, mind you, but starting and going the entire way for the American League. ..." — *Rick Ferrell*

Boston Red Sox and Washington Senators en route to a .281 career average. Ferrell could handle the bat, as he demonstrated in hit-and-run situations and with his ability to move runners. Not blessed with great physical skills, he literally built himself into a complete player.

Ferrell arrived on the major league scene with the Browns in 1929, two years after his brother Wes made his pitching debut for Cleveland. The North Carolina-raised brothers, who would later form a battery in Boston and Washington, might have become the game's first Hall of Fame brother battery if Wes, a six-time 20-game winner, had not injured his arm.

Ferrell, a seven-time All-Star selection, enjoyed the distinction of catching all nine innings of baseball's first All-Star Game in 1933 while Bill Dickey and Mickey Cochrane watched from the bench. In 1944 and '45, he caught Washington's all-knuckleballer rotation of Dutch Leonard, Roger Wolff, Johnny Niggeling and Mickey Haefner.

FERRELL

ROLAND GLEN FINGERS
OAKLAND, A.L., 1968-1976
SAN DIEGO, N.L., 1977-1980
MILWAUKEE, A.L., 1981-1985
CAREER EPITOMIZED EMERGENCE OF MODERN-DAY
RELIEF ACE AS HE APPROACHED LEGENDARY STATUS
WITH CONSISTENT EXCELLENCE COMING OUT OF
BULLPEN. RELIED UPON SINKING FAST BALL TO
BECOME ALL-TIME MAJOR LEAGUE LEADER WITH
341 CAREER SAVES. APPEARED IN 16 WORLD SERIES
GAMES FOR OAKLAND, WINNING 2 AND SAVING 6.
A.L. MVP AND CY YOUNG AWARDEE IN 1981.

Player/Year elected: 1992, 81.2 percent of vote

ROLLIE FINGERS

Born: 8-25-46, Steubenville, Ohio **Height/Weight:** 6-4/195 **Bats/Throws:** R/R **Position:** Pitcher **Career statistics:** 114-118, 2.90 ERA, 341 saves **Teams:** Athletics 1968-76; Padres 1977-80; Brewers 1981-82, 1984-85 **Major awards:** A.L. Cy Young, 1981; A.L. MVP, 1981

"He gives you that anchor. I don't know of one guy, with the exception of Nolan Ryan, who is as tough to hit in the seventh or eighth inning as at the start of a game. You need that guy like Rollie to win pennants." — *Sal Bando*

get the final few outs to protect a lead and he worked as often as needed.

Instead of banishing pitchers who couldn't make it as starters to the bullpen, teams began grooming late-inning specialists in the Fingers mold. They were influenced by the way the rubber-armed Ohioan anchored Oakland's five division title winners (1971-75) and three straight World Series champions (1972-74) while saving games for Catfish Hunter, Kenny Holtzman and Vida Blue.

The handlebar mustache made him look like the villain from a silent movie. His loose, carefree demeanor added a half inch to the smile hitters tried hard to suppress every time he strolled to the mound. But one fastball or slider from Rollie Fingers changed amusement to desperation and made it clear to everybody that a tense situation was under control.

The fun-loving, mustache-twirling, sometimes-flaky Fingers spent 17 major league seasons dousing late-inning fires as the premier relief pitcher of his era. Not only did the lanky 6-foot-4 righthander thrive from 1968 through 1985 with the Oakland Athletics, San Diego Padres and Milwaukee Brewers, he redefined the role that late-inning specialists would play in years to come. Fingers became the closer who could

The amazing thing about Fingers was his durability and consistency over a long period. He used a lively fastball with a natural drop, the slider and a devastating forkball to carve out 341 career saves, 107 relief wins (fourth all time) and a 2.90 ERA. He pitched in five All-Star Games and was named MVP of the 1974 World Series after recording a win and two saves against the Los Angeles Dodgers.

The Oakland championships were nice, but Fingers posted his best saves totals with San Diego (35 and 37) and received his greatest honor after the strike-shortened 1981 season when he became the first reliever to win both the Cy Young and MVP awards in the same season. That was the reward for a 28-save, 1.04-ERA performance at the tender age of 35.

FINGERS

CARLTON ERNEST FISK
"PUDGE"
BOSTON, A.L., 1969, 1971-80
CHICAGO, A.L., 1981-93

A COMMANDING FIGURE BEHIND THE PLATE FOR A RECORD 24 SEASONS, HE CAUGHT MORE GAMES (2,229) AND HIT MORE HOME RUNS (351) THAN ANY CATCHER BEFORE HIM. HIS GRITTY RESOLVE AND COMPETITIVE FIRE EARNED HIM THE RESPECT OF TEAMMATES AND OPPOSING PLAYERS ALIKE. A STAUNCH TRAINING REGIMEN EXTENDED HIS DURABILITY AND ENHANCED HIS PRODUCTIVITY—AS EVIDENCED BY A RECORD 72 HOME RUNS AFTER AGE 40. HIS DRAMATIC HOME RUN TO WIN GAME SIX OF THE 1975 WORLD SERIES IS ONE OF BASEBALL'S UNFORGETTABLE MOMENTS. WAS THE 1972 AMERICAN LEAGUE ROOKIE OF THE YEAR AND AN 11-TIME ALL-STAR.

Player/Year elected: 2000, 79.6 percent of vote

CARLTON FISK

Born: 12-26-47, Bellows Falls, Vt. **Height/Weight:** 6-2/220 **Bats/Throws:** R/R **Primary position:** Catcher **Career statistics:** .269 avg., 2,356 hits, 1,276 runs, 376 HR, 1,330 RBIs **Teams:** Red Sox 1969, 1971-80; White Sox 1981-93 **Major awards:** A.L. Rookie of Year, 1972

Like a crouching tiger, hidden dragon, Carlton Fisk squatted, growled, snarled, fumed and breathed fire into the hearts of unfocused teammates for 24 major league seasons. He was a marathon man at baseball's most grueling position, a blue-collar catcher who demanded all-out effort all of the time. Fisk's legacy was his durability and gritty determination; his defining memory was a freeze-frame World Series home run that has become part of the game's special lore.

The sight of a frantic Fisk, waving his long drive fair in the 12th inning of a Game 6 victory over Cincinnati at Fenway Park, is a 1975 Series classic. But the 6-foot-2, 220-pound "Pudge" wasn't about mouth-watering talent and late-inning dramatics. He was about showing up day after day, season after season, and pushing himself to catch 2,226 games—more than any man in history.

And he did it his way. Over 11 American League seasons in Boston and 13 more in Chicago, pitchers remember Fisk, always in control, pushing them and embarrassing them with his booming voice. His frequent trips to the mound were agonizingly slow and his words harsh, but he never spared his body behind the plate and he made pitchers better with his game-calling skills. Anybody, friend or foe, who didn't run hard could count on a Fisk tirade.

Fans also remember a powerful righthanded pull hitter who pounded 376 home runs, a record 351 as a catcher, compiled a respectable .269 career average and stole a surprising 128 bases. A dangerous run-producer who hit 37 homers for the White Sox at age 37, Fisk was infamous for his snail-paced at-bats and ability in the clutch. From his 1972 breakthrough as the A.L.'s first unanimous Rookie of the Year to his 1993 retirement at age 45, Fisk was a serious offensive threat.

A Vermont-born workout fanatic who overcame several career-threatening injuries, Fisk played in 10 All-Star Games but made only one postseason appearance after '75—in the 1983 Championship Series with Chicago.

"Just being around a guy like (Fisk) makes a difference. It's his attitude, his presence." —*Ozzie Guillen*

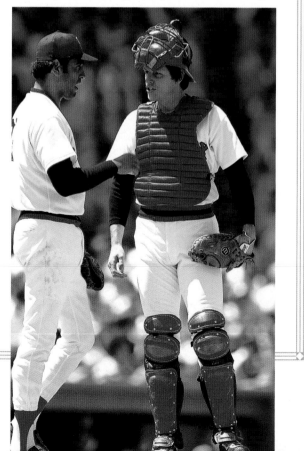

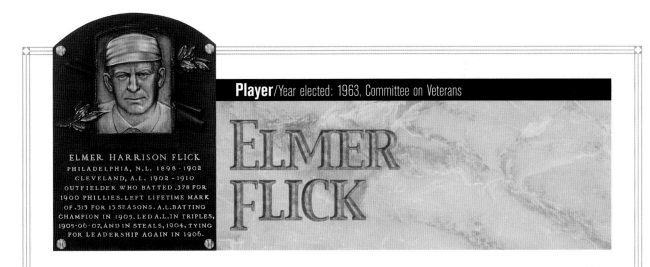

ELMER HARRISON FLICK
PHILADELPHIA, N.L. 1898-1902
CLEVELAND, A.L. 1902-1910
OUTFIELDER WHO BATTED .378 FOR
1900 PHILLIES. LEFT LIFETIME MARK
OF .315 FOR 13 SEASONS. A.L. BATTING
CHAMPION IN 1905, LED A.L. IN TRIPLES,
1905-06-07, AND IN STEALS, 1904, TYING
FOR LEADERSHIP AGAIN IN 1906.

Player/Year elected: 1963, Committee on Veterans

ELMER FLICK

Born: 1-11-1876, Bedford, Ohio **Died:** 1-9-71 **Height/Weight:** 5-9/160 **Bats/Throws:** L/R **Primary position:** Outfield
Career statistics: .313 avg., 1,752 hits, 330 steals **Teams:** Philadelphia 1898-1902; Indians 1902-10 **Batting champion:** A.L., 1905

As a naive farmboy from Ohio in 1898, he replaced Big Sam Thompson in the Philadelphia Phillies' vaunted outfield. Nine years later, the Detroit Tigers were turned down when they tried to get him from Cleveland in an even-up trade for Ty Cobb. Timing was everything in the 13-year career of Elmer Flick, a superb turn-of-the-century star who quietly built one of the game's more interesting legacies.

Flick was a slightly built (5-foot-9, 160 pounds) lefthanded hitter who arrived at his first major league camp with a homemade, thick-handled bat and soft-spoken confidence that he could wield it effectively against anybody in the National League. Time would prove him right while also revealing a well-rounded outfielder who could run, throw and handle himself on the bases.

Flick's timing was perfect as he moved into right field alongside Dick Cooley and Ed Delahanty, replacing ailing Phillies star Thompson. He batted .302 as a rookie, .342 as a second-year man and .367 with 11 home runs in 1900, finishing second in the

"I could hit anybody. They called me, 'Elmer Flick, the Demon of the Stick.' " —*Elmer Flick*

N.L. to Honus Wagner (.381) and Herman Long (12).

Flick's timing wasn't so good in 1902 when he jumped to the American League's Philadelphia A's and became embroiled in a court case involving the Phillies' rights to star second baseman Nap Lajoie and other league jumpers. Flick eventually ended up in Cleveland where he led the A.L. in triples three straight years and topped .300 four times, including a .308 average in 1905 that would stand for 63 years as the lowest to win a batting championship.

Perhaps the greatest complement to Flick's steady and reliable play came in the spring of 1907 when Tigers manager Hughie Jennings offered Cobb, his abrasive young outfielder, to the Indians and was rejected—an understandable but unwise decision. Flick batted .302 that season and then developed a mysterious stomach ailment that forced him to the sideline in 1908 and into premature retirement two years later. He left with a .313 career mark and 330 stolen bases.

WHITEY FORD

EDWARD CHARLES FORD
"WHITEY"
NEW YORK A.L. 1950-1967
POSTED BEST WINNING PERCENTAGE (690)
AMONG TWENTIETH CENTURY PITCHERS
WITH 200 OR MORE DECISIONS. HAD 236
VICTORIES AND 106 LOSSES' LIFETIME EARNED
RUN AVERAGE 2.74 PACED A.L. IN VICTORIES
AND WINNING PCT. THREE TIMES AND IN
EARNED-RUN AVERAGE AND SHUTOUTS
TWICE. WON CY YOUNG AWARD IN 1961. SET
WORLD SERIES STANDARDS FOR GAMES
PITCHED, 22; INNINGS, 146; WINS, 10, AND
STRIKEOUTS, 94. AND WITH 33⅔ CONSECUTIVE
SCORELESS INNINGS.

Born: 10-21-28, New York, N.Y. **Height/Weight:** 5-10/180 **Bats/Throws:** L/L **Position:** Pitcher **Career statistics:** 236-106, 2.75 ERA, 1,956 strikeouts **Teams:** Yankees 1950, 1953-67 **Major awards:** M.L. Cy Young, 1961

He may not have been baseball's original "crafty little lefthander," but Whitey Ford sure fit the description as well as anybody who pitched before or after him. The blond-headed, 5-foot-10, 180-pound New Yorker also was the ace for a New York Yankees juggernaut that captured 11 American League pennants and six World Series titles with him at the pitching controls between 1950 and 1964.

"(Ford) is always around the plate. He's so easy to catch I could do it while sitting in a rocking chair." —*Yogi Berra*

What Ford's left arm lacked in power his head made up for with guile, determination and instinct. He delivered his fastball, curve, sinker and slider with overhand, three-quarters and sidearm motions, rarely giving the hitter the same look on consecutive pitches. His control was outstanding; his confident demeanor never wavered; his pickoff move froze embarrassed baserunners, and his bulldog determination seemed to toughen as the situation warranted.

Supported by a series of powerful Yankees lineups, Ford parlayed his pitching prowess into an incredible .690 career winning percentage, the best in major league history for a 200-game winner. His 25-4 record earned him a 1961 Cy Young Award and he posted ERA titles in 1956 and 1958. His 236-106 career mark could have been even better if not for the two peak seasons (1951 and '52) he lost to military service during the Korean War.

Ford, praised by longtime manager Casey Stengel as the best money pitcher in baseball, was at his best in postseason play. He still holds World Series records for wins (10), strikeouts (94), games (22) and innings pitched (146) and he once worked a fall classic-record 33 straight scoreless innings. His two shutouts in a 1961 five-game win over Cincinnati earned him MVP honors.

Ford, a six-time All-Star Game performer who threw 45 career shutouts, was known for his sense of humor and the clever one-line quips that brought back memories of Hall of Famer Lefty Gomez among longtime Yankee fans. He also was known for the nightlife he enjoyed to extremes with longtime friends and teammates Mickey Mantle and Billy Martin.

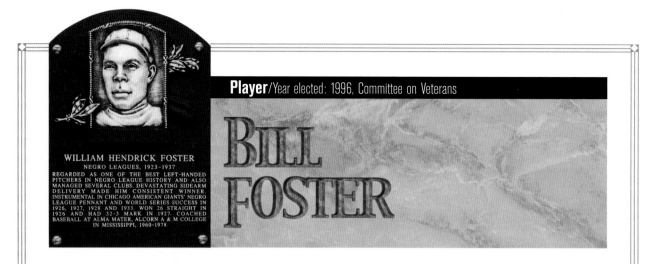

WILLIAM HENDRICK FOSTER
NEGRO LEAGUES, 1923-1937
REGARDED AS ONE OF THE BEST LEFT-HANDED
PITCHERS IN NEGRO LEAGUE HISTORY AND ALSO
MANAGED SEVERAL CLUBS. DEVASTATING SIDEARM
DELIVERY MADE HIM CONSISTENT WINNER.
INSTRUMENTAL IN CHICAGO AMERICAN GIANTS' NEGRO
LEAGUE PENNANT AND WORLD SERIES SUCCESS IN
1926, 1927, 1928 AND 1933. WON 26 STRAIGHT IN
1926 AND HAD 32-3 MARK IN 1927. COACHED
BASEBALL AT ALMA MATER, ALCORN A & M COLLEGE
IN MISSISSIPPI, 1960-1978

Player/Year elected: 1996, Committee on Veterans

BILL FOSTER

Born: 6-12-04, Calvert, Tex. **Died:** 9-16-78 **Height/Weight:** 6-1/195 **Bats/Throws:** B/L **Position:** Pitcher **Teams (1923-38):** Memphis Red Sox; Chicago American Giants; Birmingham Black Barons; Homestead Grays; Kansas City Monarchs; Cole's American Giants; Pittsburgh Crawfords

> ## "Bill Foster was my star pitcher, the greatest pitcher of our time, not even barring Satchel. Rube taught him, I didn't teach him. The art of pitching he learned from Rube."
>
> *—Dave Malarcher, from the book Voices from the Great Black Baseball Leagues*

They say he could pick the buttons off a batter's uniform—with any one of his five pitches. What Bill "Willie" Foster might have lacked in raw speed he more than made up for with guile, control and finesse. He was by many accounts the best lefthander in black baseball history, a big-game pitcher with a workhorse mentality.

The 6-foot-1, 195-pound Texan did his best work for the Chicago American Giants, a team organized years earlier by black baseball legend Rube Foster, his older half brother. Twenty-five years apart, the brothers never saw eye to eye, a relationship strained by Rube's initial refusal to give Willie a job and his demanding lectures once he did. The youngster never tasted success until 1926, the year Rube retired because of illness.

But there was no stopping him after that. The lanky lefty attacked hitters with a good fastball, slider, drop, sidearm curve and change, all thrown from the same motion. Like Rube so many years earlier, Willie would start his delivery from an erect position with ball held directly behind his head. A long stride brought his release point uncomfortably closer to a batter who never knew what to expect.

Foster's control was impeccable and pressure only seemed to strengthen his resolve. In 1926, he reportedly won 26 straight games against all levels of competition while compiling an 11-4 league record for the Giants. Down three-games-to-two in a pennant playoff against the Kansas City Monarchs, Foster beat Bullet Joe Rogan in both ends of a doubleheader and then posted a 21-3 league mark in 1927 while leading the Giants to another pennant.

Over a career that stretched through 1938, Foster became known for his duels against Satchel Paige and his big-game performances. He was a complete-game winner in the first East-West All-Star Game in 1933 and he won the majority of his starts against white major league teams. Aside from the American Giants, Foster played briefly with the Homestead Grays, Monarchs and Pittsburgh Crawfords.

RUBE FOSTER

ANDREW (RUBE) FOSTER

RATED FOREMOST MANAGER AND EXECUTIVE IN
HISTORY OF NEGRO LEAGUES. ACCLAIMED TOP
PITCHER IN BLACK BASEBALL FOR NEARLY A
DECADE IN EARLY 1900s. FORMED CHICAGO
AMERICAN GIANTS IN 1911 AND BUILT THEM
INTO MIDWEST'S DOMINANT BLACK TEAM. IN
1920 HE ORGANIZED NEGRO NATIONAL LEAGUE.
HEADED LEAGUE AND MANAGED CHICAGO TEAM
UNTIL RETIREMENT FOLLOWING 1926 SEASON.

Born: 9-17-1879, Calvert, Tex. **Died:** 12-9-30 **Height/Weight:** 6-2/210 **B/T:** R/R **Primary positions:** Pitcher, first base
Teams played (1902-14): Chicago Union Giants; Cuban X Giants; Philadelphia Giants; Leland Giants; Chicago American Giants
Teams managed (1907-26): Leland Giants; Chicago American Giants **Executive career:** Owner Chicago American Giants, 1910-26;
founder Negro National League, 1920

He could overwhelm you with his bulk, mesmerize you with his baritone voice or inspire you with his enthusiasm for the game he obviously loved. Andrew "Rube" Foster was called the "Father of Black Baseball," and for good reason. Nobody could match his contributions as outstanding pitcher, team builder, innovative manager and organizer of the first black league in a career that stretched from 1902-26.

Foster was a 6-foot-2, 210-pound Texas-born righthanded submariner with a big fastball and nasty screwball when he began his professional career with the Cuban X Giants in 1902. Soon he was attracting attention on black baseball's exhibition trail, where he won fame for defeating Philadelphia A's superstar Rube Waddell and formed a friendship with New York Giants manager John McGraw.

McGraw's influence was obvious when Foster began managing in 1907 for the Leland Giants. He preached speed and defense, employing a "racehorse" style with heavy emphasis on bunting, the hit-and-run, basestealing and aggressiveness. When he organized

"(Foster is) the most finished product I've ever seen in the pitcher's box." — *Frank Chance*

his own team in 1910, he stocked it with the best run-and-gun talent of the era and renamed it the Chicago American Giants, a name that would sustain prominence for decades.

Foster, a stern disciplinarian, outstanding teacher and adept handler of players, never stopped promoting black baseball, a talent he better exploited after ending his pitching career. He arranged for his Giants to play in Chicago's Southside Park, which had been abandoned by the White Sox, and took on all comers. The American Giants won the first three pennants when Foster formed the eight-team Negro National League in 1920—a venture some credit with saving black baseball.

Working 15-hour days with little compensation, Foster struggled to keep his ship afloat. Now a 250-pound "teddy bear," he shifted players from team to team to maintain competitive balance, lent money (often his own) to failing franchises and preached the need to be prepared for integration. The strain eventually caught up. In 1926, Foster suffered a nervous breakdown and died four years later at age 51.

F
O
S
T
E
R

Player/Year elected: 1997, Committee on Veterans

NELLIE FOX

JACOB NELSON FOX
"NELLIE"
PHILADELPHIA, A.L., 1947-1949
CHICAGO, A.L., 1950-1963
HOUSTON, N.L., 1964-1965
SURE-HANDED SECOND BASEMAN AND SKILLFUL BATSMAN WAS
A CATALYST FOR THE "GO-GO" WHITE SOX OF THE 1950s. A
12-TIME AMERICAN LEAGUE ALL-STAR WHO NEVER STRUCK OUT
MORE THAN 18 TIMES IN A SEASON, HIS STRIKEOUT TO AT BAT
RATIO BEING THIRD BEST ALL-TIME. ONCE WENT RECORD 98
GAMES WITHOUT A STRIKEOUT. PLAYED RECORD 798 CONSECUTIVE
GAMES AT SECOND. LED LEAGUE IN HITS FOUR TIMES, PUTOUTS
10 TIMES, FIELD PCT. SIX TIMES. WON 1959 A.L. MVP HONORS
BY HELPING CHICAGO TO FIRST FLAG IN 40 YEARS.

Born: 12-25-27, St. Thomas, Pa. **Died:** 12-1-75 **Height/Weight:** 5-9/160 **Bats/Throws:** L/R **Primary position:** Second base **Career statistics:** .288 avg., 2,663 hits, 1,279 runs **Teams:** Athletics 1947-49; W. Sox 1950-63; Astros 1964-65 **Major awards:** A.L. MVP, 1959

The big wad of tobacco, stuffed tightly into his left cheek, distorted a boyish face. His contagious enthusiasm and scrappy playing style defined a remarkably successful career. Nellie Fox, all 5-foot-9, 160 pounds of him, was a 19-year baseball marvel, a sandlot dreamer who hustled his way to Hall of Fame glory as an inspirational leader for the 1950s-era Go-Go White Sox.

Fox looked like a boy among men, but there was no denying the energy he brought to the field every game. When the first pitch was thrown, he became a bouncing, bobbing, chattering sparkplug, whether snagging would-be hits from his second base position, slapping, slashing and driving pitches with his lefthanded swing or running the bases, which he did aggressively if not with great speed.

Fox was a self-made hitter who choked up on the bat and simply guided the ball where it was pitched. He slashed out 2,663 hits, never striking out more than 18 times or hitting more than six home runs in a season,

"I hate to play a single game without him. It's like trying to run an auto without spark plugs. He's the heart of the team." —*Marty Marion, 1955*

and he was a masterful bunter who moved runners and disrupted defenses with his hit-and-run ability. The six-time .300 hitter also was a three-time Gold Glove winner who led the American League six times in fielding percentage while commiting only 209 errors.

But Fox's intangibles transcend mere numbers. He had the heart of a lion and was always in the lineup, playing 798 straight games over one stretch, and he was a model citizen—hard working, never complaining, a team-first cheerleader. Fox and shortstop Luis Aparicio formed the heart and soul of Chicago's "Go-Go" pennant winners of 1959 when "Little Nell" earned A.L. MVP honors with a .306 average and then batted .375 in his only World Series, a six-game loss to Los Angeles.

Fox, who played in 13 All-Star Games, began his career at age 19 with the Philadelphia Athletics and ended it in 1965 at Houston—after 14 seasons as one of the greatest second basemen in Chicago history.

FOX

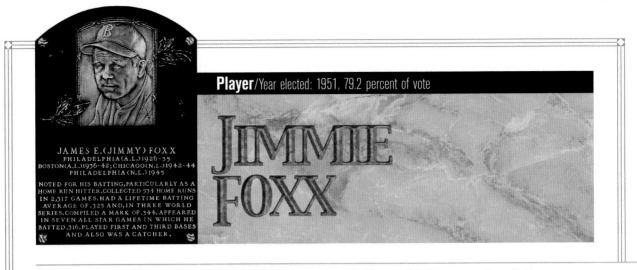

JIMMIE FOXX

JAMES E.(JIMMY) FOXX
PHILADELPHIA(A.L.)1926-35
BOSTON(A.L.)1936-42;CHICAGO(N.L.)1942-44
PHILADELPHIA(N.L.)1945
NOTED FOR HIS BATTING,PARTICULARLY AS A
HOME RUN HITTER.COLLECTED 534 HOME RUNS
IN 2,317 GAMES.HAD A LIFETIME BATTING
AVERAGE OF .325 AND,IN THREE WORLD
SERIES.COMPILED A MARK OF .344. APPEARED
IN SEVEN ALL STAR GAMES IN WHICH HE
BATTED .316.PLAYED FIRST AND THIRD BASES
AND ALSO WAS A CATCHER.

Born: 10-22-07, Sudlersville, Md. **Died:** 7-21-67 **Height/Weight:** 5-11/195 **Bats/Throws:** R/R **Primary position:** First base
Career statistics: .325 avg., 2,646 hits, 1,751 runs, 534 HR, 1,922 RBIs **Teams:** Athletics 1925-35; Red Sox 1936-42; Cubs 1942, 1944;
Phillies 1945 **Batting champion:** A.L., 1933, '38 **HR champion:** A.L., 1932, '33, '35, '39 **Major awards:** A.L. MVP, 1932, '33, '38

There was nothing quite like a Jimmie Foxx home run: powerful, muscular arms whipping a 37-ounce bat into a pitch with incredible speed; ball rocketing from home plate to places beyond even faster. Blink and you might miss the split-second experience. Watch closely and you might even see the vapor trail.

Unlike a Babe Ruth homer that was majestic and almost serene, a Foxx homer was brute force. Such power generated from a 5-foot-11, 195-pound former Maryland farmboy, who emerged in 1925 as the srong-man of Connie Mack's Philadelphia Athletics lineup and the first serious challenger to Ruth's power-hitting dominance. Foxx was a menacing figure when he stood at the plate with a fixed glare, waving the bat with biceps that bulged from sleeves cut deliberately short.

From his breakthrough 1929 season with the A's through 1940, his fifth season with the Boston Red Sox, Foxx never failed to hit 30 homers or drive in 100 runs, a remarkable 12-year stretch. He also led the A's to three pennants and two World Series championships, won two batting titles, topped the 50-homer plateau twice and won a 1933 Triple Crown with his .356 average, 48 homers and 163 RBIs. But 1932 was Foxx's masterpiece, his brush with baseball immortality.

That was the season "Double X" batted .364, drove in 169 runs and exploded for 58 home runs, just two short of Ruth's 1927 single-season record. It earned

> **"He was the only hitter I ever saw who could hit balls on his fist and still get them out of the park. He had muscles on his muscles."**—*Lefty Gomez*

him the first of consecutive MVP awards and became the signature season in a 20-year career that produced 534 home runs, a total that ranked second all-time to Ruth for many years. Foxx, who teamed with Ted Williams in the Boston lineup after leaving Philadelphia in 1936, ended his career in 1945 with a .325 average and a record-tying 13 100-RBI seasons.

Foxx, a friendly, popular clubhouse figure and a notorious night owl, was much more than a plodding slugger. His defensive versatility allowed managers to use him at catcher, first and third base, and in the outfield with full confidence in his abilities.

FOXX

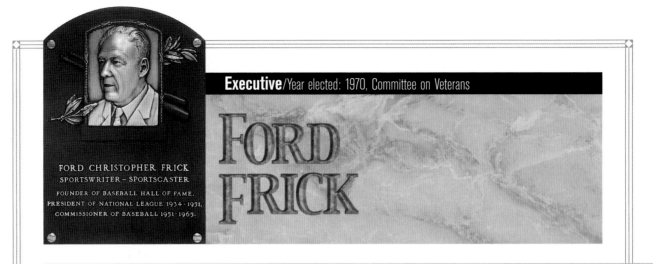

FORD FRICK

FORD CHRISTOPHER FRICK
SPORTSWRITER – SPORTSCASTER
FOUNDER OF BASEBALL HALL OF FAME.
PRESIDENT OF NATIONAL LEAGUE 1934-1951.
COMMISSIONER OF BASEBALL 1951-1965.

Born: 12-19-1894, Wawaka, Ind. **Died:** 4-8-78 **Executive career:** Head of National League Service Bureau, 1934; N.L. president, 1934-51; Baseball's third commissioner, 1951-65

He was baseball's third commissioner, a former part-time journalist who clawed his way to the top of the sports world. What Ford Frick might have lacked in baseball pedigree he made up for with honesty, hard work and devotion to the game. From his selection as National League president in 1934 until his retirement as commissioner in 1965, the boy from rural Indiana directed baseball's transformation from game to big business.

Frick, a serious, scowling, no-nonsense protector of baseball's integrity, is best remembered for his infamous "asterisk ruling" of 1961, a declaration that made life difficult for New York Yankees slugger Roger Maris in his chase of Babe Ruth's home run record. But Frick's legacy goes much deeper than that. He ushered baseball into a new, prosperous era with his innovative, supportive and sometimes visionary leadership.

It was Frick, as N.L. president in 1947, who supported Brooklyn's signing of Jackie Robinson and snuffed out widespread player revolt with the dire warning, "If you do this, you are through, and I don't care if it wrecks the league for 10 years." It was Frick's idea to create a Hall of Fame, which came to fruition with the first induction and museum dedication at Cooperstown, N.Y., in 1939.

As commissioner, Frick smoothed the way for five franchise shifts (including the Dodgers and Giants to California), oversaw expansion, negotiated the game's first multi-million dollar television package and set up the mechanics for free agency. Not bad for a former college teacher-turned-sportswriter who once acted as ghost writer for Yankees slugger Ruth.

Frick was a recognized New York writer and broadcaster when Giants manager John McGraw recommended him to oversee N.L. public relations in February 1934. When league president John Heydler retired later that year, Frick, at age 40, was tabbed to replace him. He presided over the N.L. for 17 years, injecting life into the struggling circuit, before succeeding Happy Chandler as commissioner, a job he held from 1951-65.

"If you do this, you are through, and I don't care if it wrecks the league for 10 years. You cannot do this because this is America."

—Ford Frick, *warning players not to strike over Jackie Robinson's historic 1947 major league debut*

FRICK

FRANK FRISCH

FRANK FRISCH
NEW YORK N.L.1919-1926
ST.LOUIS N.L.1927-1938
PITTSBURGH N.L.1940-1946
JUMPED FROM COLLEGE TO THE MAJORS,
THE "FORDHAM FLASH" WAS AN OUTSTANDING
INFIELDER, BASE-RUNNER AND BATTER.
HAD A LIFETIME BATTING MARK OF .316.
HOLDS MANY RECORDS. PLAYED IN 50
WORLD SERIES GAMES. MANAGED ST.LOUIS
FROM 1933 THROUGH 1938 AND WON WORLD
SERIES IN 1934. MANAGED PITTSBURGH
FROM 1940 THROUGH 1946.

Born: 9-9-1898, Bronx, N.Y. **Died:** 3-12-73 **Height/Weight:** 5-11/165 **Bats/Throws:** B/R **Primary position:** Second base
Career statistics: .316 avg., 2,880 hits, 1,532 runs 1,244 RBIs, 419 steals **Teams played:** Giants 1919-26; Cardinals 1927-37
Teams managed (1,138-1,078): Cardinals 1933-38; Pirates 1940-46; Cubs 1949-51 **Major awards:** N.L. MVP, 1931

He was the heart of the New York Giants' 1920s pennant-winning machine and the soul of St. Louis' Gashouse Gang in the 1930s. Frank Frisch was addicted to winning, a craving he filled with eight World Series appearances. As a hard-nosed second baseman and one of baseball's original switch-hitters, he was a throwback to the intense, aggressive, daring, reckless style of baseball practiced at the turn of the century.

The stocky, strong-armed Frisch, a speedy four-sport star at Fordham University, never played a minor league game before stepping into a Giants lineup that produced four consecutive National League pennants — and two World Series championships — from 1921-24. Frisch brought leadership to the field, whether knocking down hot grounders with his thick chest, diving in the dirt for balls hopelessly out of reach, running the bases with flawless instinct or baiting umpires and opponents with a razor-edged tongue.

Hitting from his natural left side, Frisch, his bat

"I won't apologize for having wanted my players to be as good as I was supposed to be. If intolerance of mediocrity is a crime, I plead guilty." — *Frank Frisch*

wagging, was aggressive and unpredictable. He was equally capable of dragging a bunt, punching an outside pitch to left field or driving a bases-loaded double into the gap. From the right side, Frisch had more power but was less aggressive. He seldom struck out (272 times in 19 seasons) and was dangerous in the clutch — a three-time 100-RBI contributor.

Frisch was center stage in the shocking 1926 trade that sent him to St. Louis for Rogers Hornsby, the best hitter in the game. It took awhile, but Frisch overcame fan resentment over the departure of the popular Hornsby and became the leader of Cardinals teams that won pennants in 1928 and '30 and the player/manager of colorful Cardinals crews that won World Series in 1931 and '34.

Frisch, a 13-time .300 hitter who posted a .316 career average, 2,880 hits and 419 stolen bases, was the first winner of the N.L. MVP award presented by the Baseball Writers' Association of America in 1931.

F
R
I
S
C
H

Player/Year elected: 1965, Committee on Veterans

PUD GALVIN

JAMES F. (PUD) GALVIN
ST. LOUIS N.A. 1875
BUFFALO N.L. 1879-1885
PITTSBURGH A.A. 1885-1886
PITTSBURGH N.L. 1887-1889 1891-1892
PITTSBURGH P.L. 1890
ST. LOUIS N.L. 1892
WON 365 GAMES. LOST 311.
WHEN ELECTED ONLY FOUR PITCHERS
HAD WON MORE GAMES.
PITCHED NO-HIT GAMES IN 1880 AND 1884.
PITCHED 649 COMPLETE GAMES.

Born: 12-25-1856, St. Louis, Mo. **Died:** 3-7-02 **Height/Weight:** 5-8/190 **Bats/Throws:** R/R **Position:** Pitcher **Career statistics:** 361-308, 2.87 ERA, 1,799 strikeouts **Teams:** Buffalo 1879-85; Pittsburgh (A.A.) 1885-86; Pittsburgh 1887-89, 1891-92; Pittsburgh (P.L.) 1890; St. Louis 1892

At 5-foot-8 and 190 pounds, James "Pud" Galvin was not your classically sculpted athlete. His rotund face, barrel chest and stocky frame camouflaged one of the most durable right arms in baseball history and his gentle nature belied a no-nonsense killer instinct. In a career that bridged the eras of underhand and overhand pitching, Galvin was an unlikely workhorse who powered his way to 361 victories and a whopping 5,941 $\frac{1}{3}$ innings.

Only Cy Young worked more innings and only five pitchers won more games than the hard-throwing Galvin, whose major league career started at Buffalo in 1879 and ended 14 years later in his hometown St. Louis — the year before the pitching distance was extended from 50 feet to 60 feet, 6 inches. Whether delivering the ball under or overhand, Galvin simply blew away hitters with his overpowering fastball.

To say he was durable is an understatement. In 1883, Galvin worked an incredible 656 $\frac{1}{3}$ innings, completed 72 of 75 starts and compiled a 46-29 record for Buffalo. A year later, he worked 636 $\frac{1}{3}$ innings,

completed 71 of 72 starts and struck out 369 en route to a 46-22 mark. Nine times he topped 400 innings and he won 20 or more games 10 times while pitching 639 complete games and 57 shutouts.

Modest, cheerful and unassuming, Galvin was a fan favorite wherever he pitched and his smiling, mustachioed face was recognizable on or off the field. While his weight fluctuated between 190 and 250, it never seemed to affect his pinpoint control (he allowed only 1.13 walks per nine innings), catlike defensive quickness or lightning move, which kept runners pinned to first base. He also was a good righthanded hitter who played occasionally in the outfield.

Over a career that took "Gentle Jeems" to three cities and three major leagues, he never played for a pennant-winner. He enjoyed the distinction of recording the first win in Pittsburgh's National League history (1887) and he was baseball's first 300-game winner, but his 308 losses rank second on the all-time list. When Galvin retired in 1892, he was the career leader in virtually every pitching category.

"When the ... mild-mannered pitcher was recognized by the crowd, it broke into a loud and continuous applause. A smile then illuminated the countenance of Gentle James and he bowed his head modestly in recognition of the tribute." — *The Buffalo Express, 1880*

GALVIN

HENRY LOUIS GEHRIG
NEW YORK YANKEES · 1923-1939
HOLDER OF MORE THAN A SCORE OF
MAJOR AND AMERICAN LEAGUE RECORDS,
INCLUDING THAT OF PLAYING 2130
CONSECUTIVE GAMES. WHEN HE RETIRED
IN 1939, HE HAD A LIFE TIME BATTING
AVERAGE OF 340.

Player/Year elected: 1939, Special election by Baseball Writers' Association

LOU GEHRIG

Born: 6-19-03, New York, N.Y. **Died:** 6-2-41 **Height/Weight:** 6-0/210 **Bats/Throws:** L/L **Primary position:** First base
Career statistics: .340 avg., 2,721 hits, 1,888 runs, 493 HR, 1,995 RBIs **Teams:** Yankees 1923-39 **Batting champion:** A.L., 1934
HR champion: A.L., 1931, tied; '34, '36 **Major awards:** League MVP, 1927

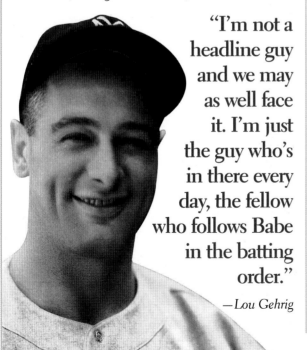

ou Gehrig will forever be lost in the glare of New York Yankees teammate Babe Ruth's vast spotlight. But nothing about Gehrig's accomplishments should be minimized, from the 2,130 consecutive games he once played as the Iron Horse to his longtime link with Ruth as the enforcer of baseball's original Bash Brothers.

Gehrig was a rock-solid 6-foot, 210-pound lefthanded slasher who rocketed line drives to all sections of the park, unlike the towering, majestic home runs that endeared Ruth to adoring fans. And unlike the gregarious Ruth, Gehrig was withdrawn, modest and unas-

> "I'm not a headline guy and we may as well face it. I'm just the guy who's in there every day, the fellow who follows Babe in the batting order."
>
> —*Lou Gehrig*

suming, happy to let his teammate drink the fruits of their tandem celebrity. But those who played with and against Gehrig understood the power he could exert over a game.

As the Yankees' first baseman, cleanup hitter and lineup protection for Ruth, Gehrig was an RBI machine. He won four American League titles and tied for another and his 184-RBI explosion in 1931 is a still-standing A.L. record. His 13 consecutive 100-RBI seasons—he averaged an incredible 147 from 1926-38—were a byproduct of 493 career home runs and a not-so-modest .340 average.

It's hard to overstate the havoc wreaked by Gehrig's bat. He topped 400 total bases in five seasons, topped 150 RBIs seven times, hit a record 23 grand slams, won a 1934 Triple Crown, hit four homers in one 1932 game and cranked out a World Series average of .361 with 10 homers and 34 RBIs. In 1927, when Ruth hit his record 60 home runs, Gehrig quietly batted .373 with 47 homers and 175 RBIs.

The Ruth-Gehrig relationship powered the Yankees to three World Series championships, and when Ruth left New York after the 1934 season, Gehrig and young Joe DiMaggio powered the team to three more. But Gehrig is best remembered for the iron-man streak that lasted from 1925-39, when a fatal disease—amyotrophic lateral sclerosis—ended his career prematurely and tugged at the heart string of a nation. Gehrig, finally accorded the recognition that long had eluded him, died two years later.

BE WISE ~ SIMONIZ

General Outdoor Adv. Co.

GEM SINGLEDGE BLADES NOW 5 for 2

OUTS

GEHRIG

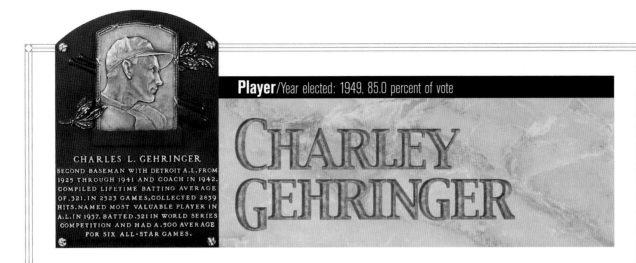

CHARLES L. GEHRINGER
SECOND BASEMAN WITH DETROIT A.L. FROM
1925 THROUGH 1941 AND COACH IN 1942.
COMPILED LIFETIME BATTING AVERAGE
OF .321, IN 2323 GAMES, COLLECTED 2839
HITS. NAMED MOST VALUABLE PLAYER IN
A.L. IN 1937. BATTED .321 IN WORLD SERIES
COMPETITION AND HAD A .500 AVERAGE
FOR SIX ALL-STAR GAMES.

CHARLEY GEHRINGER

Born: 5-11-03, Fowlerville, Mich. **Died:** 1-21-93 **Height/Weight:** 6-0/180 **Bats/Throws:** L/R **Primary position:** Second base **Career statistics:** .320 avg., 2,839 hits, 1,774 runs, 1,427 RBIs **Teams:** Tigers 1924-42 **Batting champion:** A.L., 1937 **Major awards:** A.L. MVP, 1937

They called him The Mechanical Man. And indeed Charley Gehringer did everything with machine-like precision — an effortless, graceful consistency that belied the competitive spirit raging within. He was always stylish, polished and quiet, prompting former teammate Mickey Cochrane to observe, "He says hello on opening day, goodbye closing day and, in between, hits .350."

All of Gehringer's in-betweens came for Detroit, where he honed his picture-book batting style under the tutelage of manager Ty Cobb from 1924-26 and began his 19-year run as one of the smoothest second basemen the game has produced. The sad-faced former Michigan farmboy made everything look easy with his classy glove, whether ranging to his left, charging rollers or retreating to the outfield for short fly balls. What the seven-time A.L. fielding percentage leader lacked in showmanship he more than made up for with a sleep-inducing consistency that fit his expressionless demeanor.

At the plate, the lefthanded-hitting Gehringer stood erect

"I've never seen one man hit in so much hard luck, consistently. Year after year, he leads the league in line drives right at somebody. No wonder he looks so sad." — *Bucky Harris*

and motionless, a cat preparing to pounce. Ever patient, he worked the pitcher hard and drove the ball to all fields with extra-base power. The 6-foot Gehringer, one of the best two-strike hitters of his era, topped the .300 mark 13 times en route to a career .320 average and won an American League batting championship (.371) and MVP award in 1937.

Gehringer could play the role of instigator (he topped 100 runs scored 12 times) or run-producer (seven 100-RBI seasons) while raining out hits with amazing consistency. In 1929 he led the A.L. in runs (131), hits (215), doubles (45) and triples (19) and he reached the magic 200-hit plateau five straight years and seven times in a nine-season stretch.

Gehringer, who played in the first six All-Star Games, was a middle-infield anchor for powerful Detroit lineups (featuring Cochrane, Hank Greenberg, Goose Goslin) that helped win 1934, '35 and '40 American League pennants and the 1935 World Series. Not surprisingly, Gehringer was a .321 hitter in fall classic play.

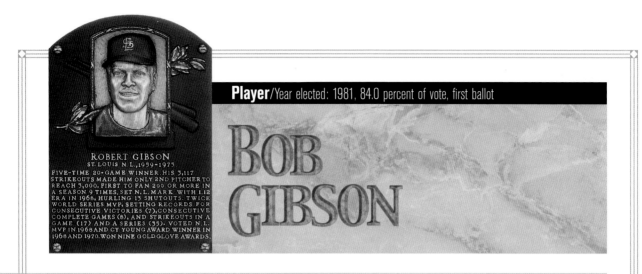

Player/Year elected: 1981, 84.0 percent of vote, first ballot

BOB GIBSON

ROBERT GIBSON
ST. LOUIS N. L., 1959-1975
FIVE-TIME 20-GAME WINNER. HIS 3,117 STRIKEOUTS MADE HIM ONLY 2ND PITCHER TO REACH 3,000. FIRST TO FAN 200 OR MORE IN A SEASON 9 TIMES. SET N.L. MARK WITH 1.12 ERA IN 1968. HURLING 13 SHUTOUTS. TWICE WORLD SERIES MVP, SETTING RECORDS FOR CONSECUTIVE VICTORIES (7), CONSECUTIVE COMPLETE GAMES (8), AND STRIKEOUTS IN A GAME (17) AND A SERIES (35). VOTED N.L. MVP IN 1968 AND CY YOUNG AWARD WINNER IN 1968 AND 1970. WON NINE GOLD GLOVE AWARDS.

Born: 11-9-35, Omaha, Neb. **Height/Weight:** 6-1/195 **Bats/Throws:** R/R **Position:** Pitcher **Career statistics:** 251-174, 2.91 ERA, 3,117 strikeouts **Teams:** Cardinals 1959-75 **Major awards:** N.L. Cy Young, 1968, '70

Bob Gibson's fastball was filled with the same intense rage as the man who launched it past helpless hitters for the better part of two decades. So was the sharp-breaking slider that some observers called the best of all time for a righthander. When Gibson was at his dazzling best, he almost made pitching seem unfair.

Look at it from the batter's point of view. Gibson, cap pulled down low over a glowering face, sets his powerful jaw and stares at his newest worst enemy. Everything about him looks mean as he begins a three-quarters delivery that will propel the ball homeward. The full-body follow-through is the killer. It begins with right leg extended sideways and ends with a full running step forward and toward the first base line. The man behind the scowl appears to be leaping toward you with hostile intent.

That intense, unfriendly style served Gibson well over the 17 seasons (1959-75) he anchored the St. Louis Cardinals' rotation, posting a 251-174 record.

"Bob wasn't just unfriendly when he pitched. I'd say it was more like hateful." — *Joe Torre*

Teammates described a man with "pride, dedication and a must-win" demeanor on the mound; a man who would bury a fastball in the batter's rib when he wanted to make a point. But they described the off-field Gibson as eloquent, bright and fun-loving, although his barbs were delivered with a cutting edge.

Gibson, an outstanding fielder (nine Gold Gloves) and dangerous hitter (24 home runs), was a five-time 20-game winner and five-time All-Star Game performer. He is best remembered for a near-legendary 1968 season that produced a 22-9 record, 13 shutouts and a 1.12 ERA—the lowest ERA of the 20th century for a pitcher with 300 or more innings. He capped it with a National League MVP and Cy Young—the first of two he would win.

Gibson was an outstanding big-game pitcher. His 7-2 World Series record and 1.89 ERA anchored two Cardinal championships in three tries and featured a dominating 17-strikeout performance against Detroit in Game 1 of the 1968 classic.

GIBSON

Player/Year elected: 1972, Special Committee on Negro Leagues

JOSH GIBSON

Born: 12-21-11, Buena Vista, Ga. **Died:** 1-20-47 **Height/Weight:** 6-1/220 **Bats/Throws:** R/R **Primary position:** Catcher

Teams (1930-46): Homestead Grays; Pittsburgh Crawfords

He was to Negro League baseball what Babe Ruth was to the all-white game of his era. The Josh Gibson legend is filled with stories of long, longer and longest home runs, other incredible batting feats and testimonials from longtime teammates and supporters that he was at least equal to the Sultan of Swat, maybe even better.

The baseball world will never know for sure because Gibson, a barrel-chested 220-pound catcher, never had the chance to test his skills in the major leagues. But those who watched him play from 1930-46 for the Homestead Grays and Pittsburgh Crawfords described an intimidating righthanded hitter who seldom struck out and powered mammoth home runs from a flat-footed stance with a simple flick of his wrists.

Gibson hit for high averages, too, but discussions about the big Georgian always focus on his legendary power. He was the king of 600-foot homers with signature blows that reportedly sailed out of such ballparks as Yankee Stadium, the Polo Grounds, Griffith Stadium

> **"He had an eye like Ted Williams and the power of Babe Ruth. He hit to all fields."** —*Monte Irvin*

and Comiskey Park. His upper-body strength was incredible; his batting marks and home run totals (a reported 75 in one season, 962 in his career) were hard to believe. And when he wasn't winning Negro League home run titles, he was amazing fans in Mexico and the Dominican Republic with his hitting feats.

Gibson, a wide-smiling quiet man with broad shoulders and thick arms, also was an outstanding rifle-arm catcher, once described by pitching great Walter Johnson as better than New York Yankees contemporary Bill Dickey. Other major league players who competed against Gibson and various other Negro League stars during offseason barnstorming games were equally impressed.

Sadly, Gibson was just 35 years old and still active when he suffered a cerebral hemorrhage and died suddenly in January 1947, a few months before Jackie Robinson would gain national attention by breaking baseball's color barrier with the Brooklyn Dodgers.

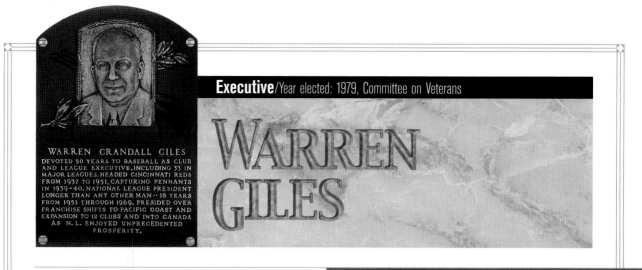

WARREN GILES

WARREN CRANDALL GILES
DEVOTED 50 YEARS TO BASEBALL AS CLUB AND LEAGUE EXECUTIVE, INCLUDING 33 IN MAJOR LEAGUES. HEADED CINCINNATI REDS FROM 1937 TO 1951, CAPTURING PENNANTS IN 1939-40. NATIONAL LEAGUE PRESIDENT LONGER THAN ANY OTHER MAN · 18 YEARS FROM 1951 THROUGH 1969. PRESIDED OVER FRANCHISE SHIFTS TO PACIFIC COAST AND EXPANSION TO 12 CLUBS AND INTO CANADA AS N.L. ENJOYED UNPRECEDENTED PROSPERITY.

Born: 5-28-1896, Tiskilwa, Ill. **Died:** 2-7-79 **Executive career:** Vice president and general manager of Reds, 1937-47; president of Reds, 1948-51; N.L. president, 1952-69; member of Hall of Fame Veterans Committee, 1970-78

He was a jovial, affable politician who could charm managers, players and umpires while taking disciplinary action against them. He was an emotional bulldog who would fight without hesitation for the interests of the National League owners he represented. It was easy to debate the decisions and leadership of Warren Giles, but nobody ever questioned the integrity and efficiency he brought to his 18-year reign as N.L. president.

Most of all, Giles was a visionary who had predicted franchise relocation and expansion long before it happened. Milwaukee fans loved him when he endorsed the Braves' proposed move there from Boston in 1953, then hated him when he didn't resist their 1966 transfer to Atlanta. Giles was an overseer for West Coast expansion and a strong proponent for the 1962 expansion that brought the New York Mets and Houston Astros into the N.L. fold.

The pink-cheeked, rotund Giles had a big heart that sometimes got in the way of disciplinary action, but he gained better compensation for umpires, paved the way

> "The easiest way to kill interest in baseball is to make it fancy, a dressy sport. Baseball prospers in an atmosphere of relaxation, a picnic type of background."
>
> —*Warren Giles*

GILES

for such innovations as domed stadiums and artificial turf and took giant steps to enhance the N.L.'s financial viability. As his N.L. gained a competitive superiority over the American League because of its faster influx of black talent, Giles strutted like a proud father.

The Illinois-born Giles came into big-league prominence as the general manager who lifted the Cincinnati Reds from 1937 also-ran status to a 1940 World Series championship. During his 15 years in Cincinnati, Giles garnered enough support to be con-sidered as the 1951 successor to commissioner Happy Chandler. That job eventually went to N.L. president Ford Frick, but Giles stepped into his vacated office and relocated its headquarters to Cincinnati.

When he finally stepped down in 1969, Giles had completed 50 years in professional baseball — 17 as a minor league executive. Giles spent nine of those years as team president at Rochester, helping Branch Rickey build his innovative St. Louis Cardinals farm system.

GILES

Player/Year elected: 1972, Committee on Veterans

LEFTY GOMEZ

VERNON LOUIS GOMEZ
"LEFTY"

NEW YORK A.L. 1930-1942
WASHINGTON A.L. 1943
WON 20 OR MORE GAMES FOUR TIMES IN
HELPING YANKEES TO WIN SEVEN
PENNANTS. LED A.L. WITH 26-5 RECORD,
2.33 EARNED RUN AVERAGE IN 1934 AND
WITH 21 VICTORIES AND 2.33 ERA IN
1937 PACED A.L. IN WINNING PCT. TWICE.
STRIKEOUTS THREE TIMES. SET WORLD
SERIES MARK BY WINNING 6 GAMES
WITHOUT A LOSS.

Born: 11-26-08, Rodeo, Calif. **Died:** 2-17-89 **Height/Weight:** 6-2/175 **Bats/Throws:** L/L **Position:** Pitcher
Career statistics: 189-102, 3.34 ERA, 1,468 strikeouts **Teams:** Yankees 1930-42; Senators 1943

His fastballs zipped across the plate with the same accuracy his one-liners zipped across the locker room. Lefty Gomez was masterful, whether serving as court jester or pitching ace for the New York Yankees' World Series machine of the 1930s. Equal parts humorist and pitcher, "El Goofy" brought fun and personality to a sport that sometimes took itself too seriously.

Gomez was a high-kicking 6-foot-2 lefthander who joined the Yankees as a 150-pound beanpole in 1930 and never weighed more than 175. But his fastball, powered by well-developed shoulder muscles, was one of the best in the game and he mesmerized hitters with a slow curve that served as his strikeout pitch. Backed by a lineup featuring Babe Ruth, Lou Gehrig and later Joe DiMaggio, he powered his way to four 20-win seasons, including a 26-5, 2.33-ERA masterpiece in 1934.

But the Gomez legend was built around the happy-go-lucky atmosphere he brought to the field. He had a special rapport with Ruth, who kidded and prodded Gomez relentlessly about his weak hitting. The high-strung Gomez, who drove manager Joe McCarthy batty with his dugout pacing and nervous energy, was famous for his one-line quips, locker-room pranks and goofy on-field antics, such as the anxious World Series moment in 1936 when he stepped off the mound to watch a plane fly overhead. Nothing was sacred to the quick-witted Lefty, who kept his teammates loose and relaxed when all around them was nervous and tense.

Clown and quipster, Gomez also was one of the best big-game pitchers in the business, a reputation enhanced by his 6-0 record in five World Series and 3-1 mark in five All-Star Games. Gomez's Hall of Fame career was cut short by a series of arm problems that limited him to 24 victories and fewer than 300 innings over his final four seasons. He pitched one game for Washington in 1943 before retiring with a 189-102 final record.

"Nobody ever hated to lose worse than I do. But when I lose, I can't see any reason for making everybody feel miserable just because I do." — *Lefty Gomez*

LEON ALLEN GOSLIN
"GOOSE"
WASHINGTON A.L. 1921 TO 1930, 1933, 1938
ST. LOUIS A.L. 1930 TO 1932
DETROIT A.L. 1934 TO 1937

BATTED .344 IN 1924, .334 IN 1925,
.354 IN 1926, .334 IN 1927. LED A.L.
IN BATTING IN 1928 WITH .379 AVERAGE.
RUNS BATTED IN FOR 1924—129.
HIT .300 OR BETTER 11 YEARS.
LIFETIME TOTAL OF 2735 HITS,
BATTING AVERAGE .316.
MADE 37 HITS IN 5 WORLD SERIES.

Player/Year elected: 1968, Committee on Veterans

GOOSE GOSLIN

Born: 10-16-00, Salem, N.J. **Died:** 5-15-71 **Height/Weight:** 5-11/185 **Bats/Throws:** L/R **Primary position:** Outfield **Career statistics:** .316 avg., 2,735 hits, 1,483 runs, 248 HR, 1,609 RBIs **Teams:** Senators 1921-30, 1933, 1938; Browns 1930-32; Tigers 1934-37 **Batting champion:** A.L. 1928

He crowded the plate with a mocking defiance, daring pitchers to take their best shot. When they did, Goose Goslin would dust himself off, lean back over the plate and invite them to do it again. The fearless, hard-swinging lefthanded hitter believed that a fastball—anybody's fastball—was worth the inconvenience and he knew what to do when he got one to hit.

Goslin was first and foremost a hitter. He attacked the ball with vengeance, playing the role of enforcer for five World Series teams in an 18-year career that started in 1921 at Washington. He was a gap hitter with power, an extraordinary run-producer who amassed 1,609 RBIs and led the American League (129) in 1924. His .316 career average was highlighted by an A.L.-leading .379 mark in 1928.

The Goose, who ran with a palms-down sway that gave his stride the appearance of a waddle, was a night-life proponent and one of the more flamboyant players of the 1920s and '30s. His

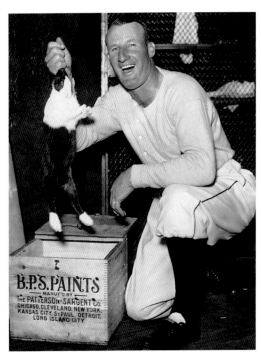

"Goslin is not only our best hitter, but he's one of the greatest natural hitters in the league." — *Bucky Harris*

swing was so hard that he often ended up sitting in the dirt when he missed connections. A bulbous nose added to his colorful persona and he sometimes treated fly balls like hand grenades. While the 5-foot-11 Goslin had an outstanding arm and worked hard to improve his defense, he never was known as a good left or right fielder.

But he offset that deficiency with his ability to drive in runs. His 11 seasons of 100 or more RBIs are tied for fifth all time and he averaged one every 5.38 at-bats, a figure topped only by Babe Ruth, Lou Gehrig, Ted Williams, Jimmie Foxx, Al Simmons and Mel Ott. He also was one of the most popular players in Washington history and a World Series hero in Detroit, where he played from 1934-37.

Goslin hit seven home runs for the Senators in three World Series (1924, '25 and '33) and his World Series-winning single gave Detroit a 1935 championship. He retired in 1938 after one season in his third stint with the Senators.

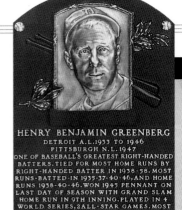

HENRY BENJAMIN GREENBERG
DETROIT A.L. 1933 TO 1946
PITTSBURGH N.L. 1947
ONE OF BASEBALL'S GREATEST RIGHT-HANDED
BATTERS. TIED FOR MOST HOME RUNS BY
RIGHT-HANDED BATTER IN 1938-58. MOST
RUNS-BATTED-IN 1935-37-40-46, AND HOME
RUNS 1938-40-46. WON 1945 PENNANT ON
LAST DAY OF SEASON WITH GRAND SLAM
HOME RUN IN 9TH INNING. PLAYED IN 4
WORLD SERIES, 2 ALL-STAR GAMES. MOST
VALUABLE A.L. PLAYER TWICE-1935-1940.
LIFETIME BATTING AVERAGE .313.

Player/Year elected: 1956, 85.0 percent of vote

HANK GREENBERG

Born: 1-1-11, New York, N.Y. **Died:** 9-4-86 **Height/Weight:** 6-4/ 215 **Bats/Throws:** R/R **Primary position:** First base **Career statistics:** .313 avg., 1,628 hits, 1,051 runs, 331 HR, 1,276 RBIs **Teams:** Tigers 1930-46; Pirates 1947 **HR champion:** A.L., 1935, tied, '38, '40, '46 **Major awards:** A.L. MVP, 1935, '40

He was a self-made superstar, the big, clumsy New York City kid who transformed his ugly-duckling awkwardness into Hall of Fame grace. What Hank Greenberg lacked in natural talent he more than made up for with unyielding desire, hard work and intense dedication to his craft. Big Hank was an overachiever, a 6-foot-4 pounder who earned baseball success through mind-over-matter determination.

Nothing came easy for Greenberg, who made his major league debut for the Detroit Tigers in 1930 as a stumbling first baseman. He wasn't fast, a shortcoming he never could overcome, but he worked hard to improve his quickness, spent hours mastering defensive fundamentals and learned to hit the curveball in early morning sessions with weary batting practice pitchers. American League pitchers felt the crunch of Hank's gritty perseverance.

His 215-pound body cut a menacing figure and his big arms and roundhouse swing pounded the ball with Ruthian-like frequency, power and run

"(Greenberg) is so powerful that he doesn't have to meet a ball squarely to drive it far and clear. All he has to do is get a piece of the ball." —*Mickey Cochrane*

production. Six times he topped 30 home runs, including a 58-homer 1938 season that left him only two short of Babe Ruth's single-season record, and four times he topped 145 RBIs, including a 183-RBI 1937 season that left him eight short of Hack Wilson's record. Greenberg, a member of two Detroit championship teams, earned two A.L. MVP awards (1935 and '40) and his .313 career average defied the conventional profile of a power hitter.

The outspoken, articulate Greenberg, who later put those qualities to use as a front-office executive, finished his career with 331 home runs—a figure that would have been considerably higher if he had not lost four-plus seasons to World War II and another to a broken wrist, giving him a real career of less than 10 years. His defining moment came in 1945, when he hit a dramatic final-day grand slam to clinch the A.L. pennant for the Tigers and complete his first half season back from military duty. He added two more homers in a World Series victory over Chicago.

Player, Manager, Executive/Year elected: 1946, Committee on Old-Timers

CLARK GRIFFITH

CLARK C. GRIFFITH
ASSOCIATED WITH MAJOR LEAGUE BASEBALL FOR MORE THAN 50 YEARS AS A PITCHER, MANAGER AND EXECUTIVE. SERVED AS A MEMBER OF THE CHICAGO AND CINCINNATI TEAMS IN THE N.L. AND THE CHICAGO, NEW YORK AND WASHINGTON CLUBS IN THE A.L. COMPILED MORE THAN 200 VICTORIES AS A PITCHER, MANAGER OF THE CINCINNATI N.L. AND CHICAGO, NEW YORK AND WASHINGTON A.L. TEAMS FOR 20 YEARS.

Born: 11-20-1869, Clear Creek, Mo. **Died:** 10-27-55 **Height/Weight:** 5-7/156 **B/T:** R/R **Position:** Pitcher **Career statistics:** 237-146
Teams played: St. L. (A.A.) 1891; Bos. (A.A.) 1891; Chi. 1893-1900; W. Sox 1901-02; Yankees 1903-07; Reds 1909; Senators 1912-14 **Teams managed (1,491-1,367):** W. Sox 1901-02; Yankees 1903-08; Reds 1909-11; Senators 1912-20 **Executive career:** Senators owner, 1920-55

From a Missouri log cabin to the center of Washington society, Clark Griffith climbed an unusual ladder of success. He won 237 games as a top-flight pitcher, 1,491 as a respected manager and thousands more as owner of baseball's most politically correct team. The "Old Fox" was equal parts player, strategist, pioneer and patriarch in a major league career that covered 65 years and linked two centuries.

At 5-foot-7 and 156 pounds, Griffith relied on guile, pinpoint control and trick pitches (curves, sliders, spitters) to carve out six straight 20-win seasons for the Chicago Nationals from 1893-1900. Then, when the American League was formed in 1901, the dashing righthander bolted to the new Chicago team and posted a 24-7 record while managing the White Sox to the A.L.'s first pennant. Over two decades of managing, Griffith kick-started the New York Yankees franchise (1903-08), spent three years in Cincinnati (1909-11) and began his long association with Washington.

By 1912, the kid who had once saddled a horse for Jesse James in wilderness Missouri was a minority stockholder in the Senators. In 1920, he purchased controlling interest and began his "third career" as Mr. Washington Baseball. A friend to presidents, senators and Supreme Court justices, Griffith became a strong

voice for the game in times of need. He was responsible for President Franklin Roosevelt's "Green Light" letter at the outbreak of World War II and the "presidential" first-pitch tradition at Griffith Stadium. He was a champion of night baseball.

Always operating on a shoestring budget, Griffith

> "He was the greatest humanitarian who ever lived and the greatest pillar of honesty baseball ever had. I never played for a better man, on the field or off." — *Bobo Newsom*

dedicated his life to keeping baseball afloat in the nation's capital. His Senators won a World Series in 1924 and pennants in 1925 and '33, but his teams generally languished in the second division. "First in war, first in peace, last in the American League" became Washington's lament as Griffith sold off star players to meet payroll.

The popularity of pitching great Walter Johnson kept the Senators going through 1927; Griffith's crafty promotions and signing of Latin players kept them viable until his death in 1955. The moribund franchise was shifted to Minneapolis five years later by Griffith's stepson, Calvin.

BURLEIGH GRIMES

BURLEIGH ARLAND GRIMES
1916 – 1934

ONE OF THE GREAT SPITBALL PITCHERS.
WON 270 GAMES, LOST 212 FOR 7 MAJOR
LEAGUE CLUBS. FIVE 20 VICTORY SEASONS.
WON 13 IN ROW FOR GIANTS IN 1927.
MANAGED DODGERS IN 1937 AND 1938.
LIFETIME E.R.A. 3.52.

Born: 8-18-1893, Emerald, Wis. **Died:** 12-6-85 **Height/Weight:** 5-10/195 **Bats/Throws:** R/R **Position:** Pitcher
Career statistics: 270-212, 3.53 ERA, 1,512 strikeouts **Teams:** Pirates 1916-17, 1928-29, 1934; Dodgers 1918-26; Giants 1927; Braves 1930; Cardinals 1930-31, 1933-34; Cubs 1932-33; Yankees 1934

Unlike most nightmares, Burleigh Grimes terror-ized his victims in broad daylight. "Old Stubblebeard" was a gruff, fear-inducing warrior, a pow-erfully built former Wisconsin lumberjack who deliv-ered his messages with hateful glares and fastballs under the chin. Every pitch was a battle, every game a war for baseball's last legal spitballer, a nomadic righthander who fought to 270 wins over a 19-season career that started in 1916 and passed through six major league cities.

"That Grimes is mean when he's out there on the rubber," said Hall of Fame second baseman Rogers Hornsby, who witnessed the intensity both as a teammate and opponent. Almost as dis-agreeable in the clubhouse as on the mound, the fierce-looking Grimes added to the intimidation by refusing to shave before starts and turning his temper on teammates who did not live up to his expectations.

Beyond the intimidation, the 5-foot-10, 195-pounder was a master psychologist who came at hit-ters from a straight overhand motion with fastballs,

curves and an outstanding spitter that sometimes dipped seven inches. Grimes, one of 17 pitchers allowed to continue throwing the pitch when it was outlawed in 1920, used slippery elm wood juice to doctor the ball and befuddled hitters by going to his mouth before every delivery, no matter what the pitch.

Grimes' confrontational per-sonality and annoying salary demands kept him from planting baseball roots. He did spend nine seasons in Brooklyn (1918-26), where he posted four of his five 20-win seasons, but his career also took him to Pittsburgh three times, St. Louis twice, Boston, Chicago and New York with both the Giants and Yankees.

Grimes, a workhorse who led the National League in complete games four times, was 23-11 for the pennant-winning Dodgers in 1920 and pitched a World Series shutout against Cleveland. He also won two Series games in 1931 for the champion Cardinals and played in two other classics for the Cardinals (1930) and Cubs (1932). He retired in 1934 at age 41 after a brief stint with the Yanks.

"I know we dealt away a fine young pitcher, but that Grimes just fights with everyone, friend or foe." — *Barney Dreyfuss, Pirates owner, 1918*

ROBERT MOSES GROVE
PHILADELPHIA A.L.1925-1933
BOSTON A.L.1934-1941
WINNER OF 300 GAMES IN THE MAJORS
OVER A SPAN OF 17 YEARS. LED A.L. IN
STRIKEOUTS SEVEN CONSECUTIVE SEASONS.
WON 20 OR MORE GAMES EIGHT SEASONS.
IN 1931, WHILE WINNING 31 GAMES AND
LOSING FOUR, COMPILED A WINNING STREAK
OF 16 STRAIGHT. WON 79 GAMES FOR THE
THREE TIME PENNANT WINNING
ATHLETICS TEAM OF 1929-30-31.

Player/Year elected: 1947, 76.4 percent of vote

LEFTY GROVE

Born: 3-6-00, Lonaconing, Md. **Died:** 5-22-75 **Height/Weight:** 6-3/200 **Bats/Throws:** L/L **Position:** Pitcher **Career statistics:** 300-141, 3.06 ERA, 2,266 strikeouts **Teams:** Athletics 1925-33; Red Sox 1934-41 **Major awards:** A.L. MVP, 1931

Opposing hitters never had a chance against a Lefty Grove fastball, which sailed past them like a meteor unleashed by some other-worldly force. Neither did teammates against the Lefty Grove temper, which erupted into legendary tantrums when things did not go just right over the virulent left-hander's 17-year major league career.

Suffice to say the lean 6-foot-3, 200-pounder was both fast and furious. And incredibly successful, thanks to that uncontrollable intensity he brought to the clubhouse and mound. When he made his big-league debut for Connie Mack's Philadelphia Athletics in 1925, his fastball was as wild as it was fast, and batters stepped into the box with trepidation.

The high-kicking Grove, who would go days without speaking to a teammate because of a defensive lapse, tamed his fastball but never lost the edge his early wildness provided. He enjoyed the first of seven straight 20-win seasons in

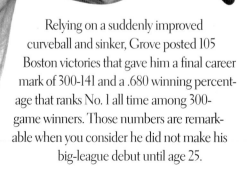

1927 and compiled a 152-41 record from 1928-33, a six-year stretch in which the A's won three American League pennants and two World Series. From 1930-33, he posted records of 28-5, 31-4, 25-10 and 24-8, earned three of his nine career ERA titles and won the last two of seven strikeout titles.

Grove's marquee effort was 1931, when he fashioned the last A.L. 30-win season until 1968. His 2.06 ERA was phenomenal in "a year of the hitter" and he capped his masterpiece with his second straight two-win World Series. In a year in which Lou Gehrig collected 46 homers and 184 RBIs and Babe Ruth amassed 46-163 totals, Grove won MVP honors.

When cost-cutting Mack traded Grove to the Red Sox after the 1933 season, he suffered an arm injury that forced him to transform from a thrower into a pitcher.

Relying on a suddenly improved curveball and sinker, Grove posted 105 Boston victories that gave him a final career mark of 300-141 and a .680 winning percentage that ranks No. 1 all time among 300-game winners. Those numbers are remarkable when you consider he did not make his big-league debut until age 25.

"Just to see that big guy glaring down at you from the mound was enough to frighten the daylights out of you." —Joe Cronin

GROVE

Player/Year elected: 1971, Committee on Veterans

CHICK HAFEY

CHARLES JAMES HAFEY
"CHICK"
ST. LOUIS N.L. 1924-1931
CINCINNATI N.L. 1932-1937
GREAT OUTFIELDER WHO COMPILED .317
LIFETIME BATTING AVERAGE. LEADING
HITTER OF N.L. WITH .349 IN 1931.
BATTED .329 OR BETTER SIX CONSECUTIVE
YEARS. EQUALLED LEAGUE RECORD OF TEN
HITS IN SUCCESSION, 1929. LIFETIME
FIELDING AVERAGE .971.

Born: 2-12-03, Berkeley, Calif. **Died:** 7-2-73 **Height/Weight:** 6-0/185 **Bats/Throws:** R/R **Primary position:** Outfield **Career statistics:** .317 avg., 1,466 hits, 833 RBIs **Teams:** Cardinals 1924-31; Reds 1932-35, 1937 **Batting champion:** N.L., 1931

He viewed the world through wire-rimmed glasses and squinted at 95-mph fastballs through defective eyes. But that didn't stop Chick Hafey from pounding out one of the most impressive hitting legacies in baseball history. Rogers Hornsby said he had never seen anybody who hit the ball harder, third baseman Pie Traynor called his line drives "savage" and John McGraw said if Hafey had been blessed with good vision, he might have been the greatest righthanded hitter of all time.

There's no doubt he could have improved on the .317 average he compiled over 13 major league seasons with the St. Louis Cardinals and Cincinnati—despite a chronic sinus condition that affected his eyes and health. In the three seasons from 1928-30, the dead pull hitter averaged .337, 27 homers and 114 RBIs despite missing 70 games and he came back in 1931 to lead National League hitters with a .349 average.

The ferocity with which Hafey attacked the ball belied his shy, soft-spoken nature. The strong 6-footer was a modest, easy-going Californian who played his first big-league game in 1924—a left fielder with a cannon arm and outstanding speed. Nobody dared run on

> **"I always thought that if Hafey had been blessed with normal eyesight and good health, he might have been the best righthanded hitter baseball had ever known."** — *Branch Rickey*

Hafey and no third baseman, fearing the vicious line drives his powerful wrists would snap down the line, dared play shallow.

Hafey thrived for awhile without glasses, but Cardinals doctors became suspicious in 1926 when he kept getting hit by pitches. Even when he became one of the game's few bespectacled players, his sinuses would flare up and double-vision would force him to the bench. Sinus surgery and glasses helped, but brightness and cold affected his sight and illness resulted in weight fluctuations.

Still, he played in four World Series and won the admiration of Cardinals teammates and fans. He was traded to the Reds in the spring of 1932 after a contentious salary dispute and played four more seasons before retiring—a retirement that was interrupted by a one-season comeback attempt in 1937.

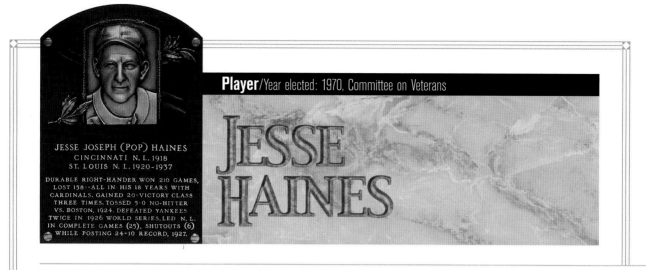

JESSE HAINES

JESSE JOSEPH (POP) HAINES
CINCINNATI N. L. 1918
ST. LOUIS N. L. 1920-1937

DURABLE RIGHT-HANDER WON 210 GAMES,
LOST 158—ALL IN HIS 18 YEARS WITH
CARDINALS. GAINED 20-VICTORY CLASS
THREE TIMES. TOSSED 5-0 NO-HITTER
VS. BOSTON, 1924. DEFEATED YANKEES
TWICE IN 1926 WORLD SERIES, LED N. L.
IN COMPLETE GAMES (25), SHUTOUTS (6)
WHILE POSTING 24-10 RECORD, 1927.

Born: 7-22-1893, Clayton, Ohio **Died:** 8-5-78 **Height/Weight:** 6-0/190 **Bats/Throws:** R/R **Position:** Pitcher
Career statistics: 210-158, 3.64 ERA, 981 strikeouts **Teams:** Reds 1918; Cardinals 1920-37

From 1920 through the devastating years of the Great Depression, there was one constant in the St. Louis Cardinals clubhouse. Wily, tough, unflappable Jesse Haines won 210 games over an 18-year association with the team while serving as inspirational leader and father figure for five pennant-winners and three World Series champions. He was "Pop" to St. Louis' 1930s-era Gashouse Gang, just plain exasperating to opponents who flailed helplessly at his dipping, darting knuckleballs.

The 6-foot righthander, a strong southwestern Ohio "country boy" who loathed the trappings of city life, was a two-pitch workhorse who posted three 20-win seasons and a 3.64 career ERA. Unable to reach the major leagues, he developed a knuckler that he gripped with the first joints of his powerful fingers and delivered with a furious motion, much faster than the fingernail flutterball thrown by later knucklers.

When Haines threw sidearm, the pitch broke down and away from righthanders. When he threw overhand, it dipped like a spitter. Haines had excellent control of the pitch, but it sometimes rubbed skin off his knuckles and forced him to the bench with bleeding fingers. One of his most memorable performances came in the seventh game of the 1926 World Series against the New York Yankees when he had to leave in the seventh inning with a 3-2 lead, setting the stage for Grover Alexander's classic bases-loaded strikeout of Tony Lazzeri and the Cardinals' first championship.

Haines was the picture of composure on the mound, working rapidly and immune to adversity. But buried within was a ferocity that sometimes exploded in the clubhouse—an intensity that rubbed off on Cardinals teammates. It's no coincidence that Haines was a key member of the first five pennant-winners in Cardinals history and a 3-1 pitcher with a 1.67 ERA in World Series play.

Haines, a 26-year-old rookie in 1920, was a 44-year-old reliever and team patriarch when he retired after the 1937 season with a 210-158 career record.

> "When I saw how hard a nice old man like Pop took losing a game, I realized why he'd been a consistent winner. I never forgot how much Haines expected of himself and others." —*Terry Moore*

HAINES

WILLIAM R. HAMILTON
PHILADELPHIA N.L. 1890-1895
BOSTON N.L. 1896-1901

HOLDS RECORDS FOR SINGLE SEASON:
RUNS SCORED, 196 IN 1894; STOLEN
BASES, 115 IN 1891. LIFETIME TOTAL
STOLEN BASES, 937. BATTED .395 IN
1893, .399 IN 1894, .393 IN 1895.
LED NATIONAL LEAGUE IN 1891 WITH
.338 AVERAGE. LIFETIME BATTING
AVERAGE OF .344. SCORED 100 OR
MORE RUNS DURING 10 SEASONS.

Player/Year elected: 1961, Committee on Veterans

BILLY HAMILTON

Born: 2-16-1866, Newark, N.J. **Died:** 12-16-40 **Height/Weight:** 5-6/165 **Bats/Throws:** L/R **Primary position:** Center field

Career statistics: .344 avg., 2,164 hits, 1,697 runs, 937 steals **Teams:** Kansas City (A.A.) 1888-89; Philadelphia 1890-95; Boston 1896-1901 **Batting champion:** N.L., 1891

He stood only 5-foot-6 and weighed 165, a chunky, stumpy-legged New Jersey kid who looked out of place in a baseball uniform. But everyone who underestimated the athleticism of Billy Hamilton got a quick dose of reality. "Sliding Billy" was a large baseball talent in a small package, an 1890s-era pioneer who helped popularize the game with his spirited play and flair for the dramatic.

The swift center fielder had a fan-friendly style. Hamilton would stand in center, half facing left field with hands clasped behind his back, peering over his shoulder at the hitter. He had an uncanny ability to race to the perfect spot at the crack of the bat and an exciting knack for making dramatic, tumbling catches. He also was an accomplished hitter and baserunner who earned ovations with his trademark head-first slides.

For two seasons in the American Association and 12 more in Philadelphia and Boston, Hamilton was the most feared leadoff man in baseball. Only once, his rookie campaign in 1888, did he have an on-base percentage under .400 and he was a 12-time .300 hitter who led the National League in walks five times. A lefthanded swinger who sprayed line drives all over the park, Hamilton posted averages of .403 (1894), .389 (1895) and .380 (1893) en route to a .344 career mark.

But his greatest renown was achieved on the bases. In an era when steals were credited to runners who took an extra base, Hamilton recorded 937 with a season high of 111. He was a run-scoring machine, topping the 100 plateau 11 times and scoring 1,697 in 1,594 games — a ratio no one has come close to duplicating. Sliding Billy scored 198 runs for Philadelphia in 1894, a still-standing record.

That 1894 Philadelphia team featured a Hall of Fame outfield of Hamilton, Ed Delahanty and Sam Thompson, which batted a combined .407 but couldn't keep the Phillies from finishing fourth. After six years in Philadelphia, Hamilton joined Hugh Duffy in Boston's outfield from 1896-1900 and helped the Beaneaters win two pennants before retiring in 1901.

"**(Jesse) Burkett was one of the greatest hitters I've ever seen. But Hamilton was one of the very best ball players.**" —*Hugh Duffy*

EDWARD HUGH HANLON
(NED)
PITTSBURGH, N.L. 1889, 1891
PITTSBURGH, P.L. 1890
BALTIMORE, N.L. 1892-1898
BROOKLYN, N.L. 1899-1905
CINCINNATI, N.L. 1906-1907
MANAGER OF FIVE PENNANT WINNING TEAMS WITH BALTIMORE
AND BROOKLYN, EMPLOYING INNOVATIVE TACTICS SUCH AS
HIT AND RUN, SQUEEZE AND 'BALTIMORE CHOP'. FOUR OF
HIS PLAYERS-McGRAW, ROBINSON, JENNINGS AND HUGGINS
THEMSELVES BECAME HALL OF FAME MANAGERS. ALSO HEADED
BASEBALL'S RULES COMMITTEE. A SPEEDY OUTFIELDER WITH
DETROIT DURING HIS PLAYING DAYS

Manager/Year elected: 1996, Committee on Veterans

NED HANLON

Born: 8-22-1857, Montville, Conn. **Died:** 4-14-1937 **Height/Weight:** 5-10/170 **Bats/Throws:** L/R **Primary position:** Outfield **Career statistics:** .264 avg., 1,347 hits **Teams played:** Cleveland 1880; Detroit 1881-88; Pittsburgh 1889, 1891; Pittsburgh (P.L.) 1890; Baltimore 1892 **Teams managed (1,312-1,164):** Pittsburgh 1889, 1891; Pittsburgh (P.L.) 1890; Baltimore 1892-98; Brooklyn 1899-1905; Cincinnati 1906-07

They tripped runners, hid extra balls in the outfield grass, flashed mirrors in the eyes of hitters and tilted the foul lines toward fair territory, all in the name of "scientific baseball." Ned Hanlon's old Baltimore Orioles were savvy, mean proponents of "whatever it takes to win." They also were accomplished tacticians who strategized, executed and hustled their way to dominance in the turn-of-the-century National League.

The Orioles were built in the image of Hanlon, a 5-foot-10, stone-faced, reticent former outfielder with a perfectly curled handlebar mustache that gave him the look of a meek office clerk. There was nothing meek about "Silent Ned's" active mind, which quickly assessed player habits and flaws and devised strategy around that information. He was demanding and precise, qualities reflected by the players he began acquiring when he became Orioles manager in 1892.

John McGraw, Hughie Jennings, Joe Kelley, Willie Keeler, Wilbert Robinson and Dan Brouthers became the backbone of the Orioles—notorious gamers who

would spare nothing in pursuit of victory. Dirty tricks aside, Hanlon also perfected such strategies as bunting, the hit-and-run, double steals and platooning. His players scratched, clawed and fought for every base, run and out.

Not surprisingly, they also won. The Orioles captured N.L. pennants in 1894, '95 and '96 and finished second the next two seasons. When Hanlon took the core of his team to Brooklyn in 1899, the Superbas won two straight pennants, giving him five in seven years. Although he never attained such success over his final seven

"He seemed not to care what anyone thought of him and that was his strength, the quality that made him a natural leader. There was an apartness about him that lent him an air of mystery—and command."

—*Burt Solomon in his 1999 book* Where They Ain't

years in Brooklyn and Cincinnati, Hanlon was recognized as one of the great tacticians and innovators in the game.

His legacy was an attention to detail and creativity that helped redefine the way baseball was played. A .264 career hitter over 13 major league seasons, he relied on the same guile and aggressiveness he looked for in the players he later managed. Hanlon finished his managerial career in 1907 with a 1,312-1,164 record and .530 winning percentage.

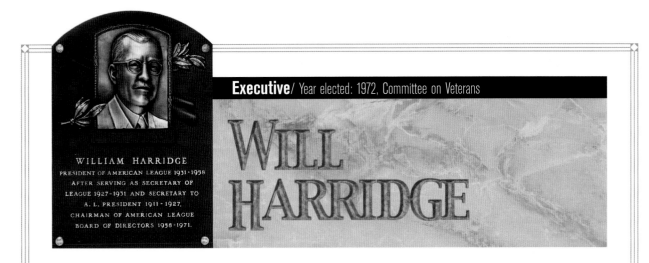

Executive/ Year elected: 1972, Committee on Veterans

WILL HARRIDGE

Born: 10-16-1883, Chicago, Ill. **Died:** 4-9-71 **Executive career:** Secretary to A.L. president Ban Johnson, 1911-27; A.L. secretary, 1927-31; A.L. president, 1931-58; A.L. chairman of the board, 1958-71

From $90-per-month railroad clerk to powerful head of the American League, Will Harridge lived a baseball fairy tale. The quiet, studious kid who had never seen or played the game evolved into one of its most indefatigable champions. Over a 28-year presidency that stretched from 1931-58, Harridge also was a guiding force that helped baseball survive a Depression, a world war and the early explosions of a technological revolution.

Friends and co-workers described Harridge as dignified and genteel, the opposite of American League founder and first president Ban Johnson. It was the tempestuous Johnson who taught the business-savvy Harridge the intricacies of the game after plucking him out of a Wabash Railroad office to be his personal secretary in 1911. Harridge learned well.

Johnson retired in 1927 and Harridge became A.L. secretary under new president E.S. Barnard. When Barnard died unexpectedly in the spring of 1931, the 45-year-old Harridge was elected as the third A.L. president and began a three-decade quest as protector of the game's integrity. The strong traditionalist supported anything he believed would promote baseball's popularity while enhancing the agenda of team owners and commissioner Kenesaw Mountain Landis.

Soft-spoken and publicity shy, the bespectacled Chicagoan never backed away from controversy. He fined and suspended Yankees catcher Bill Dickey ($1,000, 30 days) in 1932 for slugging and breaking the jaw of Washington's Carl Reynolds after a home plate collision, drawing the ire of team owner Jacob Ruppert, and he fined manager Jimmy Dykes 37 times. After early misgivings, Harridge embraced night base-

> ## "There's never been a morning in my life that I didn't look forward to going to my office."
>
> —*Will Harridge*

ball and helped the game come to terms with such post-World War II issues as integration, team relocation, radio, television and travel.

Harridge, a dedicated administrator who maintained headquarters in Chicago, was the moving force behind the All-Star Game. But he hated gimmicks and fought the showmanship efforts of colorful owner Bill Veeck. After stepping down as president in 1958, Harridge served as A.L. chairman of the board until his death in 1971.

Manager/Year elected: 1975, Committee on Veterans

BUCKY HARRIS

Born: 11-8-1896, Port Jervis, N.Y. **Died:** 11-8-77 **Height/Weight:** 5-10/156 **Bats/Throws:** R/R **Primary position:** Second base
Career statistics: .274 avg., 1,297 hits **Teams played:** Senators 1919-28; Tigers 1929, 1931 **Teams managed (2,157-2,218):** Senators 1924-28, 1935-42, 1950-54; Tigers 1929-33, 1955-56; Red Sox 1934; Phillies 1943; Yankees 1947-48 **World Series titles:** 1924, '47

He traded angry gibes with Ty Cobb, delivered hip checks to Babe Ruth and took fastballs to his body for the good of the team. But scrappy, fearless Bucky Harris will always be remembered as the 27-year-old "Boy Wonder" second baseman who guided the Washington Senators to their only World Series championship. It was a memorable beginning to a managerial career that would take him through 29 major league seasons in five cities.

For the 5-foot-10, 156-pound son of a New York coal miner, 1924 was a signature season. The managerial call came midway through his solid 12-year playing career and he responded by leading the formerly hapless Senators to their first pennant and World Series appearance. In an exciting fall classic victory over the New York Giants, Harris batted .333, hit two home runs and collected seven RBIs, three in the 4-3 Game 7 clincher. He also out-managed the master tactician, John McGraw.

Over the next three decades, Harris would join the ranks of managerial greats. Unlike the McGraws, McCarthys and Stengels who built their reputations with top-notch talent, Harris gained stature while working primarily with weak teams. He was popular with his players, a masterful handler of young talent, but his overachieving squads seldom were good enough to contend.

The always-outspoken Harris, who hid his fierce competitive drive beneath a mild-mannered exterior, guided 20 second-division teams—12 in Washington, seven in Detroit while serving three different hitches for Calvin Griffith's Senators and two for the Tigers. Only twice did he taste success after 1924—his 1925 Senators won a pennant and his 1947 New York Yankees defeated Brooklyn in a memorable World Series—but he never lacked for suitors.

When Harris, a .274 career righthanded hitter, retired in 1956, his 2,157 career wins ranked fourth on the

> ## "If you can't play for Bucky, you don't belong in the major leagues." —*Joe DiMaggio*

all-time list, his 29 managerial seasons ranked behind only Connie Mack and McGraw and his 2,218 losses were topped only by Mack.

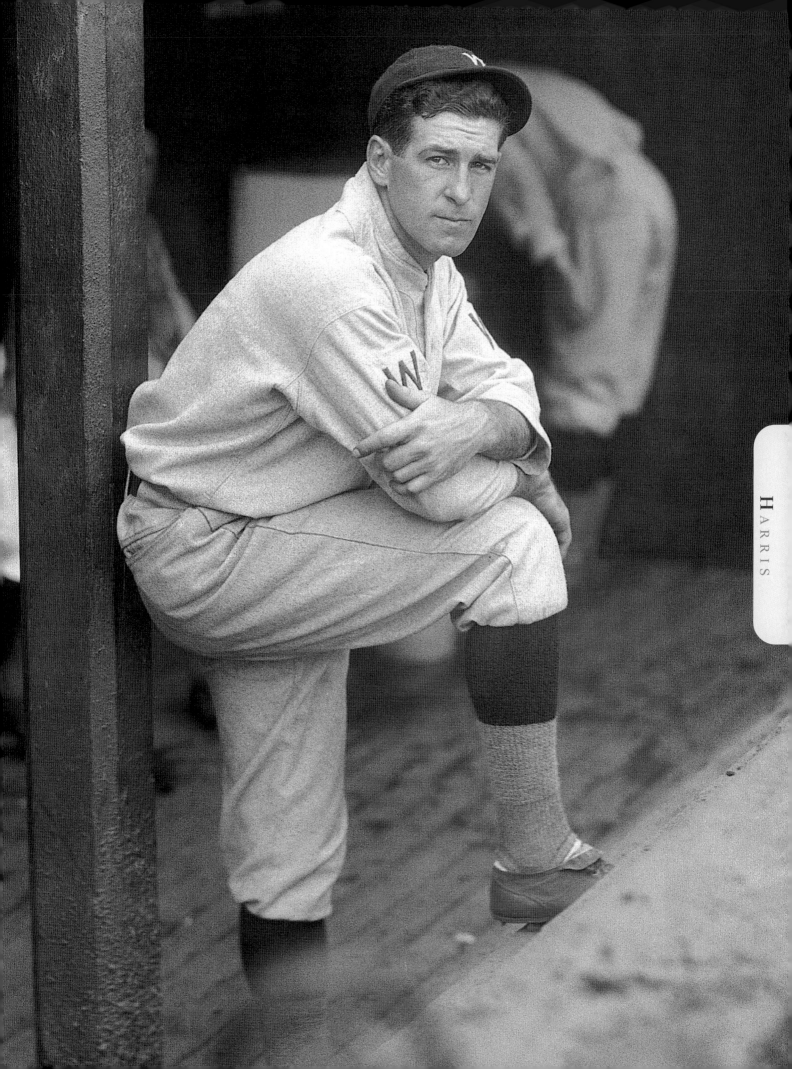

GABBY HARTNETT

CHARLES LEO (GABBY) HARTNETT
CHICAGO N.L.1922 TO 1940
NEW YORK N.L.1941
CAUGHT 100 OR MORE GAMES PER SEASON
FOR 12 YEARS, EIGHT IN SUCCESSION, 1930
TO 1937 FOR LEAGUE RECORD. SET MARK
FOR CONSECUTIVE CHANCES FOR CATCHER
WITHOUT ERROR, 452 IN 1933-34. HIGHEST
FIELDING AVERAGE FOR CATCHER IN 100 OR
MORE GAMES IN 7 SEASONS; MOST PUTOUTS
N.L. 7292; MOST CHANCES ACCEPTED N.L.
8546. LIFETIME BATTING AVERAGE .297.

Born: 12-20-00, Woonsocket, R.I. **Died:** 12-20-72 **Height/Weight:** 6-1/210 **Bats/Throws:** R/R **Primary position:** Catcher **Career statistics:** .297 avg., 1,912 hits, 236 HR, 1,179 RBIs **Teams:** Cubs 1922-40; Giants 1941 **Major awards:** N.L. MVP, 1935

His friendly, round Irish face was wedged between oversized ears and his dimpled grin transformed easily into a roaring laugh that shook the world around him. There was no mistaking the burly, chest-thrusting confidence and enthusiasm Gabby Hartnett brought to his 19 seasons as Chicago Cubs catcher and spiritual leader. Equal parts charmer, slugger and defensive wizard, Hartnett made baseball fun and entertaining throughout a career that stretched from 1922-41.

Behind the incessant chatter and jovial demeanor was an intensity that separated the 6-foot-1, 210-pound Rhode Islander from his peers. Slow afoot, he moved with surprising agility behind the plate and few runners dared test his powerful arm—maybe the best of his era. Pitchers loved the way he took charge and fans loved his hustle and trademark ball-pumping yell after every enemy strikeout.

Hartnett, nicknamed "Old Tomato Face" because of his florid complexion, was a legitimate "slugger" who seldom struck out—a six-time .300 hitter who belted 37 home runs in

"I rated Gabby the perfect catcher. He was super smart and nobody could throw with him. And he also was an outstanding clutch hitter." —*Joe McCarthy*

1930 but never fanned more than 77 times. Hartnett moved runners as adeptly as he produced runs, a combination that helped him win National League MVP honors in 1935 when he batted .344. The Cubs won a pennant that season, the third of four they won during Hartnett's career.

Hartnett, promoted to player-manager in 1938, delivered one of the great moments in baseball history—a late-season, ninth-inning drive into the looming darkness of Wrigley Field, the famed "Homer in the Gloamin'" that beat Pittsburgh and helped the Cubs secure a pennant. He also was behind the plate in the 1932 World Series when Babe Ruth hit his "called shot" homer and in the 1934 All-Star Game when Carl Hubbell struck out six straight American League sluggers.

Whether Hartnett, a six-time All-Star selection, was the equal of A.L. contemporaries Bill Dickey and Mickey Cochrane is debatable. But there's no denying his credentials: six-time leader in fielding percentage, .297 career average, 1,912 hits, 236 home runs and 1,179 RBIs.

HARTNETT

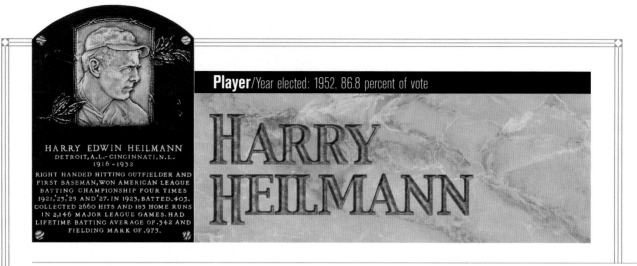

Player/Year elected: 1952, 86.8 percent of vote

HARRY HEILMANN

HARRY EDWIN HEILMANN
DETROIT, A.L.-CINCINNATI, N.L.
1916 - 1932
RIGHT HANDED HITTING OUTFIELDER AND
FIRST BASEMAN, WON AMERICAN LEAGUE
BATTING CHAMPIONSHIP FOUR TIMES
1921,'23,'25 AND '27. IN 1923, BATTED.403.
COLLECTED 2660 HITS AND 183 HOME RUNS
IN 2,146 MAJOR LEAGUE GAMES. HAD
LIFETIME BATTING AVERAGE OF .342 AND
FIELDING MARK OF .975.

Born: 8-3-1894, San Francisco, Calif. **Died:** 7-9-51 **Height/Weight:** 6-1/195 **Bats/Throws:** R/R **Primary position:** Outfield **Career statistics:** .342 avg., 2,660 hits, 1,291 runs, 183 HR, 1,539 RBIs **Teams:** Tigers 1914, 1916-29; Reds 1930, 1932 **Batting champion:** 1921, '23, '25, '27

He was slow afoot, his defense was sometimes suspect and his personality was overshadowed by Detroit outfield partner Ty Cobb. But, oh, could Harry Heilmann hit! He proved that over 17 major league seasons, competing with the likes of Cobb, Rogers Hornsby, George Sisler, Babe Ruth, Tris Speaker and Lou Gehrig for batting superiority in the 1920s.

"Old Slug," a nickname bestowed by Heilmann's Detroit teammates because of his lack of speed, was a 6-foot-1 righthanded hitter who slashed line drives around American League ballparks with alarming frequency from 1914-32. He attacked the pitch from a slight crouch and moved his hands up and down the bat, one of many hitting tricks he learned from Cobb in his formative years. Heilmann never ranked high on the home run charts (his best season was 21), but he consistently showed up among leaders in doubles and triples and he topped the 100-RBI plateau eight times in a productive nine-season span.

Heilmann's legacy will always be his bat and noth-

> "People nowadays just don't realize how great a hitter Harry was. Next to Rogers Hornsby, he was the best righthanded hitter of them all." — *Ty Cobb*

ing personifies hitting excellence more than the four A.L. batting titles he captured in the decade of the hitter — with lofty averages of .394 (1921), .403 (1923), .393 (1925) and .398 (1927). He was only nine well-placed hits (one in 1927, four in 1921 and '25) away from being a four-time .400 hitter and his career .342 average ranks among the top 10 all time. Heilmann cranked out 2,660 hits, the final 161 of which came with the Cincinnati Reds over his last two seasons.

The personable, outgoing Heilmann was a favorite of Detroit fans, who needed him as a buffer for their long-standing love/hate relationship with the controversial Cobb. Long after retirement in 1932, Heilmann remained a close personal friend of both Cobb and Ruth, two of the game's most colorful and divergent personalities. Heilmann, who never played on a Detroit pennant-winner, was not around when his Hall of Fame election was announced in 1952. He had died seven months earlier of lung cancer.

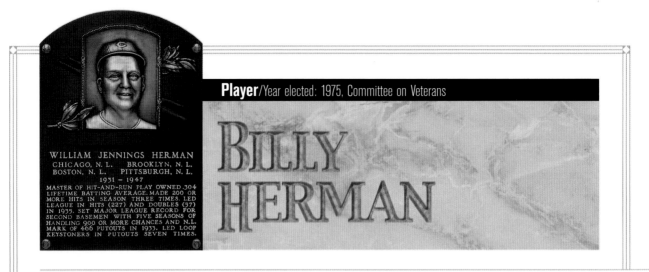

Player/Year elected: 1975, Committee on Veterans

BILLY HERMAN

Born: 7-7-09, New Albany, Ind. **Died:** 9-5-92 **Height/Weight:** 5-11/180 **Bats/Throws:** R/R **Primary position:** Second base
Career statistics: .304 avg., 2,345 hits, 1,163 runs **Teams:** Cubs 1931-41; Dodgers 1941-43, 1946; Braves 1946; Pirates 1947

Billy Herman was a con man, a sly, sneaky, ever-lurking practitioner of baseball subterfuge. Sign-stealing, trick plays, clever dekes of unsuspecting baserunners, psychological ploys—nothing escaped the game's most creative second baseman. Herman was to the middle infield of the Chicago Cubs what Ty Cobb had been to the offense of the Detroit Tigers—an inspirational warrior, always prepared for battle.

Casey Stengel called Herman "one of the two or three smartest players ever to come into the league" and the kid from Indiana spent 15 major league seasons proving him right. His ability to steal signs was uncanny and opponents were always mystified how Cubs hitters seemed to know what pitch was coming. It was no coincidence that Herman's ground balls consistently found vacated spots on his trademark hit-and-run plays.

The 5-foot-11, 180-pound righthanded hitter was not fast and didn't have much power, so he embraced bat control. Working from the No. 2 spot in Chicago's order, he sprayed hit-and-run singles to all fields, plugged gaps with see-ing-eye line drives and moved runners with unerring consis-tency. He hit 57 doubles in both 1935 and '36 en route to .341 and .334 averages and he parlayed his batting style into eight .300 seasons, 2,345 hits and a career .304 mark.

From 1932 through 1938, Herman and Billy Jurges anchored a middle infield that helped the Cubs win three National League pennants. When he was traded to Brooklyn early in the 1941 season, Dodgers boss Larry MacPhail declared, "I just bought a pennant" and then watched Herman mesh beautifully with young shortstop Pee Wee Reese as Brooklyn won its first flag in 21 years.

Herman, a five-time 100-run scorer who played in 10 All-Star Games and lost two seasons to World War II, was a serious student of the game who made up for lack of range with near-flawless positioning. The durable Herman topped N.L. second basemen seven times in putouts over a career that ended in 1947 as player-manager of the Pittsburgh Pirates.

> "If I were managing a team, I'd never let my catcher give signs with Herman on sec-ond base. I'd have some other player give them. But even then I couldn't bet Billy wouldn't steal them."
>
> —*Larry MacPhail*

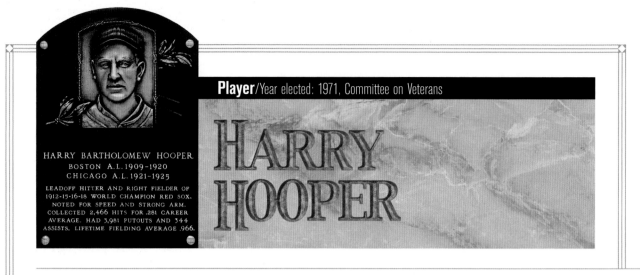

HARRY BARTHOLOMEW HOOPER
BOSTON A.L. 1909-1920
CHICAGO A.L. 1921-1925

LEADOFF HITTER AND RIGHT FIELDER OF
1912-15-16-18 WORLD CHAMPION RED SOX.
NOTED FOR SPEED AND STRONG ARM.
COLLECTED 2,466 HITS FOR .281 CAREER
AVERAGE. HAD 3,981 PUTOUTS AND 344
ASSISTS. LIFETIME FIELDING AVERAGE .966.

Player/Year elected: 1971, Committee on Veterans

HARRY HOOPER

Born: 8-24-1887, Bell Station, Calif. **Died:** 12-18-74 **Height/Weight:** 5-10/168 **Bats/Throws:** L/R **Primary position:** Right field
Career statistics: .281 avg., 2,466 hits, 1,429 runs, 375 steals **Teams:** Red Sox 1909-20; White Sox 1921-25

Former teammate Babe Ruth called him the best right fielder he had ever seen. John McGraw listed him on his all-time American League team. Harry Hooper might not have been blessed with superstar flair, but he did not lack for supporters who recognized such intangibles as grit, determination, intelligence and guile. Most of all he was a winner, that clutch performer who comes through when the game's on the line.

Hooper's value was magnified in four World Series with Boston—all of them winners. But the 5-foot-10, 168-pound Californian preferred to stay below the radar screen, which he managed to do for most of his 17 years with the Red Sox and Chicago White Sox. Hooper was the unsung leadoff man for 12 Boston seasons (1909-20) and a six-year member of an outstanding outfield that included Tris Speaker and Duffy Lewis.

The numbers don't knock you over. The five-time .300 hitter ended his career with 2,466 hits and a .281

"The best outfield trio I ever saw? That's easy. (Tris) Speaker, (Duffy) Lewis and Hooper— and the greatest of those was Hooper."

—Bill Carrigan, former Red Sox manager

average and he never led the A.L. in any statistical category. But he was adept at getting on base, a speedy and smart baserunner whose 1,429 career runs suggest he set the table well for teammates. A lefthanded hitter who sprayed the ball to all fields and seldom struck

out, Hooper made up for lack of power with quiet, team-first intangibles.

He was at his best in the large right field at Fenway Park, cutting off balls in the gap and gunning out runners with a rifle arm that produced 344 career assists. Hooper perfected a sliding catch that allowed him to jump quickly to his feet in throwing position, and teammates marveled at how effortlessly he handled Fenway's sometimes-brutal sunfield.

Everybody marveled in 1912 when Hooper made a World Series-saving Game 8 catch against McGraw's New York Giants—a home run-robbing barehanded grab as he tumbled into the stands. In 1915, he decided the Series against Philadelphia with a ninth-inning Game 5 homer—his second of the game.

ROGERS HORNSBY

NATIONAL LEAGUE BATTING CHAMPION
7 YEARS - 1920 TO 1925; 1928. LIFETIME
BATTING AVERAGE .358 HIGHEST IN
NATIONAL LEAGUE HISTORY. HIT .424 IN
1924, 20TH CENTURY MAJOR LEAGUE RECORD.
MANAGER 1926 WORLD CHAMPION ST. LOUIS
CARDINALS. MOST-VALUABLE-PLAYER
1925 AND 1929.

Player/Year elected: 1942, 78.1 percent of vote

ROGERS HORNSBY

Born: 4-27-1896, Winters, Tex. **Died:** 1-5-63 **Height/Weight:** 5-11/175 **B/T:** R/R **Primary position:** Second base **Career statistics:** .358 avg., 2,930 hits, 1,579 runs, 301 HR, 1,584 RBIs **Teams:** Cardinals 1915-26, 1933; Giants 1927; Braves 1928; Cubs 1929-32; Browns 1933-37 **Batting champion:** N.L., 1920, '21, '22, '23, '24, '25, '28 **HR champion:** N.L., 1922, '25 **Major awards:** League MVP, 1922, '25

"I don't like to sound egotistical, but every time I stepped up to the plate with a bat in my hands, I couldn't help but feel sorry for the pitcher." — *Rogers Hornsby*

As a man, Rogers Hornsby was truculent, aloof and a self-absorbed loner who always spoke his mind and seldom worried about the consequences. As a ballplayer, "Rajah" lived up to his nickname — proud, brash and majestic, especially when he stepped to the plate and let his never-silent bat do the talking.

Hornsby possessed cat-like reflexes and sprinter speed, qualities that doubled his impact as a devastating hitter and one of the best-fielding second basemen of the first half century. He stood deep in the box and rocketed line drives to all fields, a hitting style that helped him string together the best six-season offensive stretch in baseball history.

Playing for the St. Louis Cardinals, Hornsby posted averages of .370, .397, .401, .384, .424 (the highest average of the century) and .403 from 1920-25, winning six straight National League batting titles, two Triple Crowns and adulation as the greatest righthanded hitter of the modern era. He also led the N.L. in slugging and on-base percentage in each of those campaigns while topping the charts four times in RBIs and hits, three times in runs and twice in homers. Hornsby was, simply stated, prolific.

In 1926, he doubled as player/manager of the Cardinals and led them to their first N.L. pennant and World Series championship. But that was the season Hornsby's confrontational style wore thin and he was shipped to the New York Giants for Frank Frisch and Jimmy Ring in a shocking December trade that transformed him into a hired gun who could always be counted on to post big numbers and defy authority figures he seemed to resent.

Over the rest of Hornsby's 23-year playing career, he changed uniforms five times, won his seventh batting title (with the Boston Braves in 1928) and helped the Chicago Cubs win a 1929 pennant. He finished his career in 1937 after five years as player/manager of the lowly St. Louis Browns, retiring with 2,930 hits and the second-highest average in history (.358).

HORNSBY

Player/Year elected: 1969, Committee on Veterans

WAITE CHARLES HOYT
"SCHOOLBOY"

NEW YORK YANKEE PITCHER 1921-1930.
LIFETIME RECORD: 237 GAMES WON, 182
GAMES LOST, .566 AVERAGE, EARNED RUN
AVERAGE 3.59. PITCHED 3 GAMES IN 1921
WORLD SERIES AND GAVE NO EARNED RUNS.
ALSO PITCHED FOR BOSTON, DETROIT AND
PHILADELPHIA A.L. AND BROOKLYN,
NEW YORK AND PITTSBURGH N.L.

WAITE HOYT

Born: 9-9-1899, Brooklyn, N.Y. **Died:** 8-25-84 **Height/Weight:** 6-0/180 **Bats/Throws:** R/R **Position:** Pitcher **Career statistics:** 237-182, 3.59 ERA, 1,206 strikeouts **Teams:** Giants 1918, 1932; Red Sox 1919-20; Yankees 1921-30; Tigers 1930-31; Athletics 1931; Dodgers 1932, 1937-38; Pirates 1933-37

His name was articulate, just like the man with the clear resonant voice and Hall of Fame right arm. Waite Hoyt played baseball much like he attacked life—with equal parts style, talent, showmanship and fan-endearing vigor. Staff ace for the powerful Yankees, nightlife companion of Babe Ruth, vaudeville singer and part-time mortician, Hoyt carved a New York niche that was hard to ignore.

As a crafty righthander with broad shoulders and a boyish face, "Schoolboy" carved up hitters with an above-average fastball, good curve, changeup and pinpoint control. His motion, like his off-field demeanor, was relaxed and borderline arrogant, a style that only enhanced his fan appeal. A teammate of Ruth in 1919 at Boston, Hoyt rejoined the Bambino in 1921 and helped kickstart the Yankees' rise to championship prominence.

From 1921 through 1928, Hoyt won 145 games as the Yankees of Ruth, Lou Gehrig and Bob Meusel won six pennants and three World Series. He was the pitching centerpiece for the 1927 and '28 Bronx Bombers, carv-

ing out consecutive 22-7 and 23-7 marks for teams some rate as the best in history. The talented 6-footer posted a 6-4 record in Series play, working 27 innings in the 1921 classic without allowing an earned run.

The son of a minstrel singer, Hoyt was an interesting study. Brooklyn born, he talked like an Ivy League graduate. He had his father's theatrical flair and sang briefly on the vaudeville stage. He worked for several years in his father-in-law's funeral home, an occupation he considered for his post-baseball career. When snappy-dresser Hoyt wasn't in uniform, he often was with Ruth, entertaining patrons of New York's speakeasies and other prominent restaurants.

After being traded by the Yankees in 1930, Hoyt played for Detroit, Philadelphia, Brooklyn, the New York Giants and Pittsburgh, reaching another World Series with the A's in 1931. When he retired in 1938 with a 237-182 record, the always-colorful, outspoken Hoyt owned the distinction of having played for all three New York teams.

> **"It's great to be young and a Yankee!"**
>
> — *Waite Hoyt*

HOYT

CAL HUBBARD

ROBERT CAL HUBBARD
UMPIRE
AMERICAN LEAGUE 1936-1951
ONE OF MOST RESPECTED, EFFICIENT AND
AUTHORITATIVE UMPIRES IN HISTORY OF
MAJORS. GENTLE GIANT BOASTED SPECIAL
KNACK FOR DEALING WITH SITUATIONS ON
FIELD. WORKED FOUR WORLD SERIES AND
THREE ALL-STAR GAMES. SERVED AS LEAGUE'S
ASSISTANT UMPIRE SUPERVISOR IN 1952 AND AS
UMPIRE SUPERVISOR FROM 1953 TO 1969.

Born: 10-31-00, Keytesville, Mo. **Died:** 10-17-77 **Height/Weight:** 6-3/255 **Years umpired:** A.L., 1936-51; assistant to A.L. supervisor of umpires, 1952-53; A.L. supervisor of umpires, 1954-69 **All-Star Games:** 1939, '44, '49 **World Series:** 1938, '42, '46, '49

From football superstar to baseball arbiter, big Cal Hubbard walked an unusual path to two-sport glory. The man who created physical mayhem for nine National Football League seasons in the 1920s and '30s became the American League's most respected peacekeeper and umpiring supervisor for 34 more. That career double earned Hubbard distinction as the only member of both the Pro Football Hall of Fame and Baseball Hall of Fame.

In an era of 200-pound linemen, the 6-foot-3, 255-pound Missouri farmboy came out of Geneva College to rule the trenches for the New York Giants and Curly Lambeau's Green Bay Packers. As a strong, agile and surprisingly swift offensive blocker and defensive enforcer, Hubbard became the driving force of four NFL champions—a player Chicago coach George Halas called "the best lineman I ever saw."

But football was not his only passion. During the summers, Hubbard doubled as a minor league umpire, a hulking giant who could maintain peace with a warning glare and

"I always hated to throw a guy out of a game, but sometimes it was necessary to keep order. When it was time for a player to go, he went." —*Cal Hubbard*

run a smooth game with his even temper, strong sense of fairness and superior knowledge of the rules. In 1936, his worlds connected. Hubbard played his final NFL season and umpired his first of 16 A.L. campaigns.

Few players challenged "His Majesty," a regal and authoritative figure wherever he worked. He patiently listened to those who did, but woe to anyone who used profanity or carried a grudge from one game to the next. Hubbard, one of the most respected umpires of the post-World War II era, worked the first of four World Series in 1938 and received the first of three All-Star Game assignments a year later.

Hubbard's umpiring career came to a sudden halt in 1951 when a hunting accident damaged his eye. A.L. president Will Harridge, a long-time admirer, groomed Hubbard to succeed Tommy Connolly as supervisor of league umpires, a job he held from 1954-69. Hubbard, the fifth umpire selected to the Baseball Hall of Fame, also holds distinction as a member of college football's Hall of Fame.

HUBBARD

CARL HUBBELL
NEW YORK N.L. 1928-1943
HAILED FOR IMPRESSIVE PERFORMANCE IN
1934 ALL-STAR GAME WHEN HE STRUCK OUT
RUTH, GEHRIG, FOXX, SIMMONS AND CRONIN
IN SUCCESSION. NICKNAMED GIANTS'
MEAL-TICKET. WON 253 GAMES IN MAJORS,
SCORING 16 STRAIGHT IN 1936. COMPILED
STREAK OF 46⅓ SCORELESS INNINGS IN
1933. HOLDER OF MANY RECORDS.

Player/Year elected: 1947. 87.0 percent of vote

CARL HUBBELL

Born: 6-22-03, Carthage, Mo. **Died:** 11-21-88 **Height/Weight:** 6-0/170 **Bats/Throws:** R/L **Position:** Pitcher
Career statistics: 253-154, 2.98 ERA, 1,677 strikeouts **Teams:** Giants 1928-43 **Major awards:** N.L. MVP, 1933, '36

Early century hitters called it the "fadeaway." Batters in the 1920s and '30s labeled it the "butterfly" or "reverse curve." By any name and by all accounts, the two kinds of screwballs Carl Hubbell delivered to National League hitters with uncanny accuracy from 1928-43 were downright nasty—and borderline unhittable.

Amazingly, the tall, Lincolnesque lefthander did not deliver his first screwgie to a major leaguer until age 25, thanks to the perception among coaches and managers that the pitch required an unnatural twisting motion that would destroy his arm. But Hubbell, who was blessed with exceptionally long and flexible wrists, refused to give in to cynics and rode his so-called "gimmick pitch" all the way to the Hall of Fame.

The high-kicking, fast-working Hubbell, the "Meal Ticket" for a New York Giants staff that produced three pennants and one

> "Hubbell is the greatest pitcher in the league, but he presents no mystery to the onlooker. The source of his skill is ... the curveball setting up the screwball." —*Waite Hoyt*

World Series championship, undressed most of the game's top hitters with a sidearm screwball that faded down and away from righthanders and an overhand screwball that came in straight before suddenly dropping into oblivion. King Carl was especially tough on righthanders and his outstanding control allowed him to throw the pitch on any count.

The mild-mannered Hubbell, son of an Oklahoma pecan farmer, fashioned an impressive five-year run (1933-37) in which he was 115-50 and earned two MVP awards. In 1933, he posted a 23-12 record and 1.66 ERA before winning twice in a World Series victory over Washington. In 1936, he was 26-6 with a 2.31 ERA before splitting two decisions in a World Series loss to the New York Yankees.

Hubbell also recorded three of baseball's most memorable feats — an 18-inning 1-0 victory over the Cardinals in 1933; consecutive strikeouts of Babe Ruth, Lou Gehrig, Jimmie Foxx, Al Simmons and Joe Cronin in the 1934 All-Star Game; and a major league-record 24 straight wins in 1936-37. Hubbell, who worked in five All-Star Games, finally succumbed to the long-predicted arm trouble in 1943, but not before carving out 253 wins and a sparkling .622 career winning percentage.

MILLER HUGGINS

MILLER JAMES HUGGINS
1904–1929
MANAGER OF ST. LOUIS CARDINALS
AND NEW YORK YANKEES.
LED YANKEES TO 6 PENNANTS
IN 1921,1922,1923,1926,1927 AND 1928 AND
3 WORLD SERIES VICTORIES 1923,1927 AND 1928.
SECOND BASEMAN IN PLAYNG DAYS
WITH REDS AND CARDINALS, 1904-1916.

Born: 3-27-1879, Cincinnati, Ohio **Died:** 9-25-29 **Height/Weight:** 5-6/140 **Bats/Throws:** B/R **Primary position:** Second base

Career statistics: .265 avg., 1,474 hits **Teams played:** Reds 1904-09; Cardinals 1910-16 **Teams managed (1,413-1,134):** Cardinals 1913-17; Yankees 1918-29 **World Series titles:** 1923, '27, '28

He was little, a 5-foot-6, 140-pound miniature, but that didn't keep Miller Huggins from peeking into baseball heaven. "Hug" enjoyed a clear view of paradise from the New York dugout where he managed the 1920s Yankees, one of the most powerful offensive machines ever assembled. Small in stature and unsteady in health, Huggins started baseball's most celebrated franchise on its glorious road to success.

Huggins spent three decades battling long odds, ill health and bigger players who tried to intimidate him with flying spikes and challenges to his authority. He endured the former for 13 seasons as a peppery, .265-hitting second baseman and leadoff man for the Cincinnati Reds and St. Louis Cardinals, and the latter for five years as player-manager of the Cardinals and 12 more as boss of the Yankees.

"We had a few battles, but there was no man that I liked better in baseball. Whatever he said to me was for my own good." — *Babe Ruth*

Huggins, a gentleman and master psychologist who owned a law degree from his hometown-based University of Cincinnati, guided the lowly Cardinals to two third-place finishes. But he is best remembered as a key figure in the Yankees' rise to American League prominence and for his off-field battles with Yankees co-owner Tillinghast Huston and slugger Babe Ruth.

Huston, who had fought the hiring of Huggins in 1918, never missed a chance to second-guess him before selling his Yankee interests to Jacob Ruppert in 1922. Ruth tested, berated and embarrassed Huggins

HUGGINS

with his sharp tongue and refusal to follow team rules. In a celebrated 1925 showdown, Huggins earned the respect of his players by fining Ruth $5,000 and suspending him indefinitely. When Ruppert and general manager Ed Barrow backed Huggins, Ruth finally apologized and mended his ways.

Under Huggins, the Yankees compiled a 1,067-719 record, winning their first six pennants and three World Series before he died suddenly of blood poisoning in September 1929. Hug's 1927 "Murderer's Row" Bombers still rank among the greatest teams in history. Yankee Stadium's first center field monument was dedicated in 1932 to Huggins and later flanked by monuments to Ruth and Lou Gehrig.

Founder/Year elected: 1995, Committee on Veterans

WILLIAM HULBERT

Born: 10-23-1832, Burlington Flats, N.Y. **Died:** 4-10-1882 **Executive career:** Founder of National League, 1876; second N.L. president, 1877-81

It was William Hulbert's idea, an 1876 brainstorm born of frustration and competitive fire. The National League was conceived in the mind of the Chicago stockbroker and created through his diligence and bulldog determination. Little did Hulbert know that his new circuit would prosper and grow into the multi-million dollar major league baseball business that we know today.

The burly, mustachioed Hulbert was president of a staggering Chicago team in the loosely organized National Association in 1875 when he broke the league's "gentleman's agreement" by recruiting star pitcher Albert Spalding and three other players from the Boston franchise. A man of conviction and pride, he was fed up with his team's shoddy play as well as the Association's gambling, drinking and scheduling problems.

Anticipating expulsion from the Association, Hulbert organized a meeting of team owners at a New York hotel in February 1876 and proposed a new "National League" with standard player contracts, enforced rules, uniform schedules and civilized behavior. He nominated Hartford owner Morgan Bulkeley, a respected businessman and future U.S. senator, as the circuit's president and collaborated with Spalding on a constitution that remains the foundation for today's game.

Hulbert's White Stockings, who eventually would become the Cubs, won the N.L.'s first pennant with a 52-14 record, but the season ended on a sour note. Two franchises, the New York Mutuals and Philadelphia Athletics, refused to play out their schedule and Bulkeley stepped down, prompting Hulbert to take over as league president.

> "It always has been the contention of the author that the role of this strong man of the Middle West in baseball has been grossly underplayed. ..."
>
> —*Fred Lieb, in his book*
> *The Baseball Story*

He expelled the Mutuals and Athletics and, when four Louisville players were accused of throwing games in 1877, he banned them from baseball. Hulbert expelled Cincinnati in 1880 for refusing to ban the sale of beer on Sundays.

Hulbert, who is credited with organizing baseball's first umpiring staff, served as president through the 1881 season, coming down hard on the rowdyism that was so prevalent in the early game. He died of heart failure shortly before the 1882 campaign at age 49.

HULBERT

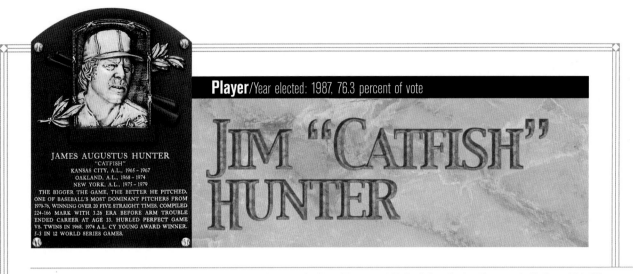

JIM "CATFISH" HUNTER

JAMES AUGUSTUS HUNTER
"CATFISH"
KANSAS CITY, A.L., 1965 – 1967
OAKLAND, A.L., 1968 – 1974
NEW YORK, A.L., 1975 – 1979
THE BIGGER THE GAME, THE BETTER HE PITCHED.
ONE OF BASEBALL'S MOST DOMINANT PITCHERS FROM
1970-76, WINNING OVER 20 FIVE STRAIGHT TIMES. COMPILED
224-166 MARK WITH 3.26 ERA BEFORE ARM TROUBLE
ENDED CAREER AT AGE 33. HURLED PERFECT GAME
VS. TWINS IN 1968. 1974 A.L. CY YOUNG AWARD WINNER.
5-3 IN 12 WORLD SERIES GAMES.

Born: 4-8-46, Hertford, N.C. **Died:** 8-30-99 **Height/Weight:** 6-0/195 **Bats/Throws:** R/R **Position:** Pitcher **Career statistics:** 224-166, 3.26 ERA, 2,012 strikeouts **Teams:** K. C. Athletics 1965-67; Oakland Athletics 1968-74; Yankees 1975-79 **Major awards:** A.L. Cy Young, 1974

He was a self-described "good 'ol country boy" from Hertford, N.C., a master craftsman who survived 15 years of bickering, battling and Bronx Zoo hijinks under the two most controversial owners in baseball history. Jim "Catfish" Hunter not only survived the craziness, he prospered. The talented righthander carved out a championship legacy for Oakland and New York teams that won six pennants and five World Series in the 1970s.

Opponents described Hunter as "a comfortable collar." His easy motion made a less-than-overpowering fastball deceptively fast and he mixed it masterfully with a slider and changeup. The 6-foot Hunter was an always-cool control artist who lived on the edge of the plate and never gave hitters what they expected. Up, down, in, out—pitches were always delivered to precise spots with plenty of movement and off-balance hitters were left scratching their heads.

To call Hunter's career colorful would be understatement. He was signed in 1964 at age 17 by Kansas City A's

"He's the Robin Roberts of this generation. He's a grinder. He's got a tremendous ERA. He's consistent. He's great to play behind because he gets rid of the ball." —*Dick Williams*

owner Charles O. Finley, who gave him the colorful nickname "Catfish." Hunter made his first national impact in 1968 when, now pitching for the A's in Oakland, he fired a perfect game at Minnesota. By 1970, Catfish was the ace of a young, bickering A's team that would win five division titles and three World Series over the next five years.

Hunter's five-year record included 106 regular-season wins, a 4-0 World Series mark, a 1974 Cy Young (25-12, 2.49 ERA) and recognition as the top righthander in baseball. After his big 1974 season, he celebrated by suing Finley for breach of contract and eventually was declared a free agent, prompting a multi-team bidding war that ended when Yankees owner George Steinbrenner gave him a five-year, $3.75 million deal.

Hunter hit the Big Apple with a vengeance in 1975, posting a 23-14 record. The rising Yankees, with Hunter in their rotation, rose up to win pennants in 1976, '77 and '78 and two World Series. Hunter retired in 1979 with a 224-166 record and 3.26 ERA.

MONTE IRVIN

MONFORD (MONTE) IRVIN
NEGRO LEAGUES 1937-1948
NEW YORK N.L., CHICAGO N.L.,
1949-1956
REGARDED AS ONE OF NEGRO LEAGUES' BEST
HITTERS. STAR SLUGGER OF NEWARK EAGLES
WON 1946 NEGRO LEAGUE BATTING TITLE.
LED N.L. IN RUNS BATTED IN AND PACED
"MIRACLE" GIANTS IN HITTING IN 1951
DRIVE TO PENNANT. BATTED .458 AND
STOLE HOME IN 1951 WORLD SERIES.

Born: 2-25-19, Columbia, Ala. **Height/Weight:** 6-1/195 **Bats/Throws:** R/R **Primary position:** Outfield **Career statistics:** .293 avg., 731 hits, 99 HR, 443 RBIs **Major league teams:** Giants 1949-55; Cubs 1956 **Negro League teams (1937-48):** Newark Eagles

The call came 10 years late, but that didn't keep Monte Irvin from providing a tantalizing glimpse of what might have been. He batted .299 in his first full major league season, played a leading role in baseball's most celebrated pennant race a year later and turned in a scintillating World Series performance. From Negro League superstar to 30-year-old rookie, Irvin's career transformation was as graceful as his outfield play.

A two-time Negro National League batting champion with the Newark Eagles, Irvin was Branch Rickey's leading candidate to break baseball's color barrier in the early 1940s. He seemed to be a perfect fit—fast, with a lightning-quick righthanded swing and a powerful arm that served him well at either shortstop or in the outfield; articulate, even-tempered and polished, a two-year college man with an easy personality.

Jackie Robinson eventually was chosen for the historic task and Irvin got lost in the integration shuffle, watching former infield mate Larry Doby and other younger blacks sign major league contracts ahead of him. The 6-foot-1, 195-pounder finally was signed in 1949 by the New York Giants—at age 30—and went on to bat .293 over eight seasons, seven for Giants

teams that won two pennants and one World Series.

New Yorkers who recall the Giants' incredible mad-dash 1951 pennant run also remember Irvin, a one-man army, lashing line drives into gaps and important home runs out of the Polo Grounds. Not only did he bat .312 and

> "Monte was the best all-round player I have ever seen. As great as he was in 1951, he was twice that good 10 years earlier in the Negro Leagues."
>
> —*Roy Campanella*

drive in a league-leading 121 runs, he hit .458 in a World Series loss to the Yankees and executed a memorable Game 1 steal of home.

Irvin also will be remembered as the mentor for young Giants center fielder Willie Mays and the left fielder in baseball's first all-black outfield with Mays and Hank Thompson. A severely broken ankle sidelined Irvin in 1952 and affected him for the rest of his career, although he did bat .329 with 97 RBIs in 1953. He retired in 1956 at age 37.

IRVIN

REGINALD MARTINEZ JACKSON
"MR. OCTOBER"
KANSAS CITY, A.L., 1967
OAKLAND, A.L., 1968-1975, 1987
BALTIMORE, A.L., 1976
NEW YORK, A.L., 1977-1981
CALIFORNIA, A.L., 1982-1986
EXCITING PERFORMER WHO PLAYED FOR 11 DIVISION WINNERS AND
FOUND SPECIAL SUCCESS IN WORLD SERIES SPOTLIGHT WITH 10 HOME
RUNS, 24 RBI'S AND .357 BATTING AVERAGE IN 27 GAMES. IN 1977
SERIES, HIT RECORD 5 HOMERS, 4 OF THEM CONSECUTIVE, INCLUDING
3 IN ONE GAME ON 3 FIRST PITCHES OFF 3 DIFFERENT HURLERS.
MAMMOTH CLOUT MARKED 1971 ALL-STAR GAME. 563 HOMERS RANK
6TH ON ALL-TIME LIST. A.L. MVP, 1973.

Player/Year elected: 1993, 93.6 percent of vote, first ballot

REGGIE JACKSON

Born: 5-18-46, Wyncote, Pa. **Height/Weight:** 6-0/200 **Bats/Throws:** L/L **Primary position:** Outfield **Career statistics:** .262 avg., 2,584 hits, 1,551 runs, 563 HR, 1,702 RBIs **Teams:** Kansas City Athletics 1967; Oakland Athletics 1968-75, 1987; Orioles 1976; Yankees 1977-81; Angels 1982-86 **HR champion:** 1973, '75, tied, '80, tied, '82, tied **Major awards:** A.L. MVP, 1973

He was charming and belligerent; cocky and self-effacing; articulate and crude; enigmatic and straightforward. You didn't just watch Reggie Jackson, you experienced him. The love-hate bond that fans, players and owners formed with the complex, often-contradictory kid from Wyncote, Pa., lasted 21 years, surviving 563 home runs and at least that many well-publicized tantrums.

Jackson, muscular and with an all-or-nothing corkscrew lefthanded swing, enjoyed several baseball lives. He was the heart and soul of an Oakland team that won three straight World Series (1972, '73 and '74); the straw that stirred a Yankees team that won two straight Series (1977 and '78); and "Mr. October," who rose to his greatest heights in the 11 League Championship Series and five World Series in which he hit 17 home runs for the A's, Yankees and California Angels.

The bottom line on Jackson was drama — and emotion, which he kept upfront for all the paying customers to see. A Jackson home run was majestic and he exulted accordingly, with a slow, measured trot.

"If I played in New York, they'd name a candy bar after me." — *Reggie Jackson, 1975*

Jackson strikeouts (all 2,597 of them) were exciting and he fumed with demonstrative vigor. Jackson's right field defense was erratic, his baserunning was daring but careless and his battles with owners, managers, teammates and even himself were legendary.

But there's no denying the charisma, which the New York media devoured for five years like a hungry shark. And there's no denying the talent, which produced at least a share of four American League home run titles, six 100-RBI seasons, 12 All-Star Game appearances and a 1973 MVP award — a campaign in which he led Oakland to its second straight championship with a .293 average, 32 home runs and 117 RBIs.

Game 6 of the 1977 World Series was typical Jackson, who had endured a season of feuding with Yankees manager Billy Martin and several teammates, especially catcher Thurman Munson. Jackson, who already had hit two Series homers, dramatically powered three more — on consecutive pitches — in a Series-clinching victory over the Los Angeles Dodgers.

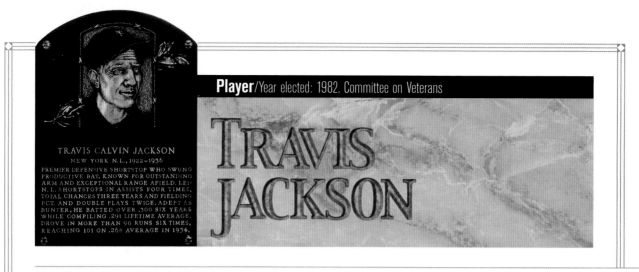

TRAVIS JACKSON

TRAVIS CALVIN JACKSON
NEW YORK N.L., 1922–1936
PREMIER DEFENSIVE SHORTSTOP WHO SWUNG
PRODUCTIVE BAT. KNOWN FOR OUTSTANDING
ARM AND EXCEPTIONAL RANGE AFIELD. LED
N.L. SHORTSTOPS IN ASSISTS FOUR TIMES,
TOTAL CHANCES THREE YEARS AND FIELDING
PCT. AND DOUBLE PLAYS TWICE. ADEPT AS
BUNTER, HE BATTED OVER .300 SIX YEARS
WHILE COMPILING .291 LIFETIME AVERAGE.
DROVE IN MORE THAN 90 RUNS SIX TIMES,
REACHING 101 ON .268 AVERAGE IN 1934.

Born: 11-2-03, Waldo, Ark. **Died:** 7-27-87 **Height/Weight:** 5-11/160 **Bats/Throws:** R/R **Primary position:** Shortstop
Career statistics: .291 avg., 1,768 hits, 929 RBIs **Teams:** Giants 1922-36

They called him "Stonewall" and that's exactly what Travis Jackson was for 15 major league seasons. Quietly, smoothly and without your typical New York fanfare, the skinny kid from Waldo, Ark., provided

"Jackson is at once the delight and despair of every manager other than John McGraw. It's a delight to see him play, but he makes you despair of ever having a shortstop like him." — *Bucky Harris*

the game and inspirational hustler who helped the Giants win four pennants and a 1933 World Series championship.

Jackson was a righthanded pull hitter who bypassed the generally preferred wagon-tongue bat for a 36-ouncer that he whipped through the strike zone quickly and with force. He learned to yank the inside pitch down the short left field line at the Polo Grounds and hit 21 home runs in 1929, a surprising total for a shortstop.

The skinny 5-foot-11, 160-pounder was a clutch hitter who topped .300 six times and ballooned to a lofty .339 in 1930, but he also was sidelined throughout his career by bad knees and such illnesses as mumps, influenza and an appendicitis. The knees got so bad in 1935 that he was moved to third base where he finished his career the following season for the N.L. champions.

a nearly impenetrable barrier on the left side of the Giants infield. John McGraw liked Jackson enough to name him team captain and National League rival Charlie Grimm raved about "the finest arm I ever saw on a shortstop."

That arm and a productive bat are what set Jackson apart from other shortstops of his era (1922-36). He played deep, increasing his already good range, and consistently gunned batters down from the hole and the edge of the outfield grass. Jackson had quick hands and led N.L. shortstops in fielding percentage two times, but he also was a college graduate, student of

But he is best remembered as McGraw's last great shortstop and a member of a Hall of Fame infield that included Bill Terry, Fred Lindstrom and second basemen Frank Frisch and Rogers Hornsby. Jackson retired with a .291 average, 1,768 hits and 929 RBIs, 101 of which came in 1934 when he played in baseball's second All-Star Game.

JACKSON

FERGUSON ARTHUR JENKINS
PHILADELPHIA, N.L., 1965-1966
CHICAGO, N.L., 1966-1973, 1982-1983
TEXAS, A.L., 1974-1975, 1978-1981
BOSTON, A.L., 1976-1977
CANADA'S FIRST HALL-OF-FAMER. 284-226
LIFETIME WITH 3,192 STRIKEOUTS AND 3.34 ERA
DESPITE PLAYING 12 OF HIS 19 YEAR CAREER IN
HITTERS' BALLPARKS-WRIGLEY FIELD AND FENWAY
PARK. WON 20 GAMES 7 SEASONS, INCLUDING 6
CONSECUTIVE, 1967 - 1972. CY YOUNG AWARD
WINNER, 1971. TRADEMARKS WERE PINPOINT CONTROL
AND CHANGING SPEEDS.

Player/Year elected: 1991, 75.4 percent of vote

FERGUSON JENKINS

Born: 12-13-43, Chatham, Ontario **Height/Weight:** 6-5/210 **Bats/Throws:** R/R **Position:** Pitcher **Career statistics:** 284-226, 3.34 ERA, 3,192 strikeouts **Teams:** Phillies 1965-66; Cubs 1966-73, 1982-83; Rangers 1974-75, 1978-81; Red Sox 1976-77 **Major awards:** N.L. Cy Young, 1971

The long right arm, an extension of Ferguson Jenkins' 6-foot-5, 210-pound body, shot forward from a smooth, easy motion—as if to reach out and touch someone. It never did, but the pitches it delivered over 19 major league seasons touched the hearts of fans in four cities where Jenkins worked. The deceptive motion was a calling card for one of baseball's ultimate craftsmen, a Canadian-born control artist with a tireless enthusiasm and rubber arm.

Jenkins was a master at changing speeds and painting corners, not unlike contemporary righthander Catfish Hunter. Not blessed with Bob Gibson-like velocity, he would spot his fastball and move in and out with curves and sliders, always thrown at different speeds. Jenkins always worked ahead in the count, seldom walked batters and dared hitters to take their best shot, which often resulted in high home run totals.

Managers learned to live with the home runs. In a six-season span from 1967-72 while pitching for mediocre Chicago teams at hitter-friendly Wrigley Field, Jenkins

"Fergie is still the best pitcher in baseball. They can talk about Tom Seaver all they want, but I'll take Fergie." —*Ken Holtzman, 1974*

won 20 or more games every year, topped 300 innings four times and led the National League three times in complete games. He was at his best in 1971 when he posted a 24-13 record, 30 complete games and 325 innings—earning the N.L. Cy Young Award.

But Jenkins' control didn't extend to his salary complaints, which were delivered fast and furious to the chagrin of Cubs management. When he slipped to 14-16 in 1973, the Cubs, apparently convinced he was nearing the end at age 30, traded him to Texas and watched as he posted a 25-12 record for the Rangers. Jenkins won 17 the next season for Texas and 110 over his final nine, which included a two-year stop in Boston and returns to both the Rangers and Cubs.

When he retired in 1983, the 40-year-old from Chatham, Ontario, had pitched 4,500 2/3 innings while compiling a 284-226 record and 3.34 ERA—outstanding figures considering he never pitched in a postseason game.

HUGHIE JENNINGS
OF BALTIMORE'S FAMOUS OLD ORIOLES,
HE WAS ONE OF THE GAME'S MIGHTY
MITES. A STAR SHORTSTOP HE WAS A
CONSTANT THREAT AT THE PLATE.
ONCE HIT .397. PILOTED DETROIT
TO THREE CHAMPIONSHIPS.

Player/Year elected: 1945, Committee on Old-Timers

HUGHIE JENNINGS

Born: 4-2-1869, Pittston, Pa. **Died:** 2-1-28 **Height/Weight:** 5-9/165 **Bats/Throws:** R/R **Primary position:** Shortstop
Career statistics: .312 avg., 1,526 hits, 359 steals **Teams played:** Louisville (A.A.) 1891; Louisville 1892-93; Baltimore 1893-1898, 1899; Brooklyn 1899-1900, 1903; Phillies 1901-02; Tigers 1907, 1909, 1912, 1918 **Teams managed (1,184-995):** Tigers 1907-20; Giants 1924-25

He is remembered for the "Ee-yah" battle cries he screetched from the third base coaching box—both arms raised skyward, one leg lifted—in celebration of a Detroit hit or run. But the colorful managing style Hughie Jennings employed over a 14-year tenure with the Tigers was merely a byproduct of the way he had played the game for 12 full major league seasons. Brash, loud, creative and always entertaining, Jennings was the 1890s-era shortstop and captain of the rough-and-tumble Baltimore Orioles.

Traded to the Orioles by Louisville in 1893, third-year major leaguer Jennings joined forces with future Hall of Famers John McGraw, Wilbert Robinson, Willie Keeler and Joe Kelley to form the nucleus of one of the most colorful teams ever assembled. Red-haired, freckle-faced and only 160 pounds, the smiling Pennsylvanian didn't fit the profile of the brawling Orioles—talented but unscrupulous gamesmen who spiked, tripped, grabbed, roughed up and bullied opponents.

With McGraw and Jennings as their ringleaders, the

"No one compared with Hughie as a shortstop." —*Honus Wagner*

Orioles won pennants in 1894, '95 and '96 and a Temple Cup playoff in '97. The 5-foot-9 Jennings led National League shortstops in fielding average all four of those seasons, stunning everyone with a cat-like quickness and sure-handed style that set a standard for the position.

As a young hitter, the righthanded Jennings had a tendency to step in the bucket. But McGraw backed him up to a wall, pitched to him and watched him develop into an outstanding contact man who posted consecutive averages of .335, .386, .401, .355 and .328. Three times he reached the 100-RBI plateau; five times he scored 100 runs. Fearless, he was hit by 49 pitches in 1896, the same season he stole a career-high 70 bases.

Jennings, Keeler and Kelley moved to Brooklyn in 1899 and the Superbas won consecutive pennants. Jennings finished as a full-time player two years later in Philadelphia, but he made occasional appearances in later years while managing the Tigers. A future lawyer, Jennings retired with a .312 average and 1,526 hits.

Executive/Year elected: 1937, Centennial Commission

BAN JOHNSON

Born: 1-5-1864, Norwalk, Ohio **Died:** 3-28-31 **Executive career:** President of Western League, 1893-1900; founder American League, 1901; president of American League, 1901-27; leader of the three-man National Commission, baseball's ruling body, 1903-20

Friends marveled at his consuming work ethic and tunnel-vision dedication; enemies complained about his tempestuous, hard-edged personality and dictatorial manner. Love him or hate him, American League founder Byron Bancroft Johnson was baseball's driving force for a quarter century, the man who gave it status as America's National Pastime.

Tall, husky and chesty, Johnson could be intimidating and confrontational. He was long on bluster and short on patience, a man who bullied opponents and usually got his way. An energetic, principled visionary who never backed down, Johnson was a tireless promoter of the game and defender of its integrity — the perfect leader to guide it into the 20th century.

A graduate of Marietta College and former Cincinnati sportswriter, Johnson built the old Western League into an eight-team circuit that eventually challenged the "major league" monopoly of the long-established National League. He claimed major league status for his renamed American League in 1901 and waged a two-plus-year war, eventually bringing N.L. owners to their knees. When peace prevailed in

"Ban Johnson was to me the most unforgettable character I've ever known. ... no person in all the history of the game has done as much to perpetuate baseball as our great national pastime." — *Billy Evans, umpire and executive*

Ban Johnson, standing (right).

1903, baseball emerged as two separate leagues operating under a three-man commission—A.L. president Johnson, N.L. president Harry Pulliam and Cincinnati owner Garry Herrmann.

Johnson dominated the commission, and baseball, for the next 20 years, carving out a legacy of growth and prosperity. His word was law and he brought discipline and dignity to the game, prohibiting liquor, profanity and any semblance of rowdyism. He gave umpires total authority and promoted baseball as a friendly entertain-ment option. The World Series became an annual insti-tution and players like Walter Johnson, Ty Cobb and Babe Ruth became national figures.

The first chink in Johnson's power base occurred in 1919, when the "Black Sox" World Series scandal taint-ed the game and led to the 1921 installation of Kenesaw Mountain Landis as its first commissioner. With Landis entrenched as the game's new "dictator," Johnson's power eroded further, leading to his bitter 1927 retirement as A.L. president.

JUDY JOHNSON

WILLIAM JULIUS JOHNSON
"JUDY"
NEGRO LEAGUES 1923-1937
CONSIDERED BEST THIRD BASEMAN OF HIS
DAY IN NEGRO LEAGUES. OUTSTANDING AS
FIELDER AND EXCELLENT CLUTCH HITTER
WHO BATTED OVER .300 MOST OF CAREER.
HELPED HILLDALE TEAM WIN THREE FLAGS
IN ROW, 1923-24-25. ALSO PLAYED FOR
1935 CHAMPION PITTSBURGH CRAWFORDS.

Born: 10-26-00, Snow Hill, Md. **Died:** 6-15-89 **Height/Weight:** 5-11/150 **Bats/Throws:** R/R **Primary position:** Third base
Teams (1918, 1921-37): Bacharach Giants; Hilldale Daisies; Homestead Grays; Pittsburgh Crawfords

He picked off hot-corner smashes with Pie Traynor-like efficiency and sprayed line drives around ballparks with Paul Waner-like force. But few fans got to witness the wonder of William "Judy" Johnson. As the proud and premier third baseman of the 1920s and '30s Negro Leagues, Johnson quietly performed his magic in baseball obscurity.

Major league scouts and barnstormers attested to Johnson's lightning-quick hands, powerful arm and dangerous righthanded bat, which always produced averages in the mid-300s. The shy 5-foot-11, 150-pounder seldom hit for power, but he was recognized as one of the most intelligent hitters of the Negro circuits, a patient and scientific slasher who was at his best with the game on the line.

Johnson was not fast, but he ran bases with the same reliable instincts that made him a popular model and steadying influence for younger players. Midway through a career that started with the Philadelphia-based Hilldale club, he became player-manager of the 1930 Homestead Grays (Josh Gibson's first team) and in 1932 joined the famed Pittsburgh Crawfords, where he captained a team that included future Hall of Famers Gibson, Satchel Paige and Cool Papa Bell.

Johnson, born in Snow Hill, Md., was a year-round player — summers in the Negro Leagues, winters with hotel teams in Florida and the Cuban Winter League. He also played against such barnstormers as Rogers Hornsby, Jimmie Foxx and Babe Ruth, never failing to impress.

Johnson's career was filled with terrible fields, inferior equipment, long trips in crowded cars and third-rate hotels, but he never complained.

It was with Hilldale in 1924 that Johnson played in the first official Negro World Series against the Kansas City Monarchs, batting .364 in a losing cause. He also played for pennant-winners with the Crawfords before retiring in 1937. In 1954, he became a scout for the Philadelphia Athletics, a major league association that had eluded him throughout his career, and he later scouted for the Braves and Phillies.

> **"No matter how much the pressure, no matter how important the play or the throw or the hit, Judy could do it when it counted."**
>
> —*Cool Papa Bell, The Negro Leagues Book*

JOHNSON

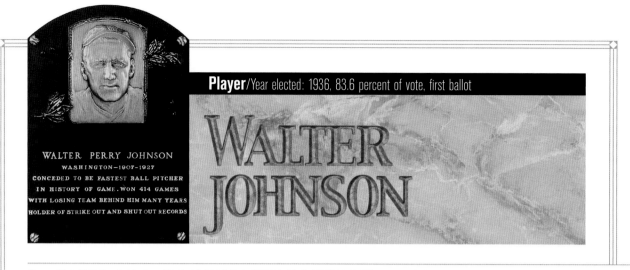

WALTER PERRY JOHNSON
WASHINGTON—1907-1927
CONCEDED TO BE FASTEST BALL PITCHER
IN HISTORY OF GAME. WON 414 GAMES
WITH LOSING TEAM BEHIND HIM MANY YEARS
HOLDER OF STRIKE OUT AND SHUT OUT RECORDS

Player/Year elected: 1936, 83.6 percent of vote, first ballot

WALTER JOHNSON

Born: 11-6-1887, Humboldt, Kan. **Died:** 12-10-46 **Height/Weight:** 6-1/200 **Bats/Throws:** R/R **Position:** Pitcher
Career statistics: 417-279, 2.17 ERA, 3,509 strikeouts **Teams:** Senators 1907-27 **Major awards:** Chalmers MVP 1913; League MVP 1924

He was the hardest-throwing pitcher of his era, the most successful fireballer in major league history. Walter Johnson was to power pitching what contemporary Ty Cobb was to bat control. And every time Johnson delivered his fastball to overmatched hitters, he delivered a dose of much-needed pride to the fans of an overmatched franchise.

The 6-foot-1, 200-pound Johnson used that fastball and pinpoint control to carve out 417 victories for the Washington Senators, a career total that ranks second all time to Cy Young. He sling-shotted his heat homeward with a long right arm from an exaggerated sidearm motion, mesmerizing befuddled hitters. For the first 15 years of his 21 major league seasons, that fastball was his only pitch—an incredible testimony to the outstanding 2.17 ERA Johnson compiled over 5,914 1/3 innings.

Johnson's success can be measured against two additional barriers that would have been the demise of many pitchers: First, he piled up his wins for the lowly Senators, a team that did not taste success until 1924

"He was the only pitcher I ever faced who made the ball whistle. You could actually hear it as it crossed the plate. Sounded like a bullet from a rifle, sort of a zing, and it made you shaky in the knees." — *Ty Cobb*

and '25—when Johnson was approaching age 40. Second, the "Big Train" never deviated from a gentlemanly demeanor that kept him from brushing back aggressive hitters, allowing them a sense of security they did not enjoy against more mean-spirited pitchers of the era.

Those handicaps never seemed to matter. Fourth-year man Johnson recorded the first of 10 straight 20-win seasons in 1910 and topped the 30 plateau in 1912 and '13—a campaign in which he recorded a 1.14 ERA. From 1910-19, he led the American League nine times in strikeouts, five times in innings and four times in ERA while pitching 78 of his record 110 career shutouts.

Johnson, baseball's first 3,000-strikeout pitcher and, amazingly, a 1-0 loser 26 times, was nearing the end of his career when the Senators finally won their first two pennants. His Game 7 relief win in 1924 gave the city its first championship and he won two games in a losing 1925 Series effort. Johnson was one of five charter members of the Hall of Fame's first class in 1936.

JOHNSON

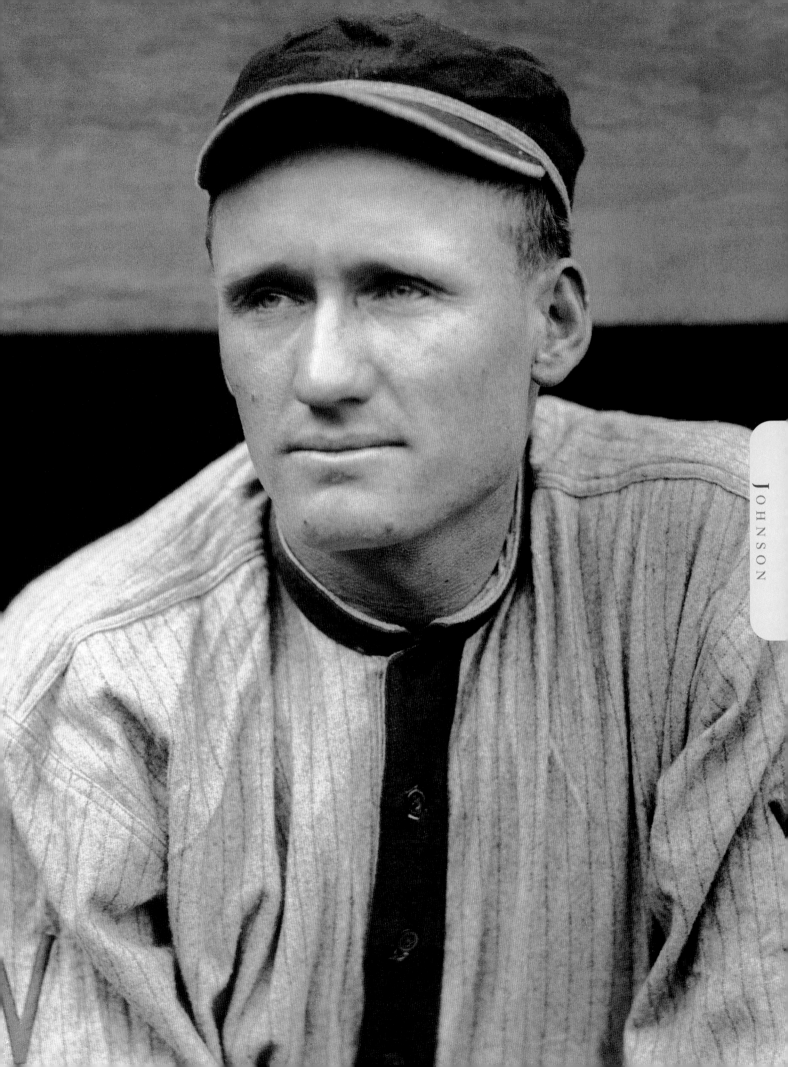

Player/Year elected: 1978, Committee on Veterans

ADDIE JOSS

ADRIAN (ADDIE) JOSS
CLEVELAND A.L., 1902-1910
ONE OF PREMIER PITCHERS OF AMERICAN
LEAGUE'S FIRST DECADE. SPEED, SHARP
CONTROL HELPED HIM TO WIN 20 OR MORE
GAMES FOUR SEASONS IN A ROW. POSTED
LEAGUE-LEADING 27 VICTORIES AND THREE
ONE-HITTERS IN 1907. HURLED PERFECT
GAME IN 1908. HAD ANOTHER NO-HITTER
IN 1910. CREDITED WITH 45 SHUTOUTS
AMONG HIS 160 CAREER VICTORIES.

Born: 4-12-1880, Woodland, Wis. **Died:** 4-14-11 **Height/Weight:** 6-3/185 **Bats/Throws:** R/R **Position:** Pitcher
Career statistics: 160-97, 1.89 ERA, 920 strikeouts **Teams:** Indians 1902-10

He arrived in 1902 with storybook flair and departed in tragedy nine years later, breaking the heart of a city. In between, Addie Joss was really something—a pinwheeling, side-arming pitching machine that won both games and fans with startling consistency. Almost a century later, Joss remains a legendary figure in Cleveland and one of the great "what if" stories in baseball history.

In his all-too-short career, the 6-foot-3 righthander compiled a 160-97 record and incredible 1.89 ERA while matching pitches with the likes of Cy Young, Ed Walsh and Walter Johnson. He threw a "smoking fastball" and infamous "jump ball" that hitters claimed would dip, level off and dip again— pitches complicated by his pivoting, back-to-the-batter motion and sidearm delivery.

Some hitters said Joss "took the ball from his hip pocket" and others merely complained about having to pick up the BBs he threw from a tangle of long arms and legs. Whatever the perception, Joss was difficult to hit and always around

the plate, allowing fewer than a runner per inning during his career. In 2,327 innings, he surrendered only 19 home runs while completing 234 of 260 career starts and pitching 45 shutouts.

Cleveland fans got their first look at Joss in April 1902 when he fanned four of the first six St. Louis batters he faced and pitched a one-hit shutout, allowing only a scratch single by Jesse Burkett. He won 17 games as a rookie, 18 as a sophomore and topped the 20-win plateau from 1905 through 1908. Joss was 24-11 in '08 with a 1.16 ERA and he recorded the second perfect game of the century—a classic 1-0 win over Chicago's Walsh, who struck out 15 Indians.

Joss, who hailed from the Wisconsin woodlands, pitched his second career no-hitter in 1910. But during the following spring training, he fainted one day on the bench, a problem diagnosed as pleurisy. Joss was sent home to Toledo where he died 11 days later of tubercular meningitis—two days after his 31st birthday.

> "When you talk about pitchers in Cleveland, there will be three names that come to mind immediately: Cy Young, Bob Feller and Addie Joss." —*Lee Allen, Hall of Fame historian*

JOSS

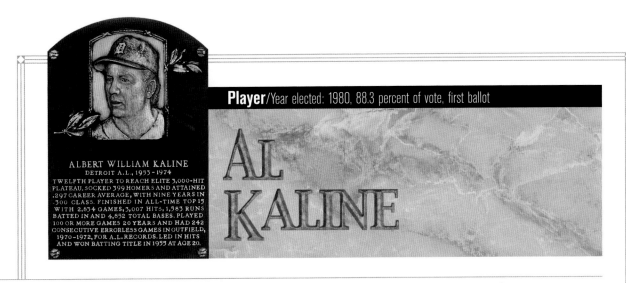

ALBERT WILLIAM KALINE
DETROIT A.L., 1953-1974
TWELFTH PLAYER TO REACH ELITE 3,000-HIT
PLATEAU. SOCKED 399 HOMERS AND ATTAINED
.297 CAREER AVERAGE, WITH NINE YEARS IN
.300 CLASS. FINISHED IN ALL-TIME TOP 15
WITH 2,834 GAMES, 3,007 HITS, 1,583 RUNS
BATTED IN AND 4,852 TOTAL BASES. PLAYED
100 OR MORE GAMES 20 YEARS AND HAD 242
CONSECUTIVE ERRORLESS GAMES IN OUTFIELD,
1970-1972, FOR A.L. RECORDS. LED IN HITS
AND WON BATTING TITLE IN 1955 AT AGE 20.

AL KALINE

Born: 12-19-34, Baltimore, Md. **Height/Weight:** 6-2/180 **Bats/Throws:** R/R **Primary position:** Right field **Career statistics:** .297 avg., 3,007 hits, 1,622 runs, 399 HR, 1,583 RBIs **Teams:** Tigers 1953-74 **Batting champion:** A.L., 1955

He guarded the right field tradition at Tiger Stadium like a jealous lover, much as former Detroit icon Ty Cobb had done more than four decades earlier. What Al Kaline might have lacked in color and charisma he more than made up for with hard work, persistence and all-around consistency. Kaline was the battery that juiced the Tigers' attack for 22 seasons and one of the premier defensive outfielders of the 1950s and '60s.

Kaline was a graceful stylist who made the game look easy. Shy and unsmiling off the field, Kaline the player spoke volumes with an aggressive, always-heady performance that reflected an intense desire to succeed. The consistency that became a Kaline trademark was best reflected by the way he cut down runners with a strong, accurate arm and the diving, wall-banging defense that earned him 10 Gold Gloves and numerous stays on the disabled list.

Kaline, a righthanded hitter who made his big-league debut at the tender age of 18, used a feet-apart, Joe DiMaggio-like stance and lightning-quick wrists to slash line drives to all fields. He provided himself a lofty career standard in 1955 when, at age 20, he hit .340 and became the youngest batting champion in history. That early success saddled Kaline with great expectations he struggled throughout his career to fulfill, but a final .297 average, 399 home runs and 3,007 hits would suggest he more than succeeded. So would his reputation as one of the most feared clutch hitters of his era.

Despite a long list of debilitating injuries, Kaline never backed off his aggressive playing style and the fans loved him for it. They also appreciated a man who achieved career success despite a childhood operation that forced him to compete with a deformed left foot. Kaline played in 16 All-Star Games but only one World Series—a 1968 classic in which he batted .379 and helped the Tigers post a seven-game victory over the St. Louis Cardinals.

"I wasn't meant to be a superstar. I'm no Willie Mays or Mickey Mantle." —*Al Kaline*

Copyright 1887.
Goodwin & Co.

New York's

OLD JUDGE CIGARETTES Goodwin & Co.,
New York.

Player/Year elected: 1964, Committee on Veterans

TIM KEEFE

Born: 1-1-1857, Cambridge, Mass. **Died:** 4-23-33 **Height/Weight:** 5-10/185 **Bats/Throws:** R/R **Position:** Pitcher
Career statistics: 342-225, 2.62 ERA, 2,564 strikeouts **Teams:** Troy 1880-82; New York (A.A.) 1883-84; New York 1885-89, 1891; New York (P.L.) 1890; Philadelphia 1891-93

It was called a "slow-ball" by 1880s-era writers and fans, a softly thrown pitch that tantalized overeager hitters. For Tim Keefe, it was simply a "change of pace" that the underhanding righthander used to frustrate opponents for 14 major league seasons. Not only was "Sir Timothy" the pioneer of off-speed deliveries, he was a master strategist who enjoyed status as the game's second 300-game winner.

The 5-foot-10, 185-pound Keefe was strong enough to overmatch many of the era's contact hitters with his fastball and curve, but it was his changeup, thrown with a fastball motion, that helped him become a big winner. He posted 32 or more wins every season from 1883-88 while pitching for New York teams in the American Association and National League, completing 333 of 343 starts and never falling below 400 innings.

Keefe was a quiet workhorse known for his bushy mustache and attention-shunning, workmanlike manner. To fans and teammates, he was a highly regarded gentleman. To opponents, he was a meticulous crafts-

> "Keefe was one of the first pitchers celebrated for his head work. Teaming with Smiling Mickey Welch, he assured the Giants of a well-pitched game almost every day."
>
> —*Lee Allen, Hall of Fame historian*

man who exploited their weaknesses. The Massachusetts-born Irishman carved up hitters with his masterful control and became the first pitcher to top 300 strikeouts three times.

Keefe, who began his career in 1880 at Troy, was best known as the pitching partner of Mickey Welch during his five seasons with the Giants. In 1886 he won 42 games while working 535 innings and in 1888 he won 35, including a record 19 straight. The Giants won the first of two straight N.L. pennants that season and Keefe posted a 1.74 ERA.

Keefe, who continued pitching underhand when the overhand motion was legalized, was a leader in the Brotherhood of Professional Base Ball Players, the players' first attempt at unionization. He jumped to the new Players League in 1890 when the Brotherhood revolted and returned briefly to the Giants in 1891 when the circuit collapsed. He spent his final years in Philadelphia, retiring in 1893 after working one season at the new 60-feet, 6-inch pitching distance. He left with a 342-225 record and 554 complete games in 594 starts.

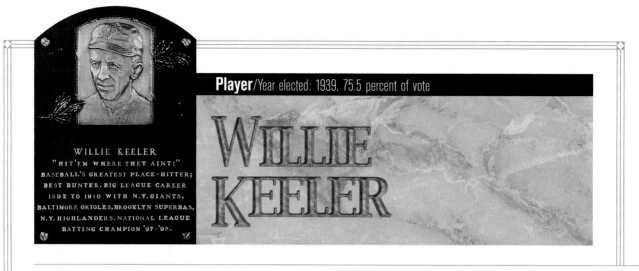

WILLIE KEELER
"HIT'EM WHERE THEY AINT!"
BASEBALL'S GREATEST PLACE-HITTER;
BEST BUNTER. BIG LEAGUE CAREER
1892 TO 1910 WITH N.Y. GIANTS,
BALTIMORE ORIOLES, BROOKLYN SUPERBAS,
N.Y. HIGHLANDERS. NATIONAL LEAGUE
BATTING CHAMPION '97-'98.

WILLIE KEELER

KEELER

Born: 3-3-1872, Brooklyn, N.Y. **Died:** 1-1-23 **Height/Weight:** 5-4/140 **Bats/Throws:** L/L **Primary position:** Outfield
Career statistics: .341 avg., 2,932 hits, 1,719 runs, 495 steals **Teams:** New York 1892-93; Brooklyn 1893, 1899-1902;
Baltimore 1894-98; Yankees 1903-09; Giants 1910 **Batting champion:** N.L., 1897, '98

He was a 5-foot-4 1/2, 140-pound package of base-ball dynamite. Light Willie Keeler's fuse and watch him run around the bases. What "Wee Willie" lacked in size and brawn he more than made up for with an explosive style that frustrated opposing pitchers and endeared him to fans of the dead-ball era.

Keeler's game was speed and he recognized the adjustments he would need to keep up with the big boys. While others tried to drive the ball into outfield gaps, Wee Willie developed a "hit 'em where they ain't" style that would make him the scourge of the National League. He choked up midway on his 29-ounce bat, leaned over the plate and drove pitchers crazy with well-placed bunts, Baltimore-chop grounders and shallow fly-ball hits. When outfielders played shallow to stop that strategy, Keeler could power a ball over their head.

Off the field, Keeler was shy, quiet and always polite, obviously embarrassed by his diminutive size. But on the field, he was an aggressive pioneer, one of base-

"I was just thinking of those suckers, the club owners, paying me for playing ball. Why, I would pay my way into their ballparks if that was the only way I had to get into a game."

—*Willie Keeler*

ball's first scientific hitters and a baserunning monster who used his speed like a club against distracted defenses. Not only did he steal 495 bases over 19 seasons, he combined with Baltimore teammate John McGraw to perfect the hit-and-run and other early strategies.

Keeler's best years were spent as a go-get-'em right fielder on the Orioles' pennant-winning teams of 1894, '95 and '96 — seasons in which he batted .371, .377 and .386. But his masterpiece was 1897, when he batted a whopping .424 and compiled a 44-game hitting streak that stood as the major league record until Joe DiMaggio broke it in 1941. In an eight-season stretch for Baltimore and Brooklyn from 1894-1901, Keeler never fell below .339 or failed to get 200 hits.

He remained a force well into the 20th century, emerging as the first real superstar for a New York Highlanders team that would gain later fame as the Yankees. Keeler retired in 1910 with a .341 career average and 2,932 hits — all but 419 of them singles.

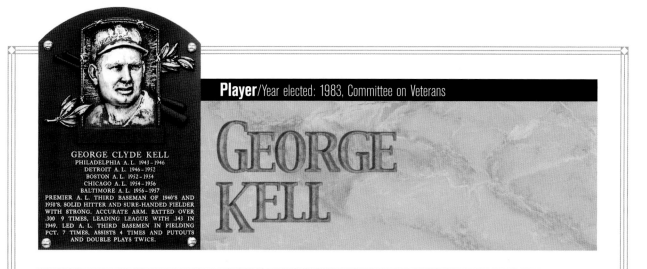

GEORGE CLYDE KELL
PHILADELPHIA A. L. 1943-1946
DETROIT A. L. 1946-1952
BOSTON A. L. 1952-1954
CHICAGO A. L. 1954-1956
BALTIMORE A. L. 1956-1957
PREMIER A. L. THIRD BASEMAN OF 1940'S AND
1950'S. SOLID HITTER AND SURE-HANDED FIELDER
WITH STRONG, ACCURATE ARM. BATTED OVER
.300 9 TIMES, LEADING LEAGUE WITH .343 IN
1949. LED A. L. THIRD BASEMEN IN FIELDING
PCT. 7 TIMES, ASSISTS 4 TIMES AND PUTOUTS
AND DOUBLE PLAYS TWICE.

Player/Year elected: 1983, Committee on Veterans

GEORGE KELL

Born: 8-23-22, Swifton, Ark. **Height/Weight:** 5-9/175 **Bats/Throws:** R/R **Primary position:** Third base **Career statistics:** .306 avg., 2,054 hits **Teams:** Athletics 1943-46; Tigers 1946-52; Red Sox 1952-54; White Sox 1954-56; Orioles 1956-57 **Batting champion:** A.L., 1949

The energy George Kell exerted while playing third base was enough to light up a ballpark and the 2,054 hits he lashed out over 15 seasons illuminated his self-made offensive prowess. Kell was a throwback, that down-and-dirty "gamer" who attacked his craft with total hustle and devotion. Slow afoot, short on power and not blessed with great natural ability, he more than made up for deficiencies with drive and enthusiasm.

From 1943 through 1957, Kell "showed" the managers and fans of five American League teams he was the real deal—a quick, efficient, sometimes-flashy third baseman and a tough-minded hitter who taught himself to drive, slash and yank singles and doubles to all fields. He studied and analyzed his play with a scientific passion that helped him match players with superior skills.

"That guy has more competitive spirit in his little finger than most players have in their whole body," said Steve O'Neill, Kell's Detroit manager from 1946-48. O'Neill liked Kell's quick reflexes, sure hands and strong, accu-

"He doesn't have the power of Joe DiMaggio or Ted Williams, but ... every time you look up, he's on the bases. Bunting, stealing and on the hit-and-run, he drives you nuts. He's a player of the old school." —*Ted Lyons*

rate arm. But he marveled at his willingness to dive, sprawl and block balls with his body, never quitting on a play. The soft-spoken Kell, who broke in with Philadelphia in 1943, led the A.L. in fielding percentage seven times.

As a righthanded hitter, the 5-foot-9, 175-pound Arkansas native was a classic contact man, never striking out more than 37 times. Kell constantly fidgeted and moved around in the box, confusing pitchers and catching defenses out of position. Traded by the A's to Detroit in 1946, he batted .322—the first of eight straight seasons he would top the .300 plateau, five of them with the Tigers.

Kell, who batted .306 in a career that also included stays in Boston, Chicago and Baltimore, edged Red Sox star Ted Williams, .3429-.3427, for the 1949 A.L. batting title and followed in 1950 with a .340 average and league-leading totals of 218 hits and 56 doubles. But the seven-time All-Star Game performer never played in a postseason contest.

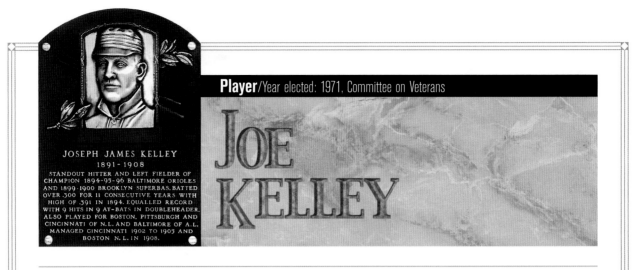

Player/Year elected: 1971, Committee on Veterans

JOE KELLEY

JOSEPH JAMES KELLEY
1891-1908
STANDOUT HITTER AND LEFT FIELDER OF
CHAMPION 1894-95-96 BALTIMORE ORIOLES
AND 1899-1900 BROOKLYN SUPERBAS. BATTED
OVER .300 FOR 11 CONSECUTIVE YEARS WITH
HIGH OF .391 IN 1894. EQUALLED RECORD
WITH 9 HITS IN 9 AT-BATS IN DOUBLEHEADER.
ALSO PLAYED FOR BOSTON, PITTSBURGH AND
CINCINNATI OF N.L. AND BALTIMORE OF A.L.
MANAGED CINCINNATI 1902 TO 1905 AND
BOSTON N.L. IN 1908.

Born: 12-9-1871, Cambridge, Mass. **Died:** 8-14-43 **Height/Weight:** 5-11/190 **Bats/Throws:** R/R **Primary position:** Outfield
Career statistics: .317 avg., 2,220 hits, 1,421 runs, 1,194 RBIs, 443 steals **Teams:** Boston 1891, 1908; Pittsburgh 1892; Baltimore 1892-98; Brooklyn 1899-1901; Baltimore (A.L.) 1902; Reds 1902-06

Love him or hate him, Joe Kelley was a perfect fit for the rough-and-tumble Baltimore Orioles powerhouse teams of the 1890s. As an outstanding left fielder, he dazzled fans with his spirited defense, exceptional speed and lively bat. As a handsome, vain and magnetic personality, he amused them by constantly sneaking peaks at the pocket mirror he kept hidden under his cap.

From 1893-98, Kelley combined with John McGraw, Hughie Jennings, Willie Keeler and Wilbert Robinson on one of the most celebrated and controversial teams ever assembled. The Orioles used every trick in the book, both fair and foul, to win games and Kelley was front and center on three straight National League pennant-winning teams (1894-96) and another that won the Temple Cup in an 1897 postseason series. A favorite Kelley trick was to hide an extra ball in the high outfield grass, just in case an opponent plugged the gap.

More times than not, however, the speedy Kelley could track down those drives, the result of a good work ethic and the patient coaching of manager Ned Hanlon in 1892 and '93. A converted pitcher, the 5-foot-11, 190-pound kid from Cambridge, Mass., would arrive at the park early every morning to work on his game and fans soon were marveling at the results.

Kelley, a compact righthanded hitter, posted his first .300 average in 1893 (.305) and never dropped below that plateau over the next 10 seasons. For the Orioles of 1894-97, Kelley batted .393, .365, .364 and .362, averaging 144 runs scored and 116 RBIs. He was an excellent bunter and a dangerous baserunner who led the N.L. with 87 steals in 1896.

When time finally ran out on the Orioles, Kelley moved with Hanlon, Jennings and Keeler to Brooklyn and helped the Superbas win pennants in 1899 and 1900. He later spent three-plus seasons as player-manager at Cincinnati and one in the same role with the Boston Braves. When he retired in 1908, he sported a .317 average and career totals of 2,220 hits and 1,194 RBIs.

> "Kelley was one of the greatest outfielders of all time. He was rated the kingpin of the Orioles outfield. He covered a lot of ground and was one of the best hitters in the league." —*Dutch Brennan, former major league scout*

GEORGE LANGE KELLY
"HIGHPOCKETS"
NEW YORK N. L., PITTSBURGH N. L.
CINCINNATI N. L., CHICAGO N. L.
BROOKLYN, N. L., 1915-1930 AND 1932
ESTABLISHED MAJOR LEAGUE RECORD BY
HITTING SEVEN HOME RUNS IN SIX CONSECUTIVE
GAMES (1924). RAPPED HOMERS IN THREE
SUCCESSIVE INNINGS (1923). DROVE IN MORE THAN
100 RUNS FOUR CONSECUTIVE YEARS, 1921-24.
SET LEAGUE RECORDS FOR CHANCES ACCEPTED
(1,862) AND PUTOUTS (1,799) BY FIRST BASEMAN
IN 1920. ALSO LED IN CHANCES ACCEPTED
1921-22-23.

Player/Year elected: 1973, Committee on Veterans

GEORGE KELLY

Born: 9-10-1895, San Francisco, Calif. **Died:** 10-13-84 **Height/Weight:** 6-4/190 **Bats/Throws:** R/R
Primary position: First base **Career statistics:** .297 avg., 1,778 hits, 1,020 RBIs **Teams:** Giants 1915-17, 1919-26;
Pirates 1917; Reds 1927-30; Cubs 1930; Dodgers 1932 **HR champion:** N.L., 1921

By 1920s standards, George Kelly was a baseball oddity—a slick-fielding first baseman trapped in a 6-foot-4, 190-pound body. If "Highpockets" looked out of place among the smaller players of his era, it was only until the game began. His long legs seemed to glide effortlessly, his long arms snagged inaccurate throws and his lively bat anchored four straight pennant-winners and two World Series champions for John McGraw's powerful New York Giants.

Kelly was at his gangly best as a smooth, agile first baseman. But McGraw was most fascinated with a cannon-like right arm that made Kelly versatile enough to play second base and all three outfield positions. While playing first, he would range far into the outfield as a cutoff man and nail runners trying to take the extra base.

"Long George," a righthanded swinger from San Francisco, was a self-made hitter who struggled for four years after reporting to the Giants in 1915. But something clicked in 1920 when he replaced Hal Chase as the regular first baseman and led the National League with 94 RBIs. From 1921 through '24, he topped the .300 and 100-RBI plateaus every season as the Giants won four straight pennants and beat the Yankees in two World Series—one of which (1921) ended dramatically when Kelly gunned down a runner at third base.

Kelly liked to crouch over the plate and wait for a high fastball he could straighten up and crunch. In 1921, he hit an N.L.-leading 23 home runs—the sec-

"Kelly made more key hits for me than any other player."

—John McGraw

ond-highest total in league history — and he was noted for his power binges. In 1923, he hit home runs in three straight innings; in 1924, he hit seven in a six-game stretch.

Kelly, forced out of his first base job by Bill Terry in 1925, was traded to Cincinnati in 1927 and finished his career with short stretches in Chicago and Brooklyn. The man McGraw called the best clutch hitter he had ever managed retired in 1932 with a .297 average and 1,020 RBIs.

MIKE KELLY

MIKE J. (KING) KELLY
COLORFUL PLAYER AND AUDACIOUS
BASE-RUNNER. IN 1887 FOR BOSTON
HE HIT .394 AND STOLE 84 BASES.
HIS SALE FOR $10,000 WAS ONE OF
THE BIGGEST DEALS OF BASEBALL'S
EARLY HISTORY.

Born: 12-31-1857, Troy, N.Y. **Died:** 11-8-1894 **Height/Weight:** 5-10/170 **Bats/Throws:** R/R **Primary positions:** Catcher, outfield
Career statistics: .314 avg., 1,868 hits, 1,357 runs, 368 steals **Teams:** Cincinnati 1878-79; Chicago 1880-86; Boston 1887-89, 1891-92; Boston (P.L.) 1890; Cincinnati (A.A.) 1891; Boston (A.A.) 1891; New York 1893 **Batting champion:** N.L., 1886

He was Chicago's "King" and Boston's "$10,000 Beauty." When handsome, dashing Mike Kelly flashed his matinee-idol smile, the entire baseball world seemed to spin a little faster. He was the game's first superstar, its most colorful personality and most innovative performer. Everybody loved Kelly, the hard-drinking, high-living Irishman who swaggered through a 16-year Hall of Fame career.

There's no denying Kelly's talent—he was a slashing righthander who could hit for average, steal bases, score runs and drive them in, all of which he did for five Chicago pennant-winners (1880-86) and three more in Boston, one in the outlaw Players League. Primarily a catcher and outfielder, Kelly could play anywhere and his versatility was accompanied by dramatic flair.

Chicagoans watched Kelly perform baseball's first hook slide, a maneuver that inspired yells of "Slide, Kelly, Slide!" and a popular song by the same name. He experimented with the head-first slide and some-

> **"Mike's only enemy is himself."** —*Cap Anson*

times is credited with inventing the hit-and-run play. He was the first catcher to use finger signals, the first outfielder to back up infield throws and one of the first players to be asked for autographs.

Fans loved Kelly's swagger and he basked in their affection. He drank with them and entertained them on vaudeville, reciting "Casey at the Bat." Kelly was known for his fancy clothes and horse track patronage. In Boston, after cost-conscious Chicago had sold his contract for the staggering sum of $10,000, he rode to games in an expensive horse-drawn carriage, saluting adoring fans as he drove past wearing his ascot, silk hat and patent-leather shoes.

On the field, Kelly was all business. He was at his best in 1886 when he posted a league-leading .388 average and scored 155 runs for the pennant-bound White Stockings. Five times he scored 100 runs and his career .314 average, 1,357 runs and 368 steals attest to his consistency. He retired in 1893, after one season in his native New York, and died a year later of pneumonia at age 36.

KELLY

Player/Year elected: 1984, 83.1 percent of vote

HARMON KILLEBREW

HARMON CLAYTON KILLEBREW
WASHINGTON A.L. 1954–1960
MINNESOTA A.L. 1961–1974
KANSAS CITY A.L. 1975
MUSCULAR SLUGGER WITH MONUMENTAL HOME RUN AND RBI SUCCESS. HIS 573 HOMERS OVER 22 YEARS RANK FIFTH ALL-TIME AND SECOND ONLY TO RUTH AMONG A.L. HITTERS. TIED OR LED A.L. IN HOME RUNS 6 TIMES, BELTED OVER 40 ON 8 OCCASIONS AND IS THIRD IN HOME RUN FREQUENCY. DROVE IN OVER 100 RUNS 9 TIMES. A.L. MVP IN 1969.

Born: 6-29-36, Payette, Idaho **Height/Weight:** 5-11/210 **Bats/Throws:** R/R **Primary positions:** Third base, first base
Career statistics: .256 avg., 2,086 hits, 1,283 runs, 573 HR, 1,584 RBIs **Teams:** Senators 1954-60; Twins 1961-74; Royals 1975
HR champion: A.L., 1959, tied, '62, '63, '64, '67, tied, '69 **Major awards:** A.L. MVP, 1969

He was raw power, 210 pounds of muscle crammed into a 5-foot-11 frame. The thick legs supported a barrel chest and shoulders that looked like something right out of a blacksmith's shop. Harmon Killebrew was the prototypical slugger, the kind of all-or-nothing run producer who found acclaim in the power-crazy 1950s and '60s.

As a home run hitter, Killebrew was very successful. He hit 573, sixth on the all-time list, topped the 40 plateau eight times and captured six American League homer titles. A righthanded hitter with a big swing, the balding, round-faced "Killer" did not hit many line-drive home runs — most of his were towering fly balls that soared into the stands anywhere from the right-center field gap to the left field line. They usually were prodigious and memorable.

So were Killebrew's run-production numbers over 22 seasons, 21 of which were spent with a Minnesota Twins franchise that shifted from Washington in 1961. He piled up nine 100-RBI seasons en

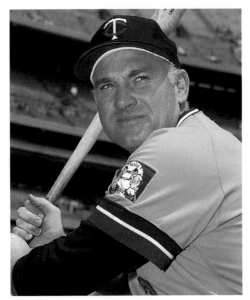

"**If Harmon Killebrew isn't this league's No. 1 player, I've never seen one. He's one of the greatest of all time.**" — *Reggie Jackson, 1969*

route to a career total of 1,584 and captured three RBI titles. Batting cleanup in a 1960s lineup that included Cesar Tovar, Tony Oliva, Rod Carew and Bob Allison, Killebrew provided the hammer for offensive-minded Twins teams that lost in the 1965 World Series to Los Angeles and claimed West Division titles in 1969 and '70.

Killebrew was slow afoot and that factored in to his .256 career average. He never batted higher than .288 in a full season and he never settled into a defensive position, shuttling throughout his career among first base, third and left field. But no matter where he played, he always performed solidly and without complaint.

That was typical for the gentle giant who started his career as a painfully shy rookie in 1954 and retired more than two decades later as a Minnesota icon. Killebrew, who played in 10 All-Star Games, enjoyed his signature season in 1969 when he belted 49 homers, drove in 140 runs and won MVP honors in the A.L.

KILLEBREW

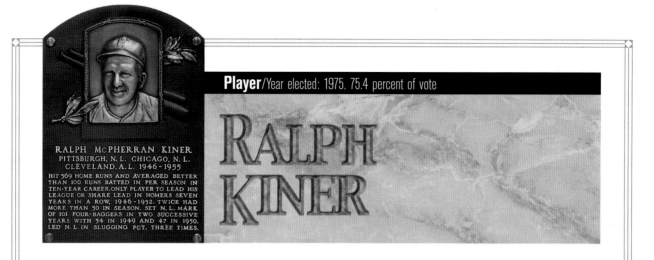

Player/Year elected: 1975, 75.4 percent of vote

RALPH KINER

RALPH McPHERRAN KINER
PITTSBURGH, N. L. CHICAGO, N. L.
CLEVELAND, A. L. 1946-1955

HIT 369 HOME RUNS AND AVERAGED BETTER
THAN 100 RUNS BATTED IN PER SEASON IN
TEN-YEAR CAREER. ONLY PLAYER TO LEAD HIS
LEAGUE OR SHARE LEAD IN HOMERS SEVEN
YEARS IN A ROW, 1946-1952. TWICE HAD
MORE THAN 50 IN SEASON. SET N. L. MARK
OF 101 FOUR-BAGGERS IN TWO SUCCESSIVE
YEARS WITH 54 IN 1949 AND 47 IN 1950.
LED N. L. IN SLUGGING PCT. THREE TIMES.

Born: 10-27-22, Santa Rita, N.M. **Height/Weight:** 6-2/195 **Bats/Throws:** R/R **Primary position:** Outfield **Career statistics:** .279 avg., 1,451 hits, 369 HR, 1,015 RBIs **Teams:** Pirates 1946-53; Cubs 1953-54; Indians 1955 **HR champion:** N.L., 1946, '47, tied, '48, tied, '49, '50, '51, '52, tied

The full, lusty swing told you everything you needed to know about Ralph Kiner's intentions. Hit the ball hard and trot slowly around the bases before it touched asphalt or concrete. Kiner was a 6-foot-2, 195-pound baseball enforcer who brought the home run back into vogue during a short-but-productive 10-year career in the late 1940s and early 1950s.

Everything about Kiner suggested power. The broad shoulders, the full-back-like arms and legs, the quick wrists that compensated for his big swing. Long-suffering Pittsburgh fans embraced their young slugger and Kiner reciprocated, enhancing his fearsome image with torrid home run binges that left opponents shaking their heads. Five in two games. Six in three games. Four in a doubleheader. And, incredibly, eight in one four-game stretch of unrelentless destruction.

The image of a smiling, wavy-haired Kiner spread quickly through National League cities as he either won or shared home run titles in each of his first seven

"I try to hit the ball as hard as I can every time I swing."

— *Ralph Kiner*

seasons. Twice he topped the 50 plateau and in five of those campaigns he topped 100 RBIs. And thanks to the early career tutoring of Hank Greenberg, Kiner never topped 100 strikeouts after his 1946 rookie season.

Greenberg's influence, however, could not help Kiner's suspect left field defense, improve the speed of one of baseball's slowest runners or ease the pain of playing for one of the game's weakest teams. But Kiner more than made up for those deficiencies with his intelligent, low-key, one-of-the-guys personality and amazingly consistent run production.

Kiner's final .279 average was respectable and his total of 369 home runs (36.9 per season) could have been considerably higher if not for the three prime seasons he missed during World War II and the back problems that forced a premature retirement at the still-productive age of 33. Kiner, who played in five All-Star Games, went on to a longer and on-going baseball career in the broadcast booth for the New York Mets.

KINER

CHARLES HERBERT KLEIN
"CHUCK"
PHILADELPHIA N.L., CHICAGO N.L.,
PITTSBURGH N.L., 1928-1944
ONLY PLAYER IN 20TH CENTURY TO COLLECT
200 OR MORE HITS IN EACH OF FIRST FIVE
FULL MAJOR LEAGUE SEASONS. ATTAINED
.320 CAREER AVERAGE AND 300 HOME RUNS.
LED N.L. IN HOMERS AND TOTAL BASES FOUR
TIMES AND IN RUNS SCORED AND SLUGGING
PCT. THREE EACH. SET LEAGUE RECORD FOR
MOST EXTRA BASE HITS IN SEASON--107 IN 1930.
VOTED MOST VALUABLE PLAYER IN 1932.

Player/Year elected: 1980, Committee on Veterans

CHUCK KLEIN

Born: 10-7-04, Indianapolis, Ind. **Died:** 3-28-58 **Height/Weight:** 6-0/185 **Bats/Throws:** L/R **Primary position:** Outfield
Career statistics: .320 avg., 2,076 hits, 1,168 runs, 300 HR, 1,201 RBIs **Teams:** Phillies 1928-33, 1936-39, 1940-44; Cubs 1934-36;
Pirates 1939 **Batting champion:** N.L., 1933 **HR champion:** N.L., 1929, '31, '32, tied, '33 **Major awards:** N.L. MVP, 1932

He clawed his way from an Indianapolis steel mill to the top of the baseball world. Over a five-year stretch with the Depression-era Philadelphia Phillies, Chuck Klein was as good as it gets. He belted, bashed and even threw his way into the record books with a consistency that earned him comparisons to Babe Ruth. Then, just as suddenly as he had risen, Klein faded out of the spotlight he had worked so hard to claim.

To get perspective on Klein, you start with the broad-shouldered, deep-chested, 6-foot body that was supported by relatively thin legs. It was all muscle, especially the powerful forearms that swung a 42-ounce bat from the left side like a toothpick. Klein had home run power, but fans were more likely to see his vicious drives bouncing into the gaps or off the 30-foot right field wall at tiny, hitter-friendly Baker Bowl.

The quiet, sometimes-withdrawn Klein jumped into the spotlight with a .356, 43-home run, 145-RBI effort in 1929 and through 1933 he

> "One reason why I've been able to play baseball well is because it's fun to me. Many players find it work." — *Chuck Klein*

never batted lower than .337 or posted fewer than 200 hits, 28 homers or 120 RBIs. His 1932 MVP performance was a warmup for the .368, 28-homer, 120-RBI Triple Crown he won a year later. He even set a still-standing 20th century defensive record in 1930 when he recorded 44 assists from his right field position.

But the numbers dropped sharply in 1934 when Klein was sent to Chicago by the financially strapped Phillies and he never rediscovered the stroke over an 11-season finish that took him back to Philadelphia, to Pittsburgh and back to Philly. He did have his moments, such as a 1935 World Series appearance with the Cubs and an electrifying four-home run explosion while playing for the Phillies in a game against Pittsburgh in 1936.

Klein, a National League starter in baseball's first All-Star Game in 1933, finished his Hall of Fame career in 1944 with a .320 average, 300 home runs and 2,076 hits.

BILL KLEM

WILLIAM J. KLEM
UMPIRE
NATIONAL LEAGUE · 1905-1951
KNOWN AS "THE OLD ARBITRATOR". UMPIRED
IN 18 WORLD SERIES. CREDITED WITH
INTRODUCING ARM SIGNALS INDICATING
STRIKES AND FAIR OR FOUL BALLS. FAMOUS
QUOTE: "BASEBALL IS MORE THAN A GAME
TO ME—IT'S A RELIGION." RETIRED AS ACTIVE
UMPIRE IN 1940. NAMED CHIEF OF N.L.
STAFF IN 1941.

Born: 2-22-1874, Rochester, N.Y. **Died:** 9-16-51 **Height/Weight:** 5-8/160 **Years umpired:** N.L., 1905-41; chief of N.L. umpires, 1941-51
All-Star Games: 1933, '38 **World Series:** 1908, '09, '11, '12, '13, '14, '15, '17, '18, '20, '22, '24, '26, '29, '31, '32, '34, '40

He was a tough, arrogant little autocrat who boldly defended his claims of infallibility. Bill Klem was never known for modesty, but he was universally accepted as the greatest umpire of all time. The "Old Arbitrator" was a brilliant technician, colorful innovator and fiery spokesman for his profession over a 36-year career, the man who helped bring it dignity and respect.

From the moment Klem stepped onto his first National League field in 1905, nobody doubted who was in charge. The 5-foot-8 New Yorker with a big voice and confident, authoritative air stood up to the rowdy elements of early century baseball and refused to back down in the face of threats or violence. He took control of games, treated everyone fairly and raised the standard for umpiring competence, especially with his work on balls and strikes.

Klem was so good behind the plate that he did nothing but call pitches for 16 years, from his days as a single umpire through 1920. He also was the go-to arbiter in the N.L., the man who worked the controversial Chicago-New York pennant-deciding makeup game of 1908 as well as a record 18 World Series and baseball's first All-Star Game in 1933.

Uncompromising and resolute, Klem also was colorful and quick with a quip. He once punctuated an argument with Giants manager John McGraw by saying, "I never missed one in my life," a statement that became the trademark of his career. When a player or manager became abusive, he drew a line in the dirt with his toe and walked away. Few dared cross it.

Klem revolutionized the profession with use of hand signals for out, safe, fair, foul, strike and ball. He was the first to straddle foul lines for better perspective and stand to the side of the catcher for a better look at pitches. He fought nonstop for better pay and working conditions. When Klem retired in 1941 to become chief of N.L. umpires, he was much more than an "Old Arbitrator." He was a baseball legend.

> ## "Baseball is more than a game to me. It's a religion."
> —*Bill Klem*

Player/Year elected: 1972, 86.9 percent of vote, first ballot

SANDY KOUFAX

SANFORD KOUFAX
"SANDY"
BROOKLYN N.L. 1955-1957
LOS ANGELES N.L. 1958-1966

SET ALL-TIME RECORDS WITH 4 NO-HITTERS
IN 4 YEARS, CAPPED BY 1965 PERFECT GAME,
AND BY CAPTURING EARNED-RUN TITLE FIVE
SEASONS IN A ROW, 1962-1966. WON 25 OR
MORE GAMES THREE TIMES, HAD 11 SHUTOUTS
IN 1963. STRIKEOUT LEADER FOUR TIMES,
WITH RECORD 382 IN 1965, FANNED 18 IN A
GAME TWICE. MOST VALUABLE PLAYER 1963.
CY YOUNG AWARD WINNER 1963-65-66.

Born: 12-30-35, Brooklyn, N.Y. **Height/Weight:** 6-2/210 **Bats/Throws:** R/L **Position:** Pitcher **Career statistics:** 165-87, 2.76 ERA, 2,396 strikeouts **Teams:** Brooklyn Dodgers 1955-57; Los Angeles Dodgers 1958-66 **Major awards:** N.L. Cy Young, 1963, '65, '66

The ball shot out of his left hand and hurtled plate-ward in a white blur. The contorted grimace on Sandy Koufax's thin face was easier to see than the missile he had just launched. Such was the plight of over-matched National League hitters who had to face the Los Angeles Dodgers' ace during the most dominant six-year pitching exhibition of the second half-century.

Simply stated, the kid from Brooklyn was not your normal, everyday lefthander, from the day in 1955 when he joined his hometown Dodgers (skipping the minor leagues) until a day in 1966 when he told stunned Los Angeles fans he was retiring after 12 seasons because of an arthritic elbow he didn't want to damage beyond repair. The decision was shocking because Koufax, at age 30, had just completed a 27-9 season and a 129-47 six-year run that had vaulted him to the top of the pitching charts.

But that was typical Koufax, an intelligent, straight-shooting pragmatist who didn't mince words off the field or pitches on it. His 6-foot-2 frame held 210 pounds of muscle that delivered a blazing fastball and nasty curve to intimidated batters. When Koufax was "on," he left a trail of wins, strikeouts and no-hitters that cut a wide swath through baseball's record book.

Koufax, who was signed out of the University of Cincinnati, struggled with control and self-confidence through six mediocre seasons before transforming into a proficient pitching machine. From 1961-66, he was close to perfection. His .733 winning percentage was complemented by a record five consecutive N.L. ERA titles, one MVP, three Cy Young Awards, four strikeout titles and a 0.95 ERA and 4-3 record in three World Series — two that produced Dodger championships.

Koufax, who combined with Don Drysdale to form one of the best 1-2 pitching punches in history, twice fanned 18 batters in a game and struck out a then-record 382 in 1965, the same year he pitched a perfect game against Chicago — one of his four no-hitters. He retired with a 165-87 record.

> **"I never saw those old-timers, but he must have the greatest stuff of any pitcher in history."** — *Ray Culp, Phillies pitcher, 1964*

K
O
U
F
A
X

NAP LAJOIE

NAPOLEON (LARRY) LAJOIE
PHILADELPHIA (N) 1896-1900
PHILADELPHIA (A) 1901
CLEVELAND (A) 1902-14
PHILADELPHIA (A) 1915-16
GREAT HITTER AND MOST GRACEFUL
AND EFFECTIVE SECOND-BASEMAN
OF HIS ERA. MANAGED CLEVELAND 4
YEARS. LEAGUE BATTING CHAMPION
1901-03-04.

Born: 9-5-1874, Woonsocket, R.I. **Died:** 2-7-59 **Height/Weight:** 6-1/200 **Bats/Throws:** R/R **Primary position:** Second base
Career statistics: .338 avg., 3,242 hits, 1,504 runs, 1,599 RBIs, 380 steals **Teams:** Philadelphia 1896-1900;
Athletics 1901-02, 1915-16; Indians 1902-14 **Batting champion:** A.L., 1901, '03, '04 **HR champion:** A.L., 1901

Stylish, graceful and handsome. Strong, intimidating and rugged. All of those seemingly contradictory descriptions applied to hard-hitting Napoleon Lajoie, a dark, bold-featured French-Canadian who left an indelible mark as one of the greatest and most important baseball stars of the 20th century's first decade.

Lajoie's historic contribution was made in 1901, his sixth major league season, when he jumped from the Philadelphia Phillies of the established National League to Connie Mack's Philadelphia Athletics of the new American League, giving the rival circuit its first superstar and instant credibility. Lajoie punctuated his controversial move by winning the century's first Triple Crown and posting a remarkable .422 average — still the highest single-season mark in A.L. history.

When the Phillies obtained an injunction prohibiting Lajoie from playing for the "other Philadelphia club" in 1902, Mack simply dealt his star to the A.L.'s franchise in Cleveland, where he remained until the final two seasons of his 21-year career — sitting out all

games in Philadelphia. Cleveland fans formed a love affair with their big Frenchman, who reigned as the early century's premier offensive and defensive second baseman.

The 6-foot-1, 200-pounder, easily recognized by his upturned collar and cap cocked stylishly to the side, glided effortlessly around the field, a graceful defender who led the A.L. in fielding percentage seven times. When Lajoie positioned himself deep in the box with his thick-handled bat, third basemen lived in fear of the vicious line drives he launched with a smooth, extended swing.

The oft-described "hardest hitter of the dead-ball era" backed up that reputation with a .338 career average, 3,242 hits, four 100-RBI seasons and three batting titles for generally weak Cleveland teams. But Lajoie is best remembered for the disputed 1910 title he lost by a fraction to Detroit rival Ty Cobb. A testimony to Lajoie's unwavering popularity was that the Indians were known as the "Naps" from 1905-09, years when he served as player/manager.

> "Lajoie was one of the most rugged hitters I ever faced. He'd take your leg off with a line drive, turn the third baseman around like a swinging door and powder the hand of the left fielder." — *Cy Young*

LAJOIE

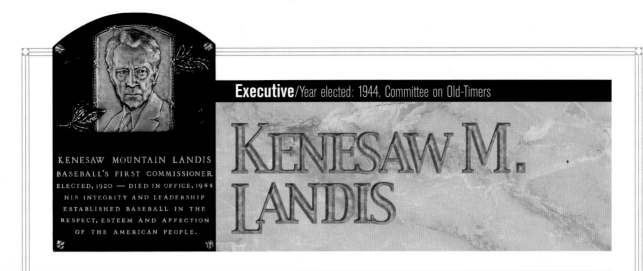

KENESAW M. LANDIS

KENESAW MOUNTAIN LANDIS
BASEBALL'S FIRST COMMISSIONER
ELECTED, 1920 — DIED IN OFFICE, 1944
HIS INTEGRITY AND LEADERSHIP
ESTABLISHED BASEBALL IN THE
RESPECT, ESTEEM AND AFFECTION
OF THE AMERICAN PEOPLE.

Born: 11-20-1866, Millville, Ohio **Died:** 11-25-44 **Executive career:** Baseball's first commissioner, 1921-44

To players and fans, he was the white-haired, craggy-faced, unsmiling symbol of baseball integrity. To the owners who had hired him, Kenesaw Mountain Landis was a ruthless dictator who would rule their sport for almost a quarter century.

Baseball's first commissioner was all that and more, a heavy-handed but honest-minded federal judge who returned dignity and trust to the field in the wake of the 1919 Black Sox scandal.

From 1921 until his sudden death in 1944, the proud Ohioan governed with an iron fist and took full advantage of the "absolute powers" he had been given. His first act was to ban for life the eight Chicago White Sox players who had been accused of consorting with gamblers to fix the 1919 World Series, even though all were cleared in court. Then he began carving his historical niche as a "player's commissioner" and arch-enemy of gambling.

Under Landis' firm hand, baseball survived a scandal and the Great Depression, dealt firmly with further threats to its integrity, created a more friendly

environment for players and fans and positioned itself to stay afloat during World War II. He suspended New York star Babe Ruth for his barnstorming activities, won power struggles against American League czar Ban Johnson and Yankees owner Jacob Ruppert and fought, unsuccessfully, Branch Rickey's concept of a farm system.

Landis, a former federal judge who had helped baseball out of a 1915 jam with his clever handling of a Federal League suit against the major leagues, was the perfect choice when the sport needed someone with decisiveness and vision. Nobody who followed would enjoy his absolute authority.

The thin, distinguished Landis was a familiar figure at World Series games, his chin resting absent-mindedly on the front-row rail. He is best remembered for his role in the 1934 fall classic, when he ordered Cardinals left fielder Joe Medwick removed from Game 7 "for his own protection" because he was being pelted with garbage by irate Detroit fans in the sixth inning.

> "We do not want baseball in America exempt from the liabilities of common life in America. We want the same rules applied and enforced on us as on everyone else." —*Kenesaw M. Landis, 1943*

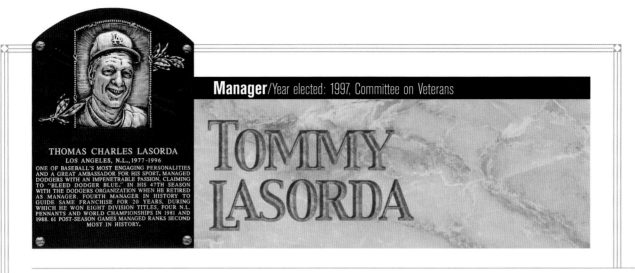

TOMMY LASORDA

THOMAS CHARLES LASORDA
LOS ANGELES, N.L., 1977-1996
ONE OF BASEBALL'S MOST ENGAGING PERSONALITIES
AND A GREAT AMBASSADOR FOR HIS SPORT. MANAGED
DODGERS WITH AN IMPENETRABLE PASSION, CLAIMING
TO "BLEED DODGER BLUE." IN HIS 47TH SEASON
WITH THE DODGERS ORGANIZATION WHEN HE RETIRED
AS MANAGER. FOURTH MANAGER IN HISTORY TO
GUIDE SAME FRANCHISE FOR 20 YEARS, DURING
WHICH HE WON EIGHT DIVISION TITLES, FOUR N.L.
PENNANTS AND WORLD CHAMPIONSHIPS IN 1981 AND
1988. 61 POST-SEASON GAMES MANAGED RANKS SECOND
MOST IN HISTORY.

Born: 9-22-27, Norristown, Pa. **Height/Weight:** 5-11/190 **Teams managed:** Dodgers 1976-96 **Career record:** 1,599-1,439, .526
World Series titles: 1981, '88 **Major awards:** N.L. Manager of Year, 1983, '88

He spread baseball goodwill with his enthusiasm, managed with his gut and communicated with his heart. A Tommy Lasorda hug was worth a thousand words, which he also delivered with unbridled passion. He was cheerleader, motivator, salesman, strategist and eternal optimist for the Los Angeles Dodgers, the team he loved, promoted and guided to eight division titles, four National League pennants and two World Series championships over a colorful 20-year period.

> "The important thing about Tommy is that he is not just a guy who makes out the lineup and decides strategy. He makes everyone feel a part of it." —*Bill Russell*

More than anything, Lasorda motivated. He cajoled players, embraced their families and made them want to share his vision of Dodger baseball. His shticks (bleeding Dodger blue, worshiping the Great Dodger in the Sky) sometimes wore thin, but not the enthusiasm he brought to the field and the messages he delivered so eloquently to fans who adored him. Lasorda could be hokey, but no one accused him of being insincere.

It's no coincidence that he managed nine N.L. Rookies of the Year, two Cy Youngs and one MVP. Or that his infield of Steve Garvey, Dave Lopes, Bill Russell and Ron Cey stayed intact for an amazing nine seasons. Lasorda was easy to play for and the atmosphere around him was electric, thanks to a constant locker room parade of Hollywood celebrities.

Lasorda's Dodger loyalty actually stretched back more than three decades — as a pitcher, scout, coach and minor league manager. As a 5-foot-11 left-hander, he was 0-4 in three brief major league stops (two with the Dodgers in the 1950s) and he won five pennants in seven seasons as a manager in the Dodgers system. His dream came true in 1976 when he replaced Walter Alston as Los Angeles manager.

The 49-year-old Lasorda was as noisy, combative and energetic as Alston was quiet and conservative. But the results were similar. The paunchy "Pasta King" won pennants in 1977 and '78, his first two full seasons, and World Series in 1981 and '88. Twelve of his 20 teams finished either first or second and he retired in 1996 with a 1,599-1,439 record.

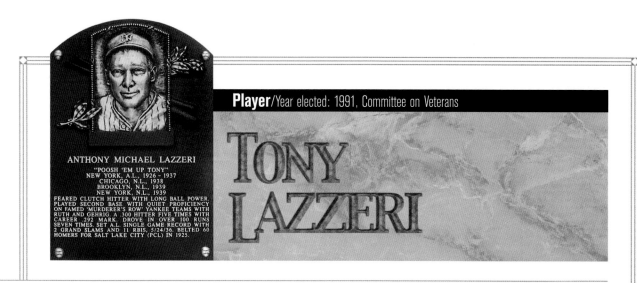

ANTHONY MICHAEL LAZZERI
"POOSH 'EM UP TONY"
NEW YORK, A.L., 1926 – 1937
CHICAGO, N.L., 1938
BROOKLYN, N.L., 1939
NEW YORK, N.L., 1939
FEARED CLUTCH HITTER WITH LONG BALL POWER.
PLAYED SECOND BASE WITH QUIET PROFICIENCY
ON FAMED 'MURDERER'S ROW' YANKEE TEAMS WITH
RUTH AND GEHRIG. A .300 HITTER FIVE TIMES WITH
CAREER .292 MARK. DROVE IN OVER 100 RUNS
SEVEN TIMES. SET A.L. SINGLE GAME RECORD WITH
2 GRAND SLAMS AND 11 RBIS, 5/24/36. BELTED 60
HOMERS FOR SALT LAKE CITY (PCL) IN 1925.

Player/Year elected: 1991, Committee on Veterans

TONY LAZZERI

Born: 12-6-03, San Francisco, Calif. **Died:** 8-6-46 **Height/Weight:** 5-11/170 **Bats/Throws:** R/R **Primary position:** Second base

Career statistics: .292 avg., 1,840 hits, 178 HR, 1,191 RBIs **Teams:** Yankees 1926-37; Cubs 1938; Dodgers 1939; Giants 1939

It was easy to miss Tony Lazzeri in the "Murderer's Row" crowd at Yankee Stadium. But over 14 major league seasons, the 5-foot-11, 170-pound second baseman carved out his own Hall of Fame niche while caddying to such heavyweights as Babe Ruth, Lou Gehrig, Bob Meusel and Joe DiMaggio. Lazzeri was the Bronx Bombers' quiet enforcer, an always-reliable link between the great New York championship teams of the late 1920s and 1930s.

It was Lazzeri, a Pacific Coast League star, who opened the San Francisco-to-New York talent pipeline, a route later followed by DiMaggio and Frank Crosetti, and he opened the gates to millions of Italians, who flocked to ballparks to see him play. The son of an Italian iron worker, "Poosh-'Em-Up Tony" was a smooth, sure-handed fielder who balanced the Yankees' flamboyance with an unobtrusive work ethic.

But it was the bat that attracted Yankee scouts. His righthanded swing, propelled by powerful wrists and boilermaker forearms, produced 60 home runs and 222 RBIs in 1925 for San Francisco of the PCL, and when Lazzeri was inserted

into New York's Murderer's Row lineup in 1926, he responded with 18 homers and 114 RBIs. Lazzeri's bases-loaded, Game 7 strikeout against St. Louis' Grover Alexander still stands as a classic World Series moment.

"(Tony) not only was a great ballplayer, he was a great man. He was a leader. He was like a manager on the field."

— *Frank Crosetti*

But that rookie failure was an illusion. From 1927 through 1937, the silent, unsmiling Lazerri was a defensive anchor and clutch run-producer for five championship teams — a six-time 100-RBI man and five-time .300 hitter. When he moved to Chicago in 1938, the Cubs won a National League pennant and Lazzeri lost to his former Yankees teammates in the World Series — his seventh fall classic.

Lazzeri, who retired in 1939 with a .292 average and 1,191 RBIs, is best remembered for the dramatic 1926 World Series strikeout. But he hit a grand slam for the Yankees in the 1936 classic and his 11-RBI explosion in a 1936 regular-season contest, fueled by three homers and two grand slams, is a still-standing American League record.

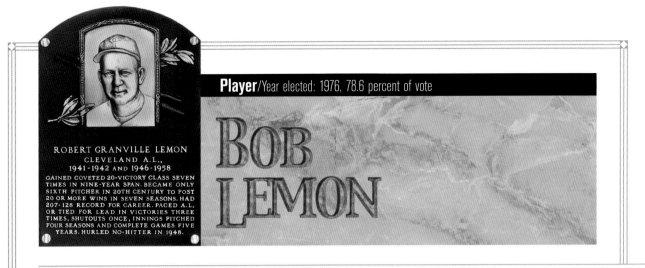

ROBERT GRANVILLE LEMON
CLEVELAND A.L.,
1941-1942 AND 1946-1958
GAINED COVETED 20-VICTORY CLASS SEVEN
TIMES IN NINE-YEAR SPAN. BECAME ONLY
SIXTH PITCHER IN 20TH CENTURY TO POST
20 OR MORE WINS IN SEVEN SEASONS. HAD
207-128 RECORD FOR CAREER. PACED A.L.
OR TIED FOR LEAD IN VICTORIES THREE
TIMES, SHUTOUTS ONCE, INNINGS PITCHED
FOUR SEASONS AND COMPLETE GAMES FIVE
YEARS. HURLED NO-HITTER IN 1948.

BOB LEMON

Born: 9-22-20, San Francisco, Calif. **Died:** 1-11-2000 **Height/Weight:** 6-0/185 **Bats/Throws:** L/R **Position:** Pitcher
Career statistics: 207-128, 3.23 ERA, 1,277 strikeouts **Teams:** Indians 1946-58

Teammates refused to play catch with him because of erratic movement on his throws. Hitters tossed bats in disgust after chasing one of his darting, dipping and fluttering deliveries. Everybody viewed Cleveland righthander Bob Lemon as a baseball "freak," an infield and outfield bust who transformed, almost overnight, into a seven-time 20-game winner.

Lemon's rags-to-riches story is nothing if not dramatic. On opening day in 1946, he was a third baseman-turned-center fielder trying to fight his way through the jungle of major league pitching. Two years later, he was a member of Cleveland's rotation, a 25-year-old bulldog who would post a 20-14 record, pitch 10 shutouts and win two World Series games for the champion Indians. It was only the beginning. Over an incredible nine-year span from 1948-56, the 6-foot Californian posted 186 wins while completing 179 of 312 starts.

Indians manager Lou Boudreau suggested the transition after watching the quiet, unpretentious young-

ster baffle Cleveland's bullpen catcher with the natural break of his throws while playing catch. Soon Lemon was learning how to control his so-called "fastball," which was more of a natural sinker, and a slider that darted down and away from righthanded hitters. He developed a big-breaking curve that set up his other pitches, which he threw at different speeds.

> "Lemon can put about four speeds on the ball, which ruins your timing. ... His fastball is a natural sinker. I'd either top it to the infield or golf it for a lousy single."
>
> — *Joe DiMaggio*

Lemon, who led the A.L. in innings four times en route to a 207-128 career record and 3.23 ERA, supplemented his new calling with a cat-like fielding prowess and dangerous bat. Unable to solve big-league pitching as a young lefthanded hitter, he belted 37 home runs and compiled a .284 average as a frequent pinch-hitter.

With a rotation of Lemon, Early Wynn, Mike Garcia and aging Bob Feller, the Indians were a threat to New York's American League superiority through 1956. Lemon, who pitched in four All-Star Games, was 23-7 in 1954 when the powerful Indians rolled to an A.L.-record 111 wins before losing to the New York Giants in a World Series shocker.

Player/Year elected: 1972, Special Committee on Negro Leagues

WALTER FENNER LEONARD
"B U C K"
NEGRO LEAGUES 1933–1950
FIRST BASEMAN OF HOMESTEAD GRAYS WHEN
TEAM WON NEGRO NATIONAL LEAGUE PENNANT
NINE YEARS IN A ROW, 1937 – 1945. TEAMED
WITH JOSH GIBSON TO FORM MOST FEARED
BATTING TWOSOME IN NEGRO BASEBALL FROM
1937 TO 1946. RANKED AMONG NEGRO HOME
RUN LEADERS. WON NEGRO NATIONAL LEAGUE
BATTING TITLE WITH .391 AVERAGE IN 1948.

BUCK LEONARD

Born: 9-8-07, Rocky Mount, N.C. **Died:** 11-27-97 **Height/Weight:** 5-10/185 **Bats/Throws:** L/L **Primary position:** First base

Teams (1933-53): Brooklyn Royal Giants; Homestead Grays; Portsmouth (Piedmont)

As one-half of the greatest 1-2 hitting punch in Negro League history, Buck Leonard made an indelible impression on a baseball community he would never be allowed to inhabit. "He was major league all the way," said Hall of Fame catcher Roy Campanella. And nobody who saw him play—black or white—would argue the point.

Unfortunately, Leonard's only contact with major league players would be in offseason barnstorming exhibitions that filled out the exhaustive year-round schedule of the pre-World War II black player. For 23 years, he competed in as many as three games per day and for 17 of those seasons he handled first base duty for the Homestead Grays, a Pittsburgh-based power that also featured catcher Josh Gibson, pitcher Satchel Paige and several other black stars.

The combination of Gibson, the Babe Ruth of the Negro Leagues, and Leonard, the so-called Lou Gehrig of the Negro Leagues, was offensive mayhem. Gibson, renowned for his long home runs, batted third; Leonard, who hit his homers frequently if not as far, batted fourth. Pitchers who worked around Gibson had to deal with a left-handed batter who uncoiled into their fastballs from a menacing crouch. He was a dead-pull hitter who produced runs and posted averages in the high .300s.

At 5-foot-10, 185 pounds, the stocky lefthander was not the prototypical first baseman. But nobody in any league could match Leonard's agility, powerful arm and ability to dig throws out of the dirt. Some observers called him quietly elegant. Others said his defense alone was worth the price of admission. His play around the bag mirrored his personality— steady, quiet and always dependable.

When baseball's color barrier fell in 1947, Leonard was 39 years old and past his prime, a self admission that reflected his unwillingness to pit diminishing talents against younger major leaguers. He was forced to settle for Hall of Fame recognition, which came in 1972 at age 64.

> "Satchel Paige and Josh Gibson got more publicity in the Negro Leagues. But Buck was just as good. Josh hit the ball farther, but Buck hit it just as often." —*Monte Irvin*

Player/Year elected: 1976, Committee on Veterans

FRED LINDSTROM

FREDERICK CHARLES LINDSTROM
NEW YORK N.L., PITTSBURGH N.L.,
CHICAGO N.L., BROOKLYN N.L.,
1924 · 1936
COMPILED LIFETIME .311 BATTING MARK,
INCLUDING SEVEN SEASONS OF .300 OR
BETTER. ONE OF ONLY THREE PLAYERS TO
AMASS 250 OR MORE HITS A YEAR TWICE.
AS YOUNGEST PLAYER (AGE 18) IN WORLD
SERIES HISTORY, HE TIED RECORD WITH
FOUR HITS IN GAME IN 1924. EQUALLED
MAJOR LEAGUE RECORD BY COLLECTING
NINE HITS IN 1928 DOUBLEHEADER.

Born: 11-21-05, Chicago, Ill. **Died:** 10-4-81 **Height/Weight:** 5-11/170 **Bats/Throws:** R/R **Primary positions:** Third base, outfield
Career statistics: .311 avg., 1,747 hits, 779 RBIs **Teams:** Giants 1924-32; Pirates 1933-34; Cubs 1935; Dodgers 1936

New York fans called Fred Lindstrom "the Boy Wonder," a tribute to his inspired World Series play at the tender age of 18. John McGraw called him one of the most reliable and versatile players he had ever managed. Lindstrom, by any description, was a brash, supremely confident New York-worthy star whose career ended prematurely after 13 memorable seasons.

Giants fans appreciated the glove and strong arm Lindstrom flashed in 1924 when, at 18, he took over for injured third baseman Heinie Groh late in the season. McGraw's Giants won the National League pennant and young Lindstrom collected 10 hits in a seven-game World Series against Washington—a classic that ended in defeat when two grounders, one in the decisive 12th-inning, hopped erratically over Lindstrom's head.

But that disappointment was short-lived. New Yorkers fell in love with the charming, blond-headed Chicago kid, one of few players who dared talk back to the authoritarian McGraw. In 1926, Lindstrom

became the full-time third baseman in a Hall of Fame infield that included Bill Terry, Frank Frisch and Travis Jackson and started a string of six straight .300 seasons. A 5-foot-11 righthanded swinger who chose bat control over power, Lindstrom lashed drives to all fields, delighted McGraw with his ability to hit behind runners and thrived in the clutch.

Lindstrom was capable as both a run-producer and table-setter for hard-hitting first baseman Terry. Twice he collected 231 hits—in 1928 when he batted .358 and two years later when he hit .379. And when McGraw needed center field help in 1931, Lindstrom conquered a new position and remained there the rest of his career.

Lindstrom, who was bitterly disappointed in 1932 when McGraw suddenly retired and chose Terry as his managerial successor, asked to be traded and spent his last four seasons in Pittsburgh, Chicago and Brooklyn. He did play in another World Series for the 1935 Cubs, but he retired a year later, at age 31, with a bad back and a .311 career average.

"My greatest thrill? That's easy. It came the day Mr. McGraw named his 20 all-time players. I'm ninth on that list and that is thrill enough to last me a lifetime."

— Fred Lindstrom

JOHN HENRY LLOYD
"POP"
NEGRO LEAGUES 1906-1932
REGARDED AS FINEST SHORTSTOP TO PLAY
IN NEGRO BASEBALL. SCIENTIFIC HITTER
BATTED OVER .400 SEVERAL TIMES DURING
HIS 27-YEAR CAREER. PERSONIFIED BEST
QUALITIES OF ATHLETE BOTH ON AND OFF
FIELD. INSTRUMENTAL IN HELPING OPEN
YANKEE STADIUM TO NEGRO BASEBALL IN
1930. MANAGED MORE THAN TEN SEASONS.

JOHN HENRY LLOYD

Born: 4-25-1884, Palatka, Fla. **Died:** 3-19-65 **Height/Weight:** 5-11/180 **Bats/Throws:** L/R **Primary position:** Shortstop
Teams (1905-31): Cuban X Giants; Philadelphia Giants; Leland Giants; Lincoln Giants; Chicago American Giants; Brooklyn Royal Giants; Columbus Buckeyes; Bacharach Giants; Kansas City Monarchs; Hilldale Daisies; Harlem Stars; New York Black Yankees; Lincoln Stars

They called him "the black Honus Wagner," a tribute to his shortstop play, and he handled a bat with Ty Cobb-like mastery, lashing out nasty line drives with his measured lefthanded swing. John Henry Lloyd not only was the class of early black baseball, he was one of the most talented players in any league. Connie Mack thought so. So did John McGraw, Babe Ruth and even Wagner, who said he was honored by the comparison.

Opponents often talked about the way Lloyd, a lanky 5-foot-11 Floridian, seemed to glide around the infield, extending his range with long arms and huge hands that scooped up balls with machine-like efficiency. In Cuba, where Lloyd played 12 winter league seasons, fans called him "El Cuchara," or "shovel," because of the way he scooped up handfuls of dirt and pebbles along with the ball that he fired to first with a strong, accurate arm.

Lloyd was versatile enough to play any position, fast enough to steal bases and a craftsman with the bat. He stood in his closed stance, bat cradled in the crook of his left elbow, and sprayed line drives with a relaxed swing. Every ball seemed to have eyes and he seldom struck out, a dead-ball era trait he took to a new level. Lloyd had power but was more likely to hurt you with a well-placed bunt or perfectly executed hit-and-run.

Lloyd was a consistent .380-plus hitter over an itinerant 27-year career (1905-31) that took him from team to team, from Chicago to New York, and on barnstorming tours that put him in contact with the game's best players. On the field, he was a fierce and aggressive competitor. Off the field, he was gentle and considerate, a patient teacher known to appreciative young players as "Pop."

The name fit black baseball's elder statesman, who retired in 1931 at age 47 and continued playing and coaching at the semipro level for another 10 years.

> ## "He looked like he was gliding over to the ball. You could hardly see his feet move."
>
> *— Judy Johnson, from the book Blackball Stars*

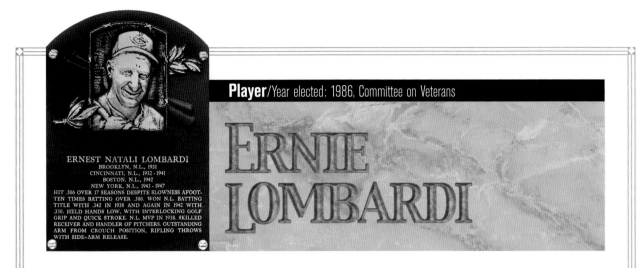

ERNEST NATALI LOMBARDI
BROOKLYN, N.L., 1931
CINCINNATI, N.L., 1932 - 1941
BOSTON, N.L., 1942
NEW YORK, N.L., 1943 - 1947
HIT .306 OVER 17 SEASONS DESPITE SLOWNESS AFOOT.
TEN TIMES BATTING OVER .300. WON N.L. BATTING
TITLE WITH .342 IN 1938 AND AGAIN IN 1942 WITH
.330. HELD HANDS LOW, WITH INTERLOCKING GOLF
GRIP AND QUICK STROKE. N.L. MVP IN 1938. SKILLED
RECEIVER AND HANDLER OF PITCHERS. OUTSTANDING
ARM FROM CROUCH POSITION, RIFLING THROWS
WITH SIDE-ARM RELEASE.

Player/Year elected: 1986, Committee on Veterans

ERNIE LOMBARDI

Born: 4-6-08, Oakland, Calif. **Died:** 9-26-77 **Height/Weight:** 6-3/230 **Bats/Throws:** R/R **Primary position:** Catcher

Career statistics: .306 avg., 1,792 hits, 190 HR, 990 RBIs **Teams:** Dodgers 1931; Reds 1932-41; Braves 1942; Giants 1943-47

Batting champion: N.L., 1938, '42 **Major awards:** N.L. MVP, 1938

The first thing you noticed about Ernie Lombardi was his thick, powerful body, a 6-foot-3, 230-pound mass of muscle complemented by an equally massive nose. The second was the ponderously slow way he ambled through life and plodded around the bases. Not so visible were the eagle eyes, the lightning-quick hands and the over-sized heart that gave him distinction as one of the great catchers of the 1930s and '40s.

Big Ernie was so slow that infielders would set up in the outfield grass, leaving little space for his line drives to fall. Lombardi never got a leg hit and he led the National League in double-play grounders four times, but that didn't stop him from compiling a career .306 average with a sledge-hammer righthanded swing that was deadly and amazingly accurate.

Fans and writers joked about the big, shy Italian with the over-sized "schnoz," but players marveled at his vicious, gap-plugging shots and the incredible hand-eye coordination (he never struck out more than 25 times) that helped him become the only catcher to win two batting championships. In 1938, his seventh

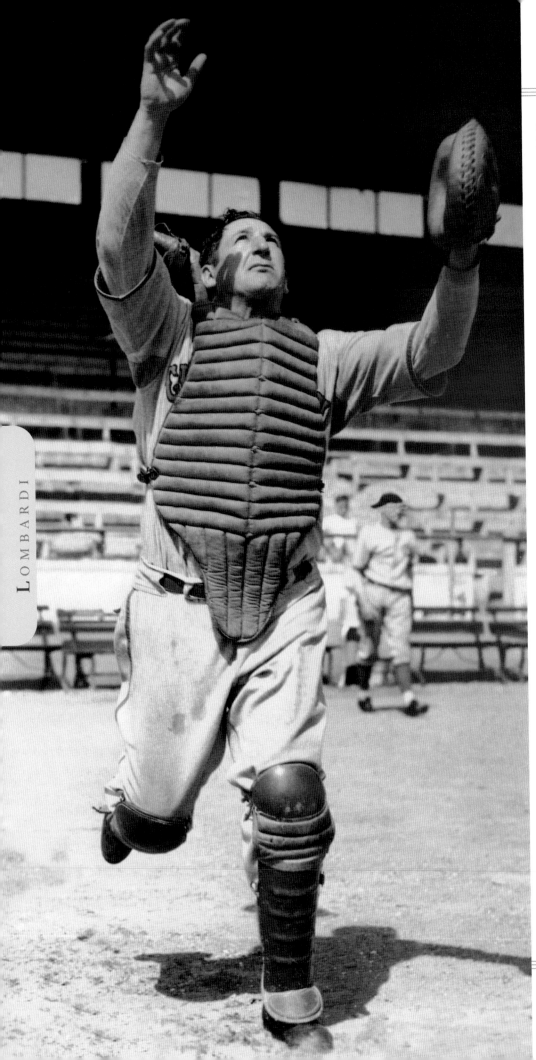

season in Cincinnati, he led the N.L. with a .342 mark while earning MVP honors, and in 1942, playing his only season in Boston, he batted .330.

Lombardi never hit more than 20 homers or drove in 100 runs, but he was a bottom-of-the-lineup force who helped the Reds win pennants in 1939 and '40. He is remembered unfairly for his Game 4 "snooze" in the 1939 World Series — a play on which New York's Joe DiMaggio circled the bases on a single as Lombardi lay dazed after a violent collision with runner Charlie Keller.

The gentle Californian, a five-time All-Star Game participant who worked Johnny Vander Meer's back-to-back no-hitters in 1938, was the prototype catcher of his era — a big, strong-armed receiver who could gun down runners without leaving his crouch. After leaving the Braves in 1940, he played five seasons with the New York Giants before ending his 17-year career in 1947.

> "He was the best righthanded hitter I ever saw. And he was an exceptional player in every way except running. If he hadn't been so slow, he would have had an even better batting average."
>
> — Harry Craft

AL LOPEZ

ALFONSO RAMON LOPEZ

RENOWNED FOR SHREWD LEADERSHIP DURING
36-YEAR BIG LEAGUE CAREER AS CATCHER
AND MANAGER. WON TWO PENNANTS AND HAD
TEN SECOND-PLACE FINISHES WITH WINNING
PCT. OF .581 IN 17 SEASONS AT HELM OF
CLEVELAND AND CHICAGO WHITE SOX. ONLY
MANAGER TO INTERRUPT YANKEES' PENNANT
DYNASTY OF 1949-1964, GUIDING INDIANS
TO '54 FLAG WITH A.L. RECORD 111 WINS
AND PILOTING WHITE SOX TO 1959 TITLE.

Born: 8-20-08, Tampa, Fla. **Height/Weight:** 5-11/165
Bats/Throws: R/R **Primary position:** Catcher
Career statistics: .261 avg., 1,547 hits **Teams played:**
Dodgers 1928, 1930-35; Braves 1936-40; Pirates 1940-46;
Indians 1947 **Teams managed (1,410-1,004):** Indians
1951-56; White Sox 1957-65, 1968-69

He was the Mr. Rogers of baseball, a smiling, friendly, calm and collected nice guy who didn't finish last. Al Lopez, the "sotto voce manager," was as beloved by players and umpires as Leo Durocher was despised. The Senor preferred to kill opponents softly with his strategic moves and analytical mind—a style that gave him status as lone challenger to Yankee dominance in the 1950s and '60s.

History remembers Lopez as the only manager to beat the New York Yankees from 1951 through 1964, a period in which the Bronx Bombers won 12 American League pennants. They failed to win only in 1954, when Lopez guided the pitching- and slugging-rich Cleveland Indians to an A.L.-record 111 victories, and 1959, when he directed Chicago's "Go Go White Sox" to a surprising pennant. In nine of the other 12 seasons in that 14-year span, Lopez's Indians and White Sox finished second.

> "Lopez knows how he wants things run and he runs them that way. He's at his best with a club that acts and plays as intelligent professionals should." —*Bill Veeck*

LOPEZ

"I handle my players the way I wanted to be handled as a player," Lopez liked to say, referring to a record-setting 19-year playing career in which he caught 1,918 games — a record that stood for four decades. The two-time All-Star and .261 career hitter was a superb handler of pitchers, team leader and student of the game while playing for Brooklyn, the Boston Braves, Pittsburgh and Cleveland, all typically second-division teams.

When Lopez took the Indians reins in 1951, he inherited a pitching staff featuring Early Wynn, Bob Lemon, Mike Garcia and Bob Feller. Cleveland responded to his gentle prodding and patriarchal guidance, powering to the 1954 pennant before losing in a shocking World Series sweep to the New York Giants. Lopez was hired by Bill Veeck in 1957 and pulled off a shocker of his own two years later. But the overachieving Sox lost to Los Angeles in the 1959 fall classic.

The always-talkative Floridian managed eight more seasons before retiring with a 1,410-1,004 record and impressive .584 winning percentage. His final two seasons were shortened by ill health.

LOPEZ

TED LYONS

THEODORE AMAR LYONS
CHICAGO A.L. 1923 TO 1946
ENTIRE ACTIVE PITCHING CAREER OF 21
SEASONS WITH CHICAGO A.L. WON 260
GAMES, LOST 230. TIED FOR LEAGUE'S MOST
VICTORIES 1923 AND 1927, BEST EARNED RUN
AVERAGE, 2.10 IN 1942 WHEN HE STARTED
AND FINISHED ALL 20 GAMES. PITCHED
NO-HIT GAME, AUG. 21, 1926 AGAINST BOSTON.
PITCHED 21-INNING GAME MAY 24, 1929.

Born: 12-28-00, Lake Charles, La. **Died:** 7-25-86 **Height/Weight:** 5-11/200 **Bats/Throws:** B/R **Position:** Pitcher

Career statistics: 260-230, 3.67 ERA, 1,073 strikeouts **Teams:** White Sox 1923-42, 1946

He was a first-class citizen for a second-class team, the primary reason Chicago didn't crash through the American League basement from 1923 through '46. Ted Lyons used his warm, friendly personality to win over White Sox fans and his efficient right arm to stabilize a franchise. Over 21 seasons, Lyons was king of Chicago's South Side — a 260-game winner for a team that finished in the second division 16 times.

"If Lyons had been with the Yankees, my guess would be that he would have won 400 games," said former New York manager Joe McCarthy. But the 5-foot-11, 200-pounder from Lake Charles, La., never complained about the weak teams for which he compiled some amazing numbers: three 20-win seasons, 356 complete games in 484 starts, 4,161 innings and a 3.67 ERA.

Lyons arrived in Chicago in 1923, a rookie straight off the Baylor University campus, and provided relief for a team still reeling from the Black Sox scandal. By 1924, he was a member of the rotation; by 1925, he was a 21-game winner. Never overpowering, his sneaky fastball, sharp-breaking curve and pinpoint control mesmerized hitters, who always seemed to be a pitch or two behind the wily righthander.

Lyons was at his crafty best in 1930, when he posted a 22-15 record and A.L.-leading totals of 29 complete games and 297$^{2}/_{3}$ innings for a team that finished 62-92. But his most impressive feat came after a 1931 shoulder injury forced him to reinvent his pitching style and turn to a career-saving knuckleball that allowed him to pitch 13 more seasons. Never again a 20-game winner, he posted 134 victories while continuing as White Sox stopper.

Most of all, Lyons was as fierce and combative on the mound as he was nice and gentlemanly off it. He was so popular that the White Sox used him late in his career as their "Sunday pitcher," the man who could attract fans. His final season was as a player-manager in 1946, after three years of duty in World War II.

"If I had the choice of any pitcher for a clutch game, the guy I'd pick would be Ted Lyons." —*Tris Speaker*

CONNIE MACK

CONNIE MACK

A STAR CATCHER BUT FAMED MORE
AS MANAGER OF THE PHILADELPHIA
ATHLETICS SINCE 1901.
WINNER OF 9 PENNANTS AND 5
WORLD CHAMPIONSHIPS.
RECEIVED THE BOK AWARD
IN PHILADELPHIA FOR 1929.

Born: 12-22-1862, East Brookfield, Mass. **Died:** 2-8-56
Height/Weight: 6-1/150 **Teams managed:** Pittsburgh 1894-96;
Athletics 1901-50 **Career record:** 3,731-3,948, .486
World Series titles: 1910, '11, '13, '29, '30 **Executive
career:** Founder, part-owner, owner of Athletics, 1901-50

He was a fixture on the baseball landscape, a physical and spiritual symbol of the game's 20th-century roots. Nobody had a more sustained impact on the National Pastime than Connie Mack, a key figure in the formation of the American League. For more than a half century, he was a player, pioneer, manager, builder and beloved owner of the team he founded, the Philadelphia Athletics.

The image still endures: a tall, thin, gaunt-faced Mack, dressed in dark business suit with high-collared shirt and derby hat, waving his folded scorecard to position his players. He was dignified, a soft-voiced, kindly gentleman who seldom lost his temper or used profanity. He was astute, a brilliant strategist and judge of talent.

Cornelius Alexander McGillicuddy, the man everyone called "Mr. Mack," learned his trade as a light-hitting catcher in the 1880s and '90s. But it was while managing in Ban Johnson's Western League that his talents as a tactician and organizer emerged. When Johnson transformed his minor circuit into the American League before the 1901 season, Mack was handed the Philadelphia franchise to build in his image, which he did, at first with the financial aid of Ben Shibe, later as majority owner.

The always cash-challenged Mack became renowned as a builder and destroyer of powerhouse teams. He won pennants in 1902 and 1905 and World

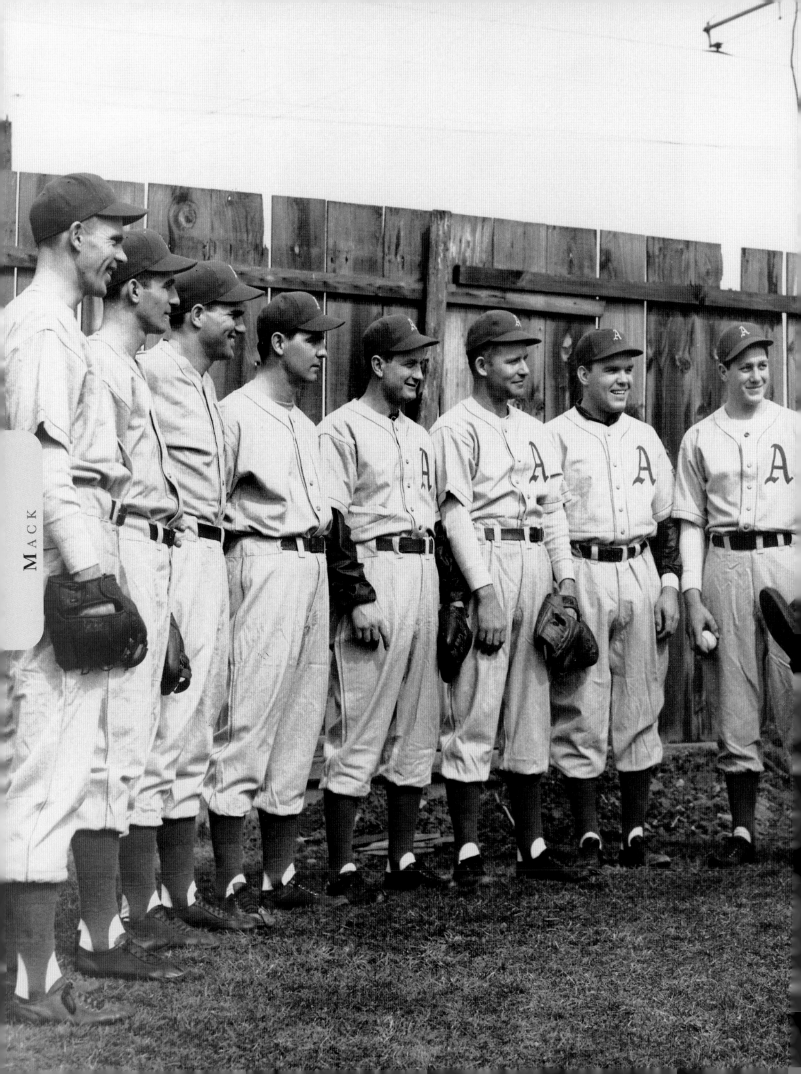

Series in 1910, '11 and '13 before being swept in the 1914 fall classic by the Boston Braves. He quickly sold off such star players as Eddie Collins, Home Run Baker and Eddie Plank and began rebuilding, a scenario that was repeated after his 1929, '30 and '31 A's won consecutive pennants and two World Series.

He never again would enjoy success. Over an incredible 50 years as A's manager, his teams won nine pennants and five World Series, finishing last 17 times. When he retired in 1950 at age 87, he owned a 3,731-3,948 managerial mark, a record for both wins and losses. Mack watched, heart-broken, in 1955 as the franchise was moved to Kansas City and died a year later at age 93.

"To me, the name of Connie Mack always has been synonymous with baseball, standing for everything that is best for the game he loved." —*Will Harridge*

Executive/Year elected: 1978, Committee on Veterans

LARRY MACPHAIL

LELAND STANFORD MacPHAIL
"LARRY"

DYNAMIC, INNOVATIVE EXECUTIVE MADE HIS MARK AS PROGRESSIVE HEAD OF THREE CLUBS—CINCINNATI REDS, BROOKLYN DODGERS AND NEW YORK YANKEES—FROM 1933 TO 1947. WON CHAMPIONSHIPS IN BOTH LEAGUES—WITH DODGERS IN 1941 AND YANKEES IN 1947. PIONEERED NIGHT BALL AT CINCINNATI IN 1935. ALSO INSTALLED LIGHTS AT EBBETS FIELD AND YANKEE STADIUM, ORIGINATED PLANE TRAVEL BY PLAYING PERSONNEL AND IDEA OF STADIUM CLUB. HELPED SET UP EMPLOYEE AND PLAYER PENSION PLANS.

Born: 2-3-1890, Cass City, Mich. **Died:** 10-1-75 **Executive career:** General manager of Reds, 1933-37; president and general manager of Dodgers, 1938-42; part-owner and general manager of Yankees, 1945-47

Proud, boisterous and tempestuous, Leland Stanford "Larry" MacPhail ran roughshod through a baseball world that revolved too slowly for his fast-forward mind. Innovative, ingenius and dynamic, he provided a nontraditional vision that helped carry the sport into a new era of prosperity. Love him or hate him, MacPhail left a colorful imprint that remains embedded in the psyche of today's National Pastime.

There was nothing subtle about the "Roaring Redhead," a bigger-than-life, hard-drinking man with an ego the size

"The baseball man who didn't have a row with Pop just wasn't going anywhere." *—Lee MacPhail*

of his native Michigan. MacPhail, who led a group of officers in an unsuccessful attempt to kidnap Kaiser Wilhelm after World War I, was opinionated and loud, always ready to browbeat or punch an opponent into submission. His ideas were so aggressive and far-reaching he became known as the "Barnum of Baseball."

Among MacPhail's contributions was night baseball, which he pioneered in 1935 when he staged the first major league game under the lights while working as general manager of the Cincinnati Reds. He later introduced to baseball such concepts as air travel, old-

timers games, plush stadium clubs, fireworks, batting helmets, daily radio broadcasts and televised games. Nothing was beyond MacPhail's vision and he doubled as master rebuilder of struggling franchises.

MacPhail, who performed his first magic with Columbus of the American Association from 1930-33, rebuilt a nearly-bankrupt Reds team that would win consecutive pennants and a World Series in 1939 and '40, a hapless Brooklyn franchise that would win a pennant in 1941 and a sagging New York Yankees team that returned to the championship stage in 1947 after an unusual three-year absence.

He also found time to serve as a colonel during World War II, install lights at three stadiums, champion Happy Chandler as baseball's second commissioner and purchase part interest in the Yankees. MacPhail's 18-year baseball association came to a stormy end during the victory celebration after the 1947 Series. His alcohol-induced rampage resulted in a brawl and prompted co-owners Dan Topping and Del Webb to buy him out the next day.

MACPHAIL

LELAND STANFORD MACPHAIL JR.
ONE OF THE LEADING EXECUTIVES IN BASEBALL HISTORY, HIS NAME IS SYNONYMOUS WITH INTEGRITY AND SPORTSMANSHIP. AS FARM DIRECTOR AND PLAYER PERSONNEL DIRECTOR OF THE YANKEES (1949-58), HELPED BUILD A SYSTEM WHICH YIELDED SEVEN WORLD CHAMPIONSHIPS. AS ORIOLES GENERAL MANAGER (1959-65), HELPED LAY THE GROUNDWORK FOR ONE OF THE GAME'S MOST CONSISTENTLY SUCCESSFUL FRANCHISES; AND HE LATER REJOINED THE YANKEES IN THE SAME CAPACITY. SERVED ADMIRABLY AS AMERICAN LEAGUE PRESIDENT (1974-1983) BEFORE CONCLUDING HIS 45-YEAR CAREER AS PRESIDENT OF THE PLAYER RELATIONS COMMITTEE. HE AND HIS FATHER LARRY FORM THE FIRST FATHER SON TANDEM IN THE HALL OF FAME.

Executive/Year elected: 1998, Committee on Veterans

LEE MACPHAIL

Born: 10-25-17, Nashville, Tenn. **Executive career:** Director of player personnel of Yankees, 1947-58; president and general manager of Orioles, 1959-66; general manager of Yankees, 1966-73; American League president 1974-83; president of Player Relations Committee, 1983-85

One was a stormy, dynamic cyclone that ripped apart the landscape of baseball in the 1930s and '40s. The other was a quiet, gentle breeze that helped carry the game through a momentous period of prosperity. Leland Stanford "Lee" MacPhail was the polar opposite of father Larry in personality, but a spitting image in terms of influence on the National Pastime he served for 45 years.

While Larry MacPhail was an innovator and pioneer who pushed his agenda by sheer force of personality, Lee was a gentleman administrator who began his baseball association with the minor league Reading club in 1941 and ended it in 1985 as president of the Player Relations Committee. In between, he served as general manager and president of the Baltimore Orioles, director of player personnel and G.M. of the New York Yankees and president of the American League.

Lee was everything his colorful father was not — dignified, calm and thoughtful, making up for lack of charisma with steady service. He rose through the

> **"Unfortunately, a person with Dad's talent comes along only once every 50 years. I've never thought of imitating him. I inherited neither his genius nor his temper. I'm just an ordinary person."** —*Lee MacPhail*

Yankees system, contributing to the organization's seven World Series championships from 1949-58, and then moved to the Orioles front office. Over eight Baltimore seasons, MacPhail laid the foundation for the team's rise to 1960s and '70s prominence, a success sealed by his 1965 acquisition of Frank Robinson from Cincinnati.

After serving as Yankees general manager from 1966-73, MacPhail was elected A.L. president — a post he held for 10 years. During that tenure, he oversaw expansion to Toronto and Seattle and was credited with bringing an end to the 1981 players' strike when he stepped in for the owners to handle stalled negotiations.

MacPhail is best remembered for overturning the umpires' ruling in the 1983 "Pine Tar" case, awarding a controversial home run to Kansas City slugger George Brett. He also is remembered as half of baseball's first father-son Hall of Fame tandem. In keeping with the bloodlines, Lee's son, Andy, has been a longtime baseball executive, first with Minnesota and currently with the Chicago Cubs.

MICKEY MANTLE

MICKEY CHARLES MANTLE
NEW YORK A.L. 1951-1968
HIT 536 HOME RUNS. WON LEAGUE HOMER TITLE
AND SLUGGING CROWN FOUR TIMES. MADE
2415 HITS. BATTED .300 OR OVER IN EACH
OF TEN YEARS WITH TOP OF .365 IN 1957.
TOPPED A.L. IN WALKS FIVE YEARS AND
IN RUNS SCORED SIX SEASONS. VOTED
MOST VALUABLE PLAYER 1956-57-62. NAMED
ON 20 A.L. ALL-STAR TEAMS. SET WORLD
SERIES RECORDS FOR HOMERS, 18; RUNS, 42;
RUNS BATTED IN, 40; TOTAL BASES, 123;
AND BASES ON BALLS, 43.

Born: 10-20-31, Spavinaw, Okla. **Died:** 8-13-95 **Height/Weight:** 5-11/200 **Bats/Throws:** B/R **Primary position:** Center field

Career statistics: .298 avg., 2,415 hits, 1,677 runs, 536 HR, 1,509 RBIs **Teams:** Yankees 1951-68 **Batting champion:** A.L., 1956

HR champion: A.L., 1955, '56, '58, 60 **Major awards:** A.L. MVP, 1956, '57, '62

When he cut his Oklahoma ties in 1949, he was called the "Commerce Comet," and when he retired from baseball 20 seasons later he was known affectionately, simply, as "The Mick." In between, a naive country boy named Mickey Mantle rose to prominence as a national icon and the centerpiece of a New York Yankees dynasty that captured 12 American League pennants and seven World Series championships over a glorious 14-year span.

The husky, blond, switch-hitting 19-year-old with blacksmith arms, sprinter speed and an unassuming, home-spun charm arrived in 1951 as the heir apparent to center fielder Joe DiMaggio, a New York idol who was playing his final season. In the Babe Ruth-Lou Gehrig-DiMaggio tradition that had helped the Yankees achieve baseball superiority for three decades, Mantle, 200 pounds of unprecedented power from both sides of the plate, eventually won over fans with his tape-measure home runs and an almost-mystical aura that would transcend his 18-year big-league career.

Mantle, who played in 16 All-Star Games, was plagued by a series of early knee problems that compromised his all-around skills and prematurely triggered a

> **"If Mickey had had good legs throughout his career, he would have been an unbelievable ballplayer."** —*Ralph Houk*

decline, but his power-hitting feats remain legendary. Fans still talk about the 565-foot Mantle blast that left Washington's Griffith Park in 1953 and the moon-shot homer that almost cleared Yankee Stadium's right field facade 10 years later. And not only were his home runs long, they were frequent.

Two times Mantle topped the 50 plateau—in 1956 when he won a Triple Crown (.353, 52 homers, 130 RBIs) and in 1961 when he hit 54 while joining teammate Roger Maris in the chase of Ruth's single-season record—en route to a career total of 536. And 10 times he complemented that power with .300-plus averages that helped him earn three MVP awards.

But Mantle's greatest legacy was written in the 12 World Series in which he set numerous fall classic records, including home runs (18), RBIs (40), runs (42), extra-base hits (26) and total bases (123).

MANTLE

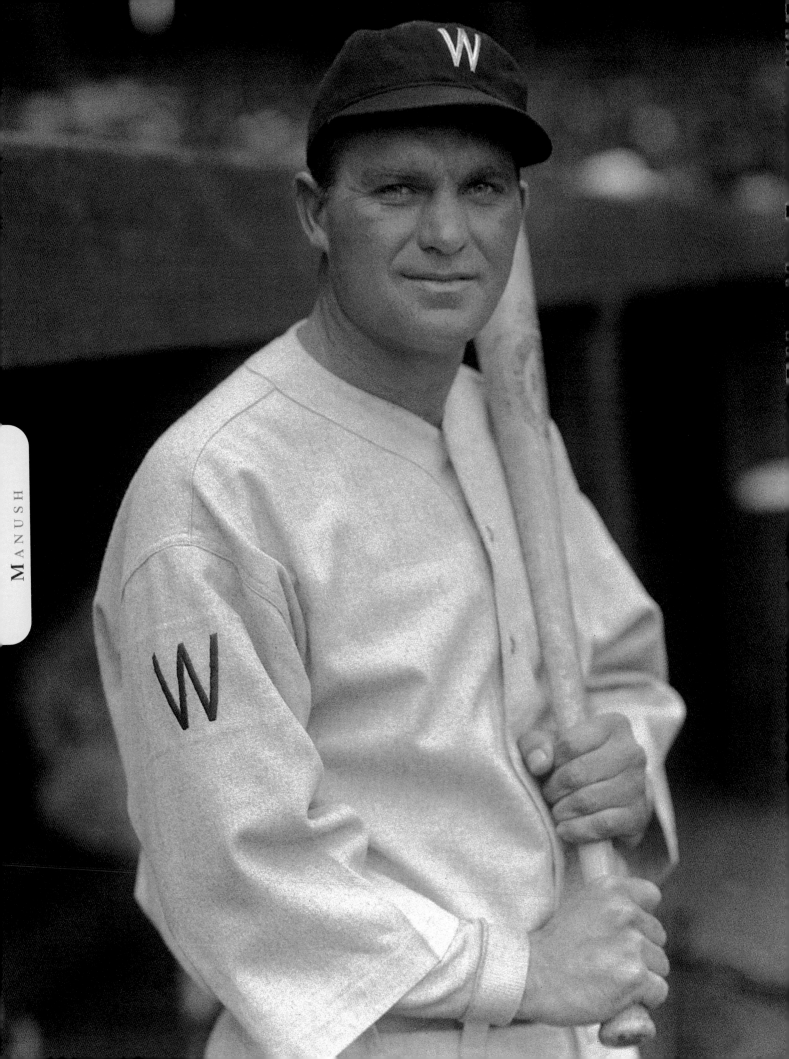

HENRY EMMET MANUSH
1923—1939
SLUGGING OUTFIELDER
FOR 6 MAJOR LEAGUE CLUBS. BATTING
CHAMPION OF A.L. AT .378 WITH 1926 TIGERS.
LIFETIME AVERAGE OF .330 IN 2,009
MAJOR LEAGUE GAMES. HAD 2,524 HITS.

Player/Year elected: 1964, Committee on Veterans

HEINIE MANUSH

Born: 7-20-01, Tuscumbia, Ala. **Died:** 5-12-71 **Height/Weight:** 6-1/200 **Bats/Throws:** L/L **Primary position:** Outfield
Career statistics: .330 avg., 2,524 hits, 1,287 runs, 1,183 RBIs **Teams:** Tigers 1923-27; Browns 1928-30; Senators 1930-35; Red Sox 1936; Dodgers 1937-38; Pirates 1938-39 **Batting champion:** A.L., 1926

He was a Ty Cobb protege, a hard-charging, spikes-flying battler with a gap-plugging left-handed swing. Heinie Manush never could match Cobb's spitfire intensity or defense-shredding speed, but he spent 17 major league seasons duplicating his unmistakable style. Like Cobb, Manush was a hitting machine, a line drive-slashing artist whose .330 career average ranks among the best of baseball's modern era.

Manush, who received batting tips from player-manager Cobb when he made his Detroit debut in 1923, choked up several inches and drove through pitches with powerful arms from an upright stance. He could look awkward, but that didn't keep him from making contact and consistently guiding missiles into the left- and right-center field gaps. Never a home run hitter, the 6-foot-1 Manush twice led the American League in doubles and pounded a league-leading 17 triples in 1933.

The center of Detroit's Hall of Fame outfield with Cobb and Harry Heilmann, Manush jumped into prominence in 1926 when he batted .378 and edged out Babe Ruth on the season's final day for the A.L. batting title. Two years later, playing

for St. Louis, he batted .378 again and lost the title on the final day to Washington's Goose Goslin. Manush was a four-time 200-hit run-producer who topped 100 RBIs twice and scored 100 runs six times.

When Cobb was ousted as Tigers manager after the 1926 season, the hard-nosed Alabaman fought with new boss George Moriarty and was traded in 1927 to the Browns. A bitter salary hassle ended his St. Louis stay in 1930 and he spent five-plus seasons in Washington, where he contributed a .336 average to a pennant-winning 1933 campaign. He retired in 1939 after short stays with the Boston Red Sox, Brooklyn and Pittsburgh.

A capable outfielder with a good arm, Manush is best remembered for a menacing bat that produced 1,457 hits over a seven-year span (208 per season) with the Browns and Senators. He finished his career with 2,524 hits and more triples (160) than home runs (110).

"Don't you believe it that old ballplayers don't care whether they get in or stay out of the Hall of Fame. It's the perfect climax to the perfect way to live—playing baseball." —*Heinie Manush*

WALTER J.V. MARANVILLE
"RABBIT"
BOSTON, PITTSBURGH, CHICAGO,
BROOKLYN AND ST. LOUIS,
NATIONAL LEAGUE, 1912 – 1935
PLAYED MORE GAMES, 2153, AT SHORTSTOP
THAN ANY OTHER NATIONAL LEAGUE PLAYER.
AT BAT TOTAL, 10078, SURPASSED BY ONLY
ONE NATIONAL LEAGUER, HONUS WAGNER.
MADE 2605 HITS IN 23 SEASONS. MEMBER
OF 1914 BOSTON BRAVES "MIRACLE TEAM"
THAT WON PENNANT, THEN WORLD SERIES
FROM ATHLETICS IN 4 GAMES.

Player/Year elected: 1954, 82.9 percent of vote

RABBIT MARANVILLE

Born: 11-11-1891, Springfield, Mass. **Died:** 1-5-54 **Height/Weight:** 5-5/155 **Bats/Throws:** R/R **Primary position:** Shortstop **Career statistics:** .258 avg., 2,605 hits, 1,255 runs, 291 steals **Teams:** Braves 1912-20, 1929-33, 1935; Pirates 1921-24; Cubs 1925; Dodgers 1926; Cardinals 1927-28

He was the Peter Pan of baseball, the hippity-hoppity little shortstop who never grew up. When Rabbit Maranville wasn't performing defensive magic and inspiring teammates, he was entertaining the world with his crazy stunts and off-the-wall antics. Clown, comedian, prankster, carouser and showman — there never was a dull moment in the 23-year career of the game's freest spirit.

The staying power of the 5-foot-5, 155-pound Maranville from 1912-35 can be attributed to the verve with which he attacked life. Fans and teammates never knew what to expect from the rabbit-eared kid from Massachusetts, who might slide through the umpire's legs one day, shadow and mimic the opposing catcher as he chased a foul popup the next. If it was raining, Rabbit might go to his position wearing rubber boots; if it was hot, he might take the field shirtless.

"Today I consider Maranville the greatest player to come into the game since Ty Cobb cracked his way into the ranks of big leaguers." —*George Stallings, manager of 1914 "Miracle Braves"*

Fans loved his vaudeville act, but they also appreciated the way he darted far and wide, gobbling up grounders and making his trademark "vest-pocket catches." He was the consummate shortstop, a five-time National League fielding average leader, and a competent righthanded singles hitter who made up for his career .258 average with an ability to move runners and deliver in the clutch.

Insiders pointed to Maranville (.246) and second baseman Johnny Evers (.279) as key figures for the "Miracle Braves" during their run to a 1914 World Series championship. And after nine seasons in Boston, Maranville remained at center stage in N.L. stops at Pittsburgh, Chicago, Brooklyn and St. Louis before a six-year return engagement with the Braves.

Through it all, he generated tales of ledge walking, river swimming and extravagant practical jokes — anything for a laugh. But when the Dodgers shuffled him to the minors in 1927, apparently signaling the end of his career, he gave up drinking, got serious and returned to the big leagues, helping the Cardinals win a 1928 pennant. When he retired in 1935, he had played 2,670 games, batted 10,078 times and collected 2,605 hits.

Player/Year elected: 1983, 83.7 percent of vote

JUAN MARICHAL

JUAN ANTONIO
MARICHAL SANCHEZ
SAN FRANCISCO N. L., 1960-1973 BOSTON A. L. 1974
LOS ANGELES N. L., 1975
HIGH-KICKING RIGHT-HANDER FROM DOMINICAN
REPUBLIC WON 243 GAMES AND LOST ONLY 142
OVER 16 SEASONS. WON 20 GAMES SIX TIMES AND
NO-HIT HOUSTON IN 1963. LED N.L. IN COMPLETE
GAMES AND SHUTOUTS TWICE AND IN ERA WITH
2.10 IN 1969. COMPLETED 244 GAMES DURING
CAREER, STRIKING OUT 2,303 AND FINISHING
WITH 2.89 ERA.

Born: 10-20-37, Laguna Verde, D.R. **Height/Weight:** 6-0/185 **Bats/Throws:** R/R **Position:** Pitcher **Career statistics:** 243-142, 2.89 ERA, 2,303 strikeouts **Teams:** Giants 1960-73; Red Sox 1974; Dodgers 1975

His leg rose up ... up ... up, until his foot was suspended over his head. Then the real run began. His leg, his right arm, his entire body swept forward in a blur and the ball swept toward home plate with unpredictable velocity and movement. Hitting against Juan Marichal was like trying to grab a fish out of a stream.

That's what it must have been like for the Philadelphia Phillies when the 22-year-old Dominican righthander made his major league debut in 1960 with a one-hit shutout. And that's what it must have been like throughout the 1960s as Marichal won 191 games, more than any other pitcher. He was the ace for a San Francisco

"This guy is a natural. He's got ideas about what he wants to do and he goes and does it. He amazes me." — *Carl Hubbell*

Giants team that won one pennant and annually battled Los Angeles and St. Louis for N.L. superiority.

The name of Marichal's game was confidence and control. He threw five basic pitches, but never at the same speed or with the same motion. He came at hitters sidearm, three-quarters or over the top and the count was inconsequential because Marichal had an uncanny

knack for painting the corner. Batters could not guess and their frustration was exacerbated by the impish grin that lit up his cherubic face and the child-like playfulness that always accompanied him to the mound.

From 1963-69, a shockingly efficient seven-year stretch, Marichal had reason to grin as he posted six 20-win seasons with such records as 25-8, 25-6 and 26-9. His ERAs were equally impressive and few pitchers could match his consistency, but he never won a Cy Young while competing against such contemporaries as Sandy Koufax, Bob Gibson and Tom Seaver.

Marichal's only weakness was an emotional fire that burned just under the surface. That emotion erupted in a 1965 bat-swinging brawl during which Marichal clubbed Dodgers catcher John Roseboro and put an indelible black mark on his image. But nothing could tarnish the .631 winning percentage (243-142) and 2.89 ERA he compiled over a 16-year career that ended in 1975 at Los Angeles.

MARICHAL

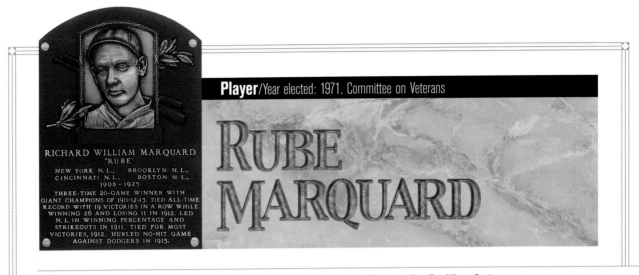

RICHARD WILLIAM MARQUARD
"RUBE"
NEW YORK N.L., BROOKLYN N.L.,
CINCINNATI N.L., BOSTON N.L.,
1908 - 1925
THREE-TIME 20-GAME WINNER WITH
GIANT CHAMPIONS OF 1911-12-13. TIED ALL-TIME
RECORD WITH 19 VICTORIES IN A ROW WHILE
WINNING 26 AND LOSING 11 IN 1912. LED
N.L. IN WINNING PERCENTAGE AND
STRIKEOUTS IN 1911. TIED FOR MOST
VICTORIES, 1912. HURLED NO-HIT GAME
AGAINST DODGERS IN 1915.

RUBE MARQUARD

Born: 10-9-1886, Cleveland, Ohio **Died:** 6-1-80 **Height/Weight:** 6-3/180 **Bats/Throws:** B/L **Position:** Pitcher
Career statistics: 201-177, 3.08 ERA, 1,593 strikeouts **Teams:** Giants 1908-15; Dodgers 1915-20; Reds 1921; Braves 1922-25

Everybody called him "Rube," but he really wasn't one. Richard "Rube" Marquard, the son of Cleveland's chief engineer, was an intelligent, flashy-dressing, sophisticated man about town who doubled as a stylish lefthander for the New York Giants and Brooklyn Dodgers. Over a career that stretched through 18 major league seasons, he was stylish and sophisticated enough to win 201 games while helping the Giants and Dodgers to five National League pennants.

The 6-foot-3, 180-pounder got his nickname from a sportswriter who compared him, physically, to American League lefty Rube Waddell, a notorious carouser, drinker and nightlife hound. But Marquard was just the opposite—a non-drinker, non-smoker who reached New York in 1908 with much fanfare and a record bonus that prompted the media to hail him as the "$11,000 beauty." Young, inexperienced and vulnerable, beauty quickly turned to an "$11,000 lemon."

By 1911, however, Giants fans were marveling at Marquard's transformation, as were hitters who flailed helplessly at a powerful fastball and sharp-breaking

"I had a lot of fun playing ball and made pretty good money, too. ... The only regret I have in baseball is that never in my life did I get to see Ty Cobb play." —*Rube Marquard*

curve that came at them from a three-quarters delivery. The fastball seemed to hop just before it reached the plate and Marquard's once-floundering career hopped with it. Forming a great 1-2 pitching punch with Christy Mathewson, he was 24-7, 26-11 and 23-10 from 1911-13 as the Giants won three straight pennants.

Those were the best seasons of Marquard's career, even though the Giants lost all three World Series—including a 1912 classic in which Marquard won two games against Boston. The handsome, dark-complexioned star enhanced his New York popularity when he reeled off a record 19-game winning streak in 1912 and his marriage to Broadway actress Blossom Seely created headlines, as did off-season appearances with her on stage.

The bubble burst in 1914 when Marquard sank to 12-22 and he was traded a year later to the Dodgers, with whom he was 13-6 and 10-7 in pennant-winning 1916 and 1920 campaigns. Again his teams failed to win the World Series and he finished his career with N.L. stops in Cincinnati (1921) and Boston (1922-25).

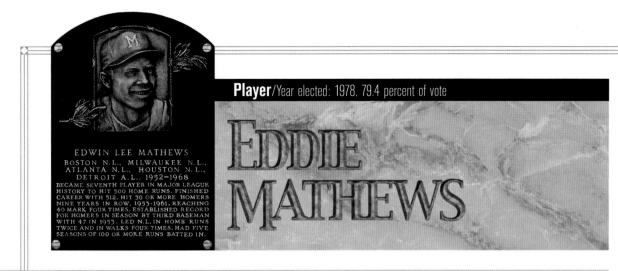

EDWIN LEE MATHEWS
BOSTON N.L., MILWAUKEE N.L.,
ATLANTA N.L., HOUSTON N.L.,
DETROIT A.L., 1952–1968
BECAME SEVENTH PLAYER IN MAJOR LEAGUE
HISTORY TO HIT 500 HOME RUNS. FINISHED
CAREER WITH 512. HIT 30 OR MORE HOMERS
NINE YEARS IN ROW, 1953-1961, REACHING
40 MARK FOUR TIMES. ESTABLISHED RECORD
FOR HOMERS IN SEASON BY THIRD BASEMAN
WITH 47 IN 1953. LED N.L. IN HOME RUNS
TWICE AND IN WALKS FOUR TIMES. HAD FIVE
SEASONS OF 100 OR MORE RUNS BATTED IN.

Player/Year elected: 1978, 79.4 percent of vote

EDDIE MATHEWS

Born: 10-13-31, Texarkana, Tex. **Died:** 2-18-01 **Height/Weight:** 6-1/200 **Bats/Throws:** L/R **Primary position:** Third base
Career statistics: .271 avg., 2,315 hits, 1,509 runs, 512 HR, 1,453 RBIs **Teams:** Boston Braves 1952; Milwaukee Braves 1953-65;
Atlanta Braves 1966; Astros 1967; Tigers 1967-68 **HR champion:** N.L., 1953, '59

The apple cheeks, dark, handsome features and Texas country-boy shyness belied the quick temper and fiery intensity Eddie Mathews brought to a diamond. So did the boyish charm that captivated fans and the mesmerizing swing that tortured pitchers for 17 major league seasons. Eddie Mathews was a baseball enigma — a sleek, fast, hungry wildcat disguised as a mild-mannered, power-hitting third baseman for the Boston/Milwaukee/Atlanta Braves.

Mathews' 6-foot-1, 200-pound, rock-solid body was a near perfect blend of speed, quickness and power. The speed was documented in 1953, his second season, when he was timed from home to first in 3.5 seconds. The quickness was critical to Mathews' development as a solid third baseman and his near-perfect lefthanded swing, which launched 512 home runs.

Early observers saw a lot of Ted Williams in Mathews' batting style. He used a slightly open stance to attack pitches with a buggy-whip swing that shot line

drives into distant stands. A dead-pull hitter who powered home runs in bunches, he formed a lethal 13-season combination in the Braves' lineup with Hank Aaron. Four times he powered 40-plus homers, 10 times he topped 30 while driving in 1,453 runs. The Aaron-Mathews tandem led Milwaukee to consecutive pennants and the city's only championship in 1957.

Mathews was an instant favorite of fans who watched him bat .302 with 47 homers and 135 RBIs in 1953 — the Braves' first Milwaukee season. That was Mathews' way of signaling elite status among such contemporary sluggers as Aaron, Mickey Mantle, Willie Mays, Duke Snider and Ralph Kiner. In the eight-year stretch from 1953-60, he averaged 39 homers and 105 RBIs while consistently ranking among league leaders in walks and runs scored.

The sometimes-moody Mathews, who won two home run crowns and played in 10 All-Star Games, was feared beyond his hitting feats. His fiery temper was exhibited in several celebrated baseball fights — none of which he lost. But former teammates cited the never-say-die hustle, personal expectations and demands he made on others as the real bottom line.

"Mathews is just as strong as Mantle. They don't hit the same — Mantle gets all his weight into his swing; Mathews uses his wrists more, like Ted Williams." — *Warren Spahn, 1953*

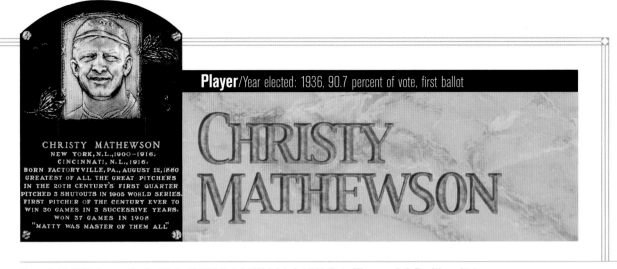

CHRISTY MATHEWSON
NEW YORK, N.L., 1900-1916.
CINCINNATI, N.L., 1916.
BORN FACTORYVILLE, PA., AUGUST 12, 1880
GREATEST OF ALL THE GREAT PITCHERS
IN THE 20TH CENTURY'S FIRST QUARTER
PITCHED 3 SHUTOUTS IN 1905 WORLD SERIES.
FIRST PITCHER OF THE CENTURY EVER TO
WIN 30 GAMES IN 3 SUCCESSIVE YEARS.
WON 37 GAMES IN 1908
"MATTY WAS MASTER OF THEM ALL"

Player/Year elected: 1936, 90.7 percent of vote, first ballot

CHRISTY MATHEWSON

Born: 8-12-1880, Factoryville, Pa. **Died:** 10-7-25 **Height/Weight:** 6-1/195 **Bats/Throws:** R/R **Position:** Pitcher
Career statistics: 373-188, 2.13 ERA, 2,507 strikeouts **Teams:** Giants 1900-16; Reds 1916

He was an unusual combination of finesse, guile and controlled intensity, a baseball artist who turned out pitching masterpieces over the first 17 years of the 20th century. Christy Mathewson was the Greg Maddux of yesteryear and his National League record-tying 373 career victories still stand as testimony to artistic efficiency.

When Mathewson threw his first pitch for John McGraw's New York Giants in the summer of 1900, he provided a breath of fresh air for the rough-and-tumble game that scared away the more genteel, educated class of would-be fan. Matty, a product of Bucknell University, helped change baseball's image and he did it without the power style that characterized most pitchers of the era.

"You could sit in a chair and catch Matty," said former Giants catcher Chief Meyers and, indeed, the righthanded Mathewson delivered his pitches with an easy overhand motion and pinpoint control. He worked with savvy, seldom walked a batter and spotted pitches, letting fielders do their job. His typical game required 80 to 90 pitches and he seldom topped 100. When in trouble, he turned to his special fadeaway curve — a modern-day screwball that mesmerized both lefthanded and righthanded hitters.

Mathewson, a first-ballot Hall of Fame selection in the charter class of 1936, also mesmerized record keepers with his numbers. He was the workhorse of Giants teams that won five pennants and a World Series from 1904-13 — a four-time 30-game winner who set a still-standing modern N.L. record with 37 victories in 1908. His pitching ledger is filled

> **"There is no doubt but that Mathewson was the greatest pitcher of all time. He was the perfect pitcher. ... He had all kinds of stuff and he knew just when to use it."** —*Roger Bresnahan*

with 20-win seasons (13), ERA titles (5), shutouts (79) and strikeout crowns (4). Matty's three straight 30-win seasons from 1903-05 were matched by only Grover Alexander among 20th century hurlers.

Mathewson is best remembered for two performances — one good, one bad. His three-shutout 1905 World Series effort against Connie Mack's Philadelphia A's has never been duplicated and he was the pitcher who lost to Chicago nemesis Three-Finger Brown in the one-game playoff that decided the infamous 1908 "Merkle's Boner" pennant race.

MATHEWSON

WILLIE HOWARD MAYS, JR.
"THE SAY HEY KID"
NEW YORK N.L., SAN FRANCISCO N.L.,
NEW YORK N.L., 1951-1973
ONE OF BASEBALL'S MOST COLORFUL AND
EXCITING STARS, EXCELLED IN ALL PHASES OF
THE GAME. THIRD IN HOMERS (660) RUNS (2,062)
AND TOTAL BASES (6,066); SEVENTH IN HITS
(3,283) AND RBI'S (1,903). FIRST IN PUTOUTS
BY OUTFIELDER (7,095). FIRST TO TOP BOTH
300 HOMERS AND 300 STEALS. LED LEAGUE IN
BATTING ONCE, SLUGGING FIVE TIMES, HOME
RUNS AND STEALS FOUR SEASONS. VOTED N.L.
MVP IN 1954 AND 1965. PLAYED IN 24
ALL-STAR GAMES - A RECORD.

Player/Year elected: 1979, 94.7 percent of vote, first ballot

WILLIE MAYS

Born: 5-6-31, Westfield, Ala. **Height/Weight:** 5-11/180 **Bats/Throws:** R/R **Primary position:** Center field **Career statistics:** .302 avg., 3,283 hits, 2,062 runs, 660 HR, 1,903 RBIs, 338 steals **Teams:** New York Giants 1951-52, 1954-57; San Francisco Giants 1958-72; Mets 1972-73

Batting champion: N.L., 1954 **HR champion:** N.L., 1955, '62, '64, '65 **Major awards:** N.L. Rookie of Year, 1951; N.L. MVP, 1954, '65

He might have been as close to baseball perfection as we'll ever get. And from the moment you walked into the stadium and took your seat, through the final out of every game, your eyes, by sheer magnetic force, were drawn to the youthful smile, the boundless enthusiasm and the graceful athleticism of Willie Mays.

The "Say Hey Kid," the former New York and San Francisco Giants star who set the lofty standard by which center fielders will forever be judged, could dominate games in ways beyond comprehension. He was the classic five-tool star

Mays with Brooklyn Dodger slugger Duke Snider.

"This man dominates a game like no other player in the history of the game. I don't think there is any play he can't make." —*Charlie Fox, Giants manager, 1971*

home run. He was a batting champion, four-time homer leader, two-time MVP and full-time offensive grinder who topped 300 total bases in 13 straight seasons.

Mays made an indelible stamp on the record books with 660 home runs (third on the all-time list), 3,283 hits (10th) and top 10 rankings in runs (2,062), RBIs (1,903), total bases (6,066) and other categories. But memories somehow gravitate toward the graceful ease with which he made difficult defensive plays look easy and the instinctive acceleration around second base on balls into the gap.

with blazing speed and equally fast instincts, powerful arms that could launch balls out of any ballpark and a sculpted 5-foot-11 body that was durable enough to withstand 13 seasons of 150-plus games.

Baseball lore is filled with accounts of incredible Mays catches and throws. He showcased his daring baserunning in a record-tying 24 All-Star Games. He was a career .302 hitter who could break up a pitching duel with an opposite-field bloop single or a 450-foot

Mays is personified by the back-to-the-infield catch he made in Game 1 of the 1954 World Series, setting the stage for the Giants' shocking sweep of Cleveland. But he also is remembered for his 1961 four-homer game at Milwaukee and numerous other spectacular moments that defined a 22-year career that stretched from 1951, when he helped the Giants stage the most dramatic pennant run in history, to a 1973 finale with the New York Mets.

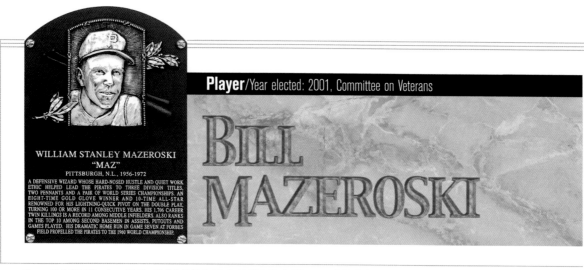

BILL MAZEROSKI

WILLIAM STANLEY MAZEROSKI
"MAZ"
PITTSBURGH, N.L., 1956-1972

A DEFENSIVE WIZARD WHOSE HARD-NOSED HUSTLE AND QUIET WORK ETHIC HELPED LEAD THE PIRATES TO THREE DIVISION TITLES, TWO PENNANTS AND A PAIR OF WORLD SERIES CHAMPIONSHIPS. AN EIGHT-TIME GOLD GLOVE WINNER AND 10-TIME ALL-STAR RENOWNED FOR HIS LIGHTNING-QUICK PIVOT ON THE DOUBLE PLAY. TURNING 100 OR MORE IN 11 CONSECUTIVE YEARS. HIS 1,706 CAREER TWIN KILLINGS IS A RECORD AMONG MIDDLE INFIELDERS. ALSO RANKS IN THE TOP 10 AMONG SECOND BASEMEN IN ASSISTS, PUTOUTS AND GAMES PLAYED. HIS DRAMATIC HOME RUN IN GAME SEVEN AT FORBES FIELD PROPELLED THE PIRATES TO THE 1960 WORLD CHAMPIONSHIP.

Born: 9-5-36, Wheeling, W. Va. **Height/Weight:** 5-11/183 **Bats/Throws:** R/R **Primary position:** Second base
Career statistics: .260 avg., 2,016 hits **Teams:** Pirates 1956-72

Now you see it, now you don't. Such was the magic of a Bill Mazeroski double-play pivot, performed with sleight-of-hand artistry by two of the quickest and surest hands in baseball history. The pivot, the range, the quick and accurate arm, the rhythm and grace—all contributed to the defensive genius of the quietly efficient second baseman Pittsburgh fans called "Maz."

"He's the best I ever saw," said former Pirates coach Johnny Pesky, a shortstop who teamed with Hall of Fame second baseman Bobby Doerr in Boston. Pesky was bedazzled by Mazeroski's routine artistry, not his occasional spectacular play. And he was impressed with his powerful arm and his penchant for always being in the right place and making tough plays look easy.

Maz was especially fun to watch on double plays, accepting throws from his shortstop or third baseman and relaying them to first in one quick and fluid motion—as if they never even touched leather. It's no coincidence that he helped turn a record

"He is one of the greatest second basemen I've ever seen. He has all the tools and he has the desire." —*George Sisler*

1,706 double plays over a 17-year career that started in 1956 at age 19 and stretched through 1972. The West Virginian also led N.L. second basemen in fielding average three times and assists on nine occasions.

Never a prolific hitter, Mazeroski gained respect for his ability to come through in the clutch. He is best remembered for his dramatic Game 7 home run that gave Pittsburgh a 1960 World Series victory over the New York Yankees—one of the most storied blasts in history—and he twice topped 80 RBIs as a bottom-of-the-lineup righthanded hitter. But mostly he was a move-the-runners contact man who posted a .260 average with 2,016 hits.

The memory of Maz—soft-spoken, friendly, crewcut, always relaxed—is indelible. The seven-time All-Star Game performer, eight-time Gold Glove winner and member of two Pirates championship teams (1960, 1971) won occasional games with his bat, but he saved a lot more with his Hall of Fame-worthy defense.

M A Z E R O S K I

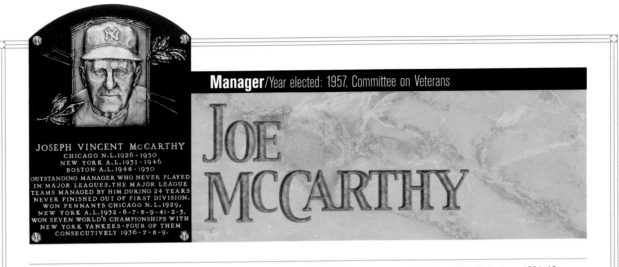

JOE MCCARTHY

JOSEPH VINCENT McCARTHY
CHICAGO N.L. 1926-1930
NEW YORK A.L. 1931-1946
BOSTON A.L. 1948-1950
OUTSTANDING MANAGER WHO NEVER PLAYED
IN MAJOR LEAGUES. THE MAJOR LEAGUE
TEAMS MANAGED BY HIM DURING 24 YEARS
NEVER FINISHED OUT OF FIRST DIVISION.
WON PENNANTS CHICAGO N.L. 1929,
NEW YORK A.L. 1932-6-7-8-9-41-2-3.
WON SEVEN WORLD'S CHAMPIONSHIPS WITH
NEW YORK YANKEES-FOUR OF THEM
CONSECUTIVELY 1936-7-8-9.

Born: 4-21-1887, Philadelphia, Pa. **Died:** 1-13-78 **Height/Weight:** 5-8/190 **Teams managed:** Cubs 1926-30; Yankees 1931-46; Red Sox 1948-50 **Career record:** 2,125-1,333, .615 **World Series titles:** 1932, '36, '37, '38, '39, '41, '43

Jimmy Dykes once called him a "push-button manager," a reference to the overabundance of talent Joe McCarthy had at his disposal with the New York Yankees. But "Marse Joe" was so much more than that. As a combination disciplinarian, handler of pitchers, strategist and winner, it's easy to make a case for him as the greatest manager of all time.

It was the square-jawed, no-nonsense Philadelphian who put the word "dynasty" into the New York vocabulary. He guided the Yankees to eight American League pennants and seven World Series championships in 16 years, including a then-unprecented four in a row (1936-39). But he also introduced the concept of "Yankee pride" to an organization that would embrace that principle well beyond his tenure as manager.

Anything less than first place was unacceptable to the 5-foot-8 former minor league second baseman and manager, who demanded teamwork over individual glory and mistake-free fundamentals over flamboyance. McCarthy expected excellence off the field

"I played under three great managers— McCarthy, (Bucky) Harris and (Casey) Stengel—and I have to put McCarthy at the top of the list. For my money, he wrote the book." —*Tommy Henrich*

as well as on and 100 percent dedication to baseball. The name "Yankees" became synonymous with "class" and players like Lou Gehrig, Joe DiMaggio, Tommy Henrich, Bill Dickey and Frank Crosetti performed with quiet dignity.

It wasn't that McCarthy couldn't handle superstars. He won a pennant in 1929, his fourth season as manager of the Chicago Cubs, while dealing with difficult Rogers Hornsby. After taking over the Yankees in 1931, he won a 1932 championship with a resentful Babe Ruth, who had been passed over for the job. In a 1948-50 career-ending managerial stint with the Boston Red Sox, McCarthy worked well with Ted Williams.

Often portrayed as colorless and humorless, McCarthy was admired and respected by players who helped him compile a 24-year legacy —2,125-1,333 in the regular season (.615), 30-13 in World Series play (.698). The first manager to make serious use of his bullpen remained with the Yankees until 1946, when he left because of ill health. McCarthy finished his career in Boston without ever having managed a second-division team.

Player/Year elected: 1946, Committee on Old-Timers

TOMMY McCARTHY

THOMAS F. McCARTHY

ONE OF BOSTON'S "HEAVENLY TWINS" UNDER MANAGER FRANK SELEE. OUTSTANDING BASE RUNNER WHO STOLE 109 BASES FOR THE BROWNS IN 1888. PIONEER IN TRAPPING FLY BALLS IN THE OUTFIELD. HOLDS N.L. RECORD FOR ASSISTS IN OUTFIELD-53 WITH BOSTON IN 1893. PLAYED 1268 GAMES IN MAJOR LEAGUES.

Born: 7-24-1863, Boston, Mass. **Died:** 8-5-22 **Height/Weight:** 5-7/170 **Bats/Throws:** R/R **Primary position:** Outfield **Career statistics:** .292 avg., 1,495 hits, 468 steals **Teams:** Boston (U.A.) 1884; Boston 1885, 1892-95; Philadelphia 1886-87; St. Louis (A.A.) 1888-91; Brooklyn 1896

He was a "Heavenly Twin," one of two 5-foot-7 dynamos the Boston Beaneaters unleashed on helpless opponents in the 1890s. If one didn't get you with his sizzling bat, the other would cut you down with his flashy glove. Tommy McCarthy, like outfield partner and soul mate Hugh Duffy, was a big-hearted Irishman in a little package—a popular Boston kid who helped bring his city two National League championships.

What McCarthy lacked in size he made up for with his take-no-prisoners hustle. He was an outstanding right fielder who could chase down line drives into the gap and gun down aggressive baserunners. Little Mack couldn't match Duffy's offensive punch, but he was a clever instigator who made consistent contact, got on base and scored runs.

It was McCarthy, working in tandem with center fielder Duffy, who helped popularize the hit-and-run and double-steal. He also was a master at threatening the bunt and slapping balls past charging fielders. An accomplished runner who once swiped 93 bases, McCarthy would turn the table on opponents by purposely letting fly balls hit the ground so he could throw ahead of "trapped" runners to start a double play—a tactic that led to the infield fly rule.

"The best man in the business at the trapped-ball trick was Tommy McCarthy. He had the play down pat, and on more than one occasion saved his team by resorting to it." —*John McGraw*

With McCarthy and Duffy leading the way, the Beaneaters captured pennants in 1892 and '93. Facing pitches from the 60-feet, 6-inch distance for the first time in 1893, McCarthy batted .346, drove in 111 runs and scored 107. He followed that with a .349-126-118 season, the seventh and final time he would score 100 runs. After McCarthy slumped to .290 in 1895, the popular Heavenly Twins tandem was broken up when he was traded to Brooklyn.

McCarthy, who made his major league debut in the one-season Union Association (1884), didn't blossom until 1888 when he helped the St. Louis Browns win an American Association pennant. But it wasn't until he returned home that he found lasting fame. McCarthy, a .292 hitter, ended his 13-year career after one Brooklyn season.

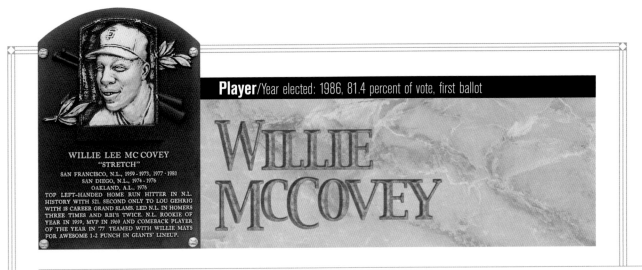

Player/Year elected: 1986, 81.4 percent of vote, first ballot

WILLIE McCOVEY

Born: 1-10-38, Mobile, Ala. **Height/Weight:** 6-4/220 **Bats/Throws:** L/L **Primary position:** First base **Career statistics:** .270 avg., 2,211 hits, 1,229 runs, 521 HR, 1,555 RBIs **Teams:** Giants 1959-73, 1977-80; Padres 1974-76; Athletics 1976 **HR champion:** N.L., 1963, tied, '68, '69 **Major awards:** N.L. Rookie of Year, 1959; N.L. MVP, 1969

Cincinnati manager Sparky Anderson called him "the most awesome man I've ever seen." Pitchers shuddered and an expectant hush enveloped the ballpark every time he stepped into the batter's box. Intimidation really wasn't Willie McCovey's style, but you couldn't convince fans or opponents who watched him stage consistently spectacular power displays over a 22-year major league career that started in 1959 and touched four decades.

In reality, the 6-foot-4, 220-pound San Francisco first baseman was a gentle Giant, amiable, soft-spoken and always respectful. But at the plate, the towering lefthanded hitter was the epitome of intimidation—massive arms sweeping a toothpick-like bat back and forth, dipping it menacingly low, as the pitcher released the ball. He didn't just hit home runs; he launched them high and far with a whiplash swing that produced 521, as well as three National League homer crowns.

McCovey is best remembered as the enforcer who protected Willie Mays for 13-plus seasons in the

> "Guys used to kid Drysdale about (McCovey). Willie was the one guy Don was reluctant to face. In the four and a half years I played with Don, I think McCovey is the only player he was afraid of physically." —*Don Sutton*

Giants' lineup (they combined for 800 home runs) and the man who hit the blistering line drive that New York Yankees second baseman Bobby Richardson snared for the heart-breaking final out in Game 7 of the 1962 World Series. But the man teammates called "Stretch" also was a solid first baseman, a three-time slugging percentage leader and a .270 career hitter who earned an MVP award in 1969—a season in which he batted .320 with 45 homers and 126 RBIs while drawing a record 45 intentional walks.

McCovey, a six-time All-Star Game performer who hit two home runs in the 1969 midsummer classic, might have posted even bigger numbers if not for some physical problems nobody could see. He played his entire career without complaint on arthritic, surgically repaired knees that hindered his running and quick movement and he later battled other injuries and intense back problems. He retired in 1980 with 18 career grand slams, second only to Lou Gehrig's all-time record of 23.

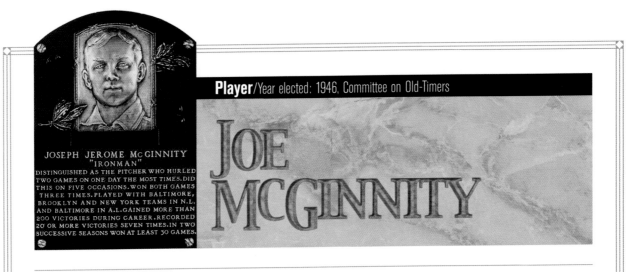

Player/Year elected: 1946, Committee on Old-Timers

JOE McGINNITY

JOSEPH JEROME McGINNITY
"IRONMAN"
DISTINGUISHED AS THE PITCHER WHO HURLED
TWO GAMES ON ONE DAY THE MOST TIMES. DID
THIS ON FIVE OCCASIONS. WON BOTH GAMES
THREE TIMES. PLAYED WITH BALTIMORE,
BROOKLYN AND NEW YORK TEAMS IN N.L.
AND BALTIMORE IN A.L. GAINED MORE THAN
200 VICTORIES DURING CAREER. RECORDED
20 OR MORE VICTORIES SEVEN TIMES. IN TWO
SUCCESSIVE SEASONS WON AT LEAST 30 GAMES.

Born: 3-19-1871, Rock Island, Ill. **Died:** 11-14-29 **Height/Weight:** 5-11/206 **Bats/Throws:** R/R **Position:** Pitcher
Career statistics: 246-142, 2.66 ERA, 1,068 strikeouts **Teams:** Baltimore 1899; Brooklyn 1900; Baltimore (A.L.) 1901-02; Giants 1902-08

Joe McGinnity's "Iron Man" nickname was forged in an 1890s foundry and cemented in baseball lore by 10 exhausting major league seasons. This was no ordinary Joe — a rubber-armed, powerfully built, jovial and brawling Irishman who was always ready to pitch. Always. McGinnity's career was short and his impact fleeting, but his legendary durability will never be forgotten.

When the blond, barrel-chested Illinois-born former iron worker signed with John McGraw's Baltimore Orioles in 1899, he was a 28-year-old rookie looking to make up for lost time. He came well armed with a sneaky fastball, a roundhouse curve he fired with a deceptive sidearm motion and a pitch he called "Old Sal" — a tricky, tantalizing "upcurve" that he delivered so far underhand his knuckles almost scraped the ground.

Facing the 5-foot-11, 206-pound McGinnity was no picnic. He distracted batters with pitches to the ribs and a constant stream of banter. His strange deliveries only complicated matters, as did his incredible durability. From his 1899 rookie season through his 1908 final campaign with McGraw's New York Giants, McGinnity topped 300 innings nine times and 400 innings twice while leading his league in games six times.

McGinnity is best remembered for the five double-headers he worked — winning both games three times in one month for McGraw's 1903 Giants. But of more significance was the 1-2 punch he formed with Christy Mathewson in a rotation that led the Giants to a National League pennant in 1904 and a World Series title in '05. McGinnity was 31-20 with 44 complete games in 1903 when Mathewson was 30-13, and he was 35-8 the following year when Matty was 33-12. Iron Joe pitched a shutout against Philadelphia in his only fall classic.

Five times McGinnity led his league in wins and only twice did he fail to top the 20 plateau — his final two New York campaigns. When he retired in 1908 with a 246-142 record, he began a second iron-man career as a minor league player-manager and continued pitching until he was 54.

> "Nothing can hurt this arm. I can throw curves like that all day. Last year, I pitched a 21-inning game for Peoria that took four hours. I never hurt my arm." — *Joe McGinnity, before his 1899 rookie season*

Umpire/Year elected: 1992, Committee on Veterans

BILL McGOWAN

Born: 1-18-1896, Wilmington, Del. **Died:** 12-9-54 **Height/Weight:** 5-10/178 **Years umpired:** A.L., 1925-54

All-Star Games: 1933, '37, '42, '50 **World Series:** 1928, '31, '35, '39, '41, '44, '47, '50

He was fiery, arrogant and confrontational, an umpire with an attitude. But Bill McGowan backed up his pugnacious style with hard work and substance. His colorful antics won him fan recognition; his hustle and near-perfect judgment earned the respect of American League managers and players who were affected by his work for 30 years.

McGowan was affectionately called "Mr. Number One" by the very players he often frustrated with his in-your-face bluntness. That's because he was generally recognized as the A.L.'s best balls-and-strikes umpire and a fair-minded official who never gave less than 100 percent on any call. He also was the iron man of umpires, once working 2,541 straight games covering 16-plus years.

It was clear when McGowan made his major league debut in 1925 the tenor of the profession was about to change. He was vigorous and aggressive, demonstrative on his gestures and ready to battle at the drop of a bat. Fans loved the way he punched out batters on called third strikes and runners on steal attempts. Other umpires copied his style while falling short in quality of work.

McGowan seemed to delight in the controversy he created, but he also was adept at restoring order before things got out of hand. Sometimes his aggressiveness backfired. Twice he was suspended by A.L. officials for over-the-edge outbursts and he often received warnings. But when the American League needed a top umpire for a big game, McGowan got the call. He worked eight World Series and four All-Star Games,

"My advice to young umpires is this: Make the players and managers respect you by your hustle. Keep on top of plays. Always try to give a manager or player a civil answer. Then walk away, tough." — *Bill McGowan*

including the inaugural midsummer classic in 1933.

But the Delaware-born McGowan was most proud of being selected umpire-in-chief for the 1948 pennant-playoff game between Boston and Cleveland, a contest he worked with unerring precision. He also was proud of the Florida-based umpiring school he founded in 1939. When McGowan retired in 1954 because of a heart problem, appreciative A.L. owners voted to double the normal $3,000 pension.

JOHN McGRAW

JOHN J. McGRAW

STAR THIRD-BASEMAN OF THE GREAT BALTIMORE ORIOLES, NATIONAL LEAGUE CHAMPIONS IN THE '90'S. FOR 30 YEARS MANAGER OF THE NEW YORK GIANTS STARTING IN 1902. UNDER HIS LEADERSHIP THE GIANTS WON 10 PENNANTS AND 3 WORLD CHAMPIONSHIPS.

Born: 4-7-1873, Truxton, N.Y. **Died:** 2-25-34 **Height/Weight:** 5-7/155 **B/T:** L/R **Primary position:** Third base **Career statistics:** .334 avg., 1,309 hits, 436 steals **Teams played:** Baltimore (A.A.) 1891; Baltimore 1892-99; St. Louis 1900; Baltimore (A.L.) 1901-02; Giants 1902-06

Teams managed (2,763-1,948): Baltimore (N.L.) 1899; Baltimore (A.L.) 1901-02; Giants 1902-32 **World Series titles:** 1905, '21, '22

McGRAW

They called him "Little Napoleon" for good reason. John McGraw was an arrogant, demanding, browbeating baseball despot, the three-decade ruler of the New York Giants. He also was the greatest manager in National League history and one of the most colorful and dominant baseball personalities of the 20th century.

It's hard to remain neutral about McGraw, who guided the Giants to 10 pennants, three World Series championships and 27 first-division finishes in 29 full seasons. He ruled his team with an iron fist and the city he served with the forcefulness of his personality. McGraw was a brilliant strategist, master psychologist and proud father figure who drove his players hard while giving them status as members of baseball's glamour franchise.

McGraw's fire-and-brimstone approach was a residue of his playing career with the legendary Baltimore Orioles, who brawled and battled their way to three straight N.L. pennants and two Temple Cup victories from 1894-97. The 5-foot-7, 155-pound third baseman was the team sparkplug, a clever trickster who would do anything to win. He also was a .334 career hitter who helped devise and perfect such strategies as the hit-and-run and double steal.

McGraw honed his managing skills in Baltimore, first with the 1899 Orioles and then with the 1901-02 entry in the new American League. At odds with A.L. president Ban Johnson over his treatment of umpires,

"McGraw men were brought up to hustle. He kept you liking the game. If he couldn't, he'd get rid of you so quick you wouldn't have time to notify the post office of your change of address."
—*Casey Stengel*

he jumped to the Giants in 1902 and took his top players with him — including pitcher Joe McGinnity. The 1904 Giants won a pennant but refused to play A.L.-champion Boston in a World Series. His Christy Mathewson-led '05 team won the Giants' first fall classic.

McGraw, one of the most vicious and relentless umpire baiters in history, enjoyed an unprecedented run from 1921-24 when the Giants won four straight pennants and two Series. But he failed to win again over his final eight years, retiring in 1932 because of ill health. McGraw left with 2,763 wins, second only to A.L.-rival Connie Mack.

Manager/Year elected: 1962, Committee on Veterans

BILL McKECHNIE

WILLIAM BOYD McKECHNIE
MANAGER OF
PITTSBURGH N.L. 1922-1926
ST. LOUIS N.L. 1928-1929
BOSTON N.L. 1930-1937
CINCINNATI N.L.1938-1946
ONLY N.L. MANAGER TO WIN PENNANTS
WITH THREE DIFFERENT CLUBS-PITTSBURGH
1925; ST.LOUIS,1928; CINCINNATI,1939,1940
WON WORLD SERIES 1925 AND 1940. NAMED
NO.1 MAJOR LEAGUE MANAGER 1937 AND
1940. ACTIVE IN BASEBALL AS MANAGER,
COACH, PLAYER, 1906 TO 1953.

Born: 8-7-1886, Wilkinsburg, Pa. **Died:** 10-29-65 **Height/Weight:** 5-10/160 **Teams managed:** Pirates 1922-26; Cardinals 1928-29; Braves 1930-37; Reds 1938-46 **Career record:** 1,896-1,723, .524 **World Series titles:** 1925, '40

Bill McKechnie didn't look, talk or act like a manager, a role he filled with dedication and dignity for a quarter century. But few could outmaneuver or match baseball wits with "Deacon Bill," who patiently preached the gospel of pitching and defense. McKechnie was a masterful tactician and psychologist, a magician who coaxed maximum effort out of talent-stretched players and teams.

At first glance, McKechnie looked like a college professor — bespectacled, slender and pale. Deeply religious and an avowed non-drinker, he was soft-spoken, personable and calm in his dealings with players and never deviated from his conservative baseball principles while posting 1,842 wins and guiding an unprecedented three different franchises to National League pennants.

McKechnie was the mastermind behind the 1925 Pittsburgh Pirates, who defeated Washington in a seven-game World Series. He led the 1928 St. Louis Cardinals to a pennant and guided Cincinnati to consecutive pennants and a 1940 Series championship. But some McKechnie fans consider an eight-year pennantless stretch from 1930-37 with the lowly Boston Braves his best work.

The Braves were so bad that a fourth-place finish was reason for celebration and McKechnie lifted them to that level in 1933 and '34. When he transformed two *thirtysomething* rookies (Lou Fette and

Jim Turner) into 20-game winners en route to a 79-73 record and fifth-place finish in 1937, he was universally saluted. It was typical McKechnie, who combined a deeply rooted knowledge of the game with understanding and unflagging patience.

That knowledge was the byproduct of a nine-year major league playing career (1907-20) that was strong on fundamentals and short on offense. A .251-hitting reserve infielder, the quiet Pennsylvanian watched and

> "He knew baseball — the complete book. He knew the percentages and he applied them to the ability of his players with amazing accuracy. I played for other good men, but McKechnie was in a class by himself." — *Paul Waner*

learned that pitching and defense were the keys to success while matching wits with the likes of John McGraw and Joe McCarthy. He never forgot.

After McKechnie ended his nine-year association with the Reds in 1946, he concluded his career with three seasons as the righthand man of young Cleveland manager Lou Boudreau. The Boudreau-McKechnie Indians won a World Series in 1948.

JOHN ALEXANDER MCPHEE
"BID"
CINCINNATI, A.A., 1882-89
CINCINNATI, N.L., 1890-99

ONE OF THE 19TH CENTURY'S PREMIER SECOND BASEMAN, HE WAS A
STANDOUT FIELDER DESPITE PLAYING BAREHANDED FOR MOST OF HIS
18-YEAR CAREER. THE LAST SECOND BASEMAN TO PLAY WITHOUT A
GLOVE, HE REGULARLY LED THE LEAGUE IN DOUBLE PLAYS, FIELDING
AVERAGE, ASSISTS AND PUTOUTS. PLAYING WITH A GLOVE FOR THE
FIRST TIME IN 1896, HIS FIELDING AVERAGE WAS .982, A MARK THAT
STOOD FOR 29 YEARS. A SKILLED LEADOFF HITTER, HE COMPILED 2,250
HITS AND TOPPED THE 100-RUN MARK 10 TIMES, INCLUDING A CAREER-
BEST 139 IN 1886. KNOWN FOR HIS SOBER DISPOSITION AND
EXEMPLARY SPORTSMANSHIP.

Player/Year elected: 2000, Committee on Veterans

BID MCPHEE

Born: 11-1-1859, Massena, N.Y. **Died:** 1-3-43 **Height/Weight:** 5-8/155 **Bats/Throws:** R/R **Primary position:** Second base **Career statistics:** .277 avg., 2,313 hits, 1,684 runs, 1,072 RBIs **Teams:** Cincinnati (A.A.) 1882-89; Cincinnati 1890-99 **HR champion:** A.A., 1886

Call him boring, but John "Bid" McPhee was a creature of habit. For 18 incredible seasons, he played the same position for the same team with the same quiet efficiency—never shying from his appointed task. If the proud New Yorker was not the 19th century's premier second baseman, he certainly was its most reliable—and, in one special way, its most unusual.

Long after most 19th-century infielders had begun using fielder's gloves, McPhee insisted on playing barehanded. Through 1896, his 15th big-league season with the Cincinnati Red Stockings, he refused to wear a glove, a macho sense of pride he backed up with amazingly consistent defensive work. Eight times he led his league in fielding percentage and he typically led or ranked near the top in double plays, assists and putouts.

When McPhee finally began using a glove in 1897, he was among the last major leaguers to do so and the final second baseman. Contemporaries insisted years later that he didn't play any better with than without. Either way, the confident Cincinnati star was surehand-ed and quick, automatic on the routine play and far-ranging for the pre-1900 era.

McPhee also was the Red Stockings' longtime instigator, a .277 career-hitting leadoff man who drew walks, stole bases and scored runs—1,684, a huge 19th-century total. The pesky righthanded spray hitter pressured opposing defenses with his speed, once stealing 95 bases, and scored 100 or more runs 10 times—his most important offensive contribution.

When McPhee got on base, the result was usually good and the four-time .300 hitter fulfilled that role for almost two decades.

Conscientious, dedicated and always ready to play, McPhee helped the Red Stockings to an American Association pennant in his 1882 rookie season and remained Cincinnati's regular second baseman through 1899, a span that included the team's 1890 transition to the National League. Some of his best offensive seasons were recorded after 1892, when baseball extended its pitching distance from 50 feet to 60-feet, 6-inches.

"This glove business has gone a little too far. True, hot-hit balls do sting a little at the opening of the season, but after you get used to it, there is no trouble on that score." —*Bid McPhee, on playing barehanded*

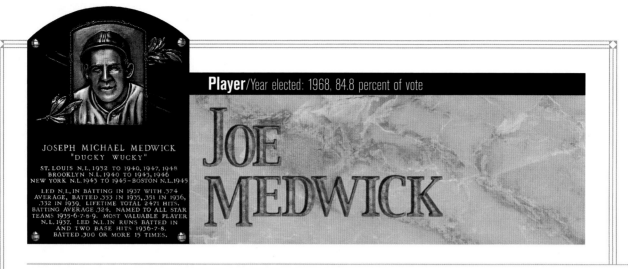

JOE MEDWICK

JOSEPH MICHAEL MEDWICK
"DUCKY WUCKY"

ST. LOUIS N.L. 1932 TO 1940, 1947, 1948
BROOKLYN N.L. 1940 TO 1943, 1946
NEW YORK N.L. 1943 TO 1945—BOSTON N.L. 1945

LED N.L. IN BATTING IN 1937 WITH .374
AVERAGE, BATTED .353 IN 1935, .351 IN 1936,
.332 IN 1939. LIFETIME TOTAL 2471 HITS,
BATTING AVERAGE .324, NAMED TO ALL STAR
TEAMS 1935-6-7-8-9. MOST VALUABLE PLAYER
N.L. 1937. LED N.L. IN RUNS BATTED IN
AND TWO BASE HITS 1936-7-8.
BATTED .300 OR MORE 15 TIMES.

Born: 11-24-11, Carteret, N.J. **Died:** 3-21-75 **Height/Weight:** 5-10/187 **Bats/Throws:** R/R **Primary position:** Outfield
Career statistics: .324 avg., 2,471 hits, 1,198 runs, 205 HR, 1,383 RBIs **Teams:** Cardinals 1932-40, 1947-48; Dodgers 1940-43, 1946; Giants 1943-45; Braves 1945 **Batting champion:** N.L., 1937 **HR champion:** N.L., 1937, tied **Major awards:** N.L. MVP, 1937

If Dizzy Dean was the heart of St. Louis' Gashouse Gang, Joe Medwick was its soul. He also was the enforcer for the colorful Cardinals who battled fate, opponents and each other during a raucous Depression-era run that produced laughs and tears, bumps and bruises and a 1934 World Series championship. What the hard-edged left fielder couldn't conquer with his lusty bat, he often challenged with his equally dangerous fists.

Medwick was a perfect fit for baseball's rugged 1930s style. Quick-tempered, he competed with an aggressive intensity that angered opponents and often befuddled his own teammates. "If you want to be a clown, join the circus," he shouted at Dean, Rip Collins, Pepper Martin and other cut-up teammates who worked him into a perpetually agitated state. Medwick released his fury with slashing line drives from a big righthanded swing that spread terror throughout the National League.

The pitch didn't have to be good; it just had to be within reach. Medwick was an offensive machine in a five-season stretch from 1935-39, piling up 1,075 hits and 657 RBIs, leading the league in doubles and RBIs three times and capturing an MVP. His .374, 31-homer, 154-RBI performance in 1937 produced the last Triple Crown in N.L. history.

"Ducky"—the nickname spoofed his duck-like walk—remained an offensive madman until 1940 when, shortly after he was traded to Brooklyn because of a salary dispute, former Cardinals teammate Bob Bowman drilled him in the head with a pitch, almost ending his career. Medwick came back to post solid numbers and helped the Dodgers win a 1941 pennant, but he never hit with the old passion.

Medwick is best remembered as the left fielder who had to be removed from the seventh game of the 1934 Series by commissioner Kenesaw Mountain Landis because he was being pelted with garbage by outraged Detroit fans. Medwick was targeted after his hard slide into Tigers third baseman Marv Owen during the Cardinals' 11-0 title-clinching win.

> "(Medwick) was the meanest, roughest guy you could imagine. He just stood up there and whaled everything within reach. Doubles, triples, home runs—he sprayed 'em all over every park." —*Leo Durocher*

JOHN ROBERT MIZE
"THE BIG CAT"
ST. LOUIS N.L., NEW YORK N.L.,
NEW YORK A. L., 1936-1953
KEEN-EYED SLUGGER SMASHED 359 HOME RUNS
AND BATTED .312 IN 15-YEAR CAREER WHILE
TOPPING .300 MARK NINE SEASONS IN A ROW.
SET MAJOR LOOP RECORDS BY HITTING THREE
HOMERS IN A GAME SIX TIMES AND TRIO IN
SUCCESSION ON FOUR OCCASIONS. WON N.L.
BATTING TITLE ONCE, LED OR SHARED LEAD
IN HOMERS AND SLUGGING PCT. FOUR TIMES,
RUNS BATTED IN AND TOTAL BASES THRICE.

Player/Year elected: 1981, Committee on Veterans

JOHNNY MIZE

Born: 1-7-13, Demorest, Ga. **Died:** 6-2-93 **Height/Weight:** 6-2/215 **Bats/Throws:** L/R **Primary position:** First base
Career statistics: .312 avg., 2,011 hits, 1,118 runs, 359 HR, 1,337 RBIs **Teams:** Cardinals 1936-41; Giants 1942, 1946-49; Yankees 1949-53 **Batting champion:** 1939 **HR champion:** 1939, '40, '47, tied, '48, tied

He stood motionless, stance closed, bat resting on his left shoulder, gray eyes staring coldly at the pitcher. The Big Cat was stalking his prey. Soon Johnny Mize would spring into action, his quick and deadly 36-inch bat driving another ball into submission, another game into the victory column and another notch into his Hall of Fame legacy.

So it was for 15 major league seasons — the 6-foot-2, 215-pound Mize deciding games with a compact left-handed swing that could pound 450-foot home runs or slash line drives to the opposite field. He was a power hitter who could transform instantly into a contact man, a hitting technician who could adjust strategy from pitch to pitch. Nothing bothered Mize, who offered the best of both offensive worlds.

As a first baseman for St. Louis and New York from 1936-49, he batted .300 nine times, drove in 100 runs eight times and produced homer totals of 51, 43 and 40. With the Cardinals, he was a straightaway hitter who sacrificed

"His bat doesn't travel as far as anybody else's. He just cocks it and slaps, and when you're as big as he is, you can slap a ball into the seats. That short swing is wonderful. ..." — *Casey Stengel*

power for the team's speed approach. With the Giants, Mize became a pull hitter to take advantage of the short right field porch at the Polo Grounds. The big, round-faced Georgian was versatile enough to win four home run crowns, three RBI titles and the 1939 N.L. batting championship (.349).

Critics panned Mize's defense, but he twice led the N.L. in fielding average and was deceptively quick. Always pleasant and affable, Mize's relaxed style gave an inaccurate impression that he wasn't always hustling. Teammates scoffed at that notion and marveled at the bat control that produced a .312 career average and kept his strikeout total from ever topping 57.

Perhaps the most memorable stage of Mize's career was 1949-53, when he served as a spot player and premier pinch-hitter for the powerful New York Yankees. The Big Cat, who played in 10 All-Star Games, was perfect for that role and helped the Yankees win a record five straight World Series championships, contributing three homers and six RBIs to their 1952 victory.

JOE MORGAN

JOE LEONARD MORGAN
HOUSTON, N.L., 1963-1971, 1980
CINCINNATI, N.L., 1972-1979
SAN FRANCISCO, N.L., 1981-1982
PHILADELPHIA, N.L., 1983
OAKLAND, A.L., 1984
IMPACT PLAYER WHO LIFTED CINCINNATI'S "BIG RED MACHINE" TO HIGHER LEVEL WITH HIS MULTI-FACETED SKILLS. TRADEMARK WAS FLAPPING LEFT ARM AS HE AWAITED PITCH. PACKED UNUSUAL POWER INTO EXTRAORDINARILY QUICK 150-LB. FIREPLUG FRAME. PLAYED 22 SEASONS AND ALSO HOLDS HOME RUN AND GAMES PLAYED RECORDS FOR 2B. N.L. MVP, 1975-76.

Born: 9-19-43, Bonham, Tex. **Height/Weight:** 5-7/155 **Bats/Throws:** L/R **Primary position:** Second base
Career statistics: .271 avg., 2,517 hits, 1,650 runs, 268 HR, 1,133 RBIs, 689 steals **Teams:** Colt .45s/Astros 1963-71, 1980; Reds 1972-79; Giants 1981-82; Phillies 1983; Athletics 1984 **Major awards:** N.L. MVP, 1975, '76

He was an equal-opportunity assassin. Joe Morgan could kill you softly with his glove, speed and quick mind. Or he could kill you savagely with a vicious line drive into the gap or a heart-piercing home run. Either way, you always wound up dead and Morgan wound up another step closer to the Hall of Fame.

That lofty height must have seemed out of reach for the 5-foot-7, 155-pound second baseman when he made his major league debut with Houston in 1963. But Morgan used his quick hands, analytical approach and game-turning speed to wreak a special kind of havoc. By the time he was traded to Cincinnati in November 1971, he was a well-oiled generator for a Big Red Machine that was ready to run roughshod through the National League.

"Little Joe," who was called the "strongest little guy I've ever been around" by former manager Sparky Anderson, was at his best from 1972 through 1977 when he helped the Reds capture four division titles and consecutive World Series. He won five Gold Gloves and

> "When he's healthy, he's the finest ballplayer I ever played with. He could win ballgames in more ways than anybody." — *Johnny Bench*

averaged .301 with 113 runs, 118 walks, 22 home runs, 84 RBIs and 60 stolen bases over that six-year stretch while earning back-to-back MVPs. The articulate, quick-to-laugh Morgan, who decided the '75 fall classic with a ninth-inning Game 7 single, simply did whatever it took to win, as illustrated by his 1976 MVP numbers — .320, 27 homers, 111 RBIs, 113 runs, 114 walks and 60 steals.

Morgan, a lefthanded hitter who distinctively flapped his left elbow before every pitch, showed a Ted Williams-like patience that allowed him to set a National League career record for walks with 1,865. But he swung often enough to rap out 2,517 hits and 268 home runs while posting eight 100-run seasons and stealing 689 bases.

Morgan's bottom line, however, was winning. The nine-time All-Star Game performer played for seven division titlists, four pennant-winners and two Series champions. His last fall classic appearance came with Philadelphia in 1983 — the second-to-last season in a 22-year career.

MORGAN

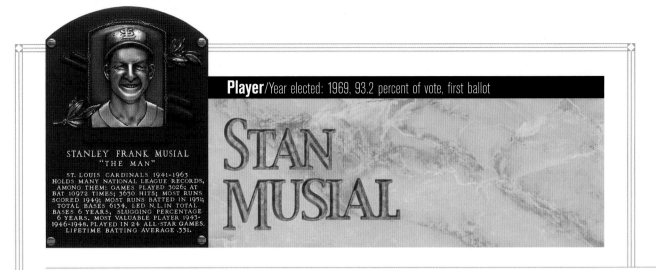

STAN MUSIAL

STANLEY FRANK MUSIAL
"THE MAN"

ST. LOUIS CARDINALS 1941-1963
HOLDS MANY NATIONAL LEAGUE RECORDS,
AMONG THEM: GAMES PLAYED 3026; AT
BAT 10972 TIMES; 3630 HITS; MOST RUNS
SCORED 1949; MOST RUNS BATTED IN 1951;
TOTAL BASES 6134. LED N.L. IN TOTAL
BASES 6 YEARS, SLUGGING PERCENTAGE
6 YEARS. MOST VALUABLE PLAYER 1943-
1946-1948. PLAYED IN 24 ALL-STAR GAMES.
LIFETIME BATTING AVERAGE .331.

Born: 11-21-20, Donora, Pa. **Height/Weight:** 6-0/175 **Bats/Throws:** L/L **Primary position:** Outfield, first base

Career statistics: .331 avg., 3,630 hits, 1,949 runs, 475 HR, 1,951 RBIs **Teams:** Cardinals 1941-44; 1946-63

Batting champion: N.L., 1943, '46, '48, '50, '51, '52, '57 **Major awards:** N.L. MVP, 1943, '46, '48

He had the menacing look of a cobra—crouched at the hips, legs close together in the back of the box with right heel elevated, bat cocked straight up, eyes peering over the right shoulder in a hypnotic search for a moving target. When the ball arrived, Stan (The Man) Musial uncoiled, driving another hit into his impressive record book.

Musial treated St. Louis fans to 3,630 of them over a 22-year career that touched three decades and produced a .331 average. He also captured the heart of an adoring city with his affable, friendly personality and quick smile—characteristics that would continue to enchant legions of admirers decades after his 1963 retirement.

That smile first was spotted in a 12-game 1941 preview and it became a fixture over his next four seasons (1945 was spent in military service) as the 6-foot, 175-pound right fielder/first baseman powered the Cardinals to four pennants and three World Series championships. He also won two of the seven National League batting titles he would claim.

While Musial was not a Ruthian-type power hitter,

"I could always hit. It's not something I ever had to think too much about. A lot of guys are very scientific about it. It just seemed to come naturally, even when I was growing up." —*Stan Musial*

careless pitchers paid for their mistakes. He muscled up for 475 career home runs, including five in a memorable 1954 double-header against the New York Giants, and finished with 1,377 extra-base hits, second only to Hank Aaron on the all-time list. Musial ranks in the top five of numerous all-time categories, he's one of four players to win three N.L. MVP awards and he appeared in a record-tying 24 All-Star Games, hitting a record six All-Star home runs.

His hitting feats are nothing less than extraordinary. Musial led the N.L in doubles eight times, in runs five times and in hits, on-base percentage and slugging percentage six times. But his greatest legacy might have been the goodwill he brought to the game and his enduring rapport with the fans. Musial was living proof that a take-no-prisoners intensity is not necessarily a prerequisite for success.

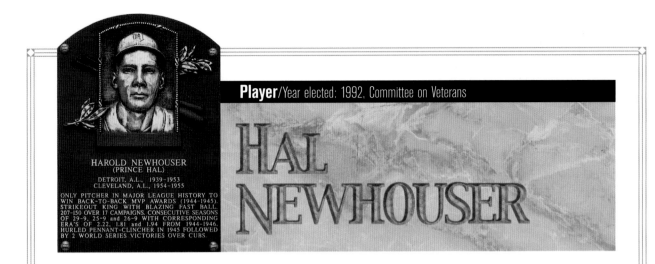

Player/Year elected: 1992, Committee on Veterans

HAL NEWHOUSER

HAROLD NEWHOUSER
(PRINCE HAL)
DETROIT, A.L., 1939-1953
CLEVELAND, A.L., 1954-1955
ONLY PITCHER IN MAJOR LEAGUE HISTORY TO
WIN BACK-TO-BACK MVP AWARDS (1944-1945).
STRIKEOUT KING WITH BLAZING FAST BALL.
207-150 OVER 17 CAMPAIGNS, CONSECUTIVE SEASONS
OF 29-9, 25-9 and 26-9 WITH CORRESPONDING
ERA'S OF 2.22, 1.81 and 1.94 FROM 1944-1946.
HURLED PENNANT-CLINCHER IN 1945 FOLLOWED
BY 2 WORLD SERIES VICTORIES OVER CUBS.

Born: 5-20-21, Detroit, Mich. **Died:** 11-10-98 **Height/Weight:** 6-2/190 **Bats/Throws:** L/L **Position:** Pitcher **Career statistics:** 207-150, 3.06 ERA, 1,796 strikeouts **Teams:** Tigers 1939-53; Indians 1954-55 **Major awards:** A.L. MVP, 1944, '45

Admirers called him Prince Hal, a tribute to the almost stately form with which he cut down American League hitters over a brilliant seven-year run from 1944-50. Victims of his early tantrums called him vain and insufferable. There never was a dull moment in the 17-year career of Detroit lefthander Hal Newhouser, who traveled a bumpy road from wartime wonder to Hall of Fame distinction.

At his best, the skinny 6-foot-2 Newhouser attacked hitters with a high leg kick, smooth overhand delivery and blazing fastball that drew comparisons to the one thrown by former star Lefty Grove. He complemented the fastball with a changeup and outstanding overhand curve, which he threw at different speeds.

At his worst, Newhouser attacked adversity with an explosive temper that also revived memories of Grove, affecting his control and costing him victories and respect. "I hate to lose," said Newhouser, who was only 18 when he made a 1939 debut with his hometown Tigers. Detroit fans endured four-plus seasons of ill-tempered medioc-

rity before something finally clicked in 1944.

That's when a suddenly mature Newhouser took control of his emotions, tamed his fastball and posted a 29-9 record that he followed with a 25-9 mark and 1.81 ERA in '45. That two-year brilliance earned him consecutive MVP awards and he capped his big 1945 season by recording two World Series wins in a seven-game triumph over the Chicago Cubs.

Critics pointed to Newhouser as a wartime phenom, but his success continued well after players had returned from the service. He was 26-9 with a 1.94 ERA in 1946 and followed that with 17-17, 21-12 and 18-11 marks. As the Tigers' workhorse piled up wins, strikeouts and innings, Ted Williams called him one of the best lefthanders he had ever faced.

A calmer and gentler Newhouser remained with Detroit until a sore arm sidelined him in 1953. The five-time All-Star Game pitcher returned to post a 7-2 record as a reliever with Cleveland in 1954 and the Indians won an A.L.-record 111 games en route to the pennant.

> "Hal has an overhand curve that nobody has got a hit off yet this season. It's the best pitch I've ever seen. ... He threw three of 'em to Joe DiMaggio and Joe couldn't even foul 'em." —*Birdie Tebbetts, 1946*

CHARLES A.(KID) NICHOLS

RIGHT HANDED PITCHER WHO WON 30 OR
MORE GAMES FOR SEVEN CONSECUTIVE
YEARS (1891-97) AND WON AT LEAST 20
GAMES FOR TEN CONSECUTIVE SEASONS
(1890-99) WITH BOSTON N.L. ALSO PITCHED
FOR ST. LOUIS AND PHILADELPHIA N.L. ONE
OF FEW PITCHERS TO WIN MORE THAN 300
GAMES, HIS MAJOR LEAGUE RECORD BEING
360 VICTORIES, 202 DEFEATS.

KID NICHOLS

Born: 9-14-1869, Madison, Wis. **Died:** 4-11-53 **Height/Weight:** 5-10/175 **Bats/Throws:** B/R **Position:** Pitcher
Career statistics: 361-208, 2.95 ERA, 1,880 strikeouts **Teams:** Boston 1890-1901; Cardinals 1904-05; Phillies 1905-06

He was a little man with a strong arm and a big heart. If Charles "Kid" Nichols didn't get you with his "jumping" fastball, he wore you down with his never-say-die grit and unflappable determination. In a career that lasted 15 years and cut across two centuries, Nichols matched numbers with the great Cy Young and staked legitimate claim as the era's premier iron man.

It's hard to fathom the durability of Nichols' right arm. Five times he topped 400 innings while pitching for the 1890s-era Boston Beaneaters and 12 times he worked more than 300. He started 562 games and finished 532, totaling 5,066 ⅓ innings. A record seven times he posted 30 or more victories, 11 times he topped 20 and he finished with 361, which ranks sixth on baseball's all-time list.

Not bad for a 5-foot-10, 175-pound Wisconsin kid who reported at age 20 to the Beaneaters in 1890 and was immediately dubbed "Kid." But nobody scoffed at the "jump ball" he delivered from a no-windup delivery that he claimed helped his control. A two-pitch hurler

(fastball and change), Nichols came straight overhand and challenged overmatched hitters.

He was an instant success, piling up victory totals of 27, 30 and 35 before making the transition from the 50-foot pitching distance to 60-feet, 6-inches. While the careers of many pitchers faltered, Nichols only got stronger, reaching the 30-win plateau in five of the next six seasons, and through the 1890s he remained the anchor for five National League pennant winners.

Nichols was a baseball paradox — a gentlemanly pitcher who relied on his arm rather than intimidation during the game's rough-and-tumble formative years. In 1892, a season in which he pitched 453 innings, he worked complete-game wins on three consecutive days in different cities. In a Temple Cup playoff series that season, he battled Cleveland's Young in a memorable 11-inning scoreless tie.

After leaving Boston in 1901, Nichols resurfaced as player-manager of the St. Louis Cardinals in 1904 and finished his career in 1906 at Philadelphia.

"You never heard of anyone with a sore arm in my day. When we weren't pitching, we either played the outfield or doubled as ticket takers. The biggest strain my arm ever underwent was at the Polo Grounds one afternoon when I counted 30,000 tickets." —Kid Nichols, 1948

NICHOLS

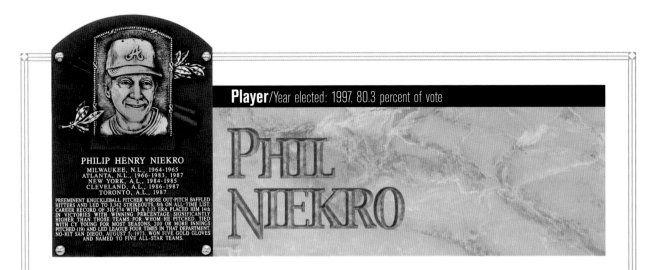

PHIL NIEKRO

PHILIP HENRY NIEKRO
MILWAUKEE, N.L., 1964-1965
ATLANTA, N.L., 1966-1983, 1987
NEW YORK, A.L., 1984-1985
CLEVELAND, A.L., 1986-1987
TORONTO, A.L., 1987

PREEMINENT KNUCKLEBALL PITCHER WHOSE OUT-PITCH BAFFLED
HITTERS AND LED TO 3,342 STRIKEOUTS, 8th ON ALL-TIME LIST.
CAREER RECORD OF 318-274 WITH A 3.35 ERA PLACED HIM 14th
IN VICTORIES WITH WINNING PERCENTAGE SIGNIFICANTLY
HIGHER THAN THOSE TEAMS FOR WHOM HE PITCHED. TIED
WITH CY YOUNG FOR MOST SEASONS, 200 OR MORE INNINGS
PITCHED (19) AND LED LEAGUE FOUR TIMES IN THAT DEPARTMENT.
NO-HIT SAN DIEGO, AUGUST 5, 1973. WON FIVE GOLD GLOVES
AND NAMED TO FIVE ALL-STAR TEAMS.

Born: 4-1-39, Blaine, Ohio **Height/Weight:** 6-1/180 **Bats/Throws:** R/R **Position:** Pitcher **Career statistics:** 318-274, 3.35 ERA, 3,342 strikeouts **Teams:** Milwaukee Braves 1964-65; Atlanta Braves 1966-83, 1987; Yankees 1984-85; Indians 1986, 1987; Blue Jays 1987

It approached the plate like a skittish white butterfly, darting, hopping, diving and dancing with no pre-planned route to its final destination. Fans and writers called it a knuckleball; catchers and opposing hitters called it more unpleasant names. For Phil Niekro, it was a butterfly he rode for 24 major league seasons—to 318 wins and Hall of Fame glory.

There was nothing mysterious about the man Atlanta fans affectionately called "Knucksie." He had a slouching, almost timid appearance and he was so relaxed teammates half expected him to fall asleep between pitches. Niekro could throw a fastball, slider and curve, but when he kicked his left knee to his waist and brought his right arm forward like a dart thrower at the local pub, everybody knew what was coming.

"It's like trying to catch a butterfly with a three-inch net," said former teammate Dave Johnson. And, indeed, hitters flailed helplessly at pitches that moved in ways even Niekro couldn't predict. The secret for the popular 6-foot-1 Ohioan was controlling the pitch he threw with the fingernails of his first two fingers, taking away the ball's natural spin. He would aim for the middle of the plate and hope for the best. When the knuckler behaved, he was almost unhittable; when it didn't, batters sat on his fastball.

Niekro wandered seven-plus seasons in the minor leagues before becoming a starter in 1967—at age 28. But from 1967-83, when he signed with the New York Yankees, Niekro failed to record double-figure win totals only once, reached the 20-win plateau three times and piled up workhorse numbers in

innings, complete games and starts. His 1.87 ERA led the National League in 1967; his 262 strikeouts did the same a decade later.

Seldom in the spotlight while working primarily for weak Braves teams, Niekro, the brother of 221-game winner Joe Niekro, pitched until age 48, ranking among all-time leaders in wins, losses, innings, strikeouts, walks and home runs.

"I just aim for the heart of the plate and hope for the best. But I don't know whether the ball will jump up or down or sideways. The best part, I guess, is that the batter doesn't know either." —*Phil Niekro*

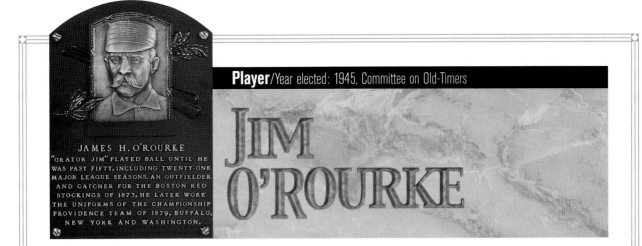

Player/Year elected: 1945, Committee on Old-Timers

JIM O'ROURKE

JAMES H. O'ROURKE
"ORATOR JIM" PLAYED BALL UNTIL HE WAS PAST FIFTY, INCLUDING TWENTY-ONE MAJOR LEAGUE SEASONS. AN OUTFIELDER AND CATCHER FOR THE BOSTON RED STOCKINGS OF 1873, HE LATER WORE THE UNIFORMS OF THE CHAMPIONSHIP PROVIDENCE TEAM OF 1879, BUFFALO, NEW YORK AND WASHINGTON.

Born: 9-1-1850, Bridgeport, Conn. **Died:** 1-8-19 **Height/Weight:** 5-8/185 **Bats/Throws:** R/R **Primary position:** Outfield
Career statistics: .313 avg., 2,340 hits, 1,446 runs, 1,010 RBIs **Teams:** Boston 1876-78, 1880; Providence 1879; Buffalo 1881-84; New York 1885-89, 1891-92, 1904; New York (P.L.) 1890; Washington 1893 **Batting champion:** N.L., 1884

The line drives he sprayed around 19th-century ball-parks were much easier to understand than his stream of four- and five-syllable words. Only a few players could match Jim O'Rourke's productive bat over a 22-year association with the professional game and nobody could match his legendary verbosity. "Orator Jim" was a baseball original, from the leagues he helped pioneer and popularize to the colorful zest he always brought to the field.

The 5-foot-8, 185-pound O'Rourke was an eloquent ambassador for the early game, dating from his four seasons in the National Association (1872-75) to major league stops in Boston, Providence, Buffalo, New York and Washington. He was dapper and confident, Irish pride literally dripping from his handlebar mustache, and intelligent enough to earn a law degree from Yale during his off-seasons.

It was that pride and intelligence that set O'Rourke apart from contemporaries and gave him status as a team leader, a quality he displayed for five pennant-winners—

two in Boston, one in Providence and two in New York. He spent most of his career playing catcher, third base and outfield, but Orator Jim was most celebrated as a slashing righthanded hitter. In 1876 while playing for Boston, he was credited with the first hit in National League history and he went on to reach the .300 plateau 12 times, winning a batting title (.347) in 1884.

O'Rourke also doubled as manager for four Buffalo seasons, at which point one of his players asked for a raise. "I'm sorry, but the exigencies of the occasion and the condition of our exchequer will not permit anything of the sort at this period of our existence," he replied with typical bombast— and the request was dropped.

After O'Rourke retired in 1893 with a .313 average, he worked as umpire, minor league manager and executive and attorney before making a one-game major league return in 1904, at age 54, with New York. O'Rourke caught one game, the Giants' pennant clincher, and collected his 2,340th career hit.

"There was no paraphernalia in the old days with which one could protect himself. No mitts; no, not even gloves; and masks, why you would have been laughed off the diamond had you worn one behind the bat. ..." —*Jim O'Rourke, 1913*

O'ROURKE

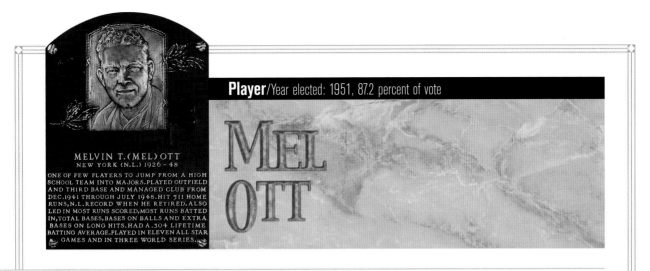

Player/Year elected: 1951, 87.2 percent of vote

MEL OTT

MELVIN T. (MEL) OTT
NEW YORK (N.L.) 1926 - 48

ONE OF FEW PLAYERS TO JUMP FROM A HIGH
SCHOOL TEAM INTO MAJORS. PLAYED OUTFIELD
AND THIRD BASE AND MANAGED CLUB FROM
DEC.1941 THROUGH JULY 1948. HIT 511 HOME
RUNS, N.L. RECORD WHEN HE RETIRED. ALSO
LED IN MOST RUNS SCORED, MOST RUNS BATTED
IN, TOTAL BASES, BASES ON BALLS AND EXTRA
BASES ON LONG HITS. HAD A .304 LIFETIME
BATTING AVERAGE. PLAYED IN ELEVEN ALL STAR
GAMES AND IN THREE WORLD SERIES.

Born: 3-2-09, Gretna, La. **Died:** 11-21-58 **Height/Weight:** 5-9.170 **Bats/Throws:** L/R **Primary position:** Right field

Career statistics: .304 avg., 2,876 hits, 1,859 runs, 511 HR, 1,860 RBIs **Teams:** Giants 1926-47

HR champion: N.L., 1932, tied, '34, tied, '36, '37, tied, '38, '42

He was a living, breathing oxymoron, a diminutive 5-foot-9, 170-pound boy wonder who dared to challenge Babe Ruth for home run-hitting superiority in New York City. When Mel Ott lifted his famous right leg and lashed into another pitch, Giants fans stationed in the Polo Grounds' short right field bleachers braced—a ritual they practiced enthusiastically for 22 seasons.

A 16-year-old Ott and his impressive lefthanded swing showed up on the Giants' doorstep in 1925 and spent a season learning the game at the side of manager John McGraw. At age 17 he played his first big-league game, at 19 he belted 18 home runs and at 20 he vaulted into prominence with a 42-homer, 151-RBI season—the first of eight 30-homer efforts that would define Ott's career.

Ottie, always smiling and personable, won over fans with his defensive hustle and cat-like quickness in right field, where he expertly played caroms off the oddly shaped wall. But most of all they loved his distinctive batting style. A .304 career hitter, he crowded the plate with feet apart and raised his right leg, about knee high, as the pitcher began his delivery. In one instantaneous motion, the bat pulled back, the foot planted and he swung.

Ott, a dead-pull hitter who seldom struck out, was tailor-made for the longball-friendly Polo Grounds (257 feet down the right field line), where he drilled 325 of his 511 career home runs. In an incredible 18-year stretch from 1928 through 1945, he led the Giants in homers every year, never falling below 18. He was the National League leader in six of those years and he topped 100 RBIs nine times as the primary run-producer for a team built around defense and pitching.

By the time Ott became the N.L.'s first 500-homer man in 1945, he also was serving as player/manager of the Giants, a role he filled for six seasons. Ott, who played in 11 All-Star Games, contributed to three New York pennant-winners, but only one World Series champion (1933).

> **"I could watch the fans yelling and laughing and I'd think, 'What an ungrateful fellow a ballplayer would be who just didn't give everything he had every moment of every inning in every game.'"** —*Mel Ott*

OTT

LEROY ROBERT PAIGE
"SATCHEL"
NEGRO LEAGUES   1926-1947
CLEVELAND A.L.   1948-1949
ST. LOUIS A.L.   1951-1953
KANSAS CITY A.L.   1965
PAIGE WAS ONE OF THE GREATEST STARS
TO PLAY IN THE NEGRO BASEBALL LEAGUES.
THRILLED MILLIONS OF PEOPLE AND WON
HUNDREDS OF GAMES. STRUCK OUT 21 MAJOR
LEAGUERS IN AN EXHIBITION GAME. HELPED
PITCH CLEVELAND INDIANS TO THE 1948
PENNANT IN HIS FIRST BIG LEAGUE YEAR
AT AGE 42. HIS PITCHING WAS A LEGEND
AMONG MAJOR LEAGUE HITTERS.

Player/Year elected: 1971, Special Committee on Negro Leagues

SATCHEL PAIGE

Born: 7-7-06, Mobile, Ala. **Died:** 6-8-82 **Height/Weight:** 6-4/180 **B/T:** R/R **Position:** Pitcher **Major League teams:** Indians 1948-49; Browns 1951-53; Athletics 1965 **Negro League teams (1926-51):** Birmingham Black Barons; Baltimore Black Sox; Cleveland Cubs; Kansas City Monarchs; Pittsburgh Crawfords; Newark Eagles; Paige's All-Stars; N.Y. Black Yankees; Memphis Red Sox; Phil. Stars; Chicago American Giants

If Satchel Paige wasn't the best pitcher in history, he might have been the most colorful. Enthusiastic, outlandish and endearing, he was a relentless showman who always made baseball fun for the multitudes who flocked to parks to see him pitch over the better part of four decades, most of which he spent dominating the 1920s, '30s and '40s Negro Leagues.

Paige was a physical anomaly who tested his rubber arm to the limit in working an estimated 2,600 games, as many as 200 in several year-round seasons. The lanky 6-foot-4 righthander delivered his blazing fastball with a windmill delivery and perfect control, often juicing up expectant fans by following through on crazy predictions and stunts (like pulling teammates off the field and then striking out the side). Ever the baseball ambassador, Paige filled ballparks for the struggling Negro Leagues while drifting from town to town and team to team, but his reputation really spread during seasons with the Pittsburgh Crawfords and Kansas City Monarchs.

It was with the Crawfords that Paige formed a Hall of Fame battery with Josh Gibson, the one black star who could almost match his popularity. And fans read stories about barnstorming games against major leaguers in which Paige outdueled such pitching stars as Dizzy Dean and Bob Feller. When an aging Paige finally was allowed to enter the white major leagues, curious fans flocked to see him pitch. Paige's fastball was dominant through most of his Negro League days, but he tantalized major leaguers with his off-speed deliveries as a 42-year-old Cleveland rookie (1948) and successful St. Louis Browns reliever (1951-53). Paige even made a curtain call in 1965 for Charlie Finley's Kansas City Athletics, working three scoreless innings against Boston—at age 59.

Although Paige did not get to test his skills at the major league level until well after his prime, he still became an American folk hero who charmed teammates and audiences with self-effacing humor and home-spun stories. And, of course, that room-lighting smile.

"Satchel Paige is the best I ever saw. I hit against Feller in his prime, but Paige ... he was just fast. Just straight overhand. He'd lift that leg and show down on you." — *Monte Irvin*

PAIGE

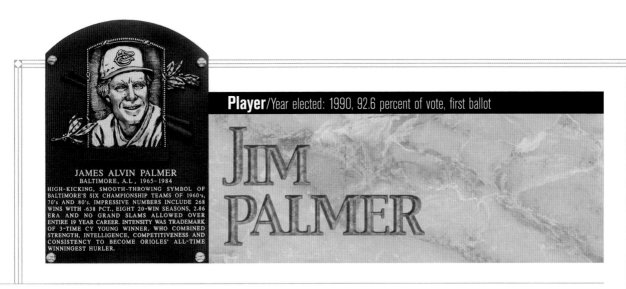

Player/Year elected: 1990, 92.6 percent of vote, first ballot

JIM PALMER

JAMES ALVIN PALMER
BALTIMORE, A.L., 1965-1984
HIGH-KICKING, SMOOTH-THROWING SYMBOL OF
BALTIMORE'S SIX CHAMPIONSHIP TEAMS OF 1960's,
70's AND 80's. IMPRESSIVE NUMBERS INCLUDE 268
WINS WITH .638 PCT., EIGHT 20-WIN SEASONS, 2.86
ERA AND NO GRAND SLAMS ALLOWED OVER
ENTIRE 19 YEAR CAREER. INTENSITY WAS TRADEMARK
OF 3-TIME CY YOUNG WINNER, WHO COMBINED
STRENGTH, INTELLIGENCE, COMPETITIVENESS AND
CONSISTENCY TO BECOME ORIOLES' ALL-TIME
WINNINGEST HURLER.

Born: 10-15-45, New York, N.Y. **Height/Weight:** 6-3/195 **Bats/Throws:** R/R **Position:** Pitcher **Career statistics:** 268-152, 2.86 ERA, 2,212 strikeouts **Teams:** Orioles 1965-67, 1969-84 **Major awards:** A.L. Cy Young, 1973, '75, '76

Every Jim Palmer pitch was a poetic revelation, from the perfectly fluid motion, traditional high leg kick and effortless delivery right down to its explosive conclusion. But everything else about the big righthander was delivered with a rough edge, from his outspoken, candid and articulate views on life in general to his frustrating complaints and verbal exchanges with Baltimore manager Earl Weaver.

On the field, the strikingly handsome New Yorker was the American League's most dominating pitcher of the 1970s, a 268-game winner over a 19-season career that started with the Orioles in 1965. Off the field, he was impetuous and unpredictable, a sometimes-aloof perfectionist who frustrated Weaver, teammates and fans with a never-ending stream of mysterious ailments.

Palmer's pitching style was determined by a rotator-cuff injury that cut him down after the 1966 World Series and cost him almost two full seasons. When he returned in 1969, he had

> "Jim had one of the most beautiful deliveries I've ever seen. It was almost like watching ballet."
>
> —*Ray Miller, former Orioles pitching coach*

transformed from a straight power pitcher into a power/finesse artist who could paint the corners with his still-dominant fastball, sharp-breaking curve and nasty changeup. Armed and dangerous once more, Palmer posted 20-win seasons in the nine-year stretch from 1970-78 while staking claim as the best righthander in the game.

During that run, he won three Cy Young Awards (1973, '75 and '76) and pitched in five All-Star Games. He was the ace of a powerful 1971 Orioles staff that featured a record-tying four 20-game winners. He led the Orioles to four division titles, two pennants and a World Series win (1970) while averaging 288 innings and pitching 44 of his 53 career shutouts.

Palmer, a member of three championship teams, recorded an 8-3 record in eight postseasons and 4-2 mark in six World Series, becoming the only pitcher to win fall classic games in three different decades. But success didn't stop the verbal war with Weaver, who prodded Palmer about imagined injuries. "The only thing Weaver knows about pitching is that he couldn't hit it," Palmer would quip in a typical response.

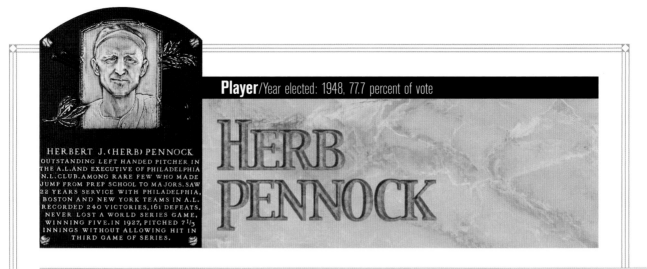

Player/Year elected: 1948, 77.7 percent of vote

HERB PENNOCK

HERBERT J. (HERB) PENNOCK
OUTSTANDING LEFT HANDED PITCHER IN
THE A.L. AND EXECUTIVE OF PHILADELPHIA
N.L. CLUB. AMONG RARE FEW WHO MADE
JUMP FROM PREP SCHOOL TO MAJORS. SAW
22 YEARS SERVICE WITH PHILADELPHIA,
BOSTON AND NEW YORK TEAMS IN A.L.
RECORDED 240 VICTORIES, 161 DEFEATS.
NEVER LOST A WORLD SERIES GAME,
WINNING FIVE. IN 1927, PITCHED 7¹/₃
INNINGS WITHOUT ALLOWING HIT IN
THIRD GAME OF SERIES.

Born: 2-10-1894, Kennett Square, Pa. **Died:** 1-30-48 **Height/Weight:** 6-0/160 **Bats/Throws:** B/L **Position:** Pitcher
Career statistics: 241-162, 3.60 ERA, 1,227 strikeouts **Teams:** Athletics 1912-15; Red Sox 1915-17, 1919-22, 1934; Yankees 1923-33

The long, thin face and Greek-statue nose looked like they belonged on a college campus. His intellectual approach and the "I-know-something-you-don't" confidence Herb Pennock took to the mound only emphasized the perception. But this tall, wispy-thin lefthander worked in a different kind of a classroom, teaching his lessons with a high leg kick and a most unlikely curriculum.

Over 22 American League seasons that included an 11-year run with the Murderer's Row Yankees of the 1920s, the 6-foot, 160-pounder posted a sparkling 241-162 record without much help from his fastball. Pennock was the consummate breaking-ball pitcher, an artist who carved up hitters with pinpoint control, masterful psychology and a strategy that exploited weaknesses.

At his best, Pennock might throw 10 fastballs per game. He studied hitters and played with their minds, giving them an assortment of curves, always with a different break, and screwballs, always thrown at different speeds. Pennock had a way of standing on the mound, staring down the fidgety batter and then fooling him with offerings that came from deceptive overhand and sidearm deliveries. Getting good wood on his pitch was difficult—and he seldom issued walks.

Pennock made his debut with the Philadelphia A's in 1912, but it wasn't until 1919—after one year of service in World War I—that he took a regular rotation spot with the Boston Red Sox. When he was traded to the Yankees in 1923, he was a 29-year-old journeyman with a 77-72 record. Over the next six seasons, Pennock would post a 115-57 mark while helping the Bronx Bombers of Babe Ruth, Lou Gehrig and Bob Meusel win four pennants and three championships.

Pennock, the son of Quaker parents from Kennett Square, Pa., never threw a thoughtless pitch over a career that extended to 1934 and covered 617 games and 3,571 ⅔ innings. He was 19-8 and 17-6 with the famed 1927 and '28 Yankees and in five World Series appearances (four with the Yankees, one with the A's) he was 5-0 with a 1.95 ERA.

"He just stands out there and looks at you ... and tugs on the bill of his cap ... and winds up and lets go. The ball never is where you think it's going to be. It was, just a split second before. But when you swing at it, the best you get is a piece of it. You fuss and fume and sweat and holler and he stands out there and looks at you ... and tugs on the bill of his cap and—aw, what's the use?"—*Bucky Harris*

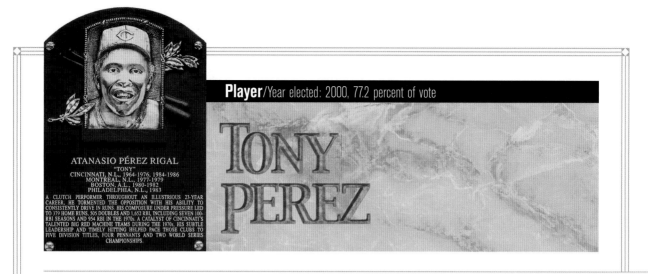

Player/Year elected: 2000, 77.2 percent of vote

TONY PEREZ

ATANASIO PÉREZ RIGAL
"TONY"
CINCINNATI, N.L., 1964-1976, 1984-1986
MONTREAL, N.L., 1977-1979
BOSTON, A.L., 1980-1982
PHILADELPHIA, N.L., 1983

A CLUTCH PERFORMER THROUGHOUT AN ILLUSTRIOUS 23-YEAR CAREER, HE TORMENTED THE OPPOSITION WITH HIS ABILITY TO CONSISTENTLY DRIVE IN RUNS. HIS COMPOSURE UNDER PRESSURE LED TO 379 HOME RUNS, 505 DOUBLES AND 1,652 RBI, INCLUDING SEVEN 100-RBI SEASONS AND 954 RBI IN THE 1970s. A CATALYST OF CINCINNATI'S TALENTED BIG RED MACHINE TEAMS DURING THE 1970s, HIS SUBTLE LEADERSHIP AND TIMELY HITTING HELPED PACE THOSE CLUBS TO FIVE DIVISION TITLES, FOUR PENNANTS AND TWO WORLD SERIES CHAMPIONSHIPS.

Born: 5-14-42, Ciego De Avila,, Cuba **Height/Weight:** 6-2/205 **Bats/Throws:** R/R **Primary position:** First base **Career statistics:** .279 avg., 2,732 hits, 1,272 runs, 379 HR, 1,652 RBIs **Teams:** Reds 1964-76, 1984-86; Expos 1977-79; Red Sox 1980-82; Phillies 1983

Like death, taxes and sunsets, Tony Perez was a sure thing for 23 major league seasons. In late innings, with runners on base and the Reds needing a key hit, Cincinnati's "Top Dog" was money in the bank. Sometimes overshadowed by a star-studded lineup in the 1970s, Perez was the motor that drove baseball's vaunted Big Red Machine.

"If a game goes long enough, Tony Perez will find a way to win it," said Dave Bristol, who managed the hard-hitting first baseman from 1966-69. And the muscular Cuban made Bristol look good. From 1967, his first full season as a regular, to 1976, his final season before being traded to Montreal, Perez drove in 1,028 runs—a 10-year average of 102.8.

More often than not, those RBIs had meaning. Sparky Anderson, Bristol's successor, tells stories of Perez's clutch two-out hits, game-winning home runs and two-strike drives into the gap. Always quick to smile, Perez lit up with men on base and the result was usually predictable. While Johnny Bench, Pete Rose

> **When there's a runner in scoring position, I can't think of any batter I'd rather have at the plate than Perez."**
>
> —*Sparky Anderson*

and Joe Morgan generated headlines, Perez labored in the trenches.

Pitchers dreaded facing the 6-foot-2, 205-pound righthander, erect in the batter's box with elbow cocked and bat angled over his shoulder. Lightning-quick wrists could yank a pitch over the left field fence, like the 15th-inning home run Perez hit off Catfish Hunter in the 1967 All-Star Game, or drive it the opposite way. Perez hit 37 homers in 1969 and 40 in 1970, when the Reds won the first of six division titles and four National League pennants in the decade.

His consistency is best demonstrated by numbers: 1,652 RBIs, 379 homers, 2,732 hits and 1,272 runs. But Perez, amazingly, never led the N.L. in any major offensive category. The seven-time All-Star Game performer played in five World Series, the last in 1983 with Philadelphia, and hit three homers in the memorable 1975 classic. He was versatile enough defensively to play third base for five Cincinnati seasons to get slugging first baseman Lee May in the lineup.

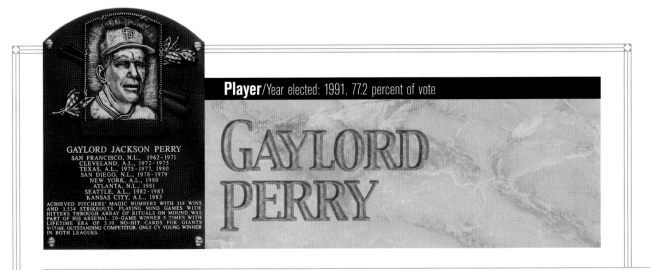

GAYLORD JACKSON PERRY
SAN FRANCISCO, N.L., 1962-1971
CLEVELAND, A.L., 1972-1975
TEXAS, A.L., 1975-1977, 1980
SAN DIEGO, N.L., 1978-1979
NEW YORK, A.L., 1980
ATLANTA, N.L., 1981
SEATTLE, A.L., 1982-1983
KANSAS CITY, A.L., 1983
ACHIEVED PITCHERS' MAGIC NUMBERS WITH 314 WINS
AND 3,534 STRIKEOUTS. PLAYING MIND GAMES WITH
HITTERS THROUGH ARRAY OF RITUALS ON MOUND WAS
PART OF HIS ARSENAL. 20-GAME WINNER 5 TIMES WITH
LIFETIME ERA OF 3.10. NO-HIT CARDS FOR GIANTS
9/17/68. OUTSTANDING COMPETITOR. ONLY CY YOUNG WINNER
IN BOTH LEAGUES.

Player/Year elected: 1991, 77.2 percent of vote

GAYLORD PERRY

Born: 9-15-38, Williamston, N.C. **Height/Weight:** 6-4/215 **Bats/Throws:** R/R **Position:** Pitcher **Career statistics:** 314-265, 3.11 ERA, 3,534 strikeouts **Teams:** Giants 1962-71; Indians 1972-75; Rangers 1975-77, 1980; Padres 1978-79; Yankees 1980; Braves 1981; Mariners 1982-83; Royals 1983 **Major awards:** A.L. Cy Young, 1972; N.L. Cy Young, 1978

He was a sleight-of-hand magician, an illusionist who misdirected the concentration of batters, managers and umpires. Gaylord Perry not only loaded up pitches with foreign substances banned by baseball rules, he loaded up the thoughts of opponents with distracting mind games. He was a 314-game winner whose success can be attributed as much to guile and intelligence as to a strong arm.

After Perry's 1983 retirement, he traced the origin of his notorious spitball to 1964, his third big-league season with the San Francisco Giants. Throughout the remainder of a 22-year career that featured stops in eight cities, he was cursed by hitters, screamed at by managers and undressed by umpires searching for evidence. The laconic, broad-shouldered North Carolinian simply accepted the flareups with his best good-old-boy smile, knowing the distractions were giving him a huge psychological edge.

Before every pitch, Perry would touch various parts of his anatomy—behind the ear, his forehead, his hair, the bill of his cap, his pants leg, his wrist—as hitters waited for the dreaded spitter, a pitch that approached the plate like a fastball and dropped abruptly. More often they got Perry's above-average fastball or slider, which cut through the strike zone like daggers. The 6-foot-4 righthander converted that psychological edge into five 20-win seasons over an amazingly durable career in which he topped 250 innings 12 times.

Perry, the first pitcher to earn Cy Young Awards in both leagues, won his first in 1972 when he recorded a 24-16 record and 1.92 ERA for Cleveland. The second came in 1978 at age 40, when he finished 21-6 for San Diego. Perry was 21-13 for Cleveland in 1974, the same season brother Jim, a 215-game big-league winner, also won 17 games for the Indians.

A five-time All-Star Game performer who recorded 3,534 strikeouts, Perry never pitched in a World Series and made only one postseason appearance. That came in 1971 when he was 1-1 for the Giants in a National League Championship Series loss to Pittsburgh.

> **"Gaylord is a great pitcher; a great, great one. But he also is a great, great competitor. Nobody wants to win more than Gaylord. He's remarkable."**
>
> —*Ken Aspromonte, Indians manager, 1974*

Player/Year elected: 1946, Committee on Old-Timers

EDDIE PLANK

Born: 8-31-1875, Gettysburg, Pa. **Died:** 2-24-26 **Height/Weight:** 5-11/175 **Bats/Throws:** L/L **Position:** Pitcher
Career statistics: 305-183, 2.37 ERA, 2,099 strikeouts **Teams:** Athletics 1901-14; Browns 1916-17

Watching Eddie Plank work was like watching grass grow. He was a frustrating anomaly in the fast-paced baseball world of the early 20th century. In an era of no-wasted-motion efficiency and two-hour games, Plank fought a war of attrition that helped him post 305 victories, most of them for Connie Mack-managed Philadelphia Athletics teams that won six American League pennants from 1901-14.

The somber-looking left-hander would hitch his cap, tug at his belt, inch forward, step off the rubber, shake off signs and fidget in numerous other ways before delivering a pitch to the waiting batter. Hitters facing Plank, not familiar with such brazen delay tactics, would fume and fret before chasing an intentionally bad pitch with predictable results. Plank also talked to himself in a distinctive nasal tone that could be heard in both dugouts.

But Plank was much more than psychological games-manship. He also was a fierce competitor who attacked hitters with a better-than-average fastball, a good curve and uncanny control that allowed him to work to spots and make hitters chase pitches on his terms. Plank also went after lefthanded batters with a devastating crossfire pitch — a wicked sidearm delivery that appeared to be coming from first base — and further helped his cause with a runner-freezing pickoff motion.

The strong-jawed, no-nonsense Plank, who graduated from Gettysburg College before pitching his first major league game at age 25, converted his unusual pitching style into seven 20-victory seasons for the A's and a 21-win 1915 campaign for St. Louis in the outlaw Federal League. His ERAs were consistently low, his strikeout totals high and he pitched 69 career shutouts, more than any other lefthander.

Plank also carved out an impressive 1.32 ERA over seven games and 54 ⅔ innings in four World Series, even though his hard-luck record was only 2-5. Plank still owns numerous pitching records in the long history of the Athletics franchise.

> "Plank was not the fastest, not the trickiest and not the possessor of the most stuff. He was just the greatest."
>
> —*Eddie Collins*

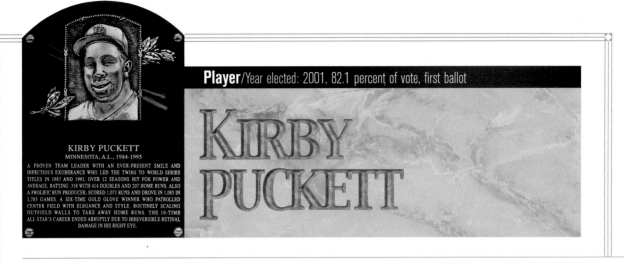

Player/Year elected: 2001, 82.1 percent of vote, first ballot

KIRBY PUCKETT

KIRBY PUCKETT
MINNESOTA, A.L., 1984-1995

A PROVEN TEAM LEADER WITH AN EVER-PRESENT SMILE AND INFECTIOUS EXUBERANCE WHO LED THE TWINS TO WORLD SERIES TITLES IN 1987 AND 1991. OVER 12 SEASONS HIT FOR POWER AND AVERAGE, BATTING .318 WITH 414 DOUBLES AND 207 HOME RUNS. ALSO A PROLIFIC RUN PRODUCER, SCORED 1,071 RUNS AND DROVE IN 1,085 IN 1,783 GAMES. A SIX-TIME GOLD GLOVE WINNER WHO PATROLLED CENTER FIELD WITH ELEGANCE AND STYLE, ROUTINELY SCALING OUTFIELD WALLS TO TAKE AWAY HOME RUNS. THE 10-TIME ALL-STAR'S CAREER ENDED ABRUPTLY DUE TO IRREVERSIBLE RETINAL DAMAGE IN HIS RIGHT EYE.

Born: 3-14-61, Chicago, Ill. **Height/Weight:** 5-8/210 **Bats/Throws:** R/R **Primary position:** Center field **Career statistics:** .318 avg., 2,304 hits, 1,071 runs, 207 HR, 1,085 RBIs **Teams:** Twins 1984-95 **Batting champion:** A.L., 1989

His smile brightened up Minneapolis and his blazing bat lit up the American League for 12 enjoyable seasons. Charisma oozed out of Kirby Puckett's Smurfian 5-foot-8 body like water out of a sponge. He brought effervescence, personality and success to a downtrodden Twins franchise while charming his way through a productive career cut short by a serious eye problem in 1996.

It was easy to love the barrel-chested, thick-necked Puckett, who signed autographs with the same enthusiasm that he drove line drives into the gap and chased down fly balls hit into his center field domain. Fans and teammates were swept away by the quick smile; opposing pitchers were swept away by the quick righthanded swing that whipped through the ball from a crouching stance. No area of the ballpark escaped the wicked drives lashed out by one of baseball's classic bad-ball hitters.

Over his 12 big-league seasons, Puckett topped

> "He has an effervescent, ingratiating personality. Kirby is a very warm, very genuine person. If he had been playing in New York or Los Angeles, they would be building statues to him."
>
> —*Andy MacPhail, former Twins G.M.*

.300 eight times and reached the 200-hit plateau four years in a row. He could finesse you with his deceptive speed or club you with his surprising power. The 1989 A.L. batting champion also was a three-time 100-RBI run-producer from his No. 3 spot in the Twins order and the catalyst for Minnesota Word Series winners in 1987 and 1991.

Puckett was at his memorable best when scaling the Metrodome's center field fence to rob hitters of home runs, a feat he pulled off with amazing regularity. Twins fans will never forget Game 6 of the 1991 World Series, when Puckett leaped above the fence in the third inning to rob Atlanta's Ron Gant and then hit a game-winning, Series-saving home run in the 11th.

Puckett, at age 35, woke up one morning before the 1996 season with blurred vision in his right eye, a condition later diagnosed as glaucoma. He never played again. The 10-time All-Star Game performer finished with a .318 average and 2,304 hits — and status alongside Harmon Killebrew as the most popular players in Minnesota history.

Player/Year elected: 1939, Committee of Old-Time Players and Writers

HOSS RADBOURN

Born: 12-11-1854, Rochester, N.Y. **Died:** 2-5-1897 **Height/Weight:** 5-9/168 **Bats/Throws:** R/R **Position:** Pitcher **Career statistics:** 309-194, 2.68 ERA, 1,830 strikeouts **Teams:** Providence 1881-85; Boston 1886-89; Boston (P.L.) 1890; Cincinnati 1891

He was a 5-foot-9, 168-pound bundle of dynamite. Stoic, brooding Charles Radbourn was a 19th-century submariner who pitched on the edge — silent and workmanlike one minute, temperamental and likely to explode the next. More than anything else, "Old Hoss" was a warrior, an inspirational workhorse who crammed 309 victories into a short-but-exciting 11-year career.

An incredible 59 came in one magic season, when Radbourn rose from the ashes of a midseason suspension to almost single-handedly win the 1884 National League pennant for the Providence Grays. After No. 2 pitcher Charles Sweeney suddenly bolted the team, the rubber-armed Radbourn came back and pitched 27 straight games, winning 26, before resting with the pennant secured. He added three wins in a post-season playoff against American Association-champion New York.

It was the stuff of legends. For many years Radbourn was credited with a final 60-12 record, but the win total later was adjusted to 59. He worked 678 ⅔ innings, com-pleted all 73 of his starts and recorded 441 strikeouts and a 1.38 ERA. By season's end, his arm was so sore he could barely comb his hair and it's probably no coincidence that he never achieved that level of success again.

At his best, Radbourn was the most complete pitcher in the game. His fastball had zip, he carved up hitters with a variety of curves and his changeup could make anybody look foolish. Radbourn, who never abandoned his underhand motion, masterfully mixed pitches and posted win totals of 25, 33 and 48 for Providence before his 1884 iron-man effort. But from 1885-91 while pitching in Providence, Boston and Cincinnati, he was 144-127 with a top victory total of 28 and three loss totals that exceeded wins. The Illinois-raised Radbourn, who pitched most of his career at the 50-foot distance, was known for his sour disposition and a fondness for saloons and night life. He also liked to hit, often playing right field on days he didn't pitch. The man who completed 488 of 502 career starts retired in 1891 with a 309-194 record.

> "Radbourn became so good with constant practice that he could throw the ball through a good-sized knothole in the fence."
>
> —*Frank Bancroft, former Providence manager*

RADBOURN

PEE WEE REESE

HAROLD HENRY "PEE WEE" REESE
BROOKLYN N.L. 1940-1957
LOS ANGELES N.L. 1958
SHORTSTOP AND CAPTAIN OF GREAT DODGER TEAMS OF 1940's AND 50's. INTANGIBLE QUALITIES OF SUBTLE LEADERSHIP ON AND OFF FIELD, COMPETITIVE FIRE AND PROFESSIONAL PRIDE COMPLEMENTED DEPENDABLE GLOVE, RELIABLE BASE-RUNNING AND CLUTCH-HITTING AS SIGNIFICANT FACTORS IN 7 DODGER PENNANTS. INSTRUMENTAL IN EASING ACCEPTANCE OF JACKIE ROBINSON AS BASEBALL'S FIRST BLACK PERFORMER.

Born: 7-23-18, Ekron, Ky. **Died:** 8-14-99 **Height/Weight:** 5-9/175 **Bats/Throws:** R/R **Primary position:** Shortstop **Career statistics:** .269 avg., 2,170 hits, 1,338 runs, 232 steals **Teams:** Brooklyn Dodgers 1940-42, 1946-57; Los Angeles Dodgers 1958

To longtime friends and family, he was Harold Henry Reese, a polite, self-effacing Kentuckian. To millions of baseball fans in Brooklyn and beyond, he was Pee Wee Reese, longtime shortstop, captain and spiritual leader of the most dominant team in the National League. Mild-mannered gentleman and Brooklyn Bum; Southern hospitality and killer instinct—the always popular Reese combined the best of two worlds.

From a baseball perspective, the "Little Colonel" was a managerial dream—a 5-foot-9, 175-pound grinder who made up for athletic deficiencies with more esoteric qualities. He was smart, a manager on the field, and he was the Dodgers' unquestioned leader, almost from his 1940 debut to his 1958 retirement after the team's first season in Los Angeles. Reese cooled tempers, dispensed advice and led by example—with key hits, sparkling defensive plays and his always-calm demeanor.

It was no coincidence the Dodgers won seven pennants and never finished lower than third in Reese's 14 years as full-time shortstop. And it was Reese, the Southerner, who mollified players and spectators when hostility surfaced over the 1947 arrival of Jackie Robinson. Reese openly befriended Robinson during his quest to break baseball's color barrier.

Reese, a righthanded swinger, was only a .269 career hitter, but he bunted, moved runners, executed hit-and-runs and worked pitchers for walks. A perfect

> "Pee Wee is the team captain and he plays the part all out. Especially in the dressing room, he knows where to be and what to say at all times."
>
> —*Jackie Robinson, 1952*

REESE

No. 2 batter who scored 94 or more runs for eight straight seasons and stole 232 bases, he had an uncanny knack for coming through in the clutch. That quality also applied to his defense. Always reliable as the anchor of the Dodgers' great infields, Reese was at his heady best with the game on the line.

Never spectacular, the eight-time All-Star Game shortstop was a regular on MVP ballots and World Series lineup cards. In 44 Series games, he collected 46 hits and batted .272—but the Dodgers won only one classic, an emotional 1955 victory over the Yankees. Contrary to popular opinion, the "Pee Wee" nickname stemmed from Reese's childhood marbles-shooting ability.

SAM RICE

EDGAR CHARLES (SAM) RICE
WASHINGTON, A.L. 1915 TO 1933
CLEVELAND, A.L. 1934
AT BAT 600 OR MORE TIMES EIGHT
DIFFERENT SEASONS. HAD 200 OR MORE HITS
IN EACH OF SIX SEASONS. BATTED .322
FOR 20-YEAR CAREER AND HAD 2987 HITS.
SET A.L. RECORD WITH 182 SINGLES IN
1925. LED A.L. IN NUMBER OF HITS 216
IN 1924 AND 1926. LED A.L. IN PUTOUTS
FOR OUTFIELDERS WITH 454 IN 1920 AND
385 IN 1922.

Born: 2-20-1890, Morocco, Ind. **Died:** 10-13-74 **Height/Weight:** 5-9/150 **Bats/Throws:** L/R **Primary position:** Outfield
Career statistics: .322 avg., 2,987 hits, 1,514 runs, 1,078 RBIs, 351 steals **Teams:** Senators 1915-33; Indians 1934

His flat, level stroke was studied and praised by Ted Williams. His durable consistency was the model by which Washington outfielders would be judged after his retirement in 1934. Edgar "Sam" Rice was the quiet, mischievous, lead-by-example hitting machine who played 19 of his 20 seasons in Washington and was a member of all three Senators pennant-winning teams.

For a wannabe pitcher who showed up on a Washington mound in 1915, Rice sure was a good hitter. So good, in fact, that Senators manager Clark Griffith decided in 1916 the 5-foot-9, 150-pounder could help him more in the outfield and made him his everyday center fielder. At age 26, the quiet, reserved Rice began a crusade that would not end until age 44, producing a .322 average and 2,987 hits.

Rice, a lefthanded hitter and righthanded thrower, stood erect at the plate and used quick wrists to slash pitches to all fields. He never swung at the first pitch and seldom fanned, once completing a 616-at-bat

> "Why worry about the first pitch? If it's no good, you're ahead of him. If he gets over a good pitch, you can be sure he'll come back with it and you're laying for it." —*Sam Rice*

season with nine strikeouts. As the ultimate contact man with the picture-perfect swing, Rice was never a home run threat. But blazing speed turned singles into doubles and his 1920 stolen base total of 63 earned him the timely nickname "Man o' War."

It's hard to argue the consistency of the little man from Morocco, Ind. Six times he topped 200 hits, the last in 1930 at age 40. Rice topped .300 in 13 full seasons and batted .334 and .350 in the pennant-winning campaigns of 1924 and '25, the first of which resulted in a World Series championship.

Rice is best remembered for his "miracle" catch in the 1925 Series against Pittsburgh—a Game 3 play in which he tumbled into the Griffith Stadium stands chasing a drive by Pirates catcher Earl Smith. After about 15 seconds, Rice emerged with the ball, precipitating an out call by the umpire and protests from the Pirates. Rice spent the rest of his life playing coy, greeting questions about whether he really caught the ball with a smile and a wink.

RICE

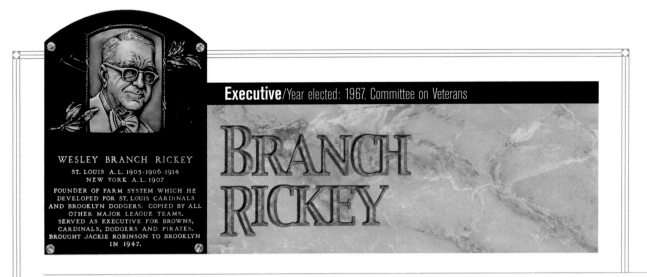

BRANCH RICKEY

WESLEY BRANCH RICKEY
ST. LOUIS A.L. 1905·1906·1914
NEW YORK A.L. 1907
FOUNDER OF FARM SYSTEM WHICH HE
DEVELOPED FOR ST. LOUIS CARDINALS
AND BROOKLYN DODGERS. COPIED BY ALL
OTHER MAJOR LEAGUE TEAMS.
SERVED AS EXECUTIVE FOR BROWNS,
CARDINALS, DODGERS AND PIRATES.
BROUGHT JACKIE ROBINSON TO BROOKLYN
IN 1947.

Born: 12-20-1881, Flat, Ohio **Died:** 12-9-65 **Teams managed (597-664):** Browns 1913-15; Cardinals 1919-25 **Executive career:** Vice-president, business manager of Browns, 1915-16; president of Cardinals, 1917, 1919-25; vice-president and business manager of Cardinals, 1925-42; president and G.M. of Dodgers, 1942-45; part owner and G.M. of Dodgers, 1945-50; vice-president and G.M. of Pirates, 1951-55

He was the esoteric "Mahatma," a visionary genius and philosopher who changed the course of baseball with his theories and innovations. Branch Rickey is remembered as the father of the farm system and the man who integrated the National Pastime, but he was so much more. He was a larger-than-life baseball giant and a colorful character who impacted the game, both on the field and off.

To hear the erudite Rickey expound his ideas and fundamentalist beliefs was a stirring experience. He was expressive and captivating, a powerful orator who loved to teach his theories of life and success. A deeply religious man who never attended a game on Sunday, the gravelly voiced Ohio farm boy also was intelligent (he held several bachelor degrees), shrewd, tough, unyielding and energetic.

It was as a theorist and thinker that Rickey made his baseball mark. Unsuccessful in a brief career as a catcher and a

> "The beetle-browed Mahatma was an unquestioned genius, a man who could have attained top rank in any business or profession. Baseball is indeed fortunate that this extraordinary person elected to channel his remarkable talents in its direction."
>
> —*Arthur Daley, New York Times*

10-year run as manager of the talent-deficient St. Louis Browns and Cardinals, he turned his attention to player acquisition. As Cardinals vice president in the 1920s, he began building baseball's first farm system, a network of minor league teams to develop talent for the parent club, and watched it flourish, along with the organization's fortunes.

Under Rickey, St. Louis teams became a force, winning pennants in 1926, '28, '30, '31, '34 and '42 and four World Series. Long after he departed for Brooklyn in 1942, his farm continued to produce talent for the powerful Cardinals. He performed his

RICKEY

"farm system" magic for the Dodgers and Pittsburgh Pirates before leaving baseball in 1959.

It was in Brooklyn that Rickey made his biggest impact with the 1945 signing of Jackie Robinson to break baseball's color barrier. Robinson's historic 1947 debut with the Dodgers opened the door for future generations of blacks and helped Brooklyn dominate the National League in the 1950s. Rickey, who tried unsuccessfully to launch a third major league in his final baseball venture, also is credited with such innovations as the sliding pit, batting cage, Ladies Day and the Knothole Gang.

EPPA RIXEY

EPPA RIXEY
PHILADELPHIA, N.L. 1912 TO 1920
CINCINNATI, N.L. 1921 TO 1933
WON 266 LOST 251 PCT. .515 ERA 3.15
SET RECORD FOR MOST VICTORIES BY
LEFT-HANDED PITCHER. LED LEAGUE IN
VICTORIES WITH 25 IN 1922. GAVE ONLY
1082 BASE ON BALLS IN 4494 INNINGS.

Born: 5-3-1891, Culpeper, Va. **Died:** 2-28-63 **Height/Weight:** 6-5/210 **Bats/Throws:** R/L **Position:** Pitcher
Career statistics: 266-251, 3.15 ERA, 1,350 strikeouts **Teams:** Phillies 1912-17, 1919-20; Reds 1921-33

One contemporary writer described Eppa Rixey's twisting, contorting delivery as "a boa constrictor twining around a mongoose." Batters facing the 6-foot-5 lefthander were further dismayed by a long-striding follow-through that simultaneously propelled ball and pitcher homeward with distracting fury. For 21 seasons in Philadelphia and Cincinnati, Rixey literally swept aside National League hitters with his deceptive motion and pinpoint control while winning 266 games.

Rixey, the product of a prominent family from Culpeper, Va., relied on guile and finesse as much as natural talent. The effectiveness of a mediocre fastball was enhanced by his unorthodox delivery and he shaved the corners with sharp-breaking curves and changeups. Rixey constantly mixed speeds and toyed with batters, who seldom saw pitches they could hit hard. And despite going deep into counts, his walk and strikeout totals were always low.

Rixey stepped off the University of Virginia campus in 1912 and began on-the-job training for a Phillies staff that featured Grover Alexander, who would dominate the city's pitching spotlight. Rixey enjoyed a 22-10 breakthrough (1.85 ERA) for Philadelphia in 1916, but it wasn't until a 1921 trade to Cincinnati that he blossomed into a consistent winner. A five-year run

> "Eppa was just great. He was great as a pitcher, fielder and competitor. I look on him as the most outstanding player I came in contact with in my entire career."
>
> —*Bubbles Hargrave, former Cincinnati catcher*

with the Reds produced 100 victories and three visits to the 20-win plateau, including a career-best 25-13 mark in 1922.

Throughout his long career, the 210-pound Rixey charmed teammates and fans with his dry wit and big Southern drawl. His nonsensical nickname "Jeptha" seemed to capture his blue-blood roots and amiable · personality. Rixey's good sense of humor helped him survive the ignominy of pitching for weak teams that finished in the second division in 12 of his 21 seasons, explaining his 251 career losses—the most by a left-hander in history.

Rixey, who allowed only 92 career home runs, made one World Series appearance for the 1915 Phillies—losing Game 5. But most of his career was spent as a durable workhorse who carved out a 3.15 ERA and worked 4,494 ⅔ innings before retiring in 1933.

PHIL RIZZUTO

PHILIP FRANCIS RIZZUTO
"SCOOTER"

NEW YORK, A.L., 1941-1942, 1946-1956

OVERCAME DIMINUTIVE SIZE (5'6", 150 LBS) TO ANCHOR SUPERB YANKEE TEAMS WHICH WON 10 PENNANTS AND 8 WORLD SERIES DURING HIS 13 MAJOR LEAGUE SEASONS. OUTSTANDING SHORTSTOP ON FIVE CONSECUTIVE WORLD CHAMPIONSHIP CLUBS. SKILLED BUNTER AND ENTHUSIASTIC BASE RUNNER WITH SOLID .273 LIFETIME BATTING AVERAGE. ALL-STAR FIVE TIMES AND A.L. MVP IN 1950 WHEN HE PEAKED AT .324 WITH 200 HITS AND A .439 SLUGGING PCT.

Born: 9-25-17, Brooklyn, N.Y. **Height/Weight:** 5-6/160 **Bats/Throws:** R/R **Primary position:** Shortstop **Career statistics:** .273 avg., 1,588 hits, 149 steals **Teams:** Yankees 1941-42, 1946-56 **Major awards:** A.L. MVP, 1950

For 13 glorious seasons, Phil Rizzuto scooted and scampered around the Yankee Stadium infield, snatching up balls like a hungry vacuum. Former manager Bucky Harris called him "a pocket-size magician"; teammates used such adjectives as "lovable," "peppy" and "inspiring." By whatever standards the diminutive former shortstop was measured, everyone agreed he was the glue that held together a championship dynasty.

What you saw with "Scooter" is what you got. He was a 5-foot-6, 160-pound bundle of energy—a dark, good-looking Italian kid who looked up to his famous teammates with open-mouth awe and played every game like it would be his last. Fans loved his enthusiasm and dedication. Players loved the gullible innocence that made him the target of good-natured jokes.

On the field, Rizzuto was quick and instinctive—a "go get 'em" shortstop who could range right, left and backward, chasing down short flies like a fourth outfielder. His hands were soft and he handled the ball like a magician, catching and throwing almost in the

"For a five-year period, I would have to take Lou Boudreau (as my shortstop). But year after year, season after season, Rizzuto was a standout." —*Paul Richards*

same motion. That same sleight-of-hand magic showed up in a righthanded batting style that focused on bunting, moving runners and slashing balls to the opposite field, depending on game situations.

The Brooklyn-born Rizzuto often was compared to contemporary Pee Wee Reese, who was performing the same shortstop magic for the cross-town Dodgers. Reese led Brooklyn to seven National League pennants after his debut in 1940; Rizzuto helped the Yankees win 10 A.L. pennants after starting in 1941. But Scooter's Yankees also won seven World Series and the career .273 hitter won an MVP when he exploded for career highs in average (.324), runs (125) and hits (200) in 1950.

It's hard to separate Rizzuto from that incredible winning legacy—or the ever-present smile that remained a New York fixture for decades in his second career as a Yankees broadcaster. Rizzuto, a five-time All-Star Game performer who lost three prime years to military service, entered the booth after his retirement in 1956.

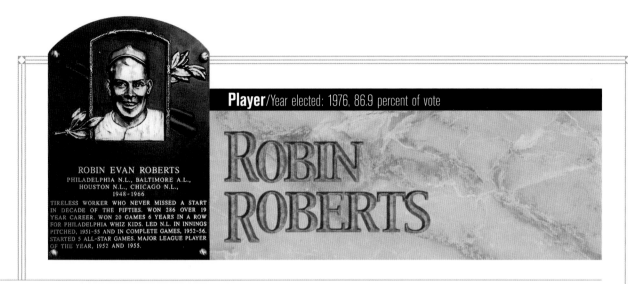

ROBIN ROBERTS

ROBIN EVAN ROBERTS
PHILADELPHIA N.L., BALTIMORE A.L.,
HOUSTON N.L., CHICAGO N.L.,
1948-1966
TIRELESS WORKER WHO NEVER MISSED A START
IN DECADE OF THE FIFTIES. WON 286 OVER 19
YEAR CAREER. WON 20 GAMES 6 YEARS IN A ROW
FOR PHILADELPHIA WHIZ KIDS. LED N.L. IN INNINGS
PITCHED, 1951-55 AND IN COMPLETE GAMES, 1952-56.
STARTED 5 ALL-STAR GAMES. MAJOR LEAGUE PLAYER
OF THE YEAR, 1952 AND 1955.

Born: 9-30-26, Springfield, Ill. **Height/Weight:** 6-0/190 **Bats/Throws:** B/R **Position:** Pitcher **Career statistics:** 286-245, 3.41 ERA, 2,357 strikeouts **Teams:** Phillies 1948-61; Orioles 1962-65; Astros 1965-66; Cubs 1966

The first distressing signs came in 1956, the year Robin Roberts became a baseball mortal. The strong right arm that had produced six consecutive 20-win, 300-inning seasons couldn't deliver fastballs with quite the same gusto or control. The legs tired quicker, the once-durable 190-pound body just would not cooperate. What had started as a race for Hall of Fame glory suddenly became a struggle for survival.

It's safe to say Roberts was remarkable—perhaps as good as any pitcher over the second half century—for that six-season stretch from 1950-55: 138 wins, 1,937 ⅔ innings, 161 complete games in 232 starts, 24 shutouts. And the temptation to ride his powerful arm to World Series success was just too strong for a downtrodden Philadelphia Phillies franchise, which overused its prodigy in an effort to make up for 35 years of postseason frustration.

Roberts, working between starts and on short rest, helped the Whiz Kids end that jinx in 1950 with a 20-11 record and he answered all calls while piling up consec-

"He's smooth fast. He throws with such ease that he doesn't seem to be bearing down very hard, and his speed takes you all the more off stride."—*Ralph Kiner*

utive win totals of 21, 28, 23, 23 and 23. But the price for that work ethic would be steep and the rewards—no more World Series, 107 wins after age 30—diminishing.

The key to success was an overpowering fastball that Roberts delivered with pin-point control from a smooth, almost-effortless motion. It was difficult for batters to time the speed of a ball that literally slid across the plate. A so-so curve was merely window dressing and a cool, calculating demeanor masked an intense competitive fire. Roberts was willing to take the mound at a moment's notice and he never gave less than 100 percent.

When he slumped to 1-10 in 1961, the Phillies severed connections with their former ace and he began a career-ending journey that would take him to Baltimore, Houston and Chicago. Depending more on guile and determination than his once-powerful fastball, Roberts carved out 52 more wins that gave him a career-ending 19-year record of 286-245. He also finished with the dubious all-time mark of 505 home runs allowed.

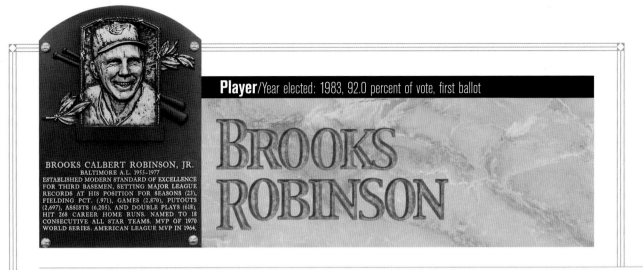

BROOKS ROBINSON

BROOKS CALBERT ROBINSON, JR.
BALTIMORE A.L. 1955-1977
ESTABLISHED MODERN STANDARD OF EXCELLENCE
FOR THIRD BASEMEN, SETTING MAJOR LEAGUE
RECORDS AT HIS POSITION FOR SEASONS (23),
FIELDING PCT. (.971), GAMES (2,870), PUTOUTS
(2,697), ASSISTS (6,205), AND DOUBLE PLAYS (618).
HIT 268 CAREER HOME RUNS. NAMED TO 18
CONSECUTIVE ALL STAR TEAMS. MVP OF 1970
WORLD SERIES. AMERICAN LEAGUE MVP IN 1964.

Born: 5-18-37, Little Rock, Ark. **Height/Weight:** 6-1/190 **Bats/Throws:** R/R **Primary position:** Third base **Career statistics:** .267 avg., 2,848 hits, 1,232 runs, 268 HR, 1,357 RBIs **Teams:** Orioles 1955-77 **Major awards:** A.L. MVP, 1964

The hunched shoulders and loping run made Brooks Robinson easy to spot. But it took a hot ground ball within hailing distance of third base to give him perspective. The eyes would flash, the reflexes would kick in and the glove would streak toward a white blur barely discernible to the human eye. Another accurate throw would complete another masterful play by baseball's "human vacuum cleaner."

Robinson's 23-year Baltimore legacy was built around scores of potential hits he stole from frustrated opponents. His 11 American League fielding-average titles offer testimony to the routine plays he always made and his 16 Gold Gloves reflect the tumbling, acrobatic gyrations he often pulled off with dramatic flair. Robinson, who made his Orioles debut in 1955 at age 18, was slow afoot and his arm was only average, but his reflexes and dexterity were exceptional and his quick release and throwing accuracy uncanny.

Robinson is best remembered for his defense, but the righthanded punch and even-keeled leadership he

added to the powerful Orioles' lineups of the 1960s and '70s cannot be overlooked. A disciplined hitter with a team-first attitude, Robinson topped 20 home runs six times and earned an A.L. MVP in 1964 when he batted .317 with 118 RBIs. He was especially dangerous in the clutch and his gracious, personable demeanor lifted him to icon status among adoring Baltimore fans.

The R&R combination of Brooks and Frank Robinson combined for 72 homers and 222 RBIs in 1966 and the Orioles won the first of four pennants and two World Series in a six-year span. The 1970 fall classic belonged to Brooks, who batted .429 and put on a defensive clinic, stealing hit after hit from the disbelieving Reds while claiming MVP honors.

"The guy can field a ball with a pair of pliers," Cincinnati star Pete Rose grumbled, expressing the frustration felt by Robinson contemporaries for almost a quarter century. A quarter century that produced still-standing third base fielding records for percentage, assists, putouts, chances and double plays.

"If (Robinson) could run, he would be the perfect ballplayer." —*Johnny Pesky*

ROBINSON

ROBINSON

FRANK ROBINSON
CINCINNATI N.L., BALTIMORE A.L.,
LOS ANGELES N.L., CALIFORNIA A.L.,
CLEVELAND A.L., 1956-1976
FIRST TO BE CHOSEN MOST VALUABLE PLAYER
IN BOTH LEAGUES -- N.L. IN 1961 AND A.L.
IN 1966. SET RECORDS BY HITTING HOMERS
IN 32 DIFFERENT PARKS AND WITH PAIR OF
GRAND-SLAMMERS IN SUCCESSIVE INNINGS IN
1970. FOURTH IN HOMERS (586), FIFTH IN
EXTRA BASES ON LONG HITS (2,430), SIXTH
IN TOTAL BASES (5,373). ON RETIRING, LED
N.L. IN SLUGGING PCT. IN 1960-61-62 AND
A.L. IN BATTING, HOMERS, RUNS BATTED IN,
TOTAL BASES AND SLUGGING PCT. IN 1966.

Player/Year elected: 1982, 89.2 percent of vote, first ballot

FRANK ROBINSON

Born: 8-31-35, Beaumont, Tex. **Height/Weight:** 6-1/195 **Bats/Throws:** R/R **Primary position:** Outfield **Career statistics:** .294 avg., 2,943 hits, 1,829 runs, 586 HR, 1,812 RBIs, 204 steals **Teams:** Reds 1956-65; Orioles 1966-71; Dodgers 1972; Angels 1973-74; Indians 1974-76

Batting champion: A.L., 1966 **HR champion:** A.L., 1966 **Major awards:** N.L. Rookie of Year, 1956; N.L. MVP, 1961; A.L. MVP, 1966

When you cut through all the superlatives, two capture the essence and intensity of the man. Frank Robinson, the self-made star with skinny legs and a big stick, was fearless and inspirational — qualities that earned him the contempt of opponents and the respect and admiration of teammates and fans over a memorable 21-year career.

There was nothing flashy about the in-your-face right fielder who made his first impressions in 1956 when he hit 38 home runs as a 20-year-old Rookie of the Year for Cincinnati. Competing for prestige in an era dominated by such names as Mays, Mantle, Aaron and Clemente, Robinson played with a recklessness, intimidating self-confidence and scowling demeanor that infuriated opponents. He always slid hard, never fraternized with the enemy and wielded a booming bat that produced 586 career homers, fourth on the all-time list.

Even his batting style was confrontational. The 6- foot-1 Robinson crowded the plate like a boxer trying to work inside, daring the pitcher to throw a strike. He crouched, leaned forward, bat pointed upward, and glared toward the mound over an upraised shoulder. Pitchers who greeted his insolence with fastballs to the ribs usually paid a price in subsequent at-bats.

Robinson was an offensive machine for the Reds from 1956-65, winning the 1961 MVP with a 37-homer, 124-RBI performance while leading Cincinnati to a pennant. Reds fans were shocked when management declared Robinson an "old 30" and traded him to Baltimore after a 1965 campaign in which he totaled 33 homers and 113 RBIs.

The young-and-talented Orioles got the outspoken clubhouse leader who would help them win four American League pennants and two World Series in a six-year span. Robinson punctuated that team success with a 1966 Triple Crown (.316, 49, 122) and distinction as the only player to win MVPs in both leagues.

The aging Robinson, who played in 11 All-Star Games, punctuated his career in 1975 with another distinction — he became Cleveland's player-manager and the first black manager in major league history. He celebrated by homering in his first "managerial" at-bat.

"I don't want people to say Mickey Mantle, Willie Mays and Hank Aaron in one breath and, in the next, Frank Robinson. I want them to say Mantle, Mays, Aaron and Robinson in the same breath." —*Frank Robinson, 1967*

JACKIE ROBINSON

JACK ROOSEVELT ROBINSON
BROOKLYN N.L. 1947 TO 1956
LEADING N.L. BATTER IN 1949. HOLDS
FIELDING MARK FOR SECOND BASEMAN
PLAYING IN 150 OR MORE GAMES WITH .992.
LED N.L. IN STOLEN BASES IN 1947 AND
1949. MOST VALUABLE PLAYER IN 1949.
LIFETIME BATTING AVERAGE .311. JOINT
RECORD HOLDER FOR MOST DOUBLE PLAYS
BY SECOND BASEMAN, 137 IN 1951.
LED SECOND BASEMEN IN DOUBLE
PLAYS 1949-50-51-52.

Born: 1-31-19, Cairo, Ga. **Died:** 10-24-72 **Height/Weight:** 5-11/204 **Bats/Throws:** R/R **Primary position:** Second base

Career statistics: .311 avg., 1,518 hits, 137 HR, 197 steals **Teams:** Dodgers 1947-56 **Batting champion:** N.L., 1949

Major awards: N.L. Rookie of Year, 1947; N.L. MVP, 1949

Jackie Robinson will be remembered as a pioneer, the man who broke baseball's color barrier for Branch Rickey's Brooklyn Dodgers in 1947 and ushered in a second half-century of hope and opportunity. But sometimes lost in the shadow of Robinson's overwhelming achievement is the marvelous athletic ability that would have been enough to get him Hall of Fame recognition in a normal, integrated baseball society.

Any assessment of Robinson's career has to be made in the context of what he endured on the field—racial epithets, name-calling, threats, spikings and other cruel admonitions. Always, as demanded by Rickey, he bit his lip and turned the other cheek, letting his hitting, baserunning and fielding reap the only revenge he would be allowed. To say that Robinson, a four-sport athlete at UCLA, performed admirably under pressure is something of an understatement.

As a hitter, the 5-foot-11 righthander was always dangerous and unpredictable, whether using his great speed to beat out a bunt, driving a ball into the gap

"He was a great competitor who could do it all. He was a great player, a manager's dream. ... If I had to go to war, I'd want him on my side." —*Leo Durocher*

or hitting behind a runner with uncanny precision. As a baserunner, he was aggressive and smart, a dancing bandit who distracted pitchers, rattled defenses and ignited the Dodgers' attack. As a second baseman, he was smooth, graceful and sure-handed, a pressure performer who made big plays in key situations.

It's no coincidence the Dodgers captured six pennants and their only Brooklyn World Series with Robinson providing the offensive spark. As a 28-year-old rookie playing under an intense spotlight, he batted .297. Two years later, he led N.L. hitters with a .342 average and drove in 124 runs. He scored 100 runs six times and his 197 career stolen bases included 19 steals of home.

But more than anything else, Robinson brought to the game a fierce pride and competitive spirit that allowed him to fight through adversity and win the respect of both teammates and opponents. That respect was manifested in his 1947 Rookie of the Year award, 1949 N.L. MVP and six All-Star Games in which he played.

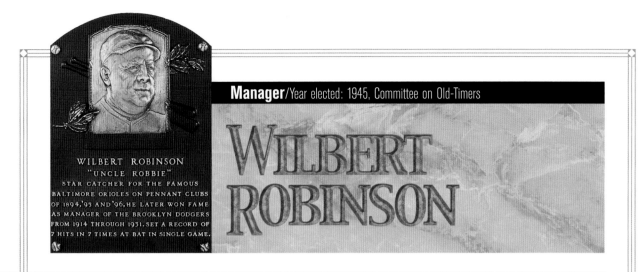

WILBERT ROBINSON

WILBERT ROBINSON
"UNCLE ROBBIE"
STAR CATCHER FOR THE FAMOUS
BALTIMORE ORIOLES ON PENNANT CLUBS
OF 1894,'95 AND'96, HE LATER WON FAME
AS MANAGER OF THE BROOKLYN DODGERS
FROM 1914 THROUGH 1931. SET A RECORD OF
7 HITS IN 7 TIMES AT BAT IN SINGLE GAME.

Born: 6-29-1863, Bolton, Mass. **Died:** 8-8-34 **Height/Weight:** 5-9/225 **Bats/Throws:** R/R **Primary position:** Catcher
Career statistics: .275 avg., 1,402 hits **Teams played:** Philadelphia (A.A.) 1886-90; Baltimore (A.A.) 1890-91; Baltimore 1892-99; St. Louis 1900; Baltimore (A.L.) 1901-02 **Teams managed (1,399-1,398):** Baltimore (A.L.) 1902; Dodgers 1914-31

Brooklyn fans remember him as "Uncle Robbie," the fun-loving, absent-minded, roly-poly manager of the 1920s "Daffiness Boys." Nothing seemed to faze Wilbert Robinson, the unpredictable leader of the zany Dodgers. But history shows another side of the man who captained one of baseball's greatest teams and managed another to 1,375 wins and two National League pennants.

The earthy, gregarious Robinson is best remembered as the man who guided the Dodgers to their first titles in 1916 and '20. But his real baseball roots were established in 1890s Baltimore, where he was catcher and captain for a three-time pennant-winning Orioles team that also featured longtime friend John McGraw. A .275 career hitter and one of two players to go 7-for-7 in a nine-inning game, Robinson later became a renowned handler of pitchers for McGraw's New York Giants before taking the Dodgers job in 1914.

He also was a simple man with little use for "scientific baseball." To him, it was a simple game of hit, pitch and throw and he managed accordingly, relying on instincts that had served him well as a player. Those instincts were good enough to get the Dodgers into two World Series and earn him lasting celebrity in Brooklyn, where his team became known as the "Robins."

The 5-foot-9 Robbie was always colorful, a fiery, profane, sometimes-comical character who waddled around the field and laughed off the crazy things that happened to his team. Three runners on third base at the same time, fly balls hitting outfielders on the head—anything was liable to happen and fans loved it. Robinson once formed a "Bonehead Club" to collect fines for stupid plays, but disbanded it after players batted out of turn because he turned in the wrong lineup card.

The Dodgers seldom contended after 1920, but the antics of Babe Herman, Dazzy Vance and Robinson were always entertaining. Robinson lasted as manager until 1931, when he was forced to resign after an 18-year association with the city. He retired with a 1,399-1,398 career record.

> "There's only one theory on pitching. Get the biggest guy you can find who can throw a ball through a two-inch plank and you got yourself a pitcher."
>
> — *Wilbert Robinson*

ROBINSON

JOE ROGAN

WILBER JOE ROGAN
(BULLET)
KANSAS CITY MONARCHS, 1920-38
A VERSATILE PERFORMER WHO WAS EQUALLY SUPERLATIVE AS A
PITCHER AND HITTER. UTILIZED A DECEPTIVELY QUICK, NO-WINDUP
DELIVERY TO LEAD KANSAS CITY TO FOUR NEGRO NATIONAL LEAGUE
TITLES. PITCHING REPERTOIRE INCLUDED A FORKBALL, CURVEBALL
AND PALMBALL, AND FEATURED A BLAZING FASTBALL AS AN
OUTPITCH. ALSO PLAYED CENTER FIELD, HITTING .343 AS HIS CLUB'S
CLEANUP HITTER AND .410 IN WORLD SERIES COMPETITION. PILOTED
THE MONARCHS IN THE DUAL ROLE OF PLAYER AND MANAGER FOR
SEVERAL SEASONS. SERVED AS AN UMPIRE IN THE NEGRO LEAGUES
FOLLOWING PLAYING CAREER.

Born: 7-28-1889, Oklahoma City, Okla. **Died:** 3-4-67 **Height/Weight:** 5-7/180 **Bats/Throws:** R/R **Primary positions:** Pitcher, outfield
Teams played (1920-38): Kansas City Monarchs **Teams managed (1926-38):** Kansas City Monarchs

He would blow you away with a fastball, freeze you with a drop curve or frustrate you with a tantalizing palmball. And then, for good measure, cleanup hitter Joe Rogan would cut out your heart with a line drive into the gap. "Bullet Joe" was wielded like a double-edged sword by the Negro National League's Kansas City Monarchs for almost two decades, a versatility only Babe Ruth and Martin Dihigo could match in modern baseball history.

The 5-foot-7 Rogan, a stocky, skinny-legged righthander who drew most of his power from a strong upper torso, had Satchel Paige-like speed with a superior assortment of hard breaking balls, off-speed pitches and occasional spitters. Bullet Joe was durable and smart, a "pitcher" who worked hitters in and out, up and down, from a no-windup, sidearm delivery. He loved the one-on-one gamesmanship of pitching and was masterful in his blending of power and finesse.

There was little finesse in Rogan's smooth righthanded swing, which typically produced .300-plus averages and high home run totals for his era (1920-38). He stood deep in the box and stepped into the ball, using powerful wrists to get the barrel of his heavy bat out front. Rogan, a deadly lowball hitter who belted a league-high 16 homers in 1922, was a key pitcher/outfielder for Monarchs teams that won three straight pennants from 1923-25.

Everybody who saw Rogan, whether in Negro League or barnstorming competition, raved about his pitching. He was, said Casey Stengel, "one of the best, if not the best, pitchers that ever lived," and Casey didn't even see him during his prime. The dour, sometimes-moody Oklahoman, who played mostly for army teams from 1911-19, did not make his Monarchs debut until age 30 and pitched until age 49, after which he spent seven years as an umpire.

Rogan doubled as Monarchs manager from 1926 through '38. He often was described as critical and demanding, a product of his military background.

"Joe Rogan was one of the world's greatest pitchers. ... He was a chunky little guy, but he could throw hard. He could throw hard as Smokey Joe Williams—yeah." *—Satchel Paige, from the book Blackball Stars*

EDD J. ROUSH
CHICAGO A.L. 1913
NEW YORK N.L. 1916, 1927 TO 1930
CINCINNATI N.L. 1916 TO 1926, 1931
LEADING N.L. BATTER IN 1917 AND 1919
BATTED .352 IN 1921, .352 IN 1922, .351
IN 1923, .348 IN 1924. BATTED OVER
.300-13 SEASONS. LIFETIME BATTING
AVERAGE OF .323. MOST OUTFIELD
PUTOUTS, 410 IN 1920. F.L. 1914-1915.

Player/Year elected: 1962, Committee on Veterans

EDD ROUSH

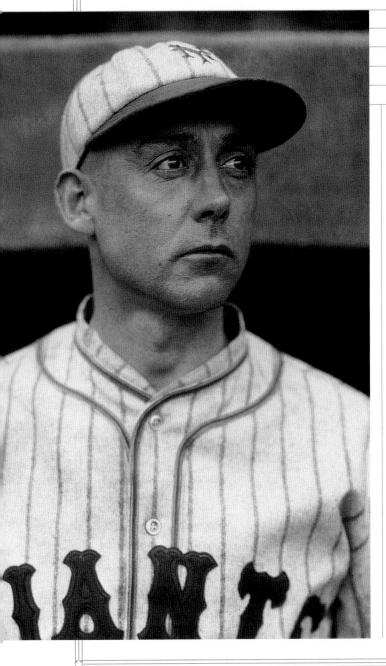

Born: 5-8-1893, Oakland City, Ind. **Died:** 3-21-88
Height/Weight: 5-11/170 **Bats/Throws:** L/L **Primary position:** Center field **Career statistics:** .323 avg., 2,376 hits, 1,099 runs, 268 steals **Teams:** White Sox 1913; Giants 1916, 1927-29; Reds 1916-26, 1931 **Batting champion:** N.L. 1917, '19

The men he worked for considered Edd Roush crusty, obstinate and unreasonable. But teammates and fans admired his center field grace and the magical way he handled a bat for 18 major league seasons. Businessman Roush was independent and defiant in defense of his principles; baseball star Roush was smooth, talented and unyielding in search of victory.

The 5-foot-11, 170-pound Roush was called the National League's Tris Speaker and it wasn't hard to figure out why. The speedy lefthander could play shallow and track down balls hit over his head and into either gap. Cincinnati fans loved the circus catches he made and the fierce pride that carried over to other facets of his game.

Roush, an Indiana country boy, was something to watch offensively. A lefthanded hitter, he would step to the plate with his huge, thick-handled, 48-ounce bat and fidget constantly with his stance, changing sometimes as the pitcher was delivering the ball. Roush, an accomplished contact man, had the uncanny ability to adjust on the fly and spray line drives to all fields. He was a master of the extra-base hit and his 182 triples rank high on the all-time list.

Roush, who spent his first two full years in the outlaw Federal League, reached the .300 plateau in each of his 10 full Cincinnati seasons and captured two batting titles — .341 in 1917 and .321 in 1919, when the Reds defeated Chicago in the infamous "Black Sox"

ROUSH

"It was a business to me. It wasn't no fun ... I played the game to win, and when you play to win, you don't play for fun." —*Edd Roush*

World Series. Fans loved Roush's toothy smile and hard-edged play, but Reds owners were less enamored with his business approach. He hated spring training and held out every year, a tactic that gave

him more time for hunting and, often, better contracts.

The Reds tested his resolve in 1922 and he remained on the sideline until late July. In 1930, the New York Giants refused to budge and Roush sat out the entire season. When he retired in 1931 after a return season with Cincinnati, Roush owned a .323 career average with 2,376 hits.

Player/Year elected: 1967, 86.9 percent of vote

RED RUFFING

Born: 5-3-04, Granville, Ill. **Died:** 2-17-86 **Height/Weight:** 6-2/205 **Bats/Throws:** R/R **Position:** Pitcher **Career statistics:** 273-225, 3.80 ERA, 1,987 strikeouts **Teams:** Red Sox 1924-30; Yankees 1930-42, 1945-46; White Sox 1947

He was a punching bag for the woeful Boston Red Sox of the late 1920s and an ace for the powerful New York Yankees in the 1930s. For Red Ruffing, baseball was a tale of two cities. In one, he was lost in the shadow of an ignominious 39-96 record; in the other, he basked in the glow of a 231-124 reincarnation.

The early Ruffing, thrust into the Red Sox rotation at age 20, was a power pitcher who fired his fastballs from an easy, three-quarters motion. He was a "thrower" who posted a 9-18 record in 1925, his first full season, and consecutive marks of 10-25 and 9-22 in 1928 and '29. In 1930, he lost his first three decisions and was traded to New York, where everything changed overnight.

Now mixing occasional curves and a changeup with fastballs that he spotted and threw at different speeds, Ruffing began piling up win-

ning seasons with a 15-5 record. He was 18-7 for the 1932 World Series champions and a 20-game winner every year from 1936-39, forming a 1-2 pitching punch with Lefty Gomez for four more Series winners. From 1928-40, the 6-foot-2 redhead never worked fewer than 220 innings while completing 264 starts.

Facing Ruffing could be intimidating. He had the look of a rugged, no-nonsense competitor, a persona that belied his well-read, articulate off-field manner. A product of Granville, Ill., the 205-pounder's vision of life as a hard-hitting outfielder had been dashed in a

mining accident that cost him four toes on his left foot. The handicap kept him from playing every day, but it didn't stop him from compiling a career .269 average with 36 home runs and 521 hits, many coming in pinch-hit roles.

Neither did it keep him from pitching 22 seasons, despite missing two years to military service, or posting a 7-2 record in seven World Series, six for the winning team. When Ruffing retired in 1947 after one season in Chicago, he owned a 273-225 record — and one of the amazing career turnarounds in baseball history.

"I always figured World Series games the easiest to pitch. The other team didn't know you ... and on the Yankees, we used to figure the National League champion only good enough to finish third or fourth in the American League." —*Red Ruffing*

AMOS RUSIE

AMOS WILSON RUSIE
"THE HOOSIER THUNDERBOLT"
INDIANAPOLIS N.L., NEW YORK N.L.,
CINCINNATI N.L., 1889-1895
1897-1898 AND 1901
GENERALLY CONSIDERED FIREBALL KING OF
NINETEENTH-CENTURY MOUNDSMEN. NOTCHED
BETTER THAN 240 VICTORIES IN TEN-YEAR
CAREER. ACHIEVED 30-VICTORY MARK FOUR
YEARS IN ROW AND WON 20 OR MORE GAMES
EIGHT SUCCESSIVE TIMES. LED LEAGUE IN
STRIKEOUTS FIVE YEARS AND LED OR TIED
FOR MOST SHUTOUTS FIVE TIMES.

Born: 5-30-1871, Mooresville, Ind. **Died:** 12-6-42 **Height/Weight:** 6-1/200 **Bats/Throws:** R/R **Position:** Pitcher
Career statistics: 246-174, 3.07 ERA, 1,950 strikeouts **Teams:** Indianapolis 1889; New York 1890-95, 1897-98; Cincinnati 1901

He was to the 1890s what Christy Mathewson later would be to the 1900s and Babe Ruth to the 1920s — a bigger-than-life, New York-worthy celebrity. Broadway actress Lillian Russell wanted to know Amos Rusie, vaudevillians performed skits celebrating his achievements and little boys saved pennies to buy a pamphlet revealing the secrets of "the World's Greatest Pitcher." Fans flocked to ballparks to see the man with the lightning fastball.

And Rusie was worth the price of admission. His powerful right arm delivered a fastball beyond imagination and an assortment of sharp-breaking curves that challenged the manhood of overmatched hitters. Not only did opponents marvel at the pitch speed when Rusie broke in with Indianapolis in 1889, they shuddered at the wildness that threatened their well being and kept the 6-foot-1, 200-pounder from thoroughly dominating the game.

Rusie, the so-called "Hoosier Thunderbolt" because of his Indiana roots, was signed by the Giants in 1890 and posted unheard-of strikeout totals of 341, 337 and 304, bewildering the slashing contact hitters of the era. He was durable as well as overpowering, topping an incredible 500 innings in all three seasons while issuing a nightmarish 821 walks. He was a pitching machine from 50 feet, rolling up win totals of 29, 33 and 32.

It probably was not a coincidence in 1893 when the pitching distance was moved to 60-feet, 6-inches — a move that generally benefited hitters. Rusie's strikeout totals shrunk, but the extra 10 feet gave his curveballs more time to break and he posted a 33-21 record, followed by a career-best 36-13 mark that he punctuated with two wins in the 1894 Temple Cup playoff against Baltimore.

Rusie pitched only nine full seasons (he sat out three in bitter financial disputes with the Giants) before arm problems forced him to retire. But in that short time he posted a 246-174 record, worked 3,778 ⅔ innings and struck out 1,950 batters while walking 1,707. When the Giants traded Rusie to Cincinnati in 1901 after two years of inactivity, they acquired a young righthander named Mathewson.

"Words fail to describe the speed with which Rusie sent the ball. ... It was like a white streak tearing past you."

— *Jimmy Ryan, Chicago outfielder, 1894*

Player/Year elected: 1936, 95.1 percent of vote, first ballot

BABE RUTH

GEORGE HERMAN (BABE) RUTH
BOSTON–NEW YORK, A.L.; BOSTON, N.L.
1915–1935
GREATEST DRAWING CARD IN HISTORY OF
BASEBALL. HOLDER OF MANY HOME RUN
AND OTHER BATTING RECORDS. GATHERED
714 HOME RUNS IN ADDITION TO FIFTEEN
IN WORLD SERIES.

Born: 2-6-1895, Baltimore, Md. **Died:** 8-16-48 **Height/Weight:** 6-2/215 **B/T:** L/L **Primary positions:** Pitcher, right field **Career statistics:** 94-46, .342 avg., 2,873 hits, 2,174 runs, 714 HR, 2,213 RBIs **Teams:** Red Sox 1914-19; Yankees 1920-34; Braves 1935 **Batting champion:** A.L., 1924 **HR champion:** A.L., 1918, tied, '19, '20, '21, '23, '24, '26, '27, '28, '29, '30, '31, tied **Major awards:** League MVP, 1923

Babe Ruth played baseball like he lived his life: with loud, gaudy, entertaining gusto. There was nothing subtle about the happy-go-lucky Sultan of Swat, who paraded through his career, forged an enduring relationship with adoring fans and then withstood the test of time as the greatest power hitter in baseball history.

Ruth's legendary home run totals — 714 in his career, 60 in 1927 — are no longer records, but they still stand as milestone numbers by which all power hitters are judged. His legendary carousing still enhances the irascible image that colors his aura. More than anything, the magnetic Ruth is hailed as the savior of the game, the man who ushered in the longball era and revitalized baseball when it was mired in the bog of the 1919 Black Sox scandal.

The Babe, a former Baltimore orphan, actually started his career as a 6-foot-2 lefthanded pitcher who carved out a 94-46 regular-season record and 3-0 World Series mark for the Boston Red Sox from 1914-19. But the real Ruth emerged in 1919 with a major league-record 29 homers and soared to a mind-boggling total of 54 in 1920, his first season as a full-time right fielder with the New York Yankees. The race was on.

Ruth became a New York icon as he powered his way through the Roaring '20s and the Great Depression, posting shocking homer totals of 59 (1921), 60 (1927) and 54 (1928) while leading the Yankees to four World Series championships and anchoring one of the most devastating lineups in history. Lost in the fog of Ruth's 12 American League home run titles, 13 slugging championships, four 50-homer seasons and six RBI titles was a career .342 average that still ranks 10th all time.

Not lost is the image of a paunchy Babe signing autographs, posing with celebrities, cavorting with kids or circling the bases with his distinctive trot. When he retired in 1935 at age 40 after one season with the Boston Braves, the Bambino owned every slugging record in the game — and enduring recognition as its most colorful and dynamic superstar.

"Ruth possessed a magnetism that was positively infectious. When he entered a clubhouse or a room, when he appeared on the field, it was as if he was the whole parade. There seemed to be flags waving, bands playing constantly." —*Waite Hoyt*

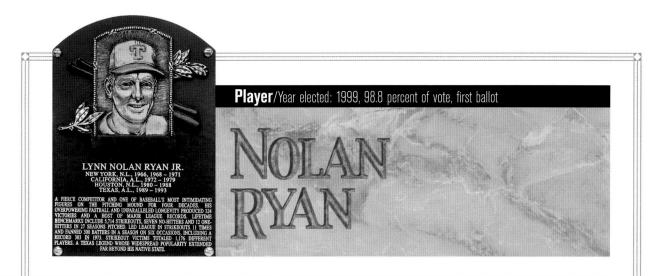

LYNN NOLAN RYAN JR.
NEW YORK, N.L., 1966, 1968 – 1971
CALIFORNIA, A.L., 1972 – 1979
HOUSTON, N.L., 1980 – 1988
TEXAS, A.L., 1989 – 1993

A FIERCE COMPETITOR AND ONE OF BASEBALL'S MOST INTIMIDATING FIGURES ON THE PITCHING MOUND FOR FOUR DECADES. HIS OVERPOWERING FASTBALL AND UNPARALLELED LONGEVITY PRODUCED 324 VICTORIES AND A HOST OF MAJOR LEAGUE RECORDS. LIFETIME BENCHMARKS INCLUDE 5,714 STRIKEOUTS, SEVEN NO-HITTERS AND 12 ONE-HITTERS IN 27 SEASONS PITCHED. LED LEAGUE IN STRIKEOUTS 11 TIMES AND FANNED 300 BATTERS IN A SEASON ON SIX OCCASIONS, INCLUDING A RECORD 383 IN 1973. STRIKEOUT VICTIMS TOTALED 1,176 DIFFERENT PLAYERS. A TEXAS LEGEND WHOSE WIDESPREAD POPULARITY EXTENDED FAR BEYOND HIS NATIVE STATE.

Player/Year elected: 1999, 98.8 percent of vote, first ballot

NOLAN RYAN

Born: 1-31-47, Refugio, Tex. **Height/Weight:** 6-2/210 **Bats/Throws:** R/R **Position:** Pitcher **Career statistics:** 324-292, 3.19 ERA, 5,714 strikeouts **Teams:** Mets 1966, 1968-71; Angels 1972-79; Astros 1980-88; Rangers 1989-93

The Nolan Ryan fastball made its first appearance on the radar gun in 1966 and was still being tracked in 1993, an amazing 27 years later. There was nothing subtle about it. At Ryan's peak, it shot to the plate at more than 100 mph. In Ryan's final season, it reached only 95—the man's one concession to age. The pitching legacy it helped produce might withstand the test of time.

Start with the strikeouts—5,714 of them, 1,578 more than second-place Steve Carlton. Then the no-hitters—seven, three more than second-place Sandy Koufax. Then the innings (5,386), victories (324), shutouts (61), one-hitters (12) and countless longevity records Ryan piled up over a career that started with the New York Mets and included long stints with the California Angels, Houston Astros and Texas Rangers.

Simply stated, Ryan was master of the attention-getting performance—a no-hitter or strikeout record waiting to happen. But unlike the great Walter Johnson, the 6-foot-2 Ryan was not a one-pitch wonder. Wild and erratic in the early years, Ryan's steady

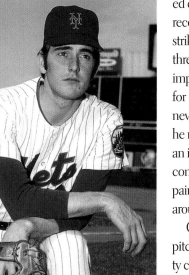

"Some guys throw hard, but not every pitch like him. He does it for nine innings. I think he has got to be the biggest superman in the league." — *Tony Oliva, 1973*

improvement drew direct parallel to his mastery of a nasty curveball that froze fastball-thinking hitters and a changeup that almost seemed unfair.

That was the perception among American League hitters in 1973 and '74 when the big righthander posted consecutive 21-16 and 22-16 records, set a single-season strikeout mark with 383, pitched three no-hitters and recorded impressive hits-per-inning marks for sub-.500 Angels teams. Ryan never again won 20 games and he never won a Cy Young, but an insatiable work ethic and commitment to conditioning painted an aura of invincibility around his bionic arm.

Once criticized as a .500 pitcher, Ryan's greatest popularity came in the 1990s when he continued to dominate batters, recorded his 300th win and added no-hitters Nos. 6 and 7— for the Rangers at ages 43 and 44. Ryan, who pitched in five All-Star Games, spent most of his years with weak teams as his 292 losses suggest, but he did pitch for the Amazin' Mets in their 1969 World Series victory over Baltimore.

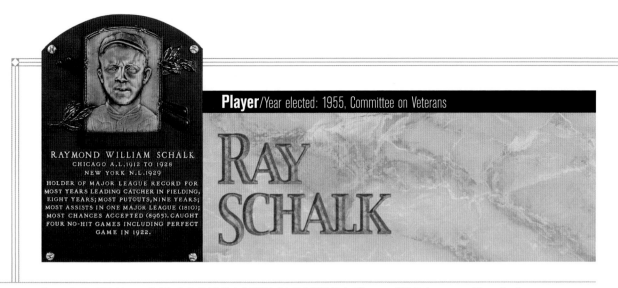

RAYMOND WILLIAM SCHALK
CHICAGO A.L. 1912 TO 1928
NEW YORK N.L. 1929
HOLDER OF MAJOR LEAGUE RECORD FOR
MOST YEARS LEADING CATCHER IN FIELDING,
EIGHT YEARS; MOST PUTOUTS, NINE YEARS;
MOST ASSISTS IN ONE MAJOR LEAGUE (1810);
MOST CHANCES ACCEPTED (6965). CAUGHT
FOUR NO-HIT GAMES INCLUDING PERFECT
GAME IN 1922.

Player/Year elected: 1955, Committee on Veterans

RAY SCHALK

Born: 8-12-1892, Harvey, Ill. **Died:** 5-19-70 **Height/Weight:** 5-8/165 **Bats/Throws:** R/R **Primary position:** Catcher
Career statistics: .253 avg., 1,345 hits **Teams:** White Sox 1912-28; Giants 1929

Like a cat ready to pounce, Ray Schalk crouched behind the plate for 18 major league seasons. He would spring up to gun down basestealers, leap on misplaced bunts, throw his body at errant pitches and sprint down the line to back up first base. Every pitch, every play was a call to arms for baseball's littlest catcher, the man Babe Ruth singled out as "the best I ever saw."

At 5-foot-8 and 165 pounds, Schalk broke the mold of burly, slow-footed catchers when he made his 1912 debut with the Chicago White Sox. He was stocky and energetic, compensating for lack of size with hustle, determination and creativity. Schalk was quick and fast, the first catcher to routinely back up throws at first and third base. He was a master at every facet of the game—a five-time American League leader in fielding percentage who recorded 1,810 assists, an A.L. record.

Not only was the man they called "Cracker" durable (he caught 121 or more games in 10 of 11 seasons from 1913-23), he routinely handled spitters, knucklers,

shine balls, emery balls and every other kind of pitch while playing through broken fingers and other nagging injuries. It's no coincidence that he caught four no-hitters, including Charlie Robertson's 1922 perfect game, and backstopped a one-season record four 20-game winners in 1920.

Schalk, a righthanded hitter from Harvey, Ill., never matched his defensive brilliance with a bat, but he compensated by moving runners, bunting and doing little things that made him valuable. In 1916, he stole 30 bases—a record for catchers that stood more than six decades. Schalk's .253 career average was overshadowed by his popularity, both in the clubhouse and among Chicago fans.

That popularity remained firmly rooted for 17 Chicago seasons, surviving the infamous 1919 World Series scandal of which Schalk was not a part and an unsuccessful 1927-28 run as player-manager. In later years, he would talk about only one World Series—the Sox's six-game victory over the New York Giants in 1917.

> **"Red Faber was ill during the (1919) Series. But if he'd been able to (pitch), we'd have beaten the Reds despite the gamblers."** —*Ray Schalk*

Player/Year elected: 1995, 96.5 percent of vote, first ballot

MIKE SCHMIDT

Born: 9-27-49, Dayton, Ohio **Height/Weight:** 6-2/200 **Bats/Throws:** R/R **Primary position:** Third base
Career statistics: .267 avg., 2,234 hits, 1,506 runs, 548 HR, 1,595 RBIs, 174 steals **Teams:** Phillies 1972-89 **HR champion:** 1974, '75, '76, '80, '81, '83, '84, tied, '86 **Major awards:** N.L. MVP, 1980, '81, '86

Brooks Robinson and Pie Traynor had the golden gloves. Eddie Mathews and Harmon Killebrew had the game-breaking power. But no third baseman in the game's long history could match the near-perfect blend of defense, run production and speed that Mike Schmidt showcased during a Hall of Fame career in Philadelphia.

Over an 18-year run that opened in 1972, the even-tempered, always-cool Schmidt used those tools to help the Phillies carve out the most successful period in franchise history. He was the clubhouse leader and driving force for a team that won five National League East Division titles, two pennants and the 1980 World Series. In the process, he also carved out a personal legacy that put him in the select company of some of the game's greatest all-around players.

Every time the 6-foot-2 Schmidt walked to the plate, there was an air of expectancy. From his righthanded upright stance with bat held high and feet spread well apart he was a home run waiting to happen—a big swing with plenty of bat speed and power to all fields. Thirteen times he hit 30 or more home runs in a season and a record eight times he led or shared N.L. home run honors en route to a career total of 548. From 1974 through 1987, which includes the strike-shortened 1981 campaign, he averaged 36.5 home runs and topped 100 RBIs nine times.

Schmidt, who played in 10 All-Star Games, also earned three MVP awards with home run-RBI combinations of 48-121 (1980), 37-119 (1986) and 31-91 (in a 102-game 1981 strike season). Sometimes lost in Schmidt's power numbers are his signature moments—a four-homer 1976 game at Chicago and a three-run, ninth-inning 1987 shot that gave the Phillies a dramatic win over Pittsburgh and Schmidt membership in baseball's elite "500 club."

But the number "10" is what really separates Schmidt from the other great power-hitting third basemen. That's how many Gold Gloves he won, second only to Robinson's 16.

> "I've tried to play the game the way it was meant to be played my entire career."
>
> —*Mike Schmidt*

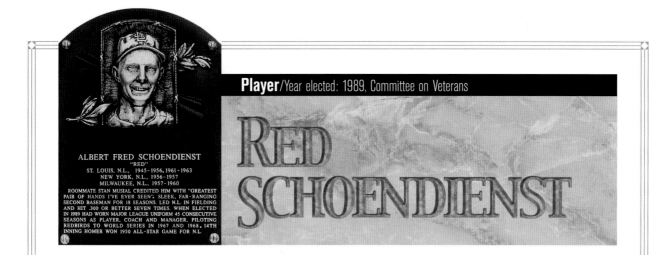

RED SCHOENDIENST

ALBERT FRED SCHOENDIENST
"RED"
ST. LOUIS, N.L., 1945-1956, 1961-1963
NEW YORK, N.L., 1956-1957
MILWAUKEE, N.L., 1957-1960
ROOMMATE STAN MUSIAL CREDITED HIM WITH "GREATEST PAIR OF HANDS I'VE EVER SEEN". SLEEK, FAR-RANGING SECOND BASEMAN FOR 18 SEASONS. LED N.L. IN FIELDING AND HIT .300 OR BETTER SEVEN TIMES. WHEN ELECTED IN 1989 HAD WORN MAJOR LEAGUE UNIFORM 45 CONSECUTIVE SEASONS AS PLAYER, COACH AND MANAGER, PILOTING REDBIRDS TO WORLD SERIES IN 1967 AND 1968. 14TH INNING HOMER WON 1950 ALL-STAR GAME FOR N.L.

Born: 2-2-23, Germantown, Ill. **Height/Weight:** 6-0/170 **Bats/Throws:** B/R **Primary position:** Second base
Career statistics: .289 avg., 2,449 hits, 1,223 runs **Teams played:** Cardinals 1945-56, 1961-63; Giants 1956-57; Braves 1957-60
Teams managed (1,041-955): Cardinals 1965-76, 1980, 1990

The flaming red hair and freckles gave him a Mark Twain-like persona that blended perfectly with his always-sunny disposition. Albert "Red" Schoendienst, all 6-feet and 170 pounds of him, was a storybook-worthy second baseman who enjoyed major league life as the toast of two cities. Not only did baseball's Huck Finn win friends and overcome adversity in a memorable 19-year career, he did it while anchoring championship teams in St. Louis and Milwaukee.

St. Louis' Big Redhead was a defensive specialist who could have thrived at almost any position. Schoendienst started as a wartime left fielder in 1945 and opened the 1946 campaign as a third baseman and shortstop before finally settling in at second — the double play partner of Marty Marion. He was slick, sure-handed and far-ranging, a sleight-of-hand magician on short-hop grounders and double-play pivots.

Six times Schoendienst led the National League in fielding percentage and year after year, fans were entranced by the grace and ease with which he handled his job. While he never matched that defensive

> "He's a plenty good batter from either side of the plate. We've thrown him everything in the book and he reads the riot act to us most every game. We consider ourselves lucky when we get him out."
>
> —*Charlie Grimm, Cubs manager,* 1947

prowess with his bat, the switch-hitting Schoendienst steadily improved — transforming himself into an excellent No. 2 hitter who would enjoy consecutive seasons of .303, .342 and .315 from 1952-54.

Schoendienst, whose upright lefthanded and righthanded stances were like mirror images, became a switch-hitter because of a teenage injury that gave him double vision in his left eye. He never let it hinder his play. In 1958, Schoendienst was diagnosed with tuberculosis after playing for the Braves in the World Series. He played five games in 1959, made a remarkable comeback with Milwaukee in 1960 and returned to St. Louis for three more years as a part-time performer and longtime manager.

When the Germantown, Ill., product retired in 1963, he was a .289 career hitter with 2,449 hits and two World Series championships — 1946 with the Cardinals, 1957 with the Braves. Not known for his power, the nine-time All-Star Game performer is remembered for winning the 1950 classic with a 14th-inning home run.

GEORGE THOMAS SEAVER
NEW YORK, N.L., 1967-1977, 1983
CINCINNATI, N.L., 1977-1982
CHICAGO, A.L., 1984-1986
BOSTON, A.L., 1986
FRANCHISE POWER PITCHER WHO TRANSFORMED
METS FROM LOVABLE LOSERS INTO FORMIDABLE
FOES. WON 311 GAMES OVER 20 SEASONS. SET N.L.
CAREER RECORD FOR STRIKEOUTS BY RHP (3,272)
AND MODERN RECORD FOR LOWEST ERA (2.73).
WHIFFED 200 OR MORE N.L. RECORD 10 TIMES
(19 IN A SINGLE GAME). N.L. ROOKIE OF YEAR,
1967 AND 3-TIME CY YOUNG AWARDEE. NO-HIT
CARDS IN 1978.

Player/Year elected: 1992, 98.8 percent of vote, first ballot

TOM SEAVER

Born: 11-17-44, Fresno, Calif. **Height/Weight:** 6-1/210 **Bats/Throws:** R/R **Position:** Pitcher

Career statistics: 311-205, 2.86 ERA, 3,640 strikeouts **Teams:** Mets 1967-77, 1983; Reds 1977-82; White Sox 1984-86; Red Sox 1986 **Major awards:** N.L. Rookie of Year, 1967; N.L. Cy Young, 1969, '73, '75

They billed him as the All-American boy and the image stayed with Tom Seaver throughout a successful 20-year career that started in New York and included stops at Cincinnati, Chicago and Boston. Articulate, handsome and intelligent off the field, Tom Terrific transformed into an intense, take-no-prisoners pitching machine when he climbed onto the mound.

Seaver charmed the tough New York market from his Rookie of the Year debut with the Mets in 1967 until he was sent to the Reds in an unpopular 1977 trade. His principle weapons were the hopping fastball, sharp-breaking curve and wicked slider he delivered with a powerful right arm and pinpoint control. But his secrets to success were the scientifically crafted delivery that saved his arm from wear and tear and the detailed book he kept on the strengths and weaknesses of every major league hitter.

Seaver literally exploded off the mound, driving hard toward the hitter with powerful legs and a well-muscled 210-pound body.

"Pitching is getting yourself ready. It's your game plan, it's finding out what you have to do that day. It's making your body do the things you want it to do."

— *Tom Seaver*

He looked like a locomotive bursting from a tunnel. The delivery was compact and so low that Seaver's right leg literally dragged the ground during his follow-through. He could be an overpowering strikeout pitcher (19 in a 1970 game, more than 200 in nine consecutive seasons) one inning, a craftsman who set up hitters with off-speed pitches the next.

Seaver's signature performance in a career that produced 311 wins, five 20-victory seasons, 61 shutouts, 3,640 strikeouts and eight All-Star Game appearances came in 1969, when he finished 25-7 and anchored a staff that pitched Gil Hodges' Amazin' Mets to a shocking National League pennant and World Series win over powerful Baltimore. He was rewarded with the first of three Cy Young Awards.

Mets fans were shocked in 1977 when Seaver, midway through his 11th New York season, was traded to Cincinnati, where he completed a 21-6 effort. He never won 20 again, but he did post solid numbers en route to the 300-win plateau, which he reached with the White Sox in 1985.

Manager/Year elected: 1999, Committee on Veterans

FRANK SELEE

FRANK GIBSON SELEE
BOSTON, N.L., 1890 – 1901
CHICAGO, N.L., 1902 – 1905

A MASTER STRATEGIST AND AN IMPECCABLE JUDGE OF TALENT WHO BECAME ONE OF THE GAME'S MOST SUCCESSFUL FIELD MANAGERS. GUIDED THE NATIONAL LEAGUE'S BOSTON BEANEATERS AND CHICAGO CUBS, COMPILING 1,284 VICTORIES OVER 16 SEASONS. HIS EXCEPTIONAL WINNING PERCENTAGE OF .598 IS FOURTH HIGHEST ALL-TIME. ASSEMBLED CHICAGO'S RENOWNED DOUBLE PLAY COMBINATION OF TINKER, EVERS AND CHANCE, AND LAID THE FOUNDATION FOR THE CUBS' THREE SUCCESSIVE PENNANTS FROM 1906 – 1908. A COURTEOUS AND MILD-MANNERED LEADER, HE CAPTURED FIVE PENNANTS AND MANAGED 12 FUTURE HALL OF FAMERS.

Born: 10-26-1859, Amherst, N.H. **Died:** 7-5-09 **Teams managed:** Boston 1890-1901; Cubs 1902-05 **Career record:** 1,284-862, .598

From factory worker to architect of two baseball dynasties, balding, taciturn Frank Selee walked a strange path to Hall of Fame glory. One day he was a baseball wannabe without a playing background; the next he was the game's most celebrated judge of talent and strategist. If not for the tuberculosis that prematurely ended his career, Selee probably would have ranked among the top five managers of all time.

His .598 career winning percentage (1,284-862) certainly merits such consideration, as do the five National League pennants he produced as Boston manager in the 1890s. When the Boston magic wore out, Selee moved on to Chicago and built a Cubs team that would win four pennants and two World Series in the five seasons after his 1905 departure because of ill health.

The curious baseball story of Selee began when he left a Waltham, Mass., factory in 1884 to form a minor league team. He was reticent, publicity shy and melancholy in appearance because of dark eyes and a thick mustache that dominated his gaunt face. But he quickly showed an ability to assess talent and put together championship teams, which landed him the Boston job in 1890. By 1893, he had three pennants to his credit.

Selee, a master of defensive shifts and the hit-and-run game, built his powerhouse by snapping up top players after the 1890 Players League collapsed. A roster filled with such names as King Kelly, Kid Nichols, Hugh Duffy, Tommy McCarthy and John Clarkson prompted *Sporting Life* to hail Selee as the "best judge of a player in America." After procuring two more titles for Boston in 1897 and '98, he reaffirmed that reputation by building the hapless Cubs into a championship contender.

He did it around such unknowns as Frank Chance, Joe Tinker, Johnny Evers and Mordecai Brown from 1902-05. But he never enjoyed the fruits of his labor. Suffering from tuberculosis, he passed on his job at age 46 to first baseman Chance and watched from afar as the 1906 Cubs began a five-year run that produced 530 wins. Selee died in 1909, the fourth year of that run.

> **"He has never failed, in minor or major league, to get together a team of winners."**
>
> — *Sporting Life, 1893*

Player/Year elected: 1977, Committee on Veterans

JOE SEWELL

JOSEPH WHEELER SEWELL
CLEVELAND A.L., NEW YORK A.L.
1920 – 1933
POSTED LIFETIME .312 BATTING AVERAGE,
TOPPING .300 IN TEN OF 14 YEARS. MOST
DIFFICULT MAN TO STRIKE OUT IN GAME'S
HISTORY. CREATED RECORDS WITH: FEWEST
CAREER STRIKEOUTS (114), FOUR SEASONS
OF FOUR WHIFFS OR LESS IN 500 AT-BATS
AND 115 GAMES IN ROW WITHOUT FANNING.
LED A.L. SHORTSTOPS IN FIELDING TWICE
AND IN PUTOUTS AND ASSISTS FOUR TIMES.

Born: 10-9-1898, Titus, Ala. **Died:** 3-6-90 **Height/Weight:** 5-7/155 **Bats/Throws:** L/R **Primary position:** Shortstop
Career statistics: .312 avg., 2,226 hits, 1,141 runs, 1,055 RBIs **Teams:** Indians 1920-30; Yankees 1931-33

He could swat a fly off the third baseman's nose with his massive 40-ounce bat and he could spot a dent on the center field fence—with pitch in mid-flight. Nobody got anything past Joe Sewell for 14 remarkable American League seasons. And nobody questioned the grit and determination he displayed while playing for World Series winners in Cleveland and New York.

Little Joe, a 5-foot-7, 155-pound bundle of energy, will always be remembered for the incredible eyesight that made him the toughest man to strike out in baseball history. His lefthanded stance was erect, his bat was huge and his ability

to hold back his chopping swing until the last possible instant was uncanny. He seldom missed—as 114 strikeouts in 7,132 career at-bats might suggest.

Not only did Sewell post at-bats-to-strikeout totals of 608-4, 578-4, 524-4 and 578-6, he delivered 2,226 hits and nine .300 seasons with his classic hit-'em-where-they-ain't style. A leadoff or No. 2 hitter most of his career, the University of Alabama graduate drove in 100 runs twice and topped 90 three other times while hitting only 49 career home runs.

"I was blessed with good eyes. I could see the ball jump off my bat." —Joe Sewell

Sewell's debut was unforgettable. It came in 1920, when the Indians were rocked by the death of shortstop Ray Chapman, who was hit on the head by a pitch from New York's Carl Mays. The desperate Indians, locked in a tight pennant race, bought the contract of a minor league shortstop named Sewell and the youngster batted .329 over the final 22 games, helping them finish first and post a seven-game World Series win over Brooklyn.

Sewell, a longtime Cleveland teammate of brother Luke, a catcher, seldom left the lineup over the next decade, running up an iron man streak of 1,103 games. A smooth shortstop who led the A.L. three times in fielding average, he moved to third base in 1929 and played that position three years later for the Yankees as they won a pennant and World Series. Sewell retired in 1933 with a .312 career average.

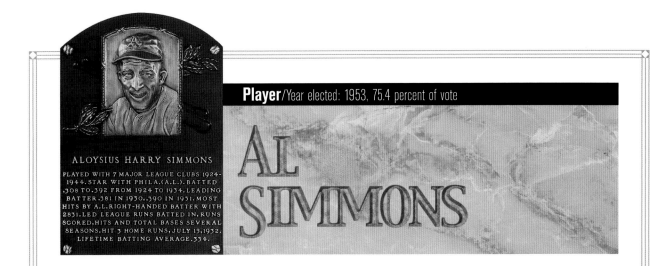

ALOYSIUS HARRY SIMMONS

PLAYED WITH 7 MAJOR LEAGUE CLUBS 1924-
1944. STAR WITH PHILA.(A.L.). BATTED
.308 TO .392 FROM 1924 TO 1934. LEADING
BATTER .381 IN 1930, .390 IN 1931. MOST
HITS BY A.L. RIGHT-HANDED BATTER WITH
2831. LED LEAGUE RUNS BATTED IN, RUNS
SCORED, HITS AND TOTAL BASES SEVERAL
SEASONS. HIT 3 HOME RUNS, JULY 15, 1932.
LIFETIME BATTING AVERAGE .334.

Player/Year elected: 1953, 75.4 percent of vote

AL SIMMONS

Born: 5-22-02, Milwaukee, Wis. **Died:** 5-26-56 **Height/Weight:** 5-11/190 **Bats/Throws:** R/R **Primary position:** Outfield
Career statistics: .334 avg., 2,927 hits, 1,507 runs, 307 HR, 1,827 RBIs **Teams:** Athletics 1924-32, 1940-41, 1944; White Sox
1933-35; Tigers 1936; Senators 1937-38; Braves 1939; Reds 1939; Red Sox 1943 **Batting champion:** A.L., 1930, '31

A haughty swagger and defiance complemented his driving-force status for one of the greatest teams ever assembled. The vicious line drives Al Simmons slashed out for 20 big-league seasons emulated the ones stroked by his boyhood hero, Ty Cobb. Some Simmons watchers called him the second-best righthanded hitter behind Rogers Hornsby; others classified him as the second-best all-around player of his era behind Cobb himself.

Simmons' .334 career average, which included 2,927 hits and 307 home runs, says a lot. But it doesn't capture the quiet confidence with which he ran the bases, played left field and gunned down aggressive runners with a shotgun arm. He seldom made a mistake, a quality not lost on Philadelphia manager Connie Mack, who made him the centerpiece of

> ## "I wish I had nine players named Al Simmons." —*Connie Mack*

his 1929, '30 and '31 pennant-winning Athletics—a star-studded team that captured two straight World Series.

Simmons' righthanded batting style was not the stuff of which instructional films are made. He stood deep in the box, feet close together, and took a long stride toward third base—as if bailing out. But "Bucketfoot Al" had the uncanny ability to keep his hips and weight in control, a discipline that allowed him to hit to the opposite field with unusual power. Two A.L. batting titles (.381 and .390) and 12 100-RBI seasons cemented Simmons' status as one of the great hitters of his time.

So did the three-year crush he delivered on A.L. pitchers during the A's pennant seasons. He batted .378 over those three years and averaged 208 hits, 124 runs, 31 homers and 150 RBIs. He added six home runs and 17 RBIs in the three World Series.

But some of the luster was lost when Mack, strapped financially by the Great Depression, sold Simmons' contract after the 1932 season, sentencing his veteran star to wander from team to team over the next decade. Simmons served as a hired gun for seven different teams, always hitting but never regaining the top form of his early years with the A's.

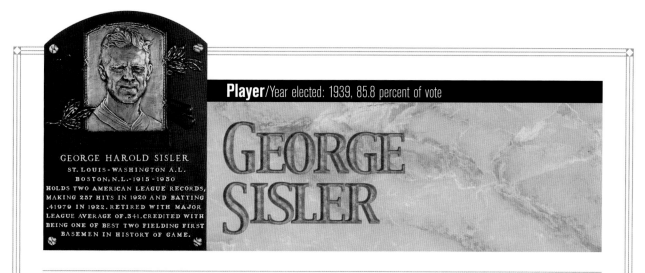

GEORGE SISLER

GEORGE HAROLD SISLER
ST. LOUIS - WASHINGTON A.L.
BOSTON, N.L.-1915-1930
HOLDS TWO AMERICAN LEAGUE RECORDS,
MAKING 257 HITS IN 1920 AND BATTING
.41979 IN 1922. RETIRED WITH MAJOR
LEAGUE AVERAGE OF .341. CREDITED WITH
BEING ONE OF BEST TWO FIELDING FIRST
BASEMEN IN HISTORY OF GAME.

Born: 3-24-1893, Manchester, Ohio **Died:** 3-26-73 **Height/Weight:** 5-11/170 **Bats/Throws:** L/L **Primary position:** First base
Career statistics: .340 avg., 2,812 hits, 1,284 runs, 1,175 RBIs, 375 steals **Teams:** Browns 1915-22, 1924-27; Senators 1928;
Braves 1928-30 **Batting champion:** A.L., 1920, '22 **Major awards:** League MVP, 1922

He was the quiet man in a league that showcased Ty Cobb and Babe Ruth and in a city that heaped its praise on St. Louis rival Rogers Hornsby. But the backseat George Sisler took to those colorful personalities was not reflected in his remarkable 15-year major league record, most of which he fashioned for the lowly St. Louis Browns.

The 170-pound Sisler, who was Hall of Fame

"He was poetry in motion, the perfect player." — *Frank Frisch*

contemporary Frank Frisch's "perfect player," brought manners and gentility to an era that was lacking in both. Modest and self-effacing, the University of Michigan grad played with a quiet self-confidence that was not lost on opponents and fans. He emerged on the big-league scene in 1915 as a lefthanded pitcher and quickly made the transition to first base — a position he mastered with grace and superior quickness.

But Sisler's real magic could be found in the 42-ounce hickory bat he used like a wand to direct balls all over the park. The choke-hitting lefthander was a line-drive slasher who could muscle mistake pitches over the right field wall. Contemporaries were most impressed by the mechanical perfection from which he seldom wavered.

Sisler batted .353, .341 and .352 from 1917-19, but that was merely an appetizer. In a remarkable three-year exhibition from 1920-22, he posted averages of .407, .371 and .420 while collecting 719 hits and striking out only 60 times. The 257 hits Sisler recorded in 1920 still stand as a major league record and the 41-game hitting streak he compiled in 1922 stood as a modern record until 1941, when Joe DiMaggio hit in 56 straight. He also averaged 110 RBIs and 132 runs while leading the American League twice in stolen bases.

Sisler was forced to sit out the 1923 season with sinusitis, a disease that caused double vision. And although he played another seven years with the Browns and Boston Braves, he never hit with the same ferocious consistency. Sisler, who compiled a .340 career average with 2,812 hits, retired in 1930 without experiencing postseason play.

ENOS SLAUGHTER

ENOS BRADSHER SLAUGHTER
"COUNTRY"
ST. LOUIS N.L. 1938-1953
NEW YORK A.L. 1954-1955, 1956-1959
KANSAS CITY A.L. 1955-1956 MILWAUKEE N.L. 1959
HARD-NOSED, HUSTLING PERFORMER WHO PLAYED
THE GAME WITH INTENSITY AND DETERMINATION.
FLAT, LEVEL SWING MADE HIM A LIFETIME .300
HITTER WHO INVARIABLY CAME THROUGH IN
CLUTCH SITUATIONS. EXCELLENT OUTFIELDER WITH
STRONG ARM. DARING BASERUNNER FAMOUS FOR
HIS MAD DASH HOME TO WIN 1946 WORLD SERIES
FOR CARDINALS. BATTED .291 IN 5 WORLD SERIES.

Born: 4-27-16, Roxboro, N.C. **Height/Weight:** 5-9/192 **Bats/Throws:** L/R **Primary position:** Right field **Career statistics:** .300 avg., 2,383 hits, 1,247 runs, 169 HR, 1,304 RBIs **Teams:** Cardinals 1938-42, 1946-53; Yankees 1954-55, 1956-59; Athletics 1955-56; Braves 1959

He was short, stocky and balding, a round-faced battler from the North Carolina hill country. But Enos Slaughter's most distinguishing features were his legs, which never stopped moving for 19 major league seasons. Those legs never walked. From the moment they hit the field, they ran . . . and ran . . . and ran some more, always in madcap pursuit of victory.

Hustling was not an option for Slaughter; it was a way of baseball life. For 13 seasons with the St. Louis Cardinals (1938-53, excluding three years of military service) and all or parts of six others with the New York Yankees, the "Old Warhorse" neither asked or gave quarter. A few years late to be a member of St. Louis' Gashouse Gang, he was one in spirit — durable, smart and willing to run through

brick walls or slide into pits of broken glass to achieve his goal.

Slaughter was a slashing lefthanded batter who reached the .300 plateau 10 times for five pennant-winning teams and four World Series champions. Not known for power, Slaughter pounded balls into the gaps, rumbled around the bases like a tank and ran over anybody who got in his way. At 5-foot-9 and 192 pounds, he was a collision waiting to happen — a daring runner who gave the Cardinals a 1946 fall classic win over Boston with his Game 7 "Mad Dash."

Slaughter also was an outstanding run-producer and strong-armed right fielder who played defense with his trademark aggressiveness. He led the National League in 1946 with 130

"I give it everything I've got. Always have played that way and I'll do it as long as I can. Anyone who don't should be sellin' peanuts up in the stands." *—Enos Slaughter*

RBIs and drove in 1,304 runs during a career many thought was over when the Cardinals traded him to the Yankees in 1954. Slaughter cried when he heard about the trade and then came off the bench to help the Yankees with three pennants and two World Series.

Teammates listened to "Country's" daily complaints about aches and pains, then watched him make game-turning plays. When he retired in 1959 at age 43, he owned a .300 average with 2,383 hits and 10 All-Star Game appearances.

HILTON LEE SMITH
NEGRO LEAGUES, 1932-1948

A QUIET BUT CONFIDENT RIGHTHANDER WHOSE DEVASTATING FASTBALL COMPLEMENTED WHAT MANY REGARD AS THE BEST SWEEPING CURVEBALL IN NEGRO LEAGUES HISTORY. AFTER BEGINNING HIS CAREER WITH THE MONROE MONARCHS, WAS CREDITED WITH 20 OR MORE WINS IN EACH OF 12 SEASONS WITH THE KANSAS CITY MONARCHS, INCLUDING A DOMINATING RECORD OF 93-11 FROM 1939 TO 1942. THE SIX-TIME ALL-STAR PITCHED A NO-HITTER VERSUS THE POWERFUL CHICAGO AMERICAN GIANTS IN 1937 AND POSTED A NEAR-PERFECT 25-1 MARK IN 1941. PLAYED ON SEVEN PENNANT WINNERS AND ONE WORLD SERIES CHAMPIONSHIP TEAM.

HILTON SMITH

Born: 2-27-12, Giddings, Tex. **Died:** 11-18-83 **Height/Weight:** 6-2/180 **Bats/Throws:** R/R **Primary positions:** Pitcher, first base, outfield **Teams (1932-48):** Monroe Monarchs; New Orleans Black Creoles; New Orleans Crescent Stars; Kansas City Monarchs

He was the man behind the curtain, the quietly efficient and grossly underappreciated wizard of Negro League baseball. Hilton Smith spent most of his career working in the rather large and flamboyant shadow of Kansas City Monarchs teammate Satchel Paige. While Satch grabbed the glory, Smith did the grunt work with a sly smile and one of the best curveballs in black baseball history.

Negro League opponents dreaded facing the 6-foot-2, 180-pound righthander, who attacked them with outstanding fastballs, curves, sinkers, sliders and changeups, all thrown from sidearm and overhand deliveries. When his curve, which he threw at different speeds, was biting, the big Texan could be almost unhittable.

In the white baseball world, Smith would have been a star. But in the 1930s and '40s Negro Leagues, where showmanship was needed to keep struggling franchises afloat, star power belonged to the Paiges, Josh Gibsons and Cool Papa Bells who attracted the fans. Smith, with his reserved personality, was forced to caddy for Paige while actually working as the ace of Monarchs teams that ranked among the best in the Negro American League.

On the Monarchs' extensive barnstorming tours, Paige often would draw the crowds, work three innings to collect his 15 percent of the gate and turn the game over to Smith. If Satch failed to show for a game, Smith would suffer the indignity of having to pretend he was Paige. But Negro League hitters knew all about Smith, who consistently racked up 20-win seasons and pitched in six straight East-West All-Star Games from 1937-42. He was outstanding in exhibitions against major leaguers, outdueling such pitchers as Bob Feller and Dizzy Dean.

Smith, a good hitter who often played first base and the outfield when not pitching, scouted and signed Jackie Robinson to a Monarchs contract. Offered a chance to sign with the Brooklyn organization after Robinson broke baseball's color barrier, he declined, saying he was too old. Smith pitched for the Monarchs until 1948.

> ## "My god, you couldn't tell the difference (between Smith and Satchel Paige)."
>
> —*Roy Campanella*

SMITH

Player/Year elected: 2002, 91.7 percent of vote, first ballot

OZZIE SMITH

OSBORNE EARL SMITH
"THE WIZARD OF OZ"
SAN DIEGO, N.L., 1978-81, ST. LOUIS, N.L., 1982-96

AN ACROBATIC, LIGHTNING-QUICK DEFENSIVE WIZARD WHO WON 13 GOLD GLOVES, MORE THAN ANY OTHER SHORTSTOP IN HISTORY. KNOWN FOR HIS INCREDIBLE RANGE, ACCURATE ARM AND ABILITY TO THROW OUT RUNNERS AFTER MAKING DIVING STOPS. A CROWD FAVORITE BECAUSE OF HIS DEFENSE, HE ALSO COLLECTED 2,460 HITS AND STOLE 580 BASES. A SOFT-SPOKEN SWITCH-HITTER AND CLUBHOUSE LEADER WHO PLAYED FOR THE CARDINALS WORLD SERIES CHAMPIONS IN 1982 AND PENNANT-WINNERS IN 1985 AND '87. STOLE 20 OR MORE BASES IN 16 OF HIS 19 SEASONS AND APPEARED IN 14 ALL-STAR GAMES.

Born: 12-26-54, Mobile, Ala. **Height/Weight:** 5-11/150 **Bats/Throws:** B/R **Primary position:** Shortstop

Career statistics: .262 avg., 2,460 hits, 1,257 runs, 580 steals **Teams:** Padres 1978-81; Cardinals 1982-96

The "Oz-zie! Oz-zie!" chants started the instant he raced to his shortstop position at St. Louis' Busch Stadium. They intensified when Ozzie Smith performed his trademark back flip, an occasional embellishment he really didn't need to earn his daily ovations. The simple thought of another sensational play was enough to electrify Cardinals fans, who have a history of tender relationships with the superstars they embrace.

Smith certainly qualified for that status. Supporters claim he was the best defensive shortstop in history; critics argue he was only one of the best. Suffice to say few games were played without the Wizard of Oz flashing the acrobatic quickness that generated oohs and aahs usually reserved for offensive feats.

Smith, who won 13 Gold Gloves, was the master at throwing on the run, whether racing behind second base or deep into the hole. He also had an uncanny knack for snaring balls with a dive, scrambling to his knees and throwing out startled runners. His range was incredible and his so-so arm was amazingly accurate.

So was the contact stroke Smith worked exhaustively to perfect from either side of the plate. A low-.200

batter in his first four seasons in San Diego, he raised his average consistently after a 1982 trade to St. Louis and finished his career as a consistent .280 threat—with 2,460 hits. Smith's ability to handle the bat and run the bases (580 career steals) enabled him to hit in the No. 2 slot and play a vital role in "Whitey Ball"—the speed game favored by Cardinals manager Whitey Herzog through most of the 1980s.

A big part of Smith's game was image, and he was as articulate in the locker room as he was with the glove. A dapper dresser with a ready smile and soft-spoken charm, Smith also was a leader on Cardinals teams that won four division titles, three National League pennants and one World Series before he retired after the 1996 season. Smith hit 28 career home runs—two for each of the 14 All-Star Games in which he appeared.

"This is a town rich in tradition. You've got the Clydesdales coming in before World Series games. People are getting off the wagon, like Stan Musial, Marty Marion and Roger Maris. Maybe some day I can come in riding on that wagon." —*Ozzie Smith*

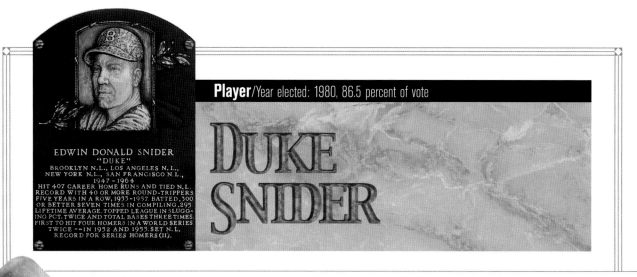

EDWIN DONALD SNIDER
"DUKE"
BROOKLYN N.L., LOS ANGELES N.L.,
NEW YORK N.L., SAN FRANCISCO N.L.,
1947-1964
HIT 407 CAREER HOME RUNS AND TIED N.L.
RECORD WITH 40 OR MORE ROUND-TRIPPERS
FIVE YEARS IN A ROW, 1953-1957. BATTED .300
OR BETTER SEVEN TIMES IN COMPILING .295
LIFETIME AVERAGE. TOPPED LEAGUE IN SLUGG-
ING PCT. TWICE AND TOTAL BASES THREE TIMES.
FIRST TO HIT FOUR HOMERS IN A WORLD SERIES
TWICE --IN 1952 AND 1955. SET N.L.
RECORD FOR SERIES HOMERS (11).

Player/Year elected: 1980, 86.5 percent of vote

DUKE SNIDER

Born: 9-19-26, Los Angeles, Calif. **Height/Weight:** 6-0/190 **Bats/Throws:** L/R **Primary position:** Center field
Career statistics: .295 avg., 2,116 hits, 1,259 runs, 407 HR, 1,333 RBIs **Teams:** Brooklyn Dodgers 1947-57;
Los Angeles Dodgers 1958-62; Mets 1963; Giants 1964 **HR champion:** N.L., 1956

"There is a helluva ballplayer. You can have Willie Mays. I'll take Snider."

—*Mayo Smith, 1955*

He was the Duke of Flatbush, a Boy of Summer and a charter member of the Dem Bums fraternity that graced Brooklyn's Ebbets Field in the late 1940s and '50s. And the image of a graceful, handsome young Duke Snider patrolling center field and driving pitches onto Bedford Avenue still burns deep in the Borough of Churches. Snider was the unofficial enforcer and most critically analyzed enigma for a franchise that dominated the National League standings through most of his career.

The prematurely gray, free-swinging Snider, a speedy lefthanded pull hitter tailored for tiny Ebbets Field, was a power source who topped 40 home runs from 1953-57 and averaged more than 100 RBIs over the same five-year stretch. He also was fast and instinctive, one of the best defensive outfielders in the

game. But no matter how Snider produced, he never could fully please demanding Brooklyn fans who thought he lacked the passion of his more intense Dodgers teammates.

Part of the image problem resulted from Snider's tell-it-like-it-is bluntness and the inner rage he directed at his own failings. It also stemmed from a sensitivity fueled by constant comparisons to two contemporary New York center fielders — Mickey Mantle and Willie Mays. But it's hard to knock Snider's .295 career average, 407 home runs and big-game efficiency — an N.L.-record 11 homers and 26 RBIs in six

World Series, two of which resulted in Dodgers championships.

Snider, who appeared in seven All-Star Games, was a force through his Brooklyn career, but his hitting dropped off in 1958 when the Dodgers moved to his hometown of Los Angeles. Frustrated by the vast right-center field dimensions of the Coliseum and playing without most of his Brooklyn teammates, Snider never topped 23 home runs or 88 RBIs again before closing his career in San Francisco. Still, he remains the Dodgers franchise record-holder for home runs (389), RBIs (1,271) and extra-base hits (814).

Player/Year elected: 1973, 83.2 percent of vote, first ballot

WARREN SPAHN

WARREN EDWARD SPAHN
BOSTON N.L., MILWAUKEE N.L.,
NEW YORK N.L., SAN FRANCISCO N.L.,
1942-1965
BECAME FIFTH BIGGEST WINNER IN MAJORS'
HISTORY WITH 363 VICTORIES. MOST
VICTORIES FOR A LEFT-HANDER. WON 20
OR MORE GAMES 13 SEASONS, SIX IN A ROW.
SET ALL-TIME RECORDS FOR YEARS LEADING
LEAGUE IN VICTORIES (8) AND COMPLETE
GAMES (9). ALSO N.L. CAREER HIGHS WITH
665 GAMES STARTED; 5,264 INNINGS;
2,853 STRIKEOUTS. PITCHED NO-HITTER
IN 1960, ANOTHER IN 1961.

Born: 4-23-21, Buffalo, N.Y. **Height/Weight:** 6-0/175 **Bats/Throws:** L/L **Position:** Pitcher **Career statistics:** 363-245, 3.09 ERA, 2,583 strikeouts **Teams:** Boston Braves 1942, 1946-52; Milwaukee Braves 1953-64; Mets 1965; Giants 1965 **Major awards:** M.L. Cy Young, 1957

Stan Musial called him "an artist with imagination." The Brooklyn Dodgers once named their new pitching machine, "The Warren Spahn." Other National League hitters simply flailed helplessly at his wide assortment of strategically placed pitches for 21 major league seasons and then retired quietly to their seat on the bench.

That's the effect Spahn had on hitters from 1946-65 as he carved out 363 victories, more than any lefthander in history and the fifth-best total all time. An artist, indeed, but more accurately a pitching scientist who could paint corners with his control and confound batters with tantalizing fastballs, curves, sinkers and screwballs barely out of the strike zone.

Spahn, a 6-footer who posted all but seven of his victories for the Boston and Milwaukee Braves, delivered those pitches from a slow, rock-back motion that fueled a high, fluid leg kick and a machine-like overhand delivery. The hitter looked for the ball amid the illusion of flailing arms and legs. No two pitches looked alike or arrived in the same spot. When Spahnie was sharp, games were fast and the results predictable.

Never more so than in the 17-year stretch from 1947-63, when Spahn reached the 20-win plateau 13 times and never failed to top 245 innings. He was a workhorse ("Spahn and Sain and pray for rain") for the 1948 pennant-winning Braves and a Cy Young winner in 1957, when Milwaukee won its only championship. Spahn was 4-3 in three World Series and 363-245 overall in a big-league career that didn't really begin until age 25 because of three years of military service in World War II.

An affable, fun-loving prankster off the field, Spahn was all business on the mound. He also was a model of consistency for two decades. In addition to three ERA titles, four strikeout crowns, 63 career shutouts and seven All-Star Game appearances, Spahn pitched two no-hitters—both after his 39th birthday. He rounded out his impressive resume by hitting 35 career home runs.

"He wasn't fast, but he was all pitcher and he had amazing control. He kept hitters off balance with his changing speeds and he never put the ball where you could get much bat on it." —*Willie Mays*

AL SPALDING

ALBERT GOODWILL SPALDING

ORGANIZATIONAL GENIUS OF BASEBALL'S PIONEER DAYS. STAR PITCHER OF FOREST CITY CLUB IN LATE 1860'S, 4-YEAR CHAMPION BOSTONS 1871-1875 AND MANAGER-PITCHER OF CHAMPION CHICAGOS IN NATIONAL LEAGUE'S FIRST YEAR. CHICAGO PRESIDENT FOR 10 YEARS. ORGANIZER OF BASEBALL'S FIRST ROUND-THE-WORLD TOUR IN 1888.

Born: 9-2-1850, Byron, Ill. **Died:** 9-9-15 **Height/Weight:** 6-1/170 **Bats/Throws:** 6-1/170 **Position:** Pitcher **Teams:** Chicago 1876-77

Executive career: Helped draft constitution for National League in 1875; president of Chicago White Stockings, 1882-90

Pitcher, pioneer, team executive, sporting goods magnate, sports book publisher and baseball ambassador—Albert Goodwill Spalding contributed to the growth of the National Pastime in more ways than any other man. Early 1870s peers regarded him as "the greatest pitcher of his day;" 1880s businessmen considered him the foremost sportsman and entrepreneur of his generation. When A.G. talked baseball, everybody listened.

From his humble Byron, Ill., roots to the top of Chicago's business world, Spalding never missed an opportunity. His early renown stemmed from his ability as a pitcher in the National Association and his role, with William Hulbert, in drafting the constitution for the National League. He went on to found a sporting goods empire with his brother, serve as president of the five-time N.L.-champion Chicago White Stockings

and organize and finance a world baseball tour.

From 1871-75, the 6-foot-1, 170-pound righthander com-

piled such records as 38-8, 41-14, 52-16 and 54-5 as the workhorse of the National Association's Boston championship team. As an underhander working from 45 feet, Spalding was 47-12 in 1876 for Hulbert's White Stockings—the N.L.'s first champions. But, unable to master the new curveball pitch, he retired from active duty in 1877 to begin his second, more lucrative, life.

His sporting goods business, which later expanded to sports other than baseball, started in Chicago and exploded into national prominence. It was official supplier of major league balls for almost a century, producer of uniforms and gear and eventually publisher of the official *Baseball Guide* and other popular "how to play" books. The business made Spalding a multimillionaire and perpetuated his name through the 20th century.

He also found time to build the White Stockings and organize an 1888-89 world tour that introduced baseball to such countries as New Zealand, Australia, Egypt, Italy, France and Great Britain. Spalding helped negotiate an end to the Players League rebellion in 1890 before leaving the game. In 1905, he returned to spearhead a commission that investigated the origin of baseball.

"**(Baseball) owes a great debt to Albert G. Spalding for the part he played in putting it on the high plane it has enjoyed as the nation's sport above all other forms of athletics.**" —*The Sporting News, 1915*

S P A L D I N G

Player/Year elected: 1937, 82.1 percent of vote

TRIS SPEAKER

TRISTRAM E. (TRIS) SPEAKER
BOSTON (A) 1909-15
CLEVELAND (A) 1916-26
WASHINGTON (A) 1927
PHILADELPHIA (A) 1928
GREATEST CENTREFIELDER OF HIS
DAY. LIFETIME MAJOR LEAGUE BATTING
AVERAGE OF .344. MANAGER IN 1920
WHEN CLEVELAND WON ITS FIRST
PENNANT AND WORLD CHAMPIONSHIP.

Born: 4-4-1888, Hubbard, Tex. **Died:** 12-8-58 **Height/Weight:** 6-0/190 **Bats/Throws:** L/L **Primary position:** Center field
Career statistics: .345 avg., 3,514 hits, 1,882 runs, 117 HR, 1,529 RBIs, 432 steals **Teams:** Red Sox 1907-15; Indians 1916-26;
Senators 1927; Athletics 1928 **Batting champion:** A.L., 1916 **HR champion:** A.L., 1912 **Major awards:** Chalmers MVP, 1912

He was easy to spot. The 6-foot, prematurely gray center fielder would position himself about 30 or 40 feet behind second base, ready to dart forward and cut off a potential hit or sprint back for anything over his head. Tris Speaker brazenly dared American League hitters to take their best shot, a challenge he answered emphatically with sure hands, lightning quickness, speed and a powerful left arm that gave him status as the best defensive player in the game.

The irony is that Speaker seldom is remembered as one of baseball's greatest hitters, thanks primarily to his unfortunate career parallel with 12-time A.L. batting champion Ty Cobb. But over a 22-year career that began in 1907 with the Boston Red Sox, the "Gray Eagle" posted a .345 average, topping the .350 mark nine times, while managing only one batting crown (1916). He collected a major league-record 792 doubles, leading the A.L. eight times, and still ranks among all-time leaders in hits (3,514), triples (222) and runs (1,882).

"There is no manlier man than Tris Speaker."
— *Joe Williams, New York sportswriter*

Speaker stood deep in the box, holding his bat hip high, and attacked the ball from a closed, crouching lefthanded stance. He was a gap-finding, extra-base machine, thanks to outstanding speed that punished momentary bobbles and helped him execute 432 steals. Only Cobb stood in the way of multiple batting titles.

Cobb, however, couldn't match Speaker's outfield cunning and nobody before or since has patrolled center field with such daring and aplomb. Believing that singles he could cut off would far outnumber triples that would sail over his head, Speaker played the shallowest center field in history, in effect serving as a fifth infielder. He loved to dart behind unsuspecting runners at second base for a pickoff and he twice tied the A.L. record with 35 assists.

Speaker was the centerpiece for three World Series champions, two with Boston (1912 and '15) and one (1920) during his eight-year run as player-manager at Cleveland. He was part of the great 1912 Boston outfield that included Duffy Lewis and Harry Hooper.

WILVER DORNEL STARGELL
"WILLIE"
PITTSBURGH, N.L., 1962 - 1982
INTIMIDATING PRESENCE BETWEEN THE LINES
AND CHARISMATIC PATRIARCH IN CLUBHOUSE
AND DUGOUT. CRUSHED 475 HOMERS, MANY
OF TAPE-MEASURE VARIETY AND HIT MOST
BY ANY PLAYER DURING 1970'S. LIKE HIS
ROUND-TRIPPERS, HIS 1,540 RBI'S ALSO MOST
EVER BY A PIRATE. BATTED .282 OVER 21
SEASONS, ALL WITH PITTSBURGH. SHARED N.L.
MVP HONORS IN 1979, AND NAMED MVP IN '79
N.L. CHAMPIONSHIP SERIES AND WORLD SERIES.

Player/Year elected: 1988, 82.4 percent of vote, first ballot

WILLIE STARGELL

Born: 3-6-40, Earlsboro, Okla. **Died:** 4-9-2001 **Height/Weight:** 6-3/225
Bats/Throws: L/L **Primary position:** First base
Career statistics: .282 avg., 2,232 hits, 1,195 runs, 475 HR, 1,540 RBIs
Teams: Pirates 1962-82 **HR champion:** 1971, '73 **Major awards:** N.L. co-MVP, 1979

The towering drives that registered 7s and 8s on baseball's Richter scale provided a stark contrast to the gentle manner in which Willie Stargell practiced his craft.

> "If I had to describe myself, it would be like a big oak tree. Good roots. A big, strong trunk. And lots of branches going off in different directions." —*Willie Stargell*

As a lumbering 6-foot-3, 225-pound, bat-waving slugger, Stargell could be frightening. As the easy-going leader of Pittsburgh's clubhouse, he could be inspiring. Nobody combined these seemingly divergent qualities more effectively than the man young Pirates players came to know affectionately as "Pops."

Stargell was a classic power hitter. He stood deep in the box with feet spread apart and attacked the pitch with a long, hard swing. The ball left his bat like a bazooka shot and he quickly gained a reputation for long home runs—two balls out of Dodger Stadium, seven out of Forbes Field, four into the upper deck at Three Rivers Stadium. He also hit a lot of them—National League-leading totals of 48 in 1971, 44 in 1973—while carving a niche alongside the top power hitters of the era.

In between his 475 career home runs and 1,936 strikeouts (No. 3 all time), Stargell collected enough hits to compile a solid .282 average over a 21-year

career that began in 1962. The seven-time All-Star Game performer also worked hard to become one of the more reliable defensive first basemen in the game. But the Stargell legacy is about much more than long homers and numbers.

The fun-loving, quick-to-smile slugger learned from early career mentor Roberto Clemente and evolved into one of the game's most influential team leaders. The Pirates captured the 1971 World Series with Clemente leading the charge, but the 1979 championship, fueled by Stargell's "We Are Family" approach, belonged to Pops.

First the 39-year-old Stargell was named N.L. co-MVP after a 32-homer, 82-RBI regular season. Then he earned MVP honors in an NLCS victory over Cincinnati with a .455 average and two home runs. He completed his MVP triple when he batted .400 and hit a World Series-deciding homer in Game 7 against Baltimore.

NORMAN THOMAS STEARNES
"TURKEY"
NEGRO LEAGUES 1923-1941

ONE OF THE NEGRO LEAGUES' MOST FEARED HITTERS, HE HIT BETTER
THAN .300 IN 14 OF 19 SEASONS, COLLECTED SIX HOME RUN TITLES AND
LED THE LEAGUE IN TRIPLES FOUR TIMES. A GRACEFUL CENTER
FIELDER AS WELL, HE PLAYED IN FOUR EAST-WEST ALL-STAR GAMES.
PLAYED 11 SEASONS FOR THE DETROIT STARS, ALSO EXCELLING WITH
THE NEW YORK LINCOLN GIANTS, KANSAS CITY MONARCHS, CHICAGO
AMERICAN GIANTS AND PHILADELPHIA STARS.

Player/Year elected: 2000, Committee on Veterans

TURKEY STEARNES

Born: 5-8-01, Nashville, Tenn. **Died:** 9-4-79 **Height/Weight:** 6-0/168 **B/T:** L/L **Primary position:** Outfield **Teams (1923-42):** Detroit Stars; Lincoln Giants; Kansas City Monarchs; Cole's American Giants; Philadelphia Stars; Chicago American Giants; Detroit Black Sox

They laughed at his unorthodox batting stance and gasped at the tape-measure home runs that shot off his lightning-quick bat. For the better part of two decades, Negro League pitchers learned there was much more to Norman "Turkey" Stearnes than met the eye. He was a big man in a 168-pound body, a home run hitter cleverly disguised as a classic leadoff man.

The first thing that fooled you was his speed, the go-get-'em type that allowed Stearnes to play center field and run the bases like contemporary Cool Papa Bell. Stearnes was a ball hawk with outstanding range and the ability to go back on anything hit over his head. He also was an accomplished basestealer who could embellish his .350-plus average with infield hits.

But it was Stearnes' batting style that defied logic. The slender 6-footer would settle into his left-handed stance with right foot open, heel twisting and toe pointed upward. He choked up on his short, 39-ounce bat like an opposite-field contact hitter, then whipped it through the strike zone with Josh Gibson-like force. If he hit it just right, the sky was the limit — or, perhaps, the upper deck at Comiskey Park.

The power came from his strong shoulders and

pitchers were well advised not to let him turn on the ball. Stearnes did often enough to rank alongside Gibson as the greatest power hitters in black baseball history. Seven times he led or tied for the Negro League homer championship (17, 10, 18, 24, etc.), most of those titles coming with the Detroit Stars from 1923-31, and his .430 mark in 1935 for the Chicago American Giants won a batting crown.

> **"Turkey Stearnes was one of the greatest hitters we ever had. He was as good as Josh. He was as good as anybody ever played ball."**
>
> —*Satchel Paige, from the book Blackball Stars*

Stearnes, a Tennessee-born loner who rarely socialized, was very particular about his bat, which he kept away from teammates and openly talked to on the bench. The talks must have worked. He was a four-time East-West All-Star Game performer and a member of pennant-winning teams in Chicago and Kansas City.

Manager/Year elected: 1966, Committee on Veterans

CASEY STENGEL

CHARLES DILLON STENGEL
"CASEY"

MANAGED NEW YORK YANKEES 1949-1960.
WON 10 PENNANTS AND 7 WORLD SERIES WITH
NEW YORK YANKEES, ONLY MANAGER TO WIN
5 CONSECUTIVE WORLD SERIES 1949-1953.
PLAYED OUTFIELD 1912-1925 WITH BROOKLYN,
PITTSBURGH, PHILADELPHIA, NEW YORK AND
BOSTON N.L. TEAMS. MANAGED BROOKLYN
1934-1936, BOSTON BRAVES 1938-1943,
NEW YORK METS 1962-1965.

Born: 7-30-1890, Kansas City, Mo. **Died:** 9-29-75 **Height/Weight:** 5-11/175 **B/T:** L/L **Primary position:** Outfield

Career statistics: .284 avg., 1,219 hits **Teams played:** Dodgers 1912-17; Pirates 1918-19; Phillies 1920-21; Giants 1921-23; Braves 1924-25 **Teams managed (1,905-1,842):** Dodgers 1934-36; Braves 1938-43; Yankees 1949-60; Mets 1962-65 **World Series titles:** 1949, '50, '51, '52, '53, '56, '58

He could tickle your funnybone, mess with your mind, test your patience or tear out your heart. But when Casey Stengel wasn't clowning or entertaining, he also could match strategies and wits with the best minds in baseball. From 1949 through 1960, the "Old Professor" forged legitimate claim as the greatest manager in history—the clever, humorous, all-knowing leader of the powerful New York Yankees.

Before and after the Yankees, Stengel was considered a baseball buffoon. He pulled imaginative pranks during a 14-year playing career, deflected criticism with colorful theatrics during an uninspiring nine-year run as manager of the Brooklyn Dodgers and Boston Braves, wore out writers with his rambling monologues—always delivered in "Stengelese," his own fractured, sometimes-unintelligible language—and served as front man for the bumbling New York Mets.

As a player from 1912-25, the 5-foot-11, bowlegged outfielder batted .284 and became notorious for his crazy stunts. Stengel, a former Kansas City dental student, once stood near home plate at Ebbets Field and doffed his hat to jeering Brooklyn fans as a bird flew out. Such antics were endearing, but

his managerial failure with weak Brooklyn and Boston teams from 1934-36 and 1938-43 did not bode well for his career.

When general manager George Weiss hired Stengel to manage the lordly Yankees in 1949, the baseball world watched in disbelief. But craggy-faced Casey, given a bottomless talent pool, guided them to a record five

> "Casey was a wonderful man. He knew what to do with the talent he had. He understood his players. I enjoyed playing for him." —*Joe DiMaggio*

straight World Series titles and never looked back. When the Yankees forced the 70-year-old Stengel to retire after his team had lost the 1960 fall classic, he owned an incredible New York legacy — 10 pennants and seven championships in 12 seasons.

A master of platooning and astute judge of talent, Stengel could be aloof with players, unlike his relationship with the New York press — "my writers" — that served him so well when he returned in 1962 as first manager of the expansion Mets. He watched his "Amazin' Mets" stumble to 340 losses in three years and 64 more in 1965 before retiring, at age 75, because of a broken hip. His 25-year managerial record was 1,905-1,842.

442

Player/Year elected: 1998, 81.6 percent of vote

DON SUTTON

DONALD HOWARD SUTTON
LOS ANGELES, N.L., 1966-80, 1988
HOUSTON, N.L., 1981-82
MILWAUKEE, A.L., 1982-84
OAKLAND, A.L., 1985
CALIFORNIA, A.L., 1985-1987
A STALWART ON THE MOUND FOR 23 MAJOR LEAGUE SEASONS, HIS IMPRESSIVE PITCHING RECORD INCLUDES 324 VICTORIES, 3,574 STRIKEOUTS AND A 3.26 ERA. STRIKEOUT TOTAL IS FIFTH BEST ALL-TIME, WHILE WIN TOTAL RANKS TIED FOR 12th. DID NOT MISS A TURN IN THE STARTING ROTATION DUE TO INJURY OR ILLNESS. CONSISTENCY AND MODEL CONTROL LED TO 15 OR MORE WINS IN 12 SEASONS AND 100 OR MORE STRIKEOUTS 21 TIMES. THE RIGHT-HANDER PITCHED IN FOUR WORLD SERIES AND WAS NAMED TO FOUR ALL-STAR TEAMS.

Born: 4-2-45, Clio, Ala. **Height/Weight:** 6-1/185 **Bats/Throws:** R/R **Position:** Pitcher **Career statistics:** 324-256, 3.26 ERA, 3,574 strikeouts **Teams:** Dodgers 1966-80, 1988; Astros 1981-82; Brewers 1982-84; Athletics 1985; Angels 1985-87

He was baseball's Energizer Bunny, the ultimate grinder and mechanic who kept going, and going, and going. Don Sutton, methodical and durable, just kept plugging away for 23 major league seasons, winning more games (324), collecting more strikeouts (3,574) and posting more innings (5,282⅓) than many of the game's more celebrated pitchers. Reliable, dependable and efficient, he was a blue-collar righthander who built a Hall of Fame career around white-collar numbers.

Sutton, a 6-foot-1, 185-pound Alabaman, was not overpowering. He spotted his fastball, handcuffed hitters with an outstanding curve and kept them off balance with occasional sliders and screwballs that he threw from an overhand motion. Every pitch was thoughtful and thrown with pinpoint control. Every game provided testimony to his supreme confidence and poise.

That poise was front and center for the Los Angeles Dodgers, who welcomed Sutton in 1966 as the heir-apparent to Sandy Koufax and aging Don Drysale and watched him post a 233-181 record and lead them to three National League pennants over the next 15 seasons. After the Dodgers let him leave as a free agent in

> "There's no way you can appreciate Don Sutton just watching him throw in practice or pitch with a 10-run lead. But put him in a big game with the tying run on third and you'll see something. Sutton thrives on pressure. ..." *— Tommy Lasorda*

1980, the 35-year-old Sutton began a five-city odyssey that would net him 91 more wins and postseason stops with the Milwaukee Brewers and California Angels.

Sutton was amazingly consistent, seldom spectacular. He never won a Cy Young and had only one 20-victory season (1976), but he reached the 15-win plateau 12 times and was a double-figure winner in 21 of his 23 seasons. Sutton, who seldom missed a start, is the only man in history to top 100 strikeouts for 21 straight years and the four-time All-Star Game performer ranks first in virtually every meaningful pitching category for the tradition-rich Dodgers.

An air of mystery always surrounded the articulate Sutton, who smiled and winked away suggestions that he doctored the ball. He was strong-minded and sometimes rubbed teammates the wrong way, but nobody ever doubted his dedication to winning — right through his final season, a 16-game return to Los Angeles in 1988.

BILL TERRY

WILLIAM HAROLD TERRY
NEW YORK N.L. 1923 TO 1941

BATTED .401 AND TIED N.L. RECORD FOR BASE HITS WITH 254 IN 1930. MADE 200 OR MORE HITS IN SIX SEASONS. RETIRED WITH LIFETIME BATTING AVERAGE OF .341, A MODERN N.L. RECORD FOR LEFT-HANDED BATTERS. MOST VALUABLE PLAYER IN 1930. SUCCEEDED JOHN McGRAW AS MANAGER IN 1932 AND WON PENNANTS IN 1933-36-37.

Born: 10-30-1898, Atlanta, Ga. **Died:** 1-9-89 **Height/Weight:** 6-2/200 **Bats/Throws:** L/L **Primary position:** First base
Career statistics: .341 avg., 2,193 hits, 1,120 runs, 154 HR, 1,078 RBIs **Teams played:** Giants 1923-36
Batting champion: N.L., 1930 **Teams managed (823-661):** Giants 1932-41 **World Series title:** 1933

The first thing you noticed about Bill Terry was the hard-edged bluntness, a glassy-eyed, no-nonsense attitude that made it perfectly clear he was about business, not pleasure. Baseball was a means to Terry's end and he pulled no punches in his legendary duels with strong-willed New York Giants manager John McGraw, his frank dealings with members of the press and his no-mercy plundering of National League pitchers.

Terry grew up in poverty, the victim of a broken home in Jacksonville, Fla., and his silent rage and obsession to succeed were magnified with every line drive he slashed into the spacious left and right-center field gaps at New York's Polo Grounds. His aloofness in the locker room transformed into competitive passion when he took the field and that passion was documented by the .341 average the graceful 6-foot-2, 200-pound first baseman carved out over a 14-year major league career.

Terry's icy glare and savage line drives through the box unnerved many pitchers, who feared the straightaway hitting

"**Bill managed like he played. It was business to him, not fun, and he was successful.**" —*Carl Hubbell*

style of the powerfully built, shoulder-hunching left-hander. His third New York season in 1925 produced a .319 average and he failed to top the .300 plateau only once over the next 11 years. He was a machine-like batsman who piled up six 200-hit seasons and topped 100 RBIs seven times. Terry's signature performance came in 1930 when he amassed 254 hits and posted an eye-catching .401 average that still stands as the last .400 season in N.L. history.

The Terry-McGraw personality clashes were legendary—they once went a year and a half without speaking to each other. But when McGraw suddenly ended his brilliant 33-year managerial run in 1932, he hand-picked Terry as his successor. It was a prudent choice.

As player-manager, Terry guided the Giants to two pennants and a 1933 World Series victory over the Washington Senators. He retired from active duty after the 1936 season, but continued in his managerial capacity until 1941, leading the Giants to one more pennant in 1937.

T
E
R
R
Y

SAMUEL LUTHER THOMPSON
DETROIT N.L. PHILADELPHIA N.L.
1885-1898; DETROIT A.L.1906
ONE OF THE FOREMOST SLUGGERS OF
HIS DAY. LIFETIME BATTING AVERAGE
.336. BATTED BETTER THAN .400 TWICE.
GREAT CLUTCH HITTER. COLLECTED
200 OR MORE HITS IN A SEASON THREE
TIMES. TOPPED N.L. IN HOME RUNS AND
RUNS BATTED IN TWICE.

SAM THOMPSON

Born: 3-5-1860, Danville, Ind. **Died:** 11-7-22 **Height/Weight:** 6-2/207 **Bats/Throws:** L/L **Primary position:** Outfield **Career statistics:** .335 avg., 2,020 hits, 1,262 runs, 126 HR, 1,305 RBIs, 232 steals **Teams:** Detroit 1885-88, 1906; Philadelphia 1889-98 **HR champion:** N.L., 1889, '95

W hen he stepped to the plate, crouching his 6-foot-2, 207-pound frame low in the box, everything stopped—all eyes focused on the intimidating form of Big Sam Thompson. Fans watched in hushed silence, fielders backed up and pitchers, only 50 feet away, fidgeted nervously. In a deadball era filled with hit-'em-where-they-ain't contact specialists, the air of anticipation hung like a thick fog over one of the game's early power hitters.

Big Sam won two home run titles with the now-modest totals of 20 and 18 over a 14-year National League career that stretched from 1885 to 1898 in Detroit and Philadelphia, but his vicious lefthanded swings, delivered with weight-shifting force as he sprang from his crouch, produced many more unsettling moments for fearful opponents. Criticized by writers as a homer-crazy slugger, his batting averages, hit totals and run-production defied such logic and placed him among the most accomplished batsmen of any era.

The mustachioed, quiet and self-effacing giant topped the 200-hit barrier three times, batted .370 or higher four times, scored 100 or more runs 10 times and was an RBI machine—1,305 in 1,410 games. In Detroit, he batted .407 and drove in 166 runs for the 1887 pennant-winning team that beat American Association champion St. Louis in a 15-game "World Series" barnstorming tour. From 1891-95 in

"Thompson belongs to that rutting class of slugging batsmen who think of nothing else when they go to the bat but that of gaining the applause of the (fans) by the novice's hit to the outfield of a 'homer,' one of the least difficult hits known to batting in Baseball. ..."
—*Spalding Guide, 1896*

Philadelphia, he played five years in a Hall of Fame outfield that included Ed Delahanty and Billy Hamilton.

In 1894, all three topped .400, right fielder Thompson checking in at .415. They also performed defensively like few outfields, before or since. Big Sam, a fast and fearless ball chaser with a powerful arm, is credited with popularizing the one-hop throw to the plate, bypassing the cutoff man.

Back problems brought a premature end to Thompson's career, limiting him to three games in 1897 and 14 in '98. At age 46, he made an eight-game comeback for the 1906 Detroit Tigers before retiring for good with a .335 average and career totals of 2,020 hits and a then-prolific 126 home runs.

Player/Year elected: 1946, Committee on Old-Timers

JOE TINKER

JOSEPH B. TINKER
FAMOUS AS A MEMBER OF ONE OF BASEBALL'S
GREATEST DOUBLE PLAY COMBINATIONS-FROM
TINKER TO EVERS TO CHANCE. A BIG LEAGUER
FROM 1902 THROUGH 1916 WITH THE CHICAGO
CUBS AND CINCINNATI REDS AND THE
CHICAGO FEDS. MANAGER CINCINNATI
1913 AND CHICAGO N.L. 1916. SHORTSTOP
ON CUBS' TEAM THAT WON PENNANTS
IN 1906, '07 '08 AND 1910.

Born: 7-27-1880, Muscotah, Kan. **Died:** 7-27-48 **Height/Weight:** 5-9/175 **Bats/Throws:** R/R **Primary position:** Shortstop
Career statistics: .263 avg., 1,560 hits, 336 steals **Teams:** Cubs 1902-12, 1916; Reds 1913

He was no ordinary Joe, as his .263 career average and 1,560 hits might suggest. Joe Tinker was the most celebrated shortstop in the early century National League, a fierce and clutch competitor for a Chicago Cubs team that won 530 games over the most prolific five-year run in baseball history. What Tinker lacked in athleticism he more than made up for with an indomitable spirit that carried him to poetic and Hall of Fame distinction.

For early Cubs fans, the middle-infield combo of Tinker and second baseman Johnny Evers was magnetic, a perfect blend of fire-and-brimstone intensity and athletic grace. Tinker liked to play deep and rely on his powerful arm; Evers was clever and a master of positioning. There seemed to be a telepathy and harmony between them, to the amazement of teammates who knew about their long off-field feud.

The poem-inspiring double-play combination of Tinker-to-Evers-to-(Frank) Chance remained intact from 1902-12, a period in

which the Cubs won four pennants and two World Series. The 5-foot-9, 175-pound Tinker also was a righthanded contact hitter and aggressive runner who did little things to help the team. The Cubs had better hitters, but few more reliable in the clutch.

Tinker, who led N.L. shortstops in fielding average four times, is remembered for his success against Christy Mathewson, the ace of New York teams that battled the Cubs for N.L. supremacy. When Fred Merkle's failure to touch second base necessitated a pennant-deciding makeup game between the teams in 1908, it was Tinker who delivered a back-breaking triple off Mathewson in the Cubs' 4-2 victory.

After leaving the Cubs, Tinker managed Cincinnati for a season and spent two years as the popular manager of Chicago's Federal League club, winning a pennant in 1915. The Kansas native, who had become a Cubs regular in 1902 at age 21, returned to the team as player-manager in 1916 before retiring at age 36.

> **"Tinker was the jolly man of the great Chicago trio. He had a keen sense of humor and ... could undress you out at second with a loud guffaw. He went right on through life that way."**
>
> —*The Sporting News, 1948*

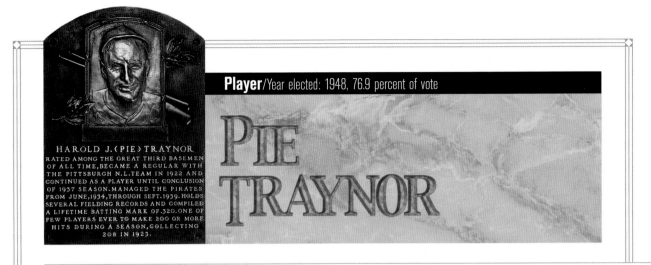

PIE TRAYNOR

HAROLD J. (PIE) TRAYNOR
RATED AMONG THE GREAT THIRD BASEMEN
OF ALL TIME, BECAME A REGULAR WITH
THE PITTSBURGH N.L. TEAM IN 1922 AND
CONTINUED AS A PLAYER UNTIL CONCLUSION
OF 1937 SEASON. MANAGED THE PIRATES
FROM JUNE, 1934, THROUGH SEPT. 1939. HOLDS
SEVERAL FIELDING RECORDS AND COMPILED
A LIFETIME BATTING MARK OF .320. ONE OF
FEW PLAYERS EVER TO MAKE 200 OR MORE
HITS DURING A SEASON, COLLECTING
208 IN 1923.

Born: 11-11-1899, Framingham, Mass. **Died:** 3-16-72 **Height/Weight:** 6-0/170 **Bats/Throws:** R/R **Primary position:** Third base
Career statistics: .320 avg., 2,416 hits, 1,183 runs, 1,273 RBIs **Teams:** Pirates 1920-37

He was tall, rangy and broad in the shoulders, an unlikely candidate for baseball immortality. But anybody who watched Pie Traynor perform his third base magic was overpowered by the experience. Lightning-quick reflexes, long, supple arms and an unfailingly accurate throw helped him set the lofty standard by which future generations of defensive third basemen would be judged.

Traynor drew his first defensive raves when he took over as Pittsburgh's regular third baseman in 1922 — his third season with the Pirates. National League players and managers had never seen anybody quite like him. Traynor would range far to his left, cutting off balls that normally skipped past overextended shortstops, or he would discourage bunters with his hardcharging gracefulness.

But he was at his best on balls hit over the bag, making lunging stops and equally acrobatic throws from awkward positions. He occasionally snared potential doubles with his bare hand, making an amazing play look easy. "Hornsby doubled

> "Pie had the quickest hands, the quickest arm of any third baseman. ... Playing first base with him was a pleasure — if you didn't stop too long to admire the plays he made." — *Charlie Grimm*

down the left field line, but Traynor threw him out," was the joke that circulated through N.L. cities.

Longtime New York manager John McGraw, moved by Traynor's incredible defense against the Giants, called him the greatest team player he had ever seen. But Traynor was more than just a pretty glove. He was a dangerous righthanded hitter who compiled a .320 career average, including a 1923 season in which he batted .338 with 208 hits, 101 RBIs and 108 runs. Typically hitting fifth in Pittsburgh's lineup, Traynor topped 100 RBIs seven times while hitting only 58 career home runs.

Traynor, easy-going, friendly and articulate, often complained that his hitting was overshadowed by his fielding. But that might have been more a product of the wide-open offensive era in which he played and his lack of power. His 17-year career, which ended as a player-manager in 1937, included two visits to the World Series — the Pirates' 1925 winner over Washington and a 1927 loss to the powerful New York Yankees.

Player/Year elected: 1955, 81.7 percent of vote

DAZZY VANCE

ARTHUR CHARLES (DAZZY) VANCE
BROOKLYN N.L. 1922 TO 1932,1935
PITTSBURGH N.L. · NEW YORK A.L.
ST.LOUIS N.L. · CINCINNATI N.L.
FIRST PITCHER IN N.L. TO LEAD IN
STRIKEOUTS FOR 7 STRAIGHT YEARS, 1922 TO
1928. LED LEAGUE WITH 28 VICTORIES IN
1924; 22 IN 1925. WON 15 STRAIGHT IN 1924.
PITCHED NO-HIT GAME AGAINST PHILLIES,
1925. MOST VALUABLE PLAYER N.L. 1924.

Born: 3-4-1891, Orient, Iowa **Died:** 2-16-61 **Height/Weight:** 6-2/200 **Bats/Throws:** R/R **Position:** Pitcher
Career statistics: 197-140, 3.24 ERA, 2,045 strikeouts **Teams:** Pirates 1915; Yankees 1915, 1918; Dodgers 1922-32, 1935; Cardinals 1933, 1934; Reds 1934 **Major awards:** League MVP, 1924

Colorful, fun-loving and witty, Dazzy Vance was the acknowledged leader of Brooklyn's "Daffiness Boys" in the 1920s. Strong-armed and lightning fast, he also mixed business with pleasure as the greatest power pitcher of the decade. Vance could cut up hitters with his well-placed one liners while cutting them down with his blazing fastballs.

The 6-foot-2 righthander was a visual paradox—red hair, round, florid face, big nose and exceptionally long arms that, combined with broad shoulders, gave him an 83-inch span. With leg kicking high and arms flailing, Vance came at batters from a sweeping overhand motion that delivered pitches like a catapult. The fastball froze hitters; a hard sweeping curve buckled their knees.

Such was the case from 1922-32, an 11-year span in which the Iowa farmboy posted 187 of his 197 career wins and won three ERA titles. Vance's 28-6 record, 2.16 ERA and 262 strikeouts were good enough to merit the League MVP award in 1924 and his 22 wins the following year led both leagues. But it was his strikeout totals

> "He gets everything behind (his delivery), including his ears." —*Wilbert Robinson*

that caught everyone's attention—and made him the N.L. leader for a record seven straight years (1922-28).

Vance's success did not come easily. He bounced around the minors for 10 years, overcoming arm and control problems before posting his first big-league win in 1922—at age 31. Most of his success was crammed into his 11 Brooklyn seasons while playing for Wilbert Robinson's weak but colorful teams. Vance, a renowned night owl, only added to the zaniness. In 1926, he was one of three runners caught at third base when teammate Babe Herman "doubled into a double play."

Vance, known for the tattered undershirt sleeve that flapped from beneath his uniform, became one of the league's top gate attractions and, as such, insisted on working every fifth day—disdaining the standard four-day rotation. Still pitching at age 43, he worked in his only World Series for the 1934 St. Louis Cardinals before retiring in 1935 after a one-season return to Brooklyn.

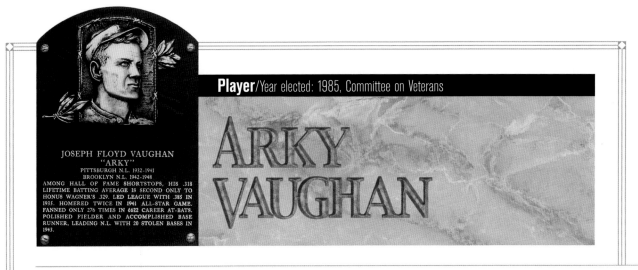

JOSEPH FLOYD VAUGHAN
"ARKY"
PITTSBURGH N.L. 1932-1941
BROOKLYN N.L. 1942-1948
AMONG HALL OF FAME SHORTSTOPS, HIS .318
LIFETIME BATTING AVERAGE IS SECOND ONLY TO
HONUS WAGNER'S .329. LED LEAGUE WITH .385 IN
1935. HOMERED TWICE IN 1941 ALL-STAR GAME.
FANNED ONLY 276 TIMES IN 6622 CAREER AT-BATS.
POLISHED FIELDER AND ACCOMPLISHED BASE
RUNNER, LEADING N.L. WITH 20 STOLEN BASES IN
1943.

ARKY VAUGHAN

Born: 3-9-12, Clifty, Ark. **Died:** 8-30-52 **Height/Weight:** 5-11/175 **Bats/Throws:** L/R **Primary position:** Shortstop
Career statistics: .318 avg., 2,103 hits, 1,173 runs **Teams:** Pirates 1932-41; Dodgers 1942-43, 1947-48 **Batting champion:** N.L. 1935

L ike a ship passing in the night, Floyd "Arky" Vaughan sailed inconspicuously through his 14-year career, avoiding fanfare with a fervor most players devote to finding it. The most complete shortstop of the 1930s also was, in the words of New York columnist Red Smith, "baseball's most superbly forgotten man." That was fine with Vaughan, who preferred to let a blazing bat and reliable glove do his talking.

Beneath Vaughan's brown hair and blue eyes was a sustained grimace that suggested business was more important than pleasure to the 5-foot-11, 175-pound Californian. He was not unfriendly; he simply was uncomfortable in the spotlight, which he gladly surrendered to more popular Pittsburgh teammates like Pie Traynor and the Waner brothers, Paul and Lloyd. But when games were being decided, Vaughan's comfort level increased dramatically.

From 1932-41, his 10 seasons with the Pirates, Vaughan never failed to bat .300. His .385 average led the National League in 1935 and he scored more than 100 runs four times. A selective lefthanded hitter

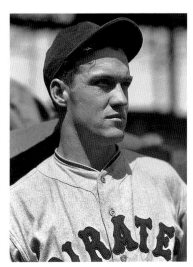

"He's not as meek as he looks. In fact, he's not meek at all. There's no brag in him, but he knows he's a good ballplayer and nobody is going to make him believe otherwise."

—*George Gibson,
Pirates manager, 1932*

with occasional power, Vaughan attacked the ball from a wide, flat-footed stance, seldom striking out and using his speed to challenge outfielders. He led the N.L. three times in triples.

The big bat, which posted a .318 career average, overshadowed Vaughan's steady work in the field. He lacked the fire and flamboyance of contemporaries Leo Durocher and Rabbit Maranville, but the results were similar. A seven-time All-Star Game performer, the Arkansas-born "Arky" hit two home runs in the 1941 midsummer classic but was upstaged by a ninth-inning, three-run homer by American Leaguer Ted Williams.

Vaughan played for Brooklyn in 1942 and his surprising 1943 dispute with manager Durocher over the suspension of another player almost caused a team revolt. At age 31, he went into voluntary retirement after the season, sat out three years and returned in 1947, batting .325 as a part-time player for the World Series-bound Dodgers. After one more Brooklyn season, Vaughan retired to his California ranch with 2,103 hits.

VAUGHAN

BILL VEECK

BILL VEECK
OWNER OF INDIANS, BROWNS AND WHITE SOX. CREATED HEIGHTENED FAN INTEREST AT EVERY STOP WITH INGENIOUS PROMOTIONAL SCHEMES, FAN PARTICIPATION, EXPLODING SCOREBOARD, OUTRAGEOUS DOOR PRIZES, NAMES ON UNIFORMS. SET M.L. ATTENDANCE RECORD WITH PENNANT-WINNER AT CLEVELAND IN 1948; WON AGAIN WITH 'GO-GO' SOX IN 1959. SIGNED A.L.'S FIRST BLACK PLAYER, LARRY DOBY IN 1947 AND OLDEST ROOKIE, 42 YEAR OLD SATCHEL PAIGE IN 1948.
A CHAMPION OF THE LITTLE GUY.

Born: 2-9-14, Chicago, Ill. **Died:** 1-2-86 **Executive career:** Part owner of Indians, 1946-49; Browns, 1951-53; White Sox, 1958-61, 1975-80

He was a beer-drinking, chain-smoking, one-legged maverick who attacked baseball with the same gusto with which he lived his life. Bill Veeck finagled, promoted and laughed his way through his some-times-controversial, always-unpredictable career as an establishment-buck-ing major league owner. Salesman, innovator and show-man, he invigorated the game with his enthusiasm and lit up four cities with his boundless energy.

Veeck with Satchel Paige.

The Chicago-born Veeck, son of longtime Cubs president Bill Veeck Sr., operated by the simple princi-ple that baseball should be fun. When it wasn't, he took steps to remedy the situation as full or part owner of the Cleveland Indians, St. Louis Browns, Chicago White Sox and minor league Milwaukee Brewers. Veeck typically worked from a shoestring budget as head of ownership syndicates and energized his fran-chises with outrageous promotions.

His masterpiece was the 1951 appearance of midget

"I want to create the greatest enjoyment for the greatest number of people, not by detracting from the ball game, but by adding a few moments of fairly simple pleasure." —*Bill Veeck*

VEECK

Eddie Gaedel in a Browns game, a stunt that infuriated American League officials. But he also entertained fans with off-the-wall giveaways (live lobsters, 200-pound blocks of ice, livestock), players in shorts, firework displays, orchids for females, clowns in the stands and even a promotion in which fans managed a game by holding up decision cards.

Veeck, the rumple-clothed, open-shirted man of the people, hobbled through life on a wooden leg, courtesy of a war injury, and enjoyed mingling with fans, either in the bleachers or at local pubs. The promotions often were attempts to prop up attendance for weak teams, but his 1948 Indians did win a World Series and his 1959 White Sox won the franchise's first pennant in 40 years.

As an innovator, Cleveland-owner Veeck broke the A.L. color barrier in 1947 with the signing of Larry Doby and he introduced the exploding scoreboard in his first of two stints as Chicago owner in 1959. But through it all, "Sport Shirt Bill" fought obstinate owners, constant health problems and financial setbacks that forced him to sell his teams four times — the Indians in 1949, Browns in 1953 and White Sox in 1961 and '80.

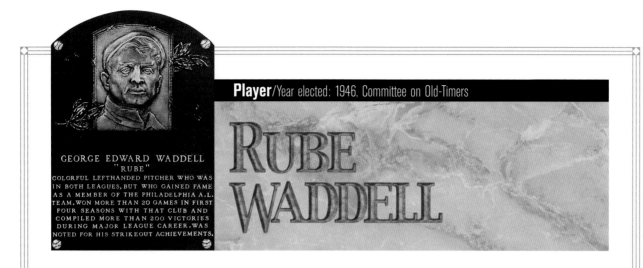

RUBE WADDELL

GEORGE EDWARD WADDELL
"RUBE"
COLORFUL LEFTHANDED PITCHER WHO WAS
IN BOTH LEAGUES, BUT WHO GAINED FAME
AS A MEMBER OF THE PHILADELPHIA A.L.
TEAM. WON MORE THAN 20 GAMES IN FIRST
FOUR SEASONS WITH THAT CLUB AND
COMPILED MORE THAN 200 VICTORIES
DURING MAJOR LEAGUE CAREER. WAS
NOTED FOR HIS STRIKEOUT ACHIEVEMENTS.

Born: 10-13-1876, Bradford, Pa. **Died:** 4-1-14 **Height/Weight:** 6-2/200 **Bats/Throws:** R/L **Position:** Pitcher **Career statistics:** 193-143, 2.16 ERA, 2,316 strikeouts **Teams:** Louisville 1897, 1899; Pirates 1900-01; Cubs 1901; Athletics 1902-07; Browns 1908-10

Big, burly, eccentric and unpredictable, Rube Waddell attacked baseball in the same free-wheeling manner he lived life. Early-century hitters feared the blazing fastballs he threw with a powerful left arm; managers and teammates endured the curves he threw with an off-centered personality. Nobody ever knew what to expect from the strong Pennsylvania country boy who won over fans with both his million-dollar talent and 10-year-old heart.

Waddell's 13-year career was legendary. He was uneducated, flaky and borderline unstable, a fun-loving "Rube" who posted a 131-82 record over the six seasons (1902-07) he pitched for Philadelphia manager Connie Mack. The patient Mack often looked the other way when the easily-distracted Waddell showed up late for games, simply dispatching an aide to search him out in the local saloons.

Often, however, Waddell could be found helping volunteer firemen, leading a parade, selling hotdogs, swimming across a river, wrestling an alligator or shooting marbles with kids. Anything was possible. He had a special fascina-tion for fire engines and was known to bolt the dugout and chase after a wailing siren.

Waddell was always likeable — but too irresponsible for disciplinarian Fred Clarke in stops at Louisville and Pittsburgh. Only Mack, who called Waddell "the best lefthander I ever saw," could live with his antics and Waddell rewarded him with consecutive seasons of 24-7, 21-16, 25-19 and 27-10. In six Philadelphia seasons, Waddell led the American League in strikeouts, posting a then single-season record 349 in 1904. His Philadelphia ERAs ranged from 1.48 to 2.44.

Hitters raved about Waddell's speed and biting curve, always thrown with pinpoint control. Fans loved his flair and came in record numbers to see him turn cartwheels after a victory. But eventually even Mack soured on the 6-foot-2 lefty and he finished his career with the St. Louis Browns, retiring in 1910 with a 193-143 record and 2.16 ERA. Waddell, who missed the 1905 World Series because he hurt his arm wrestling, contacted tuberculosis while fighting a Kentucky flood and died in 1914 at age 37.

> "What pitcher had the best combination of speed and a curveball? My goodness, I think that's quite simple. His name is Rube Waddell." — *Connie Mack*

WADDELL

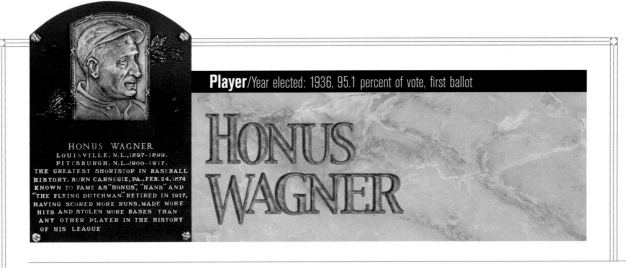

Player/Year elected: 1936, 95.1 percent of vote, first ballot

HONUS WAGNER

Born: 2-24-1874, Chartiers, Pa. **Died:** 12-6-55 **Height/Weight:** 5-11/200 **Bats/Throws:** R/R **Primary position:** Shortstop

Career statistics: .328 avg., 3,420 hits, 1,739 runs, 1,733 RBIs, 723 steals **Teams:** Louisville 1897-99; Pirates 1900-17

Batting champion: N.L. 1900, '03, '04, '06, "07, '08, '09, '11

The 5-foot-11, 200-pound gorilla-like frame featured a thick, massive chest, long arms and legs so bowed you could roll a barrel between them. Hall

"That damn Dutchman is the only man in the game I can't scare." — *Ty Cobb*

of Fame pitcher Lefty Gomez, who enjoyed the good fortune of never having to face Honus Wagner, once quipped, "He was the only ballplayer who could tie his shoelaces without bending down."

Wagner, a.k.a. the Flying Dutchman, was nobody's prototypical athlete. But when he stepped onto a baseball field, he magically transformed into one of the most versatile players in the history of the game. Wagner could pitch or play any infield or outfield position, but he is most fondly remembered as the first great shortstop of the 20th century and the National League's most proficient batsman of his era.

Wagner was to Pittsburgh what Ty Cobb was to Detroit and Babe Ruth to New York. From 1900-17, he enchanted Pirates fans with his deceptive range, the oversized, shovel-like hands that sucked every ground ball into his undersized mitt and a rifle arm that allowed him to make plays from deep in the hole — and beyond. Outstanding contact hitters of the deadball era knew better than to hit the ball to the left side of Pittsburgh's infield.

Offensively, Wagner overmatched the usually dominant pitchers of his era. His career total of 3,420 hits ranks sixth all time and his .327 average produced a National League record-tying eight batting titles. He led the league in doubles seven times, runs twice, RBIs five times, extra-base hits seven times, triples three times, slugging six times and he even captured five stolen base crowns. There was, simply, nothing

Wagner couldn't do.

Not surprisingly, the Dutchman's proficiency sparked the Pirates to four N.L. pennants and a 1909 World Series victory over Cobb's Tigers. When the first Hall of Fame class was selected in 1936, Wagner and Ruth tied for second in the voting, behind only Cobb and ahead of Christy Mathewson and Walter Johnson.

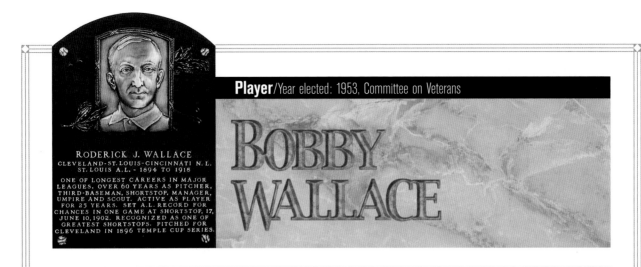

RODERICK J. WALLACE
CLEVELAND-ST.LOUIS-CINCINNATI N.L.
ST. LOUIS A.L. - 1894 TO 1918
ONE OF LONGEST CAREERS IN MAJOR
LEAGUES. OVER 60 YEARS AS PITCHER,
THIRD-BASEMAN, SHORTSTOP, MANAGER,
UMPIRE AND SCOUT. ACTIVE AS PLAYER
FOR 25 YEARS. SET A.L. RECORD FOR
CHANCES IN ONE GAME AT SHORTSTOP, 17,
JUNE 10, 1902. RECOGNIZED AS ONE OF
GREATEST SHORTSTOPS. PITCHED FOR
CLEVELAND IN 1896 TEMPLE CUP SERIES.

Player/Year elected: 1953, Committee on Veterans

BOBBY WALLACE

Born: 11-4-1873, Pittsburgh, Pa. **Died:** 11-3-60 **Height/Weight:** 5-8/170 **Bats/Throws:** R/R **Primary position:** Shortstop **Career statistics:** .268 avg., 2,309 hits, 1,057 runs, 1,121 RBIs, 201 steals **Teams:** Cleveland 1894-98; St. Louis 1899-1901, 1917-18; Browns 1902-16

He was the prototypical defensive shortstop, a turn-of-the-century magician who helped define the position for future generations. Bobby Wallace was to the fledgling American League what Honus Wagner was to the National—without the blazing bat. Over 25 major league seasons, Wallace forged a Hall of Fame career out of grit and determination, 15 of those as "Mr. Shortstop" of the St. Louis Browns.

The 5-foot-8, 170-pound Pittsburgh native was a 1970s shortstop in early-century clothing. He was graceful and mobile, sure-handed and able to gun down runners from deep in the hole. While National League counterpart Wagner was an aggressive, bulldog-like shortstop, Wallace looked like something straight out of the ballet. Results were the same, but the styles were vastly different.

Wallace, a converted pitcher and third baseman who played eight big-league seasons for the Cleveland Spiders and St. Louis Cardinals before moving to the Browns in 1902, is credited with inventing the scoop-

"We were in Philadelphia when manager Tebeau shifted me from third to short, and right off the bat I knew I had found my dish. I suddenly felt I had sprouted wings."

—*Bobby Wallace, 1899*

and-toss play—fielding slow grounders and making an underhand throw to first in virtually the same motion. He also was known for his quiet leadership and ability to make the clutch defensive play with games on the line.

Wallace's bat never measured up to his defense, although he did post a .335 average and drive in 112 runs for the 1897 Spiders and followed that two years later with a .295, 108-RBI season for the Cardinals. But Wallace, a righthander who choked up on his bottle bat and slashed at the ball from a spread-legged stance, was primarily a move-the-runners, dead-ball-style hitter while posting a .268 career average.

Defense was Wallace's game and he generally was recognized as the A.L.'s best shortstop from 1902 through 1911, when he served briefly as Browns player-manager. Wallace, a St. Louis institution who never played for a pennant-winner over 20 seasons with the Browns and Cardinals, stayed active as a role player through 1918 before retiring with 2,309 hits in 2,383 games.

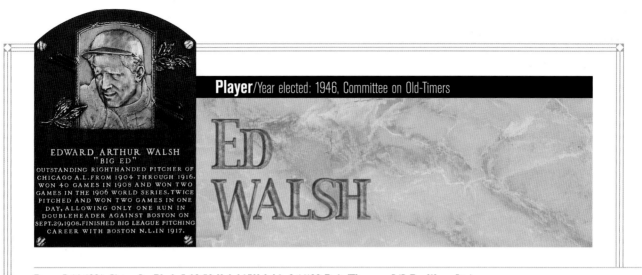

Player/Year elected: 1946, Committee on Old-Timers

EDWARD ARTHUR WALSH
"BIG ED"
OUTSTANDING RIGHTHANDED PITCHER OF
CHICAGO A.L. FROM 1904 THROUGH 1916.
WON 40 GAMES IN 1908 AND WON TWO
GAMES IN THE 1906 WORLD SERIES. TWICE
PITCHED AND WON TWO GAMES IN ONE
DAY, ALLOWING ONLY ONE RUN IN
DOUBLEHEADER AGAINST BOSTON ON
SEPT. 29, 1908. FINISHED BIG LEAGUE PITCHING
CAREER WITH BOSTON N.L. IN 1917.

ED WALSH

Born: 5-14-1881, Plains, Pa. **Died:** 5-26-59 **Height/Weight:** 6-1/190 **Bats/Throws:** R/R **Position:** Pitcher
Career statistics: 195-126, 1.82 ERA, 1,736 strikeouts **Teams:** White Sox 1904-16; Braves 1917

He was strong, cocky and confident, qualities that served him well as one of the most prolific workhorse pitchers of the early 1900s. But a little less swagger and considerably more restraint might have prolonged Ed Walsh's fleeting moment in the spotlight and allowed him to challenge the career numbers posted by Christy Mathewson, Walter Johnson and other turn-of-the-century greats.

The 6-foot-1 Walsh was a rubber-arm righthander and king of the legal spitballers. He also was a dapper, fun-loving, happy-go-lucky charmer who approached his work with youthful exuberance and defiance. An above-average fastball and mediocre curve got him to the major leagues in 1904, but it wasn't until he unleashed his devastating spitter in 1906 that he joined the baseball elite.

That was the season he posted a 17-13 regular-season record for the Hitless Wonder White Sox and keyed a World Series victory over the powerful Cubs with two more wins in the all-Chicago classic. Buoyed by that success and a spitball that "dropped like a

"The spitball was easy on the arm. ... If I'd pitched every third day, I'd have lasted five or six years longer. I wore myself out working in and out of turn." —*Ed Walsh*

10-pound brick," Walsh became a pitching machine, working scheduled starts and providing between-start relief.

The more work the better, and Walsh upped his win total to 24 in 1907 and his innings count to a whopping 422 1/3. That set the stage for the most prolific season of the modern era. In a memorable 1908 campaign, Walsh compiled a 40-15 record, completed 42 of 49 starts, appeared in a league-leading 66 games and struck out 269 batters in a modern-record 464 innings. Despite his yeoman effort and 1.42 ERA, the White Sox could finish no better than third in the American League.

Walsh never reached that height again, but he did post consecutive 27-win records in 1911 and '12 while completing a 168-112 seven-year run in which he worked 2,526 1/3 innings—an average of 361. Big Ed battled a tired arm for five more seasons, winning only 13 times and never again topping 100 innings. Walsh's 195-126 career mark was impressive, but his 1.82 ERA over 14 seasons is the lowest in modern history.

WALSH

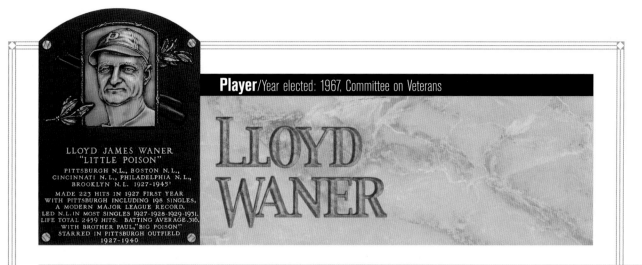

LLOYD WANER

LLOYD JAMES WANER
"LITTLE POISON"
PITTSBURGH N.L., BOSTON N.L.,
CINCINNATI N.L., PHILADELPHIA N.L.,
BROOKLYN N.L. 1927-1945'
MADE 223 HITS IN 1927 FIRST YEAR
WITH PITTSBURGH INCLUDING 198 SINGLES,
A MODERN MAJOR LEAGUE RECORD.
LED N.L. IN MOST SINGLES 1927-1928-1929-1931.
LIFE TOTAL 2459 HITS. BATTING AVERAGE .316.
WITH BROTHER PAUL,"BIG POISON"
STARRED IN PITTSBURGH OUTFIELD
1927-1940

Born: 3-16-06, Harrah, Okla. **Died:** 7-22-82 **Height/Weight:** 5-8/150 **Bats/Throws:** L/R **Primary position:** Center field **Career statistics:** .316 avg., 2,459 hits, 1,201 runs **Teams:** Pirates 1927-41, 1944-45; Braves 1941; Reds 1941; Phillies 1942; Dodgers 1944

To Pittsburgh fans, he was Little Poison — the quietly efficient half of baseball's most renowned brother act. Lloyd Waner was the wispy, fleet-footed shadow of older brother Paul — Big Poison's offensive set-up man and the Pirates' defensive stopper. Lloyd was like an annoying mosquito that buzzed around major league ballparks for 18 seasons, slapping out hits and taking a bite out of rallies with his flashy glove.

The Oklahoma-born Waners lived, fought and played side-by-side from 1927 through 1940 in Pittsburgh's outfield, Lloyd in center and Paul in right. Paul was officially listed at 5-foot-8 ½, a quarter inch taller than Lloyd, and he outweighed him, 153-150. Their facial resemblance was striking, but there was no mistaking the batting styles that carried them to Hall of Fame glory.

Paul was the better hitter, a run-producer who whipped vicious line drives all over the park. Lloyd, a classic lefthanded leadoff man, choked up on the bat and simply layed it on the ball, challenging fielders to throw him out. The National

League's fastest runner rarely struck out and he was an artist at finding holes, blooping balls into the outfield and turning the slightest bobbles into infield hits.

Lloyd also was a smooth center fielder who complemented his go-get-'em speed with a strong right arm. But his defensive prowess was overshadowed by the Waner offensive magic, which produced a combined 5,611 career hits and a .326 average. In 1927, '28 and '29, Lloyd's first three seasons, he collected 678 hits and the brothers combined for 1,338, a whopping average of 446.

Lloyd batted .355 with a rookie-record 223 hits and N.L.-leading 133 runs in 1927 as the Pirates won a pennant and lost to the powerful New York Yankees in the World Series. He continued to post high averages but never again experienced postseason play in a career that included N.L. stops in Boston, Cincinnati, Philadelphia and Brooklyn before a Pittsburgh return in 1944 and '45. The .316 career hitter managed 2,459 hits, 2,033 of which were singles.

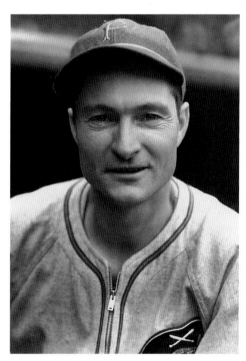

"He unjustly lived and played in Paul's shadow. Paul was a great ballplayer, but so was Lloyd." — *Pie Traynor*

Player/Year elected: 1952, 83.3 percent of vote

PAUL WANER

PAUL GLEE WANER
(BIG POISON)
PITTSBURGH-BROOKLYN-BOSTON, N.L.
NEW YORK, A.L.
1926-1945
LEFT HANDED HITTING OUTFIELDER BATTED
.300 OR BETTER 14 TIMES IN NATIONAL
LEAGUE. ONE OF SEVEN PLAYERS EVER TO
COMPILE 3,000 OR MORE HITS. SET MODERN
N.L. RECORD BY COLLECTING 200 OR MORE
HITS EIGHT SEASONS. MOST VALUABLE PLAYER
IN 1927 AND FOUR TIMES SELECTED FOR
ALL STAR GAME.

Born: 4-16-03, Harrah, Okla. **Died:** 8-29-65 **Height/Weight:** 5-9/153 **Bats/Throws:** L/L **Primary position:** Right field
Career statistics: .333 avg., 3,152 hits, 1,627 runs, 1,309 RBIs **Teams:** Pirates 1926-40; Dodgers 1941, 1943-44;
Braves 1941-42; Yankees 1944-45 **Batting champion:** N.L., 1927, '34, '36 **Major awards:** League MVP, 1927

He was the marquee half of the most offensive brother act ever to take the baseball stage. Hits simply oozed out of Paul Waner's oversized bat, and all the leftovers he passed on to brother Lloyd. The sprightly Waner brothers, Paul in right and Lloyd in center, were like gnats buzzing the faces of National League pitchers for the 14 incredible seasons (1927-40) they spent together as speedy flychasers in Pittsburgh's outfield.

The 5-foot-8 ½, 153-pound Paul (Big Poison) was a better hitter than his 5-8 ¼, 150-pound younger brother (Little Poison), but not by much. Lloyd, the Pirates' leadoff hitter, would slap a single and Paul would shoot a drive down the line or into a gap, scoring his brother or sending him to third. That combination carried the Pirates to the 1927 World Series, a classic they lost in four games to the powerful New York Yankees.

Paul was a lefthanded-swinging bat-control artist who stepped into the pitch from a close-footed stance, driving some balls to the opposite field, tomahawking others to right. He was fast enough to beat out infield rollers and quick enough to fend off the nastiest of pitches. Waner seldom struck out (34 times in his worst season) and managed eight 200-hit seasons, a figure topped only by Pete Rose and Ty Cobb. His three N.L. batting titles were the result of .380, .362 and .373 efforts.

Waner, who compiled 3,152 hits and a .333 average over 20 seasons, topped the .300 plateau in his first 12 years and earned the League MVP award in 1927 when he complemented his first batting title with a league-leading 18 triples and 131 RBIs. He also was an outstanding right fielder with speed, instincts and a strong, accurate arm.

Waner's only weakness was an affinity for the carousing nightlife that kept Yankees contemporary Babe Ruth in hot water. But it never seemed to affect Waner's performance or the scientific hitting approach he later passed on to Ted Williams and countless other players who sought his batting counsel.

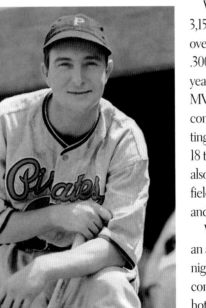

"Why shouldn't he be a great hitter? He's got eyes like a cat." —*Wilbert Robinson*

WANER

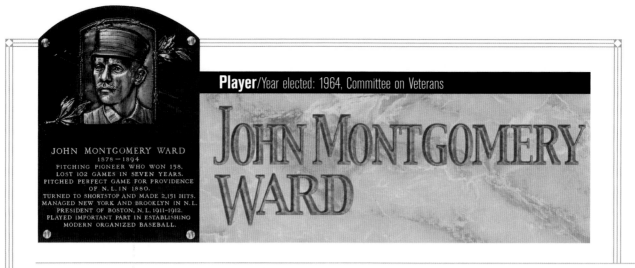

Player/Year elected: 1964, Committee on Veterans

JOHN MONTGOMERY WARD

JOHN MONTGOMERY WARD
1878 — 1894
PITCHING PIONEER WHO WON 158,
LOST 102 GAMES IN SEVEN YEARS.
PITCHED PERFECT GAME FOR PROVIDENCE
OF N.L. IN 1880.
TURNED TO SHORTSTOP AND MADE 2,151 HITS.
MANAGED NEW YORK AND BROOKLYN IN N.L.
PRESIDENT OF BOSTON, N.L. 1911-1912.
PLAYED IMPORTANT PART IN ESTABLISHING
MODERN ORGANIZED BASEBALL.

Born: 3-3-1860, Bellefonte, Pa. **Died:** 3-4-25 **Height/Weight:** 5-9/165 **Bats/Throws:** L/R **Primary positions:** Pitcher, shortstop
Career statistics: 164-103, 2.10 ERA, .278 avg., 2,136 hits, 1,410 runs, 540 steals **Teams:** Providence 1878-82; New York 1883-89, 1893-94; Brooklyn (P.L.) 1890; Brooklyn 1891-92

He was dashing, popular and versatile, a remarkable 19th-century player and organizer who helped define the course of baseball history. Nobody impacted the early game in more ways than John Montgomery Ward, both on the field and off. From pitching great, star shortstop and 1880s fan idol to champion of players' rights, Ward walked an interesting path to Hall of Fame recognition.

"Monte" won 22 games as an 18-year-old righthander for Providence in 1878 and followed with 47-19 and 39-24 marks that vaulted him to National League prominence. Then, after arm problems cut short his pitching career in 1884, Ward became the shortstop and captain of a New York Giants team that won consecutive pennants in 1888 and '89. Ward was the ultimate team leader, a .278 career lefthanded hitter and two-time basestealing champion over 17 major league seasons.

By the mid-1880s, the 5-foot-9, 165-pound Ward also was one of the game's most glamorous players. He was a suave, articulate society man, married to actress Helen Dauvray, and a capable attorney who had used his offseasons to earn a degree from Columbia Law School. When nine Giants players formed the Brotherhood of Professional Base Ball Players in 1885, Ward was elected president and established chapters in each N.L. city.

The Brotherhood took center stage in 1890, when owners continued to ignore grievances, forming the Players League—a "co-op" circuit that attracted more than 100 contract jumpers from the N.L. and American Association. Ward played for and managed the league's Brooklyn team while arguing and winning most of the suits and injunctions filed against it in court. But the league collapsed after one season and players returned to their reserve contracts.

The sometimes-temperamental Pennsylvanian played and managed two seasons for Brooklyn and two more for the Giants before retiring in 1894 to practice law. Among his notable career numbers were 164 pitching wins—including an 1880 perfect game—2,136 hits and 1,410 runs. An outstanding amateur golfer in his post-baseball life, Ward briefly was part owner of the Boston Braves.

> "So there he is—perfect game pitcher, hard-hitting shortstop, manager, organizer and owner. And, now, Hall of Famer. He is a welcome addition to the pantheon."
>
> *—Lee Allen, Hall of Fame historian, 1964*

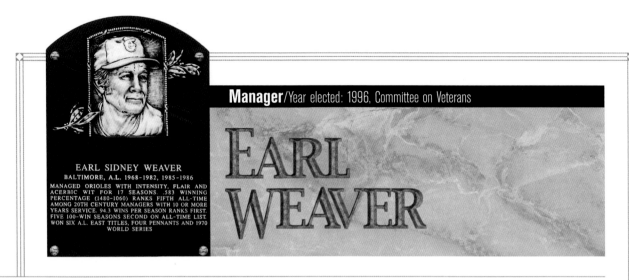

Manager/Year elected: 1996, Committee on Veterans

EARL WEAVER

Born: 8-14-30, St. Louis, Mo. **Height/Weight:** 5-8/165 **Teams managed:** Orioles 1968-82; 1985-86
Career record: 1,480-1,060, .583 **World Series titles:** 1970

He was the umpire's worst nightmare, an in-your-face bantam with attitude and theatrical flair. Earl Weaver also was known to antagonize the players he managed while entertaining fans and writers with his honest assessments and caustic humor. Love him or hate him, "The Earl of Baltimore" was a baseball demon, the master of an Orioles' universe that engulfed the American League in the 1970s.

Fans saw him as explosive and temperamental, a cocky 5-foot-8 scrapper who would charge out of the dugout, hands on hips, and scream away, earning another ejection from the game. Invariably, his 98 career exits were colorful and creative. Weaver's post-game humor could be biting and he didn't pull punches with players, who seemed to play harder to spite him.

But those players also recognized Weaver as a superb strategist and masterful handler of pitchers, despite his legendary battles with ace Jim Palmer, who liked to tell writers, "The only thing he knows about pitching is that he couldn't hit it." It's no coincidence that 22 Weaver-managed pitchers were 20-game winners and six won Cy Youngs, aided by his pioneering use of computer charts. He platooned players, disdained the sacrifice bunt and played for the big inning, although few teams could match the Orioles in fundamentals.

At age 31, the longtime minor league second baseman and manager designed an instructional program that became the bible of the Orioles organization. Seven years later, midway through the 1968 season, he replaced Hank Bauer as Baltimore manager. From 1969-79, his teams recorded four 100-win seasons while winning six division titles, four pennants and one World Series.

When Weaver retired for the first time in 1982, only two of his 14 full-season teams had finished below second place. He returned in 1985 for two seasons before leaving for good with a 1,480-1,060 record and superb .583 winning percentage — a figure enhanced by the fact that only one of his 17 teams finished below .500.

"Winning, that's the big thing. I never worry about getting fired or anything like that. I just think about winning. If you win, everyone loves you." —*Earl Weaver*

W
E
A
V
E
R

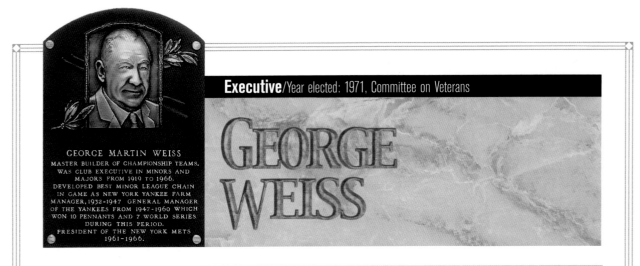

Executive/Year elected: 1971, Committee on Veterans

GEORGE MARTIN WEISS
MASTER BUILDER OF CHAMPIONSHIP TEAMS.
WAS CLUB EXECUTIVE IN MINORS AND
MAJORS FROM 1919 TO 1966.
DEVELOPED BEST MINOR LEAGUE CHAIN
IN GAME AS NEW YORK YANKEE FARM
MANAGER, 1932-1947 GENERAL MANAGER
OF THE YANKEES FROM 1947-1960 WHICH
WON 10 PENNANTS AND 7 WORLD SERIES
DURING THIS PERIOD.
PRESIDENT OF THE NEW YORK METS
1961-1966.

GEORGE WEISS

Born: 6-23-1895, New Haven, Conn. **Died:** 8-13-72 **Executive career:** Director of minor league operations of Yankees, 1932-45; vice president/player personnel of Yankees, 1946-47; vice president/general manager of Yankees, 1947-60; president of Mets, 1961-66

He was the "empire builder," the shy, moon-faced, business-savvy genius behind the New York Yankees. No one could argue the impact George Weiss had on baseball, first as farm director and then general manager of the game's model franchise. His legacy was success: 19 American League pennants and 15 World Series championships over 29 incredible seasons atop Mount Olympus.

Ed Barrow might have been the architect of the Yankee dynasty, but Weiss was the man who sustained it through four decades. The longtime minor league executive was hired in 1932 by owner Jacob Ruppert and spent 16 years building the game's premier farm system. Weiss was an amazing judge of talent, signing and developing such players as Joe Gordon, Charlie Keller, Phil Rizzuto, Yogi Berra, Mickey Mantle and Whitey Ford. It was Weiss who fought for the 1936 signing of Joe DiMaggio after other organizations had backed off because of a knee injury.

With Weiss supplying the talent, the Yankees won nine pennants and eight World Series from 1932-47. Then he became G.M. and spearheaded a drive to 10 more pennants and seven Series titles, all under the direction of Casey Stengel—the much-maligned "clown manager" Weiss hired in 1949. Weiss masterfully helped Stengel by signing and trading for players (Roger Maris, Johnny Mize, Enos Slaughter) who fit snugly into his championship puzzle.

The portly, publicity-shy Weiss often was portrayed as ruthless, unemotional and aloof. More than anything, he was a proud businessman who didn't let sentiment get in the way of sound decisions. New Yorkers were shocked in 1960 when the Yankees, after losing a tough World Series to Pittsburgh, announced a youth movement and forced both Weiss (65) and Stengel (71) to retire.

Weiss returned to baseball as president of the expansion New York Mets from 1961-66, reuniting with Stengel to help lay groundwork for a World Series winner in 1969. The Yankees, still sustained by Weiss-supplied talent, won four straight pennants and two more World Series after his departure before beginning a long rebuilding process.

"He was high class. He knew how to pick men. Why, you can't stay in baseball that long by pulling players out of the icebox." —*Casey Stengel*

MICKEY WELCH

MICHAEL FRANCIS WELCH
"SMILING MICKEY"
TROY N.L. 1880·1882
NEW YORK N.L. 1883·1892
CREDITED WITH MORE THAN 300 VICTORIES
DURING 13 SEASONS IN MAJORS. WON 17
GAMES IN A ROW IN 1885 WHILE COMPILING
44·11 RECORD FOR LEAGUE·LEADING .800
WINNING PERCENTAGE, TOPPED 30·VICTORY
TOTAL IN FOUR YEARS.

Born: 7-4-1859, Brooklyn, N.Y. **Died:** 7-30-41 **Height/Weight:** 5-8/160 **Bats/Throws:** R/R **Position:** Pitcher
Career statistics: 307-210, 2.71 ERA, 1,850 strikeouts **Teams:** Troy 1880-82; New York 1883-92

He was a New York original, a Brooklyn-born righthander who helped the Giants franchise gain credibility over a 13-year career that spanned two cities and two pitching distances. Mickey Welch was a little big man who could overpower or finesse — often on the same pitch. Before time finally caught up with his overworked arm, "Smiling Mickey" crammed 307 wins and 4,802 innings into a short-but-sweet big-league run that gave him status among the greats of 19th-century baseball.

The 5-foot-8 Welch was given his nickname by a New York cartoonist, who played off his crooked smile and the good-natured approach he took to his job. When asked the secret of his success, Welch smiled and attributed it to drinking beer. More likely it had to do with the fastball, curve and changeup he masterfully mixed while carving up hitters — and an unusual screwball he might have been the first to throw.

Welch, a 45-foot pitcher when he started with Troy in 1880 and a 50-footer when the team moved to New York three years later, was a crafty strategist who worked to hitters' weaknesses and racked up high strikeout totals for the period. But more than anything, he was renowned for high victory and inning totals that linked his name with such contempories as Pud Galvin, John Clarkson, Hoss Radbourn and Tim Keefe.

Welch, who pitched 574 innings in a 34-win rookie season, became so concerned about overuse that he negotiated a contract clause that limited his appearances to every other day. Still, he recorded five more seasons of 425-plus innings and he seldom left games, completing 525 of 549 career starts. His big season was 1885 when he finished 44-11, pitched 492 innings and struck out 258, winning 17 straight games over one stretch.

Welch was 26-19 and 27-12 in 1888 and '89, combining with Keefe to pitch the Giants to their only pre-1900 pennants. He became baseball's third 300-win pitcher in 1890, a 17-14 season that set the stage for his 1892 retirement. He finished with a 307-210 record.

> ## "Pure elixir of malt and hops, beats all the drugs and all the drops."
>
> — *Mickey Welch's secret of success*

WELCH

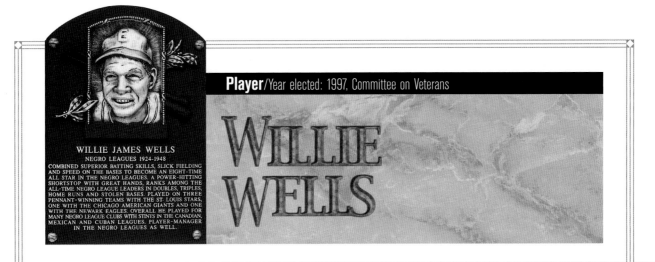

WILLIE JAMES WELLS
NEGRO LEAGUES 1924-1948
COMBINED SUPERIOR BATTING SKILLS, SLICK FIELDING AND SPEED ON THE BASES TO BECOME AN EIGHT-TIME ALL STAR IN THE NEGRO LEAGUES. A POWER-HITTING SHORTSTOP WITH GREAT HANDS, RANKS AMONG THE ALL-TIME NEGRO LEAGUE LEADERS IN DOUBLES, TRIPLES, HOME RUNS AND STOLEN BASES. PLAYED ON THREE PENNANT-WINNING TEAMS WITH THE ST. LOUIS STARS, ONE WITH THE CHICAGO AMERICAN GIANTS AND ONE WITH THE NEWARK EAGLES. OVERALL HE PLAYED FOR MANY NEGRO LEAGUE CLUBS WITH STINTS IN THE CANADIAN, MEXICAN AND CUBAN LEAGUES. PLAYER-MANAGER IN THE NEGRO LEAGUES AS WELL.

Player/Year elected: 1997, Committee on Veterans

WILLIE WELLS

Born: 8-10-05, Austin, Tex. **Died:** 1-22-89 **Height/Weight:** 5-8/160 **Bats/Throws:** R/R **Primary position:** Shortstop

Teams (1924-54): St. Louis Stars; Detroit Wolves; Homestead Grays; Kansas City Monarchs; Cole's American Giants; Newark Eagles; Chicago American Giants; Memphis Red Sox; New York Black Yankees; Baltimore Elite Giants; Indianapolis Clowns; Birmingham Black Barons

He was a little guy with bandy legs and a weak throwing arm. But anybody who underestimated the athletic abilities and desire of Willie Wells paid a stiff price. "The Devil," they used to say, could beat you in a dozen ways, which he boldly and subtly demonstrated over his three decades as the premier shortstop of the black professional leagues.

Wells was to the 1930s and '40s Negro Leagues what John Henry Lloyd was to the early black game—a ballhawking wizard. At a squatty 5-foot-8 and 160 pounds, he ranged with amazing quickness, aggressively charged toppers and grabbed erratic bounces with lightning hands. What he lacked in arm strength he made up for with quick release and uncanny positioning.

Wells displayed the same instincts with his bat, constantly adjusting his righthanded swing to fit the pitcher and situation. On one at-bat, he might slap a line drive to right or up the middle, maybe execute the hit-and-run. On the next, he might become a dangerous pull hitter. Wells, a consistent .300 threat who played for the St. Louis Stars from 1924-31, took advantage of a short left field in 1929 and hit a Negro League-record 27 home runs—in 88 games.

Wells was smart and cunning, a sign-stealer who would swipe bases, deke runners and psyche out opposing pitchers. Always upbeat and full of life, he was a Negro League legend who played with Ray Dandridge on the left side of Newark's "million-dollar infield" in the late 1930s and later managed the Eagles, prepping such stars as Monte Irvin, Larry Doby and Don Newcombe for major league play.

Wells, like most black players of his era, followed the sun and supplemented his Negro League summers with winters in Latin America, Cuba and Mexico. The eight-time East-West All-Star, who also played in the Canadian black leagues before retiring in 1954, was a pioneer of the batting helmet—a coal miner's hard hat without the gas jet.

> "The most consistent player—that was Willie Wells. Very seldom he'd strike out. Could hit righthanded or lefthanded pitching. And he would play day in and day out." —*Buck Leonard*

WELLS

Born: 5-23-1888, Hamilton, Mo. **Died:** 3-11-72 **Height/Weight:** 5-10/170 **Bats/Throws:** L/R **Primary position:** Left field **Career statistics:** .317 avg., 2,884 hits, 1,289 runs, 1,248 RBIs **Teams:** Dodgers 1909-26; Athletics 1927 **Batting champion:** N.L., 1918

He was Brooklyn's first baseball superstar and, more than seven decades after his retirement, Zack Wheat still ranks No. 1 in numerous franchise offensive categories. Only the popularity that once rivaled New York idol Babe Ruth has faded, like the yellowed newspaper clippings that heralded his achievements. Wheat was the original "Artful Dodger," a do-everything left fielder with an attitude to match.

The rock-hard 5-foot-10, 170-pounder was a friendly, mild-mannered family man who won over Brooklyn fans with his simple values and down-home Missouri charm. It didn't hurt that he could lash line drives to every section of the park with a smooth lefthanded swing, chase down fly balls with grace and speed or cut down runners with a powerful right arm. Fans took a quick liking to Wheat when he made his 1909 debut and the love affair lasted 18 standout seasons.

It wasn't unusual to see him talking to fans in the left field bleachers between pitches and advertisers attested to his popularity with personalized billboards and ads on the outfield walls at Ebbets Field. Wheat never stopped hustling, a quality that was even more endearing than his 14 seasons with a .300-plus average.

An outstanding curveball hitter, Wheat batted cleanup for generally weak Brooklyn teams known more for zany antics than baseball prowess. The Dodgers won pennants in 1916 and 1920, but Wheat spent most of his career providing the voice of reason in a Brooklyn madhouse. He won a batting title with a .335 mark in 1918 and made a successful transition from the dead-ball era to the lively ball, posting consecutive seasons of .375 and .359 in 1924 and '25 — the latter at age 37.

Wheat, whose brother Mack was a Brooklyn teammate from 1915-19, was released after the 1926 season and played one more year for the Philadelphia Athletics, batting .324 in 88 games. A .317 career batter who retired with 2,884 hits and 1,248 RBIs, Wheat remains the Dodgers' all-time leader in games, at-bats, hits, doubles, triples and total bases.

> "I could never see any sense in cursing an umpire. With them, it means you're out of the game. And I came to play." —*Zack Wheat*

WHEAT

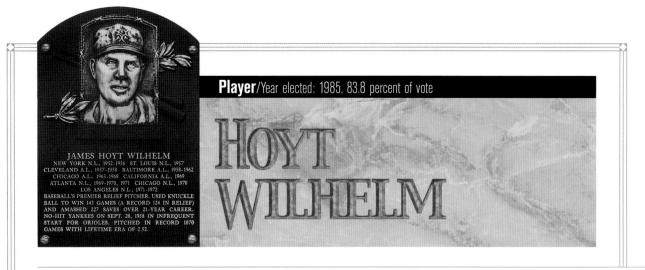

Player/Year elected: 1985, 83.8 percent of vote

HOYT WILHELM

JAMES HOYT WILHELM
NEW YORK N.L., 1952-1956 ST. LOUIS N.L., 1957
CLEVELAND A.L., 1957-1958 BALTIMORE A.L., 1958-1962
CHICAGO A.L., 1963-1968 CALIFORNIA A.L., 1969
ATLANTA N.L., 1969-1970, 1971 CHICAGO N.L., 1970
LOS ANGELES N.L., 1971-1972
BASEBALL'S PREMIER RELIEF PITCHER. USED KNUCKLE
BALL TO WIN 143 GAMES (A RECORD 124 IN RELIEF)
AND AMASSED 227 SAVES OVER 21-YEAR CAREER.
NO-HIT YANKEES ON SEPT. 20, 1958 IN INFREQUENT
START FOR ORIOLES. PITCHED IN RECORD 1070
GAMES WITH LIFETIME ERA OF 2.52.

Born: 7-26-23, Huntersville, N.C. **Height/Weight:** 6-0/195 **Bats/Throws:** R/R **Position:** Pitcher **Career statistics:** 143-122, 2.52 ERA, 1,610 strikeouts, 227 saves **Teams:** Giants 1952-56; Cardinals 1957; Indians 1957-58; Orioles 1958-62; White Sox 1963-68; Angels 1969; Braves 1969-70, 1971; Cubs 1970; Dodgers 1971-72

He "threw like an old washerwoman," relied almost exclusively on a "gimmick pitch" and was as hard on catchers as he was opposing hitters. But Hoyt Wilhelm calmly, patiently, doggedly ignored critics for 21 seasons, most of which he spent as baseball's first Hall of Fame reliever. From minor league wanderer to major league prominence, Wilhelm floated, like a well-thrown knuckleball, through a defining and trendsetting career.

The 6-foot righthander with the North Carolina drawl was not baseball's first knuckleballer, but he was the first to throw it almost to exclusion of other pitches. Wilhelm gripped the ball with the tips of his first two fingers and threw both sidearm and three-quarters at different speeds. Pitcher, catcher and batter were helpless to predict the course of a pitch that might dart from side to side or drop as much as a foot. Making contact was difficult; solid contact could be impossible.

Facing Wilhelm was an adventure. He would stand on the mound, head cocked toward his right shoulder to compensate for a lifelong eye problem. His motion was effortless and the wear on his arm minimal. From 1952-72, after seven minor league seasons and three years in the military, he appeared in a then-record 1,070 games with the Giants, Cardinals, Indians, Orioles, White Sox, Angels, Braves, Cubs and Dodgers before retiring at age 49.

It was Giants manager Leo Durocher who, in 1952, converted the 28-year-old from a minor league starter into a big-league reliever. Wilhelm appeared in a National League-leading 71 games that season, compiling a 2.43 ERA and 15-3 record. Used exclusively in relief in 16 of his 21 seasons, the four-time All-Star still pitched a no-hitter (1958) and won 19 games as a starter.

Wilhelm, who made two scoreless appearances for the Giants in the 1954 World Series, retired in 1972 with a record 124 relief wins, 227 saves and a 2.52 ERA. Baseball's first great reliever also is remembered for hitting his only home run in his first big-league at-bat.

> "When a pitcher was batting, some pitchers would give you a fastball on the first pitch, trying to get ahead on the count. But not Wilhelm. You didn't get any break from him."
>
> —*Billy Pierce*

Player/Year elected: 1987, 85.7 percent of vote

BILLY WILLIAMS

BILLY LEO WILLIAMS
CHICAGO, N.L., 1959 – 1974
OAKLAND, A.L., 1975 – 1976
SOFT-SPOKEN, CLUTCH PERFORMER WAS ONE OF
MOST RESPECTED HITTERS OF HIS DAY. BATTED SOLID
.290 OVER 18 SEASONS SOCKING 426 HOME RUNS. HIT 20
OR MORE HOMERS 13 STRAIGHT SEASONS. 1961 N.L.
ROOKIE OF YEAR. 1972 N.L. BATTING CHAMPION WITH
.333. HELD N.L. RECORD FOR CONSECUTIVE GAMES
PLAYED WITH 1117.

Born: 6-15-38, Whistler, Ala. **Height/Weight:** 6-1/175 **Bats/Throws:** L/R **Primary position:** Left field **Career statistics:** .290 avg., 2,711 hits, 1,410 runs, 426 HR, 1,475 RBIs **Teams:** Cubs 1959-74; Athletics 1975-76 **Batting champion:** N.L., 1972

Major awards: N.L. Rookie of Year, 1961

It was that swing, a wrist-snapping, picture-perfect blend of power and grace. Billy Williams didn't just hit the ball, he punished it with a short, compact stroke that resembled a man cracking his whip. Artistic and poetic; quick and efficient — the bat talked loudly and eloquently over 18 major league seasons for the Chicago Cubs' quiet man.

When Williams made contact from his erect lefthanded stance, the ball jumped on a vicious line to distant parts of Wrigley Field — and beyond. The 6-foot-1, 175-pound Alabaman packed serious muscle in his slender frame and his wrists generated lightning-like bat speed. Williams could pull the ball or ram it to the opposite field, a power approach that produced 14 seasons of 20 or more home runs and a career high of 42 in 1970.

"Billy is the best lefthanded hitter I ever saw," marveled longtime Pittsburgh star Willie Stargell, and former Cubs teammate Ernie Banks marveled at his run production and durability. Seemingly unemotional and seldom out of the lineup, Williams drove in 90 or

more runs 10 times and played in a then-National League record 1,117 straight games from 1963-70.

Williams, a hard-working but unspectacular defender, took over left field in his Rookie of the Year 1961 campaign and began working quietly behind the scenes, happy to let teammates Banks and Ron Santo dominate the Chicago spotlight. In 1964, he reached the .300 plateau for the first time. In 1970, he joined the N.L. elite with a .322, 42-homer, 129-RBI performance. Two years later, he led the N.L. with a .333 average and pounded 37 homers.

No one seemed to notice, especially MVP voters who opted for players on division and pen-nant-winning teams. The Cubs never finished higher than second place during Williams' stay and he made his only postseason appearance in the 1975 ALCS — the first of his career-ending two-season swing as an Oakland DH. Williams, who played in six All-Star Games, retired with a .290 average and career totals of 426 homers, 2,711 hits and 1,475 RBIs.

> "He can hit the good pitches for home runs. All of us can hit the bad pitches, the mistakes. But Billy Williams can hit the good pitches." —*Ernie Banks*

WILLIAMS

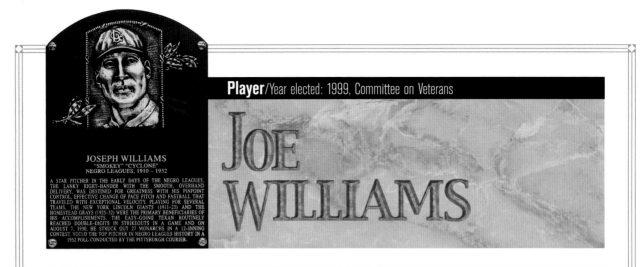

JOSEPH WILLIAMS
"SMOKEY" "CYCLONE"
NEGRO LEAGUES, 1910 – 1932

A STAR PITCHER IN THE EARLY DAYS OF THE NEGRO LEAGUES, THE LANKY RIGHT-HANDER WITH THE SMOOTH, OVERHAND DELIVERY, WAS DESTINED FOR GREATNESS WITH HIS PINPOINT CONTROL, EFFECTIVE CHANGE OF PACE PITCH AND FASTBALL THAT TRAVELED WITH EXCEPTIONAL VELOCITY. PLAYING FOR SEVERAL TEAMS, THE NEW YORK LINCOLN GIANTS (1911–23) AND THE HOMESTEAD GRAYS (1925–32) WERE THE PRIMARY BENEFICIARIES OF HIS ACCOMPLISHMENTS. THE EASY-GOING TEXAN ROUTINELY REACHED DOUBLE-DIGITS IN STRIKEOUTS IN A GAME AND ON AUGUST 7, 1930, HE STRUCK OUT 27 MONARCHS IN A 12-INNING CONTEST. VOTED THE TOP PITCHER IN NEGRO LEAGUES HISTORY IN A 1952 POLL CONDUCTED BY THE PITTSBURGH COURIER.

Player/Year elected: 1999, Committee on Veterans

JOE WILLIAMS

Born: 4-6-1886, Seguin, Tex. **Died:** 3-12-46 **Height/Weight:** 6-4/190 **Bats/Throws:** R/R **Primary positions:** Pitcher, first base, outfield **Teams (1905-32):** San Antonio Bronchos; Leland Giants; Chicago Giants; Lincoln Giants; Mohawk Giants; Chicago American Giants; Bacharach Giants; Hilldale Daisies; Brooklyn Royal Giants; Homestead Grays; Detroit Wolves

Contrary to popular belief, Joe Williams could not throw his fastball through a wall — or a color barrier. But he could fire it, with head-shaking force, past overmatched hitters, who flailed unsuccessfully at his offerings for more than two decades. "Smokey Joe" was to early black baseball what Satchel Paige was to later Negro Leagues — a powerful, dominating and eloquent ambassador for the "other game."

From 1910, when he joined the Chicago Giants, through 1932, when he worked, at age 47, for the Homestead Grays, Williams blew away hitters with a fastball contemporaries called the equal of Walter Johnson's. The hawk-nosed 6-foot-4, 190-pound physical specimen would lull them to sleep with his slow, overhand motion and explode the ball homeward with his long right arm, a precision laser that cut through the strike zone with monotonous accuracy.

Stories about 20-strikeout games, extra-inning no-hitters and other pitching feats were passed from generation to generation, verbal testaments to Williams' domination in the black summer leagues and winter visits to Cuba. But more fascinating were his legendary battles in barnstorming exhibitions against

some of the best players major league baseball had to offer.

Negro League historian John B. Holway reports that Williams recorded a 22-7-1 record in such games between 1912 and 1932. Among his victims were Grover Alexander, Johnson, Chief Bender, Rube Marquard and Waite Hoyt, all Hall of Famers. Two of his losses came at age 45; two others were by scores of 1-0. Williams reportedly fired a 10-inning no-hitter, striking out 20, against the 1917 National League-champion New York Giants, only to lose on an error.

Williams' best seasons were from 1911-23, when he pitched primarily for the New York Lincoln Giants. The proud Texan, a half Indian who used guile and a reasonable curveball to set up hitters looking for his heater, was tough to hit. In a 1952 *Pittsburgh Courier* survey to pick the best pitcher in Negro League history, Williams outpolled Paige by a single vote.

"He chewed tobacco. You'd throw him a white ball and it would come back brown. But it didn't make any difference. He could throw about the hardest I ever saw."

— *Judy Johnson, from the book Blackball Stars*

THEODORE SAMUEL WILLIAMS
"TED"
BOSTON RED SOX A.L. 1939-1960
BATTED .406 IN 1941, LED A.L. IN BATTING
6 TIMES; SLUGGING PERCENTAGE 9 TIMES;
TOTAL BASES 6 TIMES; RUNS SCORED 6 TIMES;
BASES ON BALLS 8 TIMES. TOTAL HITS 2654
INCLUDED 521 HOME RUNS. LIFETIME BATTING
AVERAGE .344; LIFETIME SLUGGING AVERAGE
.634; MOST VALUABLE A.L. PLAYER 1946 & 1949.
PLAYED IN 18 ALL STAR GAMES. NAMED PLAYER
OF THE DECADE 1951-1960.

Player/Year elected: 1966, 93.4 percent of vote, first ballot

TED WILLIAMS

Born: 8-30-18, San Diego, Calif. **Height/Weight:** 6-3/205 **Bats/Throws:** L/R **Primary position:** Left field **Career statistics:** .344 avg., 2,654 hits, 1,798 runs, 521 HR, 1,839 RBIs **Teams:** Red Sox 1939-42, 1946-60 **Batting champion:** A.L., 1941, '42, '47, '48, '57, '58 **HR champion:** 1941, '42, '47, '49 **Major awards:** A.L. MVP, 1946, '49

Nobody was more dedicated to the art of putting bat on ball than Ted Williams, a human hitting machine equipped with near-perfect eyesight, lightning reflexes, powerful forearms and unnerving patience. The "Splendid Splinter" also came with a heavy dose of arrogance and self-confidence, the most conspicuous traits of a baseball maverick who terrorized American League pitchers from 1939-60.

If Williams wasn't the greatest pure hitter of all time, he certainly was of his era. A lefthanded swinger, he stood erect, hands holding bat in a vice-like grip, straight up and close to his left shoulder. Williams would throw his gangly body forward, always keeping his hands back, until a blurry, split-second swing whipped out another line drive. Always a perfectionist, Williams refused to swing at a bad pitch, a discipline that made him one of the three most-walked hitters in history and a

"(Williams) is the most remarkable hitter I ever saw. ... I never saw a hitter who could swing as late as he does and hit the ball as good." —*Bill Dickey*

WILLIAMS

12-time leader in on-base percentage.

But the self-discipline that so defined Williams the hitter often was lost on Williams the man. Quick-tempered, cocky, opinionated and independent, the sensitive Williams, a sometimes-erratic defender in left field, fought career-long battles against critical sportswriters and fickle Boston fans. His feud with the media might have cost him three MVP awards — in 1941 when he posted baseball's last .400 average (.406) but lost out to New York's Joe DiMaggio; in 1942 and '47 when he won two Triple Crowns but lost out in voting to Yankees Joe Gordon and DiMaggio.

The Williams bottom line still is filled with superlatives — two MVPs, six batting crowns, 2,654 hits, a .344 average, 18 All-Star Games, 521 home runs, four homer titles and five RBI crowns — numbers that could have been considerably higher if he had not lost four prime seasons to military service during World War II and the Korean War.

Williams never played for a World Series champion, but he did retire with dramatic flair in 1960, hitting a home run at Fenway Park in his final at-bat.

Player/Year elected: 1995, Committee on Veterans

VIC WILLIS

Born: 4-12-1876, Cecil County, Md. **Died:** 8-3-47 **Height/Weight:** 6-2/185 **Bats/Throws:** R/R **Position:** Pitcher
Career statistics: 249-205, 2.63 ERA, 1,651 strikeouts **Teams:** Boston 1898-1905; Pirates 1906-09; Cardinals 1910

Tall, thin and long of arm, Vic Willis gracefully delivered 13 years-worth of bad news to National League hitters. The "Delaware Peach" was exactly that—a tastefully delectable combination of motion, power and guile, wrapped in a 6-foot-2, 185-pound package. Willis was a turn-of-the-century curveballer, a finesse dead-ball pitcher who carved out a 249-205 legacy with the Boston Beaneaters and Pittsburgh Pirates.

The first problem hitters faced against the tall righthander was finding the ball. Willis came at them with a straight overhand delivery and a high release, like a slingshot from above. A medium-range fastball was deceptive and difficult to pick up. But Willis did most of his damage with a sweeping curve that froze some batters and reduced others to futile defensive swings.

Willis, who was raised near Wilmington, Del., broke in with a bang in 1898, posting a 25-13 record for the pennant-bound Beaneaters—the first of eight 20-win seasons he would record. A 27-8 record in 1899 was his masterpiece, but Willis was at his workhorse best in 1902 when he finished 27-20 and posted league highs in strikeouts (225), innings (410) and complete games (45), a 20th century N.L. record.

Willis' career winning percentage might have been higher if not for consecutive 18-25 and 12-29 seasons for weak 1904 and '05 Boston teams that were depleted by the bidding war between the National and American leagues. But after a 1905 trade to Pittsburgh, he rebounded to post records of 23-13, 21-11, 23-11 and 22-11—his final 20-win campaign coming in the Pirates' 1909 run to a World Series championship.

Willis failed to win in the fall classic, but Pittsburgh defeated Detroit in seven games behind the three-win pitching of rookie Babe Adams. At age 33, Willis was dispatched in a surprising offseason trade to St. Louis, where he struggled through a 9-12 campaign before retiring with a career 2.63 ERA, 3,996 innings and 388 complete games in 471 starts.

> "Willis was a tall, graceful pitcher with a sweeping curveball, which he pitched down at a batsman."
>
> —*The Sporting News, 1947*

HACK WILSON

LEWIS ROBERT WILSON
"HACK"
NEW YORK N.L., CHICAGO N.L.,
BROOKLYN N.L., PHILADELPHIA N.L.,
1923 - 1934
ESTABLISHED MAJOR LEAGUE RECORD OF 190
RUNS BATTED IN AND NATIONAL LEAGUE HIGH
OF 56 HOMERS IN 1930. LED OR TIED FOR N.L.
HOMER TITLE FOUR TIMES. COMPILED LIFETIME
.307 BATTING AVERAGE AND DROVE IN 100 OR
MORE RUNS SIX YEARS. HIT TWO HOMERS IN
INNING IN 1925 AND THREE IN GAME IN 1930.

Born: 4-26-00, Ellwood City, Pa. **Died:** 11-23-48 **Height/Weight:** 5-6/195 **Bats/Throws:** R/R
Primary position: Outfield **Career statistics:** .307 avg., 1,461 hits, 244 HR, 1,063 RBIs **Teams:** Giants 1923-25;
Cubs 1926-31; Dodgers 1932-34; Phillies 1934 **HR champion:** 1926, '27, '28, '30

From the top of his large, round head to the bottom of his size-5 1/2 feet, Lewis "Hack" Wilson was a baseball oddity. Short, stump-like legs that anchored a 5-foot-6, 195-pound, barrel-chested frame amused fans and teammates; powerful shoulders and arms that launched rocket-shot home runs inspired and amazed them. In a 12-year career from 1923-34, the hard-living, free-spirited Wilson carved out a short but colorful slugging legacy.

Wilson was nothing if not eye-catching. His thick upper body looked like it was carved from granite; his size-18 neck connected an oversized head to bull-like shoulders. Strong arms generated intensive power through a vicious righthanded swing that attacked the ball, driving it forcefully to any part of the ballpark. An undisciplined bad-ball hitter who still managed a .307 career average, Wilson seldom got cheated.

When he missed, he could look clumsy; when he connected, he did so with Babe Ruth-like results. The hard-edged, two-fisted Pennsylvanian batted

"How do I hit 'em? I just go up there with the intention of knocking the ball out of the park, and swing." —*Hack Wilson*

.356 for the Chicago Cubs in 1930 and blasted 56 home runs, a National League record that stood for 68 years. His incredible 191-RBI explosion is a still-standing, seldom-threatened major league mark.

The four-time N.L. homer champion was a run-producing machine for the Cubs and Brooklyn Dodgers from 1926-32, after three unproductive seasons with the New York Giants. He drove in 892 runs (127 per season) over that span and established himself as a surprisingly fast and competent outfielder. He will always be remembered as the Cubs center fielder who lost two fly balls in the sun during a 10-run Philadelphia inning in Game 4 of the 1929 World Series, a rally that insured the A's victory.

Wilson also will be remembered as one of the Depression era's top gate attractions, a popular star whose career was short-circuited by his affection for drink and the Chicago and New York nightlife. When his career faded prematurely at age 34, he retired with 244 home runs and 1,063 RBIs.

WILSON

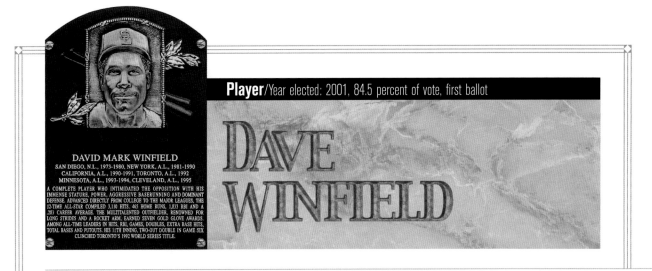

Player/Year elected: 2001, 84.5 percent of vote, first ballot

DAVE WINFIELD

Born: 10-3-51, St. Paul, Min. **Height/Weight:** 6-6/220 **Bats/Throws:** R/R **Primary position:** Outfield

Career statistics: .283 avg., 3,110 hits, 1,669 runs, 465 HR, 1,833 RBIs, 223 steals **Teams:** Padres 1973-80; Yankees 1981-90; Angels 1990-91; Blue Jays 1992; Twins 1993-94; Indians 1995

The gap-toothed smile and soft, easy-listening voice created a false sense of security. Then Dave Winfield stood up, all 6-feet, 6-inches of him, and began swinging a bat that looked like a toothpick in his massive hands. The tall, lean body, with broad shoulders anchoring long arms, was enough to intimidate any pitcher with hopes of living through another day.

But Winfield was more than just another burly home run hitter. He was an athlete—a superior athlete—who could run, hit, throw and perform just about any other baseball skill imaginable. A college athlete at Minnesota who was drafted in three professional sports, Winfield covered plenty of ground with his long, loping stride as a left or right fielder and ended rallies with his powerful arm. He was an instinctive baserunner who got plenty of practice because of his ability to put bat on ball.

Winfield's big righthanded swing produced 3,110 hits, 465 home runs and 1,833 RBIs over a 22-year career, most of which was divided between San Diego and New York. He was a run-producer extraordinaire, first over an eight-season stint for weak Padres teams (1973-80), then for Yankees teams that benefited from a consistent string of 25-homer, 100-RBI performances.

From 1981 through '88, Winfield was a model of consistency, winning five of his seven Gold Gloves and fueling the Yankees with six 100-RBI efforts. He continued to produce while feuding publicly with owner

> "Dave Winfield is my utility player. He plays anyplace —anyplace he wants." —*Gene Michael*

George Steinbrenner about contracts, performance and more personal matters. The articulate, image-conscious Winfield kept his cool through difficult times and maintained a delicate balance between his professional life and off-field charity work.

At least part of Steinbrenner's dissatisfaction stemmed from Winfield's less-than sterling performance and .045 average in a 1981 World Series loss to Los Angeles. But Winfield earned personal redemption 11 years later when he supplied the Series-deciding hit for Toronto in Game 6 of the 1992 fall classic. The 12-time All-Star Game performer retired in 1995, after short stints for California, Toronto, Minnesota and Cleveland.

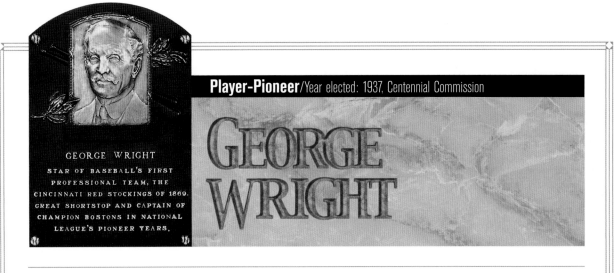

GEORGE WRIGHT

GEORGE WRIGHT

STAR OF BASEBALL'S FIRST
PROFESSIONAL TEAM, THE
CINCINNATI RED STOCKINGS OF 1869.
GREAT SHORTSTOP AND CAPTAIN OF
CHAMPION BOSTONS IN NATIONAL
LEAGUE'S PIONEER YEARS.

Born: 1-28-1847, Yonkers, N.Y. **Died:** 8-21-37 **Height/Weight:** 5-9/150 **Bats/Throws:** R/R **Primary position:** Shortstop
Career statistics: .255, 383 hits **Teams:** Boston 1876-78, 1880-81; Providence 1879, 1882

He was the playing half of baseball's pioneering Wright brothers, the dashing, curly-haired shortstop for the first professional team. George Wright not only helped spread baseball's gospel to America's hinterlands, he showed it could be played with flair and enthusiasm. His legacy remains front and center more than a century after he played — a string of "firsts" that helped define the game we know today.

Wright, a member of the first all-star team published in 1868 by Henry Chadwick, was exciting and graceful, a barehanded fielder who snared line drives, raced left or right to pick off grounders and made difficult over-the-shoulder catches. His strong arm allowed him to play well behind the baseline, a pioneering tactic that extended his range, and he was the first shortstop to cover second base on balls hit to the right.

The 5-foot-9, 150-pound New Yorker also was the first infielder to trap balls, perhaps inspiring the infield-fly rule, and the shortstop for brother Harry's first professional team, the 1869 Cincinnati Red Stockings. When the National Association, baseball's first major league, was formed in 1871, Wright played for Harry's Boston entry and, when the National League began play in 1876, he claimed distinction as its first batter — he grounded to shortstop.

But more than anything, Wright was the sport's first legitimate star, a slick-fielding, hard-hitting right-hander with a showman's flair. He batted .629 as the highest paid and most popular player for the undefeated Red Stockings (57-0) in 1869 and never dipped below .300 in five National Association seasons. He played on seven pennant-winning teams in nine full professional campaigns before falling victim to the more sophisticated curveballs of improving pitchers.

Wright left baseball in 1882 and devoted full attention to a sporting goods business that would introduce the first tennis and golf equipment to the Boston area. Wright, an outstanding cricket player, was part of landmark baseball tours to England in 1874 and various other countries in 1888.

"He called short field his home position, but when called upon, he was equally at home on any of the bases. He could catch as well as the best catchers of his day and was a fine emergency pitcher."

—Al Spink, from his book The National Game

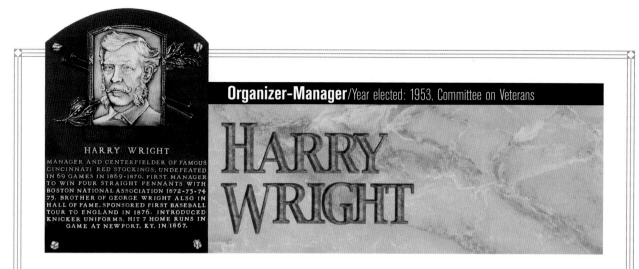

Born: 1-10-1835, Sheffield, England **Died:** 10-3-1895 **Height/Weight:** 5-10/157 **Teams managed:** Boston 1876-81; Providence 1882-83; Philadelphia 1884-93 **Career record:** 1,225-885, .581

"Every player is indebted to him for inaugurating an occupation by which he gains livelihood, and the country at large for adding one more industry to furnish employment." —*Sporting Life*, 1895

Harry Wright was the brains behind the 19th century's premier baseball brother act, the man who turned a simple game into a full-time business. As a visionary thinker, strategist and organizer, no one did more to insure the new sport's acceptance as America's national pastime. If Henry Chadwick was the "Father of Baseball," Wright had to be "Father of the Professional Game."

Unlike younger brother George, one of the brightest stars of baseball's formative era, Harry was intrigued by the game's strategic and business potential. He was a striking gentleman with long sideburns, a thick mustache and a tuft of beard that gave him a proper, clerical look. The 5-foot-10 Wright, a one-time member of the Knickerbocker Base Ball Club of New York, had ranked among the better pitchers of the 1860s, primarily because he developed one of the game's first changeups.

It was while working in Cincinnati as a cricket instructor that the England-born Wright came into baseball prominence. He organized the amateur Cincinnati

Red Stockings, gradually added star players and in 1869 unveiled baseball's first totally professional team. With George playing shortstop, center fielder and manager Harry toured the midwest with his star-studded group and compiled a 57-0 record. Paying fans flocked to see the great Red Stockings.

In 1871, Wright helped form baseball's first professional league, the National Association, and he helped organize the National League in 1876. He directed four pennant winners in the former and two more in the N.L. over a 23-year managerial career that produced 1,225 wins in Boston, Providence and Philadelphia. Wright was respected for his integrity (he always demanded sobriety and discipline) and was well known for his innovations.

It was Wright who designed the basic uniform that is still worn today and he patented the first scorecard for fans. He introduced the concepts of pregame practice, backing up throws and adjusting defenses to hitters' tendencies. Wright also spearheaded many rules changes and the move to overhand pitching.

WRIGHT

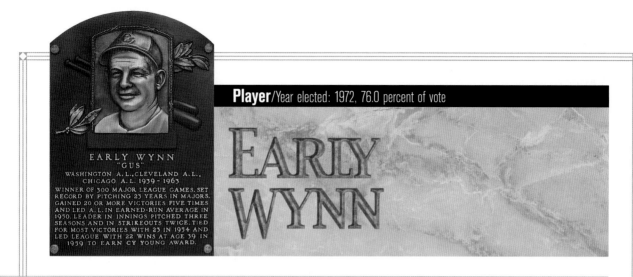

EARLY WYNN
"GUS"
WASHINGTON A.L., CLEVELAND A.L.,
CHICAGO A.L. 1939 - 1963
WINNER OF 300 MAJOR LEAGUE GAMES. SET
RECORD BY PITCHING 23 YEARS IN MAJORS.
GAINED 20 OR MORE VICTORIES FIVE TIMES
AND LED A.L. IN EARNED-RUN AVERAGE IN
1950. LEADER IN INNINGS PITCHED THREE
SEASONS AND IN STRIKEOUTS TWICE. TIED
FOR MOST VICTORIES WITH 23 IN 1954 AND
LED LEAGUE WITH 22 WINS AT AGE 39 IN
1959 TO EARN CY YOUNG AWARD.

Player/Year elected: 1972, 76.0 percent of vote

EARLY WYNN

Born: 1-6-20, Hartford, Ala. **Died:** 4-4-99 **Height/Weight:** 6-0/210 **Bats/Throws:** B/R **Position:** Pitcher
Career statistics: 300-244, 3.54 ERA, 2,334 strikeouts **Teams:** Senators 1939, 1941-44, 1946-48; Indians 1949-57, 1963; White Sox 1958-62 **Major awards:** M.L. Cy Young, 1959

The raging eyes, masked by a sneering glare, was enough to unnerve any hitter. So was his reputation as one of the fiercest and meanest competitors ever to set foot on a pitching rubber. Every time Early Wynn stepped onto a major league mound, his one simple goal was to win—no matter what it took.

"That son of a bitch is so mean he'd knock you down in the dugout," former New York Yankees great Mickey Mantle once complained—and that pretty much defined the powerfully built righthander. Wynn was a Depression-era throwback who thrived with above-average stuff and a take-no-prisoners style over a 23-year career that touched parts of four decades.

There was nothing fancy about the durable 6-foot, 210-pound wide body who viewed every hitter as the enemy and constantly looked for the intimidation edge with rib-threatening fastballs. That mean streak, combined with a driving intensity, a good fastball, a curve he learned in mid-career and a knuckleball, helped "Gus"

"Put a bat in a guy's hand, he feels like God's gift to the world. A batter just won't listen to you when he's standing up. So you got to get him sitting down. When he's sitting down, he'll listen."

— *Early Wynn*

forge 300 career wins—72 for weak Washington teams in the 1940s, 164 in Cleveland, where he posted four of his five 20-win records, and 64 for the Chicago White Sox.

Wynn, who worked in seven All-Star Games, is best remembered as part of a powerful 1950s Cleveland rotation that included Bob Lemon, Bob Feller and Mike Garcia. Wynn and Lemon both won 23 games for the 1954 Indians, who recorded an American League-record 111 victories—only to lose in the World Series to the New York Giants. Wynn came back in 1959, at age 39, to record a 22-10 mark for the pennant-bound White Sox. He was rewarded with a Cy Young.

As affable off the field as he was tough on it, Wynn once took a line drive to the chin that knocked out seven teeth—and he wanted to stay in the game. He showed that same toughness over his last three seasons as he battled to win 16 games and reach the 300-win plateau—a goal he finally achieved in 1963 at age 43.

CARL YASTRZEMSKI

CARL MICHAEL YASTRZEMSKI
"YAZ"
BOSTON, A.L., 1961-1983
SUCCEEDED TED WILLIAMS IN FENWAY'S LEFT FIELD
IN 1961 AND RETIRED 23 YEARS LATER AS ALL-TIME
RED SOX LEADER IN 8 CATEGORIES. PLAYED WITH
GRACEFUL INTENSITY IN RECORD 3,308 A.L. GAMES.
ONLY A.L. PLAYER WITH 3,000 HITS AND 400 HOMERS.
3-TIME BATTING CHAMPION. WON MVP AND TRIPLE
CROWN IN 1967 AS HE LED RED SOX TO "IMPOSSIBLE
DREAM" PENNANT.

Born: 8-22-39, Southampton, N.Y. **Height/Weight:** 5-11/182 **Bats/Throws:** L/R **Primary position:** Left field
Career statistics: .285 avg., 3,419 hits, 1,816 runs, 452 HR, 1,844 RBIs **Teams:** Red Sox 1961-83
Batting champion: 1963, '67, '68 **HR champion:** 1967 **Major awards:** A.L. MVP, 1967

His career was filled with Hall of Fame accomplishments. But nobody had to work harder for his rewards than Carl Yastrzemski. As keeper of the left field tradition at Boston's Fenway Park for 23 seasons, Yaz climbed a steep mountain to hero status, scratching and clawing to earn the esteem that should have naturally accompanied his considerable accomplishments.

Yastrzemski's often-strained relationship with Red Sox fans could be traced to 1961, when he accepted the left field baton passed to him by Boston icon Ted Williams. The Fenway faithful were skeptical when Yaz produced, quick to boo when he didn't. The 5-foot-11 New Yorker didn't understand their reluctance to embrace a player who would claim among his career achievements 3,419 hits, 452 home runs, a Triple Crown, an American League MVP, seven Gold Gloves, 18 All-Star Game selections and three batting titles.

Unlike the more natural hitters of the 1960s and '70s, Yaz was a grinder who spent hours in the cage and studied the game with a dedication few players could match. As a left-handed batter with an upright stance and corkscrew swing that slashed line drives to any section of the park, he was devastating in the clutch. When things were going right, Yaz was easy to live with; when they weren't, he was moody and distant. But he never stopped working—especially defensively, as protector of Fenway's Green Monster left field wall.

Yaz reached his pinnacle in 1967, when he fueled Boston's "Impossible Dream" pennant with the last Triple Crown performance in history—a .326, 44-homer, 121-RBI masterpiece that he followed with a three-homer World Series in a loss to St. Louis. He came back in 1968 with a .301 average that ranks as the lowest ever to win a batting crown. Yaz's only other World Series appearance came in 1975, when the Red Sox dropped a seven-game heart-breaker to Cincinnati.

When Yastrzemski retired in 1983 with distinction as the first A.L. player to amass 400 homers and 3,000 hits, only Baltimore's Brooks Robinson could match his 23-year stay with one team.

"Carl does everything there is to do in this game exceptionally well. He is the best player in this league, and he would be the best at some other position if he played there." —*Dick Williams, 1969*

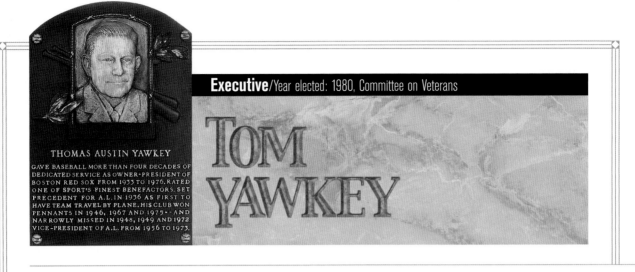

TOM YAWKEY

THOMAS AUSTIN YAWKEY

GAVE BASEBALL MORE THAN FOUR DECADES OF
DEDICATED SERVICE AS OWNER-PRESIDENT OF
BOSTON RED SOX FROM 1933 TO 1976. RATED
ONE OF SPORT'S FINEST BENEFACTORS. SET
PRECEDENT FOR A.L. IN 1936 AS FIRST TO
HAVE TEAM TRAVEL BY PLANE. HIS CLUB WON
PENNANTS IN 1946, 1967 AND 1975--AND
NARROWLY MISSED IN 1948, 1949 AND 1972.
VICE-PRESIDENT OF A.L. FROM 1956 TO 1973.

Born: 2-21-03, Detroit, Mich. **Died:** 7-9-76 **Executive career:** Owner of Red Sox, 1933-76

To the players who worked for him, Tom Yawkey was the perfect owner. To those who didn't, he was the visible, enthusiastic, ever-smiling No. 1 fan of the Boston Red Sox. Yawkey doted over his team like a proud father for 44 years, using his vast fortune to build one of the game's most revered franchises and chase a World Series championship he never caught.

Yawkey was so much more than an owner to the hundreds of players and other employees who served under him from 1933, when he plunked down $1.5 million for the struggling Red Sox, until 1976, when he died of leukemia. He was a friend, benefactor and father figure who was criticized by fellow owners for overpaying and pampering his stars.

Ted Williams, one of Yawkey's favorites, talked about "a heart the size of a watermelon" when his longtime boss died. The sentiment was shared by many. He helped players in times of need, paid for the college education of several batboys and gave millions to charity. But nothing pleased Yawkey more than

"I hope in my 16 years with the Red Sox that my play on the field gave him as much satisfaction as I had just knowing him." —*Carl Yastrzemski, 1976*

working out and mingling with his players at Fenway Park before games.

Yawkey, an avid sportsman and Yale graduate, was the adopted son of William Yawkey, the multi-millionaire former owner of the Detroit Tigers. When he purchased the Red Sox, he made it clear he intended to build a winner, hiring Eddie Collins as his general manager and acquiring such superstar talent as Joe Cronin, Lefty Grove, Jimmie Foxx, Williams and Bobby Doerr. Boston formed a passionate love affair with Yawkey and his Red Sox, but the powerful New York Yankees kept them out of the winner's circle.

Three times Yawkey got close, winning American League pennants in 1946, 1967 and 1975. But each time the Red Sox lost in seven-game World Series. Yawkey, who served as A.L. vice president from 1956-73, also watched his 1948 Sox lose a one-game pennant playoff to Cleveland. When Yawkey died, his widow, Jean, continued to run the Red Sox until her death in 1992.

YAWKEY

DENTON T. (CY) YOUNG
CLEVELAND (N) 1890-98
ST. LOUIS (N) 1899-1900
BOSTON (A) 1901-08
CLEVELAND (A) 1909-11
BOSTON (N) 1911
ONLY PITCHER IN FIRST HUNDRED
YEARS OF BASEBALL TO WIN 500 GAMES.
AMONG HIS 511 VICTORIES WERE 3
NO-HIT SHUTOUTS, PITCHED PERFECT
GAME MAY 5, 1904, NO OPPOSING
BATSMAN REACHING FIRST BASE.

CY YOUNG

Born: 3-29-1867, Gilmore, Ohio **Died:** 11-4-55 **Height/Weight:** 6-2/210 **Bats/Throws:** R/R **Position:** Pitcher **Career statistics:** 511-316, 2.63 ERA, 2,803 strikeouts **Teams:** Cleveland 1890-98; St. Louis 1899-1900; Red Sox 1901-08; Indians 1909-11; Braves 1911

His name is synonymous with masterful pitching and career success often is measured by an award bearing his name. If Cy Young wasn't the greatest pitcher in baseball history, he certainly was the game's most consistently prolific hurler and the first one destined for immortality that transcends what he accomplished on the field.

Denton True Young, a Civil War baby boomer who delivered his first pitches with oranges on his father's Ohio farm, burst upon the major league scene with the Cleveland Spiders in 1890 and began piecing together a 22-year pitching legacy that would include five 30-win seasons and 15 with 20 or more. For turn-of-the-century hitters, the 6-foot-2, 210-pound righthander was a magician who could work every other day and seemed to sense their every weakness.

Young's secret was a photographic memory that allowed him to mentally chart every batter and an assortment of pitches that kept them guessing and flailing weakly at his pinpoint deliveries. He used four motions, all of which started with his back to the plate,

> ## "I don't expect to see a second Cy Young. Men who combine his coordinated talents of mind and arm are not born often." — *John McGraw*

and his fastball was among the fastest of the period. He threw two curves, a big breaker from an overhand motion and a "swerve" that was delivered sidearm. A superb changeup also was part of an act that baffled hitters until 1911.

The amazing thing about Young was his consistency. In the 19-year stretch from 1891-1909, he dipped below 18 wins only once and 300 innings three times. His career bridged baseball's 50-foot pitching distance and such turn-of-the-century stars as Christy Mathewson, Walter Johnson and Ty Cobb. He threw three no-hitters, one a 1904 perfect game, while pitching 12 seasons with Cleveland, St. Louis and Boston in the N.L.; 10 with Boston and Cleveland in the A.L.

Young is most celebrated for his career-record 511 wins, but just as amazing are his career marks for innings (7,356), 300-inning seasons (16) and complete games (749). He also was the starter and loser for the Red Sox in baseball's first World Series game in 1903.

Player/Year elected: 1972, Committee on Veterans

ROSS YOUNGS

ROSS MIDDLEBROOK YOUNGS
"PEP"
NEW YORK N.L. 1917-1926
STAR RIGHT FIELDER OF CHAMPION GIANTS
OF 1921-22-23-24 WHEN HE BATTED .327,.331,
.336,AND.356 COMPILED LIFETIME AVERAGE
OF .322.TOPPING .300 IN NINE OF TEN YEARS.
TWICE MADE 200 OR MORE HITS IN A SEASON.
LED LEAGUE IN DOUBLES IN 1919 AND RUNS
SCORED IN 1923. LED N.L. OUTFIELDERS
IN ASSISTS TWICE AND TIED ONCE.

Born: 4-10-1897, Shiner, Tex. **Died:** 10-22-27 **Height/Weight:** 5-8/165 **Bats/Throws:** L/R **Primary position:** Outfield
Career statistics: .322 avg., 1,491 hits, 812 runs, 153 steals **Teams:** Giants 1917-26

Waite Hoyt called him "a smaller Ty Cobb." Frank Frisch recalled his "all-out hustle" and the "savage crossblocks" he threw at infielders while breaking up double plays. To John McGraw, the guru of early-century New York baseball, Ross Youngs was the ultimate man and player — "the greatest outfielder I ever saw" and the key figure in four straight Giants pennants in the early 1920s.

History remembers Youngs as a do-everything right fielder who might have attained Babe Ruth-like status if not for a fatal illness that cut short his career at age 29. The slashing switch-hitter topped .300 eight times, ran the bases with Cobb-like zeal, chased down balls with superior speed and terrorized runners with his powerful right arm. McGraw's affection for the likeable Texan was manifested by the only two pictures that hung in his Polo Grounds office — Youngs and the great Christy Mathewson.

The man they called "Pep" was a stocky 5-foot-8 former football star who played with ruggedness and enthusiasm, qualities McGraw valued. Never a home run threat, he lashed balls into the gaps and performed the duo role of run-producer and setup man, driving in 102 runs for the 1921 Giants and scoring 100 or more three straight years. Youngs batted a career-high .356 and scored 112 runs in 1924 as the Giants won their last pennant of the decade.

From 1921, when Youngs was playing his fourth full season, through 1924, his third-to-last, the Giants won four pennants and two World Series. Youngs

> "He was a smaller Ty Cobb. He was built like Enos Slaughter, had the same hustle—and even more ability." —*Waite Hoyt*

batted .375 in a 1922 fall classic win over the cross-town Yankees, .348 in a 1923 loss to the same Bronx Bombers. But he watched his average drop to .264 while battling a severe kidney problem in 1925 and played only 95 games in 1926 while grooming young Mel Ott in the subtleties of playing the tricky Polo Grounds right field.

Bedridden through most of 1927, Youngs slipped to 120 pounds and died in October of Bright's disease. He took with him a career .322 average.

YOUNGS

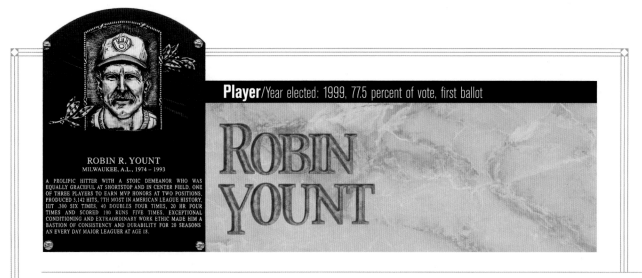

ROBIN R. YOUNT
MILWAUKEE, A.L., 1974 – 1993

A PROLIFIC HITTER WITH A STOIC DEMEANOR WHO WAS
EQUALLY GRACEFUL AT SHORTSTOP AND IN CENTER FIELD. ONE
OF THREE PLAYERS TO EARN MVP HONORS AT TWO POSITIONS.
PRODUCED 3,142 HITS, 7TH MOST IN AMERICAN LEAGUE HISTORY.
HIT .300 SIX TIMES, 40 DOUBLES FOUR TIMES, 20 HR FOUR
TIMES AND SCORED 100 RUNS FIVE TIMES. EXCEPTIONAL
CONDITIONING AND EXTRAORDINARY WORK ETHIC MADE HIM A
BASTION OF CONSISTENCY AND DURABILITY FOR 20 SEASONS
AN EVERY DAY MAJOR LEAGUER AT AGE 18.

Player/Year elected: 1999, 77.5 percent of vote, first ballot

ROBIN YOUNT

Born: 9-16-55, Danville, Ill. **Height/Weight:** 6-0/170 **Bats/Throws:** R/R **Primary positions:** Shortstop, center field **Career statistics:** .285 avg., 3,142 hits, 1,632 runs, 251 HR, 1,406 RBIs, 271 steals **Teams:** Brewers 1974-93 **Major awards:** A.L. MVP, 1982, '89

He arrived in 1974 as a curly-headed, 18-year-old shortstop and departed 20 years later as a 3,142-hit center fielder. In between, Robin Yount quietly, passionately carved his Hall of Fame career out of athleticism and such basic values as loyalty, dedication and hard work. He could beat you with his glove, bat, arm and legs; he could charm you with his all-out effort and bashful brilliance.

That Yount played his entire career for the small-market Milwaukee Brewers says a lot. He liked playing in the shadows and did it well, winning American League MVP awards while playing two of the game's most challenging positions. Yount, the Gold Glove shortstop, batted .331 with 210 hits, 29 home runs and 114 RBIs while leading the 1982 Brewers to their first World Series. Yount, the center fielder, batted .318 with 103 RBIs in 1989.

For 1,479 games, the 6-foot, 170-pound Illinois native rated in the upper echelon of big-league shortstops. He moved laterally with ease and grace, attacked slow bouncers aggressively and gunned down runners with his powerful arm. When career-threatening shoulder surgery forced him to the outfield in 1985, he made a smooth transition without complaint.

That was the Yount way—team first, without complications. He reached Milwaukee because of his glove,

"He can beat you four ways—with his glove, with his arm, with his bat, with his legs. He's probably the best baserunner in the league as far as instincts are concerned." —*Harry Dalton, Brewers G.M., 1983*

but turned himself into one of the game's most feared righthanded hitters, a fundamentally sound bulldog who went with the pitch and never gave away an at-bat. The atypical shortstop who combined power and defense, Yount batted .300 six times, drove in 100 runs three times and scored 90 or more runs on eight occasions. Twice he led the A.L. in triples while stealing 271 bases.

Yount, a career .285 hitter and three-time All-Star Game performer, was a pure player who thanked the baseball gods every day for his ability. He was a reluctant star, but a willing leader — durable enough to play 2,856 games. In his only brush with the postseason spotlight, Yount batted .414 against St. Louis in the 1982 Series with two four-hit games.

HALL OF FAME INDEX BY CLASS

Name	Class	Page	Name	Class	Page	Name	Class	Page
Chick Hafey	1971	214	Eddie Mathews	1978	322	Bill Veeck	1991	458
Harry Hooper	1971	230	Warren Giles	1979	200	Rollie Fingers	1992	170
Joe Kelley	1971	270	Willie Mays	1979	326	Bill McGowan	1992	337
Rube Marquard	1971	320	Hack Wilson	1979	492	Hal Newhouser	1992	352
Satchel Paige	1971	360	Al Kaline	1980	262	Tom Seaver	1992	416
George Weiss	1971	476	Chuck Klein	1980	278	Reggie Jackson	1993	246
Yogi Berra	1972	60	Duke Snider	1980	430	Steve Carlton	1994	84
Josh Gibson	1972	198	Tom Yawkey	1980	502	Leo Durocher	1994	156
Lefty Gomez	1972	202	Rube Foster	1981	179	Phil Rizzuto	1994	382
Will Harridge	1972	221	Bob Gibson	1981	196	Richie Ashburn	1995	38
Sandy Koufax	1972	282	Johnny Mize	1981	344	Leon Day	1995	134
Buck Leonard	1972	294	Hank Aaron	1982	22	William Hulbert	1995	241
Early Wynn	1972	498	Happy Chandler	1982	92	Mike Schmidt	1995	412
Ross Youngs	1972	506	Travis Jackson	1982	248	Vic Willis	1995	491
Roberto Clemente	1973	102	Frank Robinson	1982	388	Jim Bunning	1996	75
Billy Evans	1973	158	Walter Alston	1983	28	Bill Foster	1996	178
Monte Irvin	1973	244	George Kell	1983	268	Ned Hanlon	1996	219
George Kelly	1973	271	Juan Marichal	1983	318	Earl Weaver	1996	474
Warren Spahn	1973	432	Brooks Robinson	1983	386	Nellie Fox	1997	180
Mickey Welch	1973	477	Luis Aparicio	1984	34	Tommy Lasorda	1997	288
Cool Papa Bell	1974	52	Don Drysdale	1984	152	Phil Niekro	1997	355
Jim Bottomley	1974	62	Rick Ferrell	1984	168	Willie Wells	1997	478
Jocko Conlan	1974	118	Harmon Killebrew	1984	274	George Davis	1998	132
Whitey Ford	1974	176	Pee Wee Reese	1984	375	Larry Doby	1998	148
Mickey Mantle	1974	310	Lou Brock	1985	70	Lee MacPhail	1998	309
Sam Thompson	1974	448	Enos Slaughter	1985	425	Joe Rogan	1998	396
Earl Averill	1975	40	Arky Vaughan	1985	456	Don Sutton	1998	444
Bucky Harris	1975	222	Hoyt Wilhelm	1985	482	George Brett	1999	68
Billy Herman	1975	228	Bobby Doerr	1986	150	Orlando Cepeda	1999	87
Judy Johnson	1975	256	Ernie Lombardi	1986	299	Nestor Chylak	1999	98
Ralph Kiner	1975	276	Willie McCovey	1986	334	Nolan Ryan	1999	406
Oscar Charleston	1976	94	Ray Dandridge	1987	131	Frank Selee	1999	418
Roger Connor	1976	121	Jim "Catfish" Hunter	1987	242	Joe Williams	1999	486
Cal Hubbard	1976	236	Billy Williams	1987	484	Robin Yount	1999	508
Bob Lemon	1976	292	Willie Stargell	1988	438	Sparky Anderson	2000	30
Fred Lindstrom	1976	296	Al Barlick	1989	48	Carlton Fisk	2000	172
Robin Roberts	1976	384	Johnny Bench	1989	54	Bid McPhee	2000	341
Ernie Banks	1977	46	Red Schoendienst	1989	414	Tony Perez	2000	366
Martin Dihigo	1977	142	Carl Yastrzemski	1989	500	Turkey Stearnes	2000	440
John Henry Lloyd	1977	298	Joe Morgan	1990	346	Bill Mazeroski	2001	330
Al Lopez	1977	301	Jim Palmer	1990	362	Kirby Puckett	2001	372
Amos Rusie	1977	401	Rod Carew	1991	80	Hilton Smith	2001	427
Joe Sewell	1977	419	Ferguson Jenkins	1991	250	Dave Winfield	2001	494
Addie Joss	1978	260	Tony Lazzeri	1991	290	Ozzie Smith	2002	428
Larry MacPhail	1978	308	Gaylord Perry	1991	368			